Coups and Revolutions

Coups and Revolutions

*Mass Mobilization, the Egyptian Military,
and the United States from Mubarak to Sisi*

AMY AUSTIN HOLMES

OXFORD

UNIVERSITY PRESS

Oxford University Press is a department of the University of Oxford. It furthers
the University's objective of excellence in research, scholarship, and education
by publishing worldwide. Oxford is a registered trade mark of Oxford University
Press in the UK and certain other countries.

Published in the United States of America by Oxford University Press
198 Madison Avenue, New York, NY 10016, United States of America.

© Oxford University Press 2019

CIP data is on file at the Library of Congress
ISBN 978–0–19–007145–5

1 3 5 7 9 8 6 4 2

Printed by Sheridan Books, Inc., United States of America

Once there was a hand-written sign in Cairo that said:
"The Egyptian revolutionary youth reached the moon in the Tahrir space shuttle."
This book is dedicated to them.

Contents

Acknowledgments

In 2008, the American University in Cairo hired me to teach courses on social movements, revolutions, development, and other courses as needed in the department. I had no idea what I was getting myself into, much less any inkling that I would soon be at the epicenter of a revolution. I had spent my doctoral student days digging through archives and conducting interviews on a wide range of opposition to American overseas military bases: labor strikes, street protests, civil disobedience, armed militant attacks, and parliamentary opposition. Beginning in January 2011, I suddenly witnessed an uprising of the kind I had hitherto only read about in books. Thanks to the Egyptian people, I became familiar with varieties of mass defiance that I had never read about anywhere, that were beyond the scope of my imagination. They expanded my understanding of what is possible in this world. For that I will remain eternally grateful.

Over the years, I developed friendships with many people spanning the breadth of Egypt, from Alexandria in the north to Aswan in the south. If I thank each and every one of them, the acknowledgements would go on and on. Given the current regime's conspiratorial proclivities—this is not the right place to thank all of them. They know who they are.

Some of those I should thank are no longer with us. On January 28, 2011, when Tahrir Square was on lockdown, I showed up in front of Pierre Sioufi's apartment after being interrogated by the police. Although I was a total stranger, he and Bea allowed me into his home without asking a single question. Pierre passed away a few years later. His solidarity with me as a stranger on his doorstep – is something that will stay with me.

I thank my students at the American University in Cairo for all they have taught me. Many of my undergraduate and graduate students have gone on to do remarkable things. They overcame obstacles that are far greater than what students in less authoritarian countries have to endure. I am proud of them. It was a privilege to have free rein to teach courses on revolutions while living through one. For that I thank AUC.

I feel lucky to have encountered many people who broke taboos or pushed boundaries. When she became the first woman to run for president in modern Egyptian history, Bothaina Kamel invited me to join her on a campaign trip to Upper Egypt. Khaled Abol Naga never behaved like the famous movie star he is, but was always humble and offering to help. Adam Mekiwi could make people laugh even on the darkest days. His gang of friends took me everywhere and made sure I didn't get lost at the *millioneya*. His family was always welcoming.

Many people shared painful personal stories with me. Mirette Bakir, whose brother Ziad was killed during the revolution while he was trying to protect the Egyptian Museum from potential looting. Ahmed Harara, who lost both of his eyes to snipers and is now entirely blind. Mohamed Soltan, who survived an assassination attempt, and spent almost two years in prison. Aya Hegazi, who spent three years in prison. The list could go on. I am in awe of their bravery and resilience. I thank them—and so many others—for trusting me.

Emmanuelle Salgues and Camilo Gomez hosted me in their guest room when it didn't seem safe for me to stay alone in my apartment. Peter Verkinderen made sure there were rooftop dance parties in Cairo, and also cycling tours through the Sinai in August. Johanneke van den Bos was always up for my schemes, and I for hers. She helped so many people, but preferred that no one knew. I am thankful for the friendship of Sally Toma, Hani Sayed, Mohamed Salah, Mohamed Saleh, Osama Diab, Severine Chavanne O'Neill, George Thabet, Giangina Orsini, Karim-Yassin Goessinger, Zachary Burk—and others who cannot be mentioned.

I forewarned my Arabic tutors, Adel and Khaled, that I would probably not be their best student, but they took me on anyway and taught me a lot. I thank them for their patience.

Brown University's Watson Institute offered me a fellowship in 2013/2014, which allowed me to write the first draft of this manuscript. I am grateful to Peter Andreas for organizing a book workshop despite the fact that the manuscript was still in its very early stages.

In the spring of 2014 I was awarded a fellowship at Harvard University's Belfer Center, but I turned it down. Instead I returned to AUC to go up for tenure. I was honored nonetheless to have received their offer, and appreciate the support of Tarek Masoud. In October 2014 I was invited to the Junior Scholars Book Development workshop at Yale University that was organized by Marc Lynch and the Project on Middle East Political Science, where I received invaluable feedback on the first five chapters of the manuscript.

I owe a tremendous debt of gratitude to the Woodrow Wilson International Center for Scholars where I was awarded a fellowship and spent my post-tenure sabbatical during the 2017/2018 academic year. I would like to thank Jane Harman, Rob Litwak, and Aaron David Miller for their support. Haleh Esfandiari and Henri Barkey, who both previously served as Director of the Middle East Program at the Wilson Center, were also very helpful. After the state-controlled media in Egypt launched a campaign that included absurd allegations about my research, the Wilson Center took the unusual step of extending my fellowship for a second year. It would behoove other institutions to follow their example, and stand up for academic freedom.

There are many colleagues at the Wilson Center who I would like to thank, including Marina and David Ottaway, Diana Negroponte, Gwen Young, and Merissa Khurma. I would also like to thank my fellow fellows: Aynne Kokas, Liz Stanley, and Katie Stallard-Blanchette.

I was fortunate to receive a visiting scholar position from Harvard University's Weatherhead Center for International Affairs during the 2018/2019 academic year. I am grateful to Michele Lamont, Melani Cammett, Kathleen Molony, Ted Gilman, and Michelle Nicholasen.

Soon after I arrived in Washington, the Project on Middle East Democracy (POMED) invited me to present some of my research. I am grateful to Amy Hawthorne, Steve McInerney, Andrew Miller, and the entire POMED staff. It was a pleasure to work with Nancy Okail and the staff at TIMEP to publish the findings of the research project I was directing.

In the spring of 2018, Nathan Brown graciously organized an informal book workshop at George Washington University. I am grateful to Michele Dunne, Diane Singerman and everyone else who read the draft manuscript. Holger Albrecht and Kevin Koehler, both former colleagues of mine at AUC, also read draft chapters. The talented Nadine Bernstein designed some of the graphs and schematic diagrams, for that I am also very thankful.

During the final year of revising the manuscript, I relied on the help of a superb assistant: Sarah ElMasry. I cannot imagine having to finish the project without her. Unless otherwise noted, the translations were provided with her help. Ahmed Atif was also exceedingly helpful; he shared some of the data he had collected as part of Wikithawra, and reviewed my draft manuscript. I learned a lot from Esraa Farouk ElGazzar about student unions at public universities, and from Mahienour El Massry about Egypt's legal system.

Angela Chnapko at Oxford University Press was a pleasure to work with, and I am grateful for all she has done. The comments by two anonymous reviewers were very insightful and helped strengthen the manuscript. Of course, I am responsible for any remaining errors.

Finally, I thank my family Ann, Bert, Doug, Kimberly, Rebekah, Kathryn, and Elijah Holmes. Throughout these turbulent years, they gave me joy, and they always had my back.

PART I
REVOLUTION

1

Introduction

Revolutionary Risings in Egypt

November 3, 2011
Cairo, Egypt

The Greek Club in downtown Cairo had become a favorite hangout for self-described revolutionaries of a certain class. I had gathered there on that Thursday evening with a group of Egyptian friends, most of whom I had met earlier in the year during the mass protests on Tahrir. The country was now being run by the Supreme Council of Armed Forces, headed by Field Marshal Mohamed Hussein Tantawi, whom officers used to secretly deride as "Mubarak's poodle." Once electrified by the revolution, many of my friends were beginning to despair. Three weeks earlier, Coptic Christians had been peacefully demonstrating in front of the state television building, demanding that their churches be protected. They were shot at by army soldiers and run over by tanks, their heads flattened and bodies dismembered. The restaurant where we gathered that evening was about halfway between Tahrir and where the Maspero massacre had occurred. At some point late in the evening after everyone had had a few drinks, my friend, whose birthday we had ostensibly gathered to celebrate, stood up and started shouting, "Yaskot, yaskot hukm el askar!" (Down with military rule!) I looked around at the others, most of them self-professed atheists but from Muslim families; without hesitating they joined in, some of them pounding their fists in the air. The festive atmosphere became tense; their voices were raw with anger. Such open displays of defiance toward the military junta first spread anonymously on the internet, then slowly at street protests—but this was a restaurant. My friends kept chanting, getting louder. No one seemed to mind that other people were staring at us, in silence. We went home. A few weeks later, on November 18, mass protests began again, leading to the uprising known as the Battle of Mohamed Mahmoud. The second wave of the revolution had begun.[1]

***

Living the Revolution

The revolution in Egypt has played out in three waves of rebellion: the first was against President Hosni Mubarak; the second, against the Supreme Council of Armed Forces (SCAF); and the third, against President Mohamed Morsi and the Muslim Brotherhood. It was the second wave that was the most radical, and yet it remains the least understood. Activists targeted the entrenched power of the American-sponsored armed forces in Egypt. At the pinnacle of this power structure stood the unelected junta, known as the SCAF. It is because of the threat of a potential fourth wave of mass mobilization against President Abdel Fattah El-Sisi, and the rise of antimilitarism under the SCAF, that the ongoing crackdown is so ferocious.

When mass protests first erupted on January 25, 2011, many hoped a transition to democracy was in the offing. Instead, the period from 2011 to 2018 is better understood as a *process of revolution and counterrevolution*. The three waves of revolutionary uprisings were followed by what I see as two distinct waves of counterrevolution. Throughout the waves of protests, there has been a three-way power struggle among three conflicting factions who have each vied to transform Egyptian society according to their own vision. Briefly, these blocs included: a largely youthful secular camp who demanded a radical democratization of Egyptian society and demilitarization of the state without attempting to take power themselves; the Muslim Brotherhood who, after winning the presidency and a majority in the parliament, proceeded to preach conservative values and place their followers in leading positions within the state, without fundamentally altering social or economic arrangements; and, finally, a powerful third group that has worked more or less consistently to shield the old regime from prosecution and then, eventually, to resurrect it. I argue that each wave was propelled forward by a fierce, antisystemic opposition that demanded more than the ouster of the ruler at the pinnacle of the regime. Secondly, each uprising represented a struggle against *three distinct forms of authoritarian rule*: the autocratic Mubarak regime and the police state that protected it, the unelected military junta with their unaudited financial holdings, and finally the religious authoritarianism of the Muslim Brotherhood.

What gave the first uprising its revolutionary character is that it went far beyond the demand to oust Mubarak. The resounding chants for "bread, freedom, and social justice" represented wide-ranging demands for economic, social, and political rights. But more than this, the protesters wanted the downfall of *the regime*. This was not merely a rhetorical device or an empty protest slogan. Often overlooked by outside observers is the fact that the Tahririans specifically named a whole slew of Mubarak cronies whom they wanted to oust from power. Activists were not content with the ouster of Mubarak but insisted that neither his son Gamal Mubarak nor spy-chief Omar Suleiman would replace him. Police stations across the country were set ablaze, and certain business tycoons panicked and fled the country, fearing prosecution.

Similarly, during the second wave of unrest, activists were not simply demanding elections or removal of Field Marshal Tantawi, the head of the SCAF. The activists exposed egregious human rights violations committed by security forces. They also uncovered the unaudited financial holdings of the armed forces, making wide-ranging demands for reform and greater accountability of the military establishment that had entrenched itself in the political system since 1952. The growth of this type of antimilitarist activism in Egypt was unprecedented. If Egypt ever transitions away from military rule, it will be because anti-SCAF activists laid the groundwork.

Finally, during the third wave of the revolution, it was not merely President Morsi who was denounced for having failed to deliver his election promises but also the larger leadership of the Muslim Brotherhood from which he hailed. I argue that the movement that toppled Morsi took the form of a large coalition that can be roughly divided into two broad wings: one that could be described as Nasserist or pro-military; and another that was opposed to the military returning to power. Although initially lauded as a pro-democracy rebellion, such categories may obscure more than they explain. While the first uprising against Mubarak may be understood as a demand for representative democracy, the third wave against Morsi displayed an impatience with electoral democracy.

While charting this power struggle, I will tackle a number of questions: How could Mubarak, an entrenched autocratic ruler who had clung to power for three decades, be toppled in a mere 18 days? Did his elite cronies turn against him? The spectacle of occupied Tahrir was clearly the focal point of revolutionary energy, but how important was it really in forcing Mubarak to step down compared to the influence of pressure from the United States? What role did these same actors (the business elite, the military, the United States, and the opposition) play during the second and third waves of revolutionary upheaval? Which social forces joined the mass mobilization against the SCAF, and then against Morsi, and which remained loyal? When did calls to end specific grievances or address certain issues change into broad demands for the fall of the regime? During the first and third waves, the armed forces were instrumental in removing Mubarak and Morsi, while during the second wave, the military itself was the target of popular rage. What is the relationship between the military and each wave of mass mobilization?

Although both Mubarak and Morsi were removed by the armed forces, to describe their ousters as conventional military coups obscures the mass mobilization of civilians that was a crucial element of what should be understood as a *historical process* rather than a singular event on a single day. Recognizing that the ousters of Mubarak and Morsi were not conventional coups, some authors have described their removal as a "democratic coup," a "popularly supported coup," or a "revolutionary coup." However, these conceptual devices suggest that the objectives of the ruling brass and the activists on the streets were aligned. But that was not the case. Furthermore, such terms conceal the fact that the military interventions precipitated large-scale repression and reversed the process of democratic opening. For this reason I have found it necessary to develop a new conceptual framework that describes not only an event but also a process in and through time. A coup may take place within the space of a single day, but a revolution does not happen so quickly.

Before we can answer these questions and begin to understand the revolution, however, we must first understand the regime against which it was directed. This requires putting the recent events in their proper historical context. Egypt, after all, has a revolutionary history. Since the late nineteenth century, Egypt has undergone five mass uprisings: the Urabi revolt in 1881–1882, the revolution in 1919, the Free Officers coup in 1952, the anti-Mubarak uprising in 2011,[2] and the anti-Morsi revolt in 2013. The twentieth century in particular was marked by mass mobilization and growth of the armed forces—which also involved the mobilization of the citizenry. Revolution and warfare both defined the twentieth century, and both involved the entry of the masses into the political arena. As Jeff Goodwin has pointed out, there were many more revolutions during the Cold War era from 1945 to 1991 than during the period from 1789 to 1848; Eric Hobsbawm has referred to the latter as the "age of revolution."[3] Indeed, the sheer number of revolutions and regime-threatening rebellions across the world over the past century makes doing any rigorous analysis an unwieldy task. And yet, as Mark Katz has argued, three countries can be singled out for their significance. This is not necessarily because of the staying power or success of their revolutions but rather because they acted as trailblazers in uncharted territory, forging a path that others attempted to follow. Katz argues that there were three great "central revolutions" of the twentieth century—and they were led by Russia, Iran, and Egypt. All of these countries were incubators of a unique and heretofore historically unprecedented type of revolution, which then triggered a revolutionary wave. The following "central revolutions" were emulated by others: the Marxist-Leninist revolution led by Russia, the Islamic revolution led by Iran, and the Arab nationalist revolution led by Egypt. After the "central revolution" led by Egypt in 1952, what Katz refers to as "affiliate revolutions" took place in Syria and Iraq in 1958, Algeria and South Yemen in 1962, and Sudan and Libya in 1969.[4] In other words, the affiliate revolutions in Sudan and Libya, inspired by Egypt's 1952 revolution, happened a full 17 years later. If we apply the same time frame to the current wave of unrest that began in Tunisia in 2010 and Egypt in 2011, the early risers of the Arab Spring, we may be seeing affiliate protests across the region until 2027 or 2028.

This means that two of the three main types of revolutionary movements had their origins in the Middle East, and yet, ironically, the Middle East has been neglected in academic research on revolutionary movements—at least until recently. The scholars who have essentially shaped the field since the 1970s, including Charles Tilly, Theda Skocpol, Sidney Tarrow, Jeff Goodwin, Eric Wolf, Jack Goldstone, Eric Selbin, John Foran, Timothy Wickham-Crowley, and others, have based their theories and models on case studies of Europe, Asia, and Latin America but largely steered clear of the Middle East.[5] And yet as Theda Skocpol herself admits, the Iranian revolution flew in the face of existing theories of revolutions.[6] The Nasserite revolution in many ways also defied existing assumptions, and it remains controversial and difficult to classify until today. In her locus classicus, *States and Social Revolutions*, Skocpol distinguished between the successful social revolutions in France, Russia, and China and the failed social revolutions in England, Germany, and Japan. But was Nasser's Arab nationalist revolution successful or unsuccessful? While the monarchy was overthrown, land reforms carried out, and the Suez Canal and certain private enterprises nationalized, was the pre-1952 bourgeoisie really uprooted?[7] The espousal of Arab Socialism notwithstanding, were class relations transformed in any significant way? Was it therefore a social revolution, a political revolution, or, in Ellen Kay Trimberger's evocative phrase, a "revolution from above"?[8] Was it in fact a revolution at all, or in reality was it a military coup? These are some of the questions that will be addressed in the next chapter.

Prior to the outbreak of the Arab revolutions in 2010, scholars of revolution had largely shied away from the Middle East; scholars of authoritarianism, however, certainly did not.[9] If one's purpose is to explain the durability or robustness of authoritarian regimes, the Middle East has long offered ample opportunities for field research. In his classic typology of different forms of government, Max Weber classified states that were dominated by a single all-powerful leader as "sultanistic," in reference to the Ottoman sultan.[10] However, this book does not seek to explain the persistence of authoritarian structures. The two chapters on the counterrevolution do, however, offer insights into how the regime was able to reconsolidate itself. While some believed that, with another military leader at the helm, Egypt had reverted to a situation of Mubarakism without Mubarak, I show how Sisi's Egypt is far more repressive than any of its predecessors. At present Egypt is currently under the command of President Abdel Fattah El-Sisi, the leader of the July 3 coup against Mohamed Morsi. Sisi's ascent to power has been accompanied by a series of crackdowns more lethal than those carried out under Mubarak. Violent terrorist attacks have skyrocketed, with over 700 attacks occurring in the 22 months after the ouster of Morsi until the spring of 2015, compared to 90 attacks in the previous 22 months.[11] And the Rabaa massacre in 2013—what Human Rights Watch referred to as Egypt's Tiananmen Square—was the biggest mass killing of civilians in modern Egyptian history.

On a single day and in broad daylight in downtown Cairo, security forces opened fire and killed 932 people who were protesting the coup.[12] Despite mounting repression, we have not (yet) witnessed a fourth wave of massive anti-regime mobilization.

In sum, the primary purpose of this book is to make an empirical, theoretical, and methodological contribution to the literature on Arab revolutions and counterrevolutions—not authoritarianism. First, I will empirically document the revolutionary process in Egypt from 2011 to 2018 and offer the first systematic analysis of what I see as the four most crucial actors in the power struggle: the Egyptian military, the business elite, the United States, and the opposition. I introduce the new activist groups that have emerged, many of which are not well known outside Egypt, as they fall outside the Muslim Brotherhood/ military dichotomy. While not claiming to peer inside the so-called deep state, by providing what I believe is heretofore the most detailed assessment of the counterrevolution, including *who* was targeted *when*, *why*, and with *what type* of state repression, I am able to provide insights into the regime's agenda even if they do not reveal it themselves. Secondly, I hope to make a modest methodological contribution to the study of contentious politics by bringing together the literature on military coups and revolutions, which are often studied separately, and the still very underdeveloped literature on counterrevolutions. While many scholars have been concerned more with the origins or outcomes of the upheaval, I provide a *micro-periodization of the revolutionary process* itself. My ethnographic observations are not mere descriptions but have fundamentally shaped many of my arguments. Theoretically, I expand upon existing concepts of the state as a social relation in order to understand the networks that exist between state and society in Egypt and how they constitute the changing pillars of the Mubarak, Tantawi, and Morsi governments. I introduce the concept of the *coup from below* as a confluence of social protest and military intervention.

Overview of the Book

This book proceeds as follows. The first part covers the period of revolution from 2011 to 2013; the second part delves into the counterrevolution and return to military rule from mid-2013 to 2018. In chapter 2 I discuss the literature on revolutions, on military coups, and on the state and regime in postcolonial Egypt, before introducing the four main social forces that I will discuss throughout the book: the Egyptian military, the business elite, the United States, and the multiheaded opposition. I develop my concept of a *coup from below* by offering a schematic comparison to the *revolution from above*, which began in 1952 with the toppling of King Farouk and expulsion of the British. The Free Officers led by Nasser were junior officers who instigated major changes in the nature of the state, its relationship to society, and its relation to external powers, a process accompanied by relatively limited mobilization or input from civilians. Opposition to Nasser was easily managed by the state through relatively routine forms of repression including detainment and surveillance. This does not mean, however, that state repression was benign. The emphasis on the Arabness of Egypt entailed the suppression of the Nubian culture and language, and the building of the Aswan High Dam led to the submersion of parts of Nubia under the waters of Lake Nasser.

By contrast, the removal of Mubarak and then Morsi happened as the result of a mass mobilization of civilians that forced the hand of senior officers, who then prevented any major changes to the regime and carried out massive repression of activists and civil society at large. The unprecedented levels of violent repression combined with continued support from Egypt's external patrons including the United States, Saudi Arabia, and the United Arab Emirates, has led to a counterrevolutionary outcome. However, episodic forms of protest continue. The transfer of the Tiran and Sanafir islands to Saudi Arabia was not uncontested. And the Nubian minority continues to advocate for their rights, including the implementation of an article in the 2014 Egyptian Constitution. I suggest that referring to the upheaval since 2011 as an Arab Spring serves to continue to erase the contributions of non-Arab minorities, and is in fact a misnomer. The concept of coup from below captures the confluence of top-down military intervention and bottom-up protest, while being inclusive of Egypt's diverse population. The schematic diagram (Figure 1.1) captures the essence

| 1952–1956 | Limited mobilization of civilians | → | Junior officers' coup | → | Fall of monarchy, change of regime | → | Limited repression | → | Revolutionary outcome |

Revolution from Above

| 2011–2018 | Mass mobilization of civilians | → | Senior officers' coup | → | Fall of president, return of regime | → | Mass repression | → | Counterrevolutionary outcome |

Coup from Below

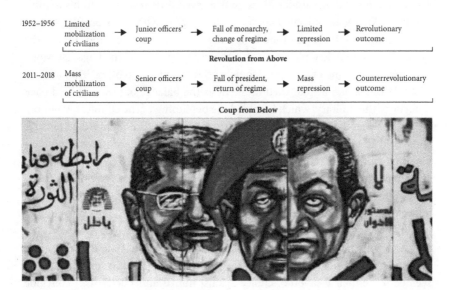

Figure 1.1

of the concepts by juxtaposing 1952–1956 with 2011–2018, while the following chapters will illustrate these points in much greater detail.

In chapter 3 I analyze the first wave of the revolution against Mubarak that took place from January 25, 2011 until February 11, 2011. Refuting arguments that focus on the role of social media or divisions among the elite and the alleged neutrality of the Egyptian military, I argue that a revolutionary coalition of the middle and lower classes created a breaking point for the regime. Key features of this mass mobilization included the refusal of protesters to be cowed by state violence, the creation of "liberated zones" occupied by the people, and "popular security" organizations that replaced the repressive security apparatus of the state, along with strikes that crippled the economy in the final days of the Mubarak era.

In chapter 4 I turn to the much less well-documented second wave of the revolution that took place while the SCAF ruled Egypt from February 12, 2011 until June 30, 2012. Here I analyze the rise of a new form of antimilitarist activism in Egypt. Of the three waves of antigovernment uprisings, this one was perhaps the most revolutionary: the goal was not to topple a single person but to dismantle military rule in Egypt. Many of these activist groups, such as No Military Trials, Kazeboon, The Campaign to End Virginity Tests, Mosireen, and others, were founded and led by women, although men also participated.

The third wave of mass mobilization against the Muslim Brotherhood is discussed in chapter 5. In this chapter I remind readers who may have forgotten that, during the first six months of Morsi's presidency, there was in fact a great deal of collaboration between Morsi and the military establishment. The Mubarak-era business elites also displayed a willingness to continue their profit-making schemes under Morsi and showed little resistance to his administration. American officials had vowed to support whoever won Egypt's first free and fair elections, and they believed a "democratic transition" was in the offing. Of my four key players, it was the citizenry who turned against Morsi first, including some of the very people who voted him into office. The summer of 2013 constituted a watershed moment as the balance of power shifted back in favor of the military, which heralded the beginning of the counterrevolution.

The first year of the counterrevolution under interim President Adly Mansour is covered in chapter 6. Although there was a civilian interim president, a civilian vice president, and a civilian prime minister, I argue that there was no civilian control of the armed forces. The goal during the first wave of the counterrevolution was not only to eliminate the Muslim Brotherhood from politics but to crush any group that could mobilize for street protests, regardless of ideology. It was the bloodiest period in modern Egyptian history. After carrying out numerous massacres of the Muslim Brotherhood, the state turned to secular and independent activists next. The Protest Law passed in November 2013 seemed to be their weapon of choice against non-Islamist activists. I conclude chapter 6 by illustrating how the concept of coup from below can be used to understand other cases such as the removal of leaders in Thailand and Burkina Faso in 2014. The coup attempt in Turkey in 2016 constitutes a negative case.

With the election of Sisi as president, the level and form of state repression changed again, which I cover in chapter 7. During the second wave of the counterrevolution, the regime turned against civil society at large, including groups that played no role in mobilizing for street protests, as well as those who had supported the coup or first wave of the crackdown. The objective seemed to be to silence independent civil society: nongovernmental organizations, charities, the media, universities, researchers, and the Nubian minority were targeted. I conclude the book in chapter 8.

2

Revolutions and Coups

Proffering an analysis of a revolution is in some ways an attempt to explain the inexplicable. Social scientists across the spectrum failed to predict the wave of unrest that became known as the Arab Spring. In the aftermath, they are still struggling to discover the key to unlocking the mystery of revolutionary upheavals. In Egypt, each of the three mass uprisings was directed at the state, hence we must first conceptualize the state apparatus and the regime that ruled it. I conceptualize the state not as a "thing" but instead as an ever-changing set of social relationships. Rather than a monolithic entity, the state is better understood as a fractured apparatus, riven with contradictions.[1]

State and Regime in Egypt

Boasting a lineage that dates back to an ancient civilization, Egypt is in some ways one of the most immutable states in the Arab world. At the same time, Egypt has also been subjected to a long history of foreign intervention or was ruled from afar, such as during the Ottoman period.[2] In 1798, Napoleon launched an ill-fated and short-lived expedition, and in 1882 Egypt was occupied by the British.[3] The emergence of the modern state in Egypt is usually traced to the reign of Muhammad Ali who came to power in 1805. The mid-twentieth century was another watershed, as governing structures were reworked once again. The members of the Free Officers Movement brought about a threefold transformation of state power as they ended the colonial period, abolished the monarchy, and established an independent republic. The Arabness of the new republic was emphasized, and the Arab Republic of Egypt became a prominent example of what Roger Owen referred to as an "Arab security state." Despite changes over time, including a period of economic opening and limited privatization, "at all times, their main function was to maintain a president in power for life."[4]

In his study of the fiscal crisis of the Mubarak regime, Samer Soliman elaborated on the classic Weberian definition of a state as an entity that monopolizes the legitimate use of coercion.[5] For Soliman, the state is "the sum total of public institutions that rule over a specific territory, with their organizational structures, laws and regulations, and formal and informal rules. It is an entity with continuity that surpasses individuals and political regimes."[6] The distinction between state and regime is important, especially in the case of Egypt, and will be returned to in the subsequent discussion. Weber further argued that states can be categorized as either bureaucratic or patrimonial. A bureaucratic state, or rational-legal bureaucracy, usually has a written set of laws and regulations and is characterized by the appointment of officials based on merit, rather than kinship or personal loyalty. In a patrimonial state, the ruler exercises power on the basis of traditional authority, usually kinship networks or patron-client relations, and is less inhibited by the existence of a codified system of laws. Officials are chosen based on their loyalty to the ruler. For almost 60 years, postcolonial Egypt was ruled by just three men: Gamal Abdel Nasser, Anwar el-Sadat, and Hosni Mubarak. Each of them presided over a state apparatus more bureaucratic than patrimonial. One of the causes of mass protests, indeed, was Mubarak's attempt to alter the fundamental nature of the state apparatus by having his son Gamal succeed him, thereby tilting more toward a form of patrimonial rule.

The question of succession in Egypt highlights the necessity of conceptually distinguishing between the state and the regime. Making this distinction is especially important in authoritarian contexts. If the state is an apparatus, the regime is the ruling group of individuals who lead the state. Whereas the state is a structure, the regime consists of actors who think, plan, and make decisions.[7] But how do we determine who belongs to any given regime? This point is a matter of some dispute, and it gets to the question of what type of authoritarian regime we are dealing with.

Just as states may be classified as being either bureaucratic or patrimonial, regimes may be classified as either exclusive or inclusive.[8] Even prior to 2011, there was no scholarly consensus on how to precisely define the Mubarak regime. For Soliman, "the regime means the president of the republic, the top security officials, the council of ministers, and the high public officials who lead and direct diverse state institutions and organs."[9] In contrast, other scholars of Egypt, such as John Waterbury (1983), Robert Springborg (1989), Eberhard Kienle (2001), and Lisa Blaydes (2011), have emphasized that the regimes of Nasser, Sadat, and Mubarak have always included individuals who were *not* members of the state apparatus.[10] At the same time, there may be individuals who, although officially employed by the state, are not part of the ruling elite group. In other words, there may be people who, through bonds of kinship, friendship, or some other informal networks, have more access to the ruler than certain high-ranking state bureaucrats. Precisely for this reason, Lisa Blaydes has urged caution in terms of pinpointing who exactly belongs to the regime, even saying that it is "impossible to precisely identify the core of individuals who make up this body."[11] Blaydes defines the regime in Egypt as including the president; his close family; and the small cadre of super elite who surround him, including senior military, party members, and intelligence officers. Her book analyzes the triad among the ruling regime, the rent-seeking elite, and the broader citizenry. In other words, although she defines "a small cadre of super elite" as belonging to the ruling regime, she considers most of the elite as distinct enough from it that she places them in a separate category. Proximity to the regime is not the same thing as being part of it.

While the importance of informal networks was a common characteristic of the Nasser, Sadat, and Mubarak regimes, there are important differences between the three. For this particular study, the most important change over time is the shift in the relative balance of power among various institutions. Although differing in their assessment of exactly how or why this process occurred, most scholars agree that the regime had become increasingly centralized over time, with power shifting to the president and away from other institutions. So, for example, under Nasser the ruling party and military were two important institutions with their own bases of power, separate and distinct from the executive. Sadat began the process of hollowing out the ruling party and removing the military from politics, a trend that Mubarak reinforced. According to Stacher, Sadat not only replaced the Arab Socialist Union (ASU) with the National Democratic Party (NDP), but he also created a "toothless version" of it.[12]

With a ruling party that had been hollowed out, a parliament that had been rendered impotent, a judiciary that could be manipulated, and a military that was allowed to oversee an economic empire at the price of political subservience, the presidency had become paramount. For three decades Mubarak sat at the apex of an authoritarian regime, and he did not tolerate even the appearance of independence. As Stacher argues, the Egyptian regime was "an executive-heavy political system where other state organizations do not maintain the ability to act independently."[13] Soliman puts it even more bluntly in saying that the president enjoyed "almost absolute power."[14]

And yet one of the paradoxes of the Egyptian case is that the amassing of ever more power in the hands of the president did not in any way preclude the development of a diverse and unruly civil society. The term "hybrid state" perhaps best describes the Mubarak regime, in which "political expression" was tolerated but "political action" was not. Samer Soliman concurs that, although freedom of expression may have increased with the advent of satellite channels, private television channels, and the spread of social media, freedom of association was more limited. The creation of independent trade unions and political parties was strictly curtailed. Nongovernmental organizations (NGOs) and charities, however, found ways to operate despite restrictions. By one estimate, the number of NGOs in Egypt had grown to around 48,000 by the end of the Mubarak era.[15]

Finally, the Mubarak regime was also bolstered by international support. Building upon the literature on domestic sources of autocracy, scholars have begun to analyze the international dimensions of authoritarianism. Jason Brownlee's book *Democracy Prevention* focuses specifically on the US-Egyptian alliance, while Oisin Tansey's *The International Politics of Authoritarian Rule* takes a comparative approach.[16] Brownlee questions many of the prevailing assumptions regarding US democracy promotion efforts overseas. In many ways his book represents a challenge to the framework developed by Steven Levitsky and Lucan Way in their book *Competitive Authoritarianism*. Levitsky and Way argue that the relative weight of domestic versus international factors in democratization processes varies in predictable ways across regions and countries. According to their analysis, the extent to which international actors can promote democratization depends on the extent of linkage and leverage that the West has vis-à-vis autocratic regimes. They define leverage as "governments' vulnerability to external democratizing pressure," while linkage to the West depends on the density of ties (economic, political, diplomatic, social, and organizational) and cross-border flows (of capital goods and services, people and information) among particular countries and the United States, the European Union, and Western-dominated multilateral institutions. In their assessment: "[I]n states with extensive ties to the West, post–Cold War international influences were so intense that they contributed to democratization even where domestic conditions were unfavorable."[17] Most of the regimes they analyze fall into the category of what they term "competitive authoritarian" regimes. Egypt, according to their assessment, was a "fully authoritarian" regime. This was in part because until then Egypt's three post-1952 presidents—Nasser, Sadat, and Mubarak—did not come to power through elections, and the elections that did take place were not competitive enough to merit the distinction of being ranked as those of a "competitive authoritarian" regime. Brownlee agrees with Levitsky and Way in categorizing Egypt as highly autocratic. Furthermore, he maintains that "there has been no autocracy more linked to and leveraged by the United States than that of Egypt."[18] This can be summarized as the following five types of linkage:

Type of linkage as defined by Levitsky and Way		Egypt
Economic linkage: flows of trade, investment, and credit.	x	Top three countries in terms of FDI in Egypt: United Kingdom, Belgium, United States (2016–2017).
Intergovernmental linkage: diplomatic and military ties, participation in Western-led treaties and organizations.	x	Egypt is a major non-NATO ally and receives the second-highest level of US military aid in the world.
Technocratic linkage: share of the country's elite that is educated in the West or has professional ties to Western universities.	x	The American University in Cairo was established in 1919, where many Egyptian elites have been educated.
Social linkage: flows of people across borders, tourism, immigration, diaspora networks.	x	Dependence on foreign tourism.
Information linkage: flows of information via telecommunications, Internet, Western media.	x	In January 2011, the official number of Internet users was 23.51 million; the number of Mobile subscribers was 71.45 million.[19]
Civil society linkage: local ties to Western-based NGOs or party organizations.	x	Many Egyptian civil society organizations have ties to the West.

Four Pillars of Regime Support

The Business Elite, the Military, the United States, and the People

Given the sprawling nature of the Egyptian state bureaucracy, the longstanding reliance on foreign aid, and the disagreement among scholars as to who or what exactly constitutes the regime, I contend that it is important to focus on which social forces matter most *during a period of revolutionary unrest*. Here it is important to distinguish between what I consider *tools of the regime* and *pillars of support for the regime*.

Despite the "executive-heavy" nature of the Mubarak regime, the president was not able to rule alone. Mubarak relied on the loyalty of his ministers and various state institutions, such as the Ministry of Interior, the Ministry of Information, the state media, and the National Democratic Party (NDP).[20] For our purposes, we may consider most of these institutions as tools of his regime that he could deploy as he pleased. When the uprising began on January 25, 2011, Mubarak could instruct his security forces to attack unarmed protesters, which they did. He could instruct the state-controlled media to report that the uprising was the result of a foreign conspiracy in which "foreign hands" were pulling the strings, which they did. As will be discussed in the following chapter, on January 28, 2011 police stations across Egypt were attacked and the headquarters of the NDP was set ablaze by protesters.[21] This happened precisely because protesters considered these institutions as part of the regime. However, Mubarak also relied on four other sources of support: a network of elite allies, the institution of the military, the United States, and the acquiescence of the citizenry. While Mubarak could usually expect them to be loyal, they also enjoyed a greater degree of agency than the Ministries of Interior and Information, the state-controlled media, or the NDP. They had the ability to decide whether or not to continue to prop up Mubarak or to pressure him to step down. For this reason, I see these institutions as the four social forces whose support or withdrawal of support for the regime was most decisive.

This theoretical framework has allowed me to incorporate insights from four broad schools of thought in the study of revolutions: the state-centered, mass mobilization, international, and Marxist approaches. In brief, the framework as a whole with the four regime pillars was inspired by the state-centered approach; I included the military as a pillar of the regime for reasons that will become clear if they are not already. I included the business elite as a second pillar of the regime, not merely because of the Marxist insistence that class matters but because business elites, which John Sfakianakis (2004) aptly referred to as "whales of the Nile," played their part in propping up the regime. In deciding to include the United States as a third important form of support, I took my cue from the international approach, but also included it because of the unceasing US military aid to Egypt. And finally, it was the *millioneya* and other large protests that convinced me it was necessary to take seriously the tactics of activists, which is of course in line with the mass mobilization approach.

The Business Elite

The Mubarak regime was "executive-heavy," and yet Mubarak could not rule by himself. He relied on a network of elite cronies that included both state bureaucrats and capitalists. During the 1990s, a class of business elites had grown enormously wealthy through the privatization program. Referred to as "whales of the Nile," John Sfakianakis (2004) identified 32 businessmen who comprised what he considered the established business elite of Egypt, with a large majority engaged mainly in import-substitution.[22] This elite sector flourished behind barriers of protection, was uncompetitive on the international market, and existed in large part due to rent-seeking operations that became more pronounced in the 1990s as the Egyptian economy expanded. More recently, Stephen Roll identified 22 businessmen with net assets exceeding $100 million, as well as seven leading media magnates as of 2011.[23] The considerable financial resources of this small business elite could, in theory, be translated into political resources if deployed for political ends. Business elites could potentially fund the opposition, and they could engage in an economic boycott of the regime. Or, on the contrary, they could use their wealth to support the regime. Although the business elites were tied to the regime through crony networks, their financial resources also gave them potential autonomy from the regime, making their actions during a period of revolutionary upheaval decisive.

In addition to economic elites, the Mubarak regime had fostered a group of state bureaucrats or political elites. Some of the most politically powerful elites were Safwat el-Sherif (Minister of Information and later NDP secretary-general), Zakaria Azmi (Mubarak's Chief of Presidential Staff for 22 years), Yousef Wali (Minister of Agriculture and later also NDP secretary-general), and Kamal el-Shazly (Minister of Parliamentary Affairs). Despite their proximity to Mubarak, their long tenure at the pinnacle of his regime, and their own vast networks, it was possible for them to be marginalized as Gamal Mubarak began his ascent within the ranks of the NDP.[24] Amr Moussa had spent 10 years serving in the Foreign Ministry and had developed his own extensive patronage networks. His outspoken criticism of US policy toward Israel and the Palestinian territories endeared him to the Egyptian population. In May 2001, he was transferred suddenly to the Arab League. Within 48 hours, his career was stunted and he was essentially removed from the sphere of domestic politics. Because the political power of elites was not institutionally based, Mubarak could change the nature of the ruling coalition relatively easily. He could bring in new elites and shed others as he pleased. Political elites knew that they could be easily replaced; indeed, as public fury mounted in early 2011, Mubarak did not hesitate to reshuffle his cabinet, dismiss high-ranking officials, and even sacrifice the political career of his own son. Financial elites, with vast economic resources, could not be as easily cast aside or replaced. And yet they were also dependent on the state for licenses and access to government contracts; they too were for the most part co-opted by the regime. Elites played a timid role in the ouster of Mubarak. This dynamic changed, however, during the third wave of the revolution against President Mohamed Morsi. Titans of the Egyptian economy such as Naguib Sawiris admit to having funded the alleged "grass-roots" campaign known as Tamarod; commissioned a music video in support of the protests; and allowed the offices of his political party, the Free Egyptians, to be used for collecting signatures.

After the ouster of Morsi and the return to military rule, it appears that money flowing from the Gulf may have been more important in shoring up the economy than Egyptian business elites, as will be discussed in chapter 7. Just days after his ascension to the presidency, Sisi called on Egyptians to donate everything they could to help solve Egypt's financial woes. By February 2016, 4.7 billion LE (about 600 million USD) had been donated, while aid flows to Egypt from the United Arab Emirates (UAE) alone totaled more than 14 billion USD from 2013 to 2015, not including funds from Saudi Arabia, Kuwait, and other countries (as will be discussed in chapter 6).[25]

The Military

The armed forces under Nasser played a crucial role in the anticolonial struggle against the British, and they have maintained a dominant position in the political scene ever since.[26] The growth of a powerful military was at least in part a legacy of the colonial period. After centuries of foreign domination, the military could claim to safeguard Egypt's independence. However, the end of the colonial period did not mean the end of foreign intervention, as the Suez Crisis in 1956 demonstrated. The fear of being reoccupied by a foreign power continued even after Egypt acquired sovereignty; it was not based on unfounded fears but on the actual experience of British, French, and Israeli aggression. This is the historical context in which the Egyptian military grew to become the strongest in the Arab world. By 2011, Egypt was estimated to be capable of mobilizing 480,000 soldiers (900,000 including reservists), 3,000 tanks, 550 fighter aircraft, 250 helicopters, and approximately 50 warships.[27] Its strength lies in the sheer number of men it can recruit and the yearly infusions of American military aid, which allow it to purchase state-of-the-art weaponry, such as F-16 fighters and M1A1 tanks.[28] The Egyptian military can claim a legacy of liberating the country and throwing off the colonial yoke and has an arsenal of advanced weaponry at its disposal. It has the ability to conscript the male population for armed service and to mobilize the entire population for other services in the name of Egyptian nationalism. Finally, the military has been allowed to develop its own businesses, giving it a stream of revenue independent of the state budget.[29] All of this means that the Egyptian armed forces have a considerable amount of political, economic, and social power independent of the executive. This independent power has most often been referred to as autonomy from the state. At the same time, however, the military is also tied to the state. Indeed, it is tied to the regime, as one of its main purposes was to safeguard against internal threats. In theory, State Security (*Amn ed-Dawla*), Central Security (*al-Amn el-Markazi*), and the intelligence services (*Mukhabarat*) were responsible for internal security, but in practice the army could also play this role.

The United States

Perhaps ironically, it is first and foremost through the institution of the armed forces, which presents itself as a guarantor against foreign domination, that the United States has obtained more leverage over Egypt than any other external actor. The influence of the United States dates back to June 1972, when Sadat expelled up to 20,000 Soviet military personnel and signaled that Egypt was turning away from the East and toward the West.[30] As the primary patron of the military since the Camp David Accords, the United States ensures a steady flow of $2 billion annually in aid, trains Egyptian officers, and has designated Egypt as a major non-NATO ally. Of course, the United States is not the only country with an interest in what goes on along the Nile. The European Union (EU) has an array of democracy promotion and economic development initiatives in Egypt whose stated goals are not fundamentally different from those of the United States. And after the ouster of Morsi, Saudi Arabia and the UAE offered to infuse the flailing Egyptian economy with billions of dollars, mainly in the form of central bank deposits and petroleum products, although the exact nature and amount of this aid is difficult to verify, as will be discussed in chapter 6.

Why have I included the United States as a pillar of support for the regime and not the EU or the Gulf states? First, the United States still acts as a hegemonic power in the region. This does not mean it will be that way forever. Precisely because states are not static entities but a set of social relationships, they can change over time. Secondly, and perhaps more importantly, however, I would follow Jason Brownlee in arguing that the full spectrum of US support for Egypt since the Camp David Accords has meant that the United States has become more of a domestic partner than an external power.[31] Briefly, the United States contributed to the stability and longevity of the Mubarak regime through sustained economic, political, and military support. This includes the provision of military aid since 1979. Egypt is one of the top recipients of US military aid in the world. According to Hillel Frisch, the Egyptian military was modernized almost solely at the expense of US taxpayers, which is especially the case with big ticket items.[32] Moheb Zaki has made the point that Mubarak preserved access to advanced weapons, training, and other benefits flowing from Washington to ensure that the army would have a direct stake in both his rule and the relationship to the United States.[33] In the early 1990s, when Egypt's economy was teetering on the brink of disaster, and an outbreak of bread riots as in 1977 was not entirely unthinkable, it was the United States who took the initiative to cancel half of Egypt's foreign debt, saving the economy and arguably prolonging Mubarak's reign. This was of course not merely an act of benevolence but an implicit form of payback for Egypt's support for the US-led First Gulf War.[34] In addition, Stacher has argued that US policies regarding Egypt have accentuated the drive toward centralization of power in the hands of the executive.[35] And finally, it is an unlikely coincidence that the first multiparty presidential elections took place in September 2005—during the height of the Bush "Freedom Agenda" and just a few months after Secretary of State Condoleezza Rice gave a speech at the American University in Cairo (AUC). In her closing remarks Rice said:

> The day is coming when the promise of a fully free and democratic world, once thought impossible, will also seem inevitable. The people of Egypt should be at the forefront of this great journey, just as you have led this region through the great journeys of the past.[36]

In sum, US support was constitutive of the Mubarak regime, and I therefore consider the United States as one of the four crucial pillars of support for the regime. If the money coming from the Gulf states continues, it may be necessary to revise the framework to include them as a major source of support for the regime. It is too early, however, to know if that will be the case.

Each of the first three actors I have discussed—the military, the business elite, and the United States—under normal circumstances support whoever is in power for however long they are in power. In the case of Mubarak, this meant almost 30 years. However, they each possess the financial, military, and political resources to potentially exert pressure on the regime. At least in theory, their resources also give them the potential autonomy that is needed to withdraw their support from the regime. Because the Egyptian military, the business elite, and the United States have a built-in ability to pressure whoever is in power, *regardless of whether or not they use this influence*, I have modified my conception of the state to include them as pillars of support for the regime.

The People and the Antiregime Opposition

The final pillar of support for the regime is the most broad and amorphous, yet arguably also the most important for any study of revolutions: the citizenry. I therefore include "the people" as a fourth pillar of support for the regime. The existence of mass protests is a defining feature of any revolutionary movement, and yet in Egypt, the sheer size and scale of street protests was truly remarkable. In 2011, Egypt experienced more protests than any other country in the world. According to the dataset compiled from newspaper reports, the top 10 countries included all 6 of the countries in the Arab world that were shaken by regime-threatening mobilizations (see Graph 2.1).

Authoritarian regimes are usually seen as less embedded in society than democratic ones, and thus they are able to rule without the active consent of the citizenry who, in democratic polities, at least have the ability to vote incumbents in or out of office. And yet this does not mean that the actions or attitudes of a population who live under authoritarian rule are entirely irrelevant. Although many in the Egyptian population may not have actively supported Mubarak,

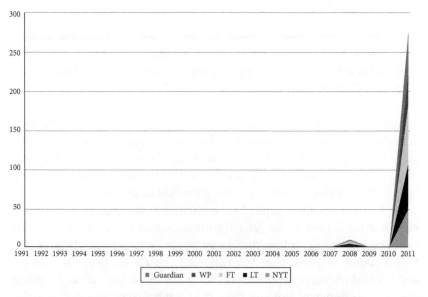

Graph 2.1 Protests in Egypt between 1991 and 2011 as reported in the *Guardian, Washington Post, Financial Times, London Times,* and *New York Times.*

Graph from Sahan Savas Karatasli et al., "Class, Crisis, and the 2011 Protest Wave: Cyclical and Secular Trends in Global Labor Unrest," in Overcoming Global Inequalities, ed. Immanuel Maurice Wallerstein and Christopher K. Chase-Dunn (London: Paradigm, 2015). https://bit.ly/2tp0kgI.

as his cronies did, by acquiescing to his tenure in power, or not attempting to overthrow him, they contributed to the longevity of his regime. Marx described the transformation from a class-in-itself to a class-for-itself as the transformation that occurs when a social class, objectively defined according to its economic position, becomes conscious of itself as a class with common interests and, with this subjective awareness, begins to act according to its economic or political interests. The citizenry undergoes a similar transformation. Perhaps the moment when this transformation was crystallized most clearly was when hundreds of thousands, perhaps millions, of Egyptians began chanting: "The people demand the downfall of the regime."

The people were transformed from an amorphous group into a collective actor who asserted its common interests. By demanding the toppling of the government, the people became a revolutionary oppositional movement. To a large extent, this opposition came about without the leadership of a revolutionary organization. The Muslim Brotherhood did not organize the protests on January 25, although some of their members did join the demonstrations, and Egypt's much smaller socialist parties and activist networks could also not claim to be leading the fray.[37] In the following chapters, I will analyze the actions of those who joined the revolutionary opposition or called for the downfall of Mubarak, the SCAF, and Morsi.

How can we begin to define or pinpoint who exactly belonged to the revolutionary opposition? Between 2011 and 2013, a whole array of social movement activism burst onto the scene—and yet, I am precisely interested in those groups who demanded the downfall of Mubarak, the SCAF, and Morsi. Other forms of activism are not included. Still, how can we begin to categorize such a diverse array of activism in which millions of people were involved?

Jeff Goodwin distinguishes between two different types of revolutionary movements that he refers to as radical or conservative. A radical revolutionary movement seeks to control the state but also aims to transform it in some fundamental way. A conservative revolutionary movement also seeks to control the state, but it wishes to preserve or only modestly reform existing economic, social, and cultural arrangements.[38] A large portion of the revolutionary activists in Egypt do not fall into either category because, although they demanded the fall of the regime, they were not trying to take control of the state themselves.[39] The Muslim Brotherhood, however, can be categorized as a conservative revolutionary movement as it did seize control of the state apparatus, but—other than placing its own members in positions of power—it did not initiate a major overhaul of economic or political arrangements. Whether the Muslim Brotherhood would have done so had it remained in power longer is, of course, a matter of speculation. The three-way power struggle was thus between a conservative revolutionary movement that was temporarily catapulted to power, a radical revolutionary movement who did not attempt to seize state power, and the old regime that viewed both conservative and radical revolutionaries as an existential threat to its own existence.

This definition of the state allows me to combine two contrasting approaches to revolutions: (1) the structural or state-centered approach that focuses on divisions within the regime and the ruling class, including external pressure on the state; and (2) a strategic or agency-based approach that focuses on the dynamic interaction between the state and the opposition.[40]

Precisely because the regime was biased toward the executive—and because the mass protests were directed against the executive (Mubarak, the SCAF, and Morsi)—I do not provide a full accounting of the role of all the other state institutions in the revolution, such as the judiciary, the state media, the Ministry of Interior, the Ministry of Social Solidarity, or other government ministries. Although these institutions are significant in other ways, I do not believe that they are as crucial as the four pillars that I discuss *during times of revolutionary mobilization*.

This can be illustrated with two examples. The judiciary and the Ministry of Interior were arguably two of the most important components of the Mubarak regime, and yet I do not include them as pillars of support for the regime— why? The pillars that I have chosen to include in my analysis are important— *not because they are components of the regime*—but rather because their *support* for the regime is not just "nice to have" but somehow of existential importance. In other words, their withdrawal of support for the regime should at least have a destabilizing impact on the regime even if not sufficient to cause it to topple. At a bare minimum, the four pillars I have included must be more than just tools of the regime: they must have the autonomy to decide whether they will support or not support the regime.

Hence, if this were a book about security-sector reform or the process of writing a new constitution, I would clearly need to put the Ministry of Interior and the judiciary at the center of my analysis. But this is a book about social mobilization. For this reason, the issue of security-sector reform (or lack thereof) and the issue of constitutional change are not front and center, but rather these issues are brought into the discussion when they become important during the uprisings. Still, the judiciary and the police may still be important for a study of social movements in other ways. For example, Mubarak was constitutionally allowed to rule indefinitely. It was the judiciary that made it possible to issue a ban on protests. And it was a court in Upper Egypt that issued several mass death sentences (all of them supporters of the deposed President Morsi) in the spring of 2014. In one case 529 defendants were sentenced to death, and in another 683 people were sentenced to death.[41] This meant that, within four months, 1,212 people had been sentenced to death in Egypt, which was more than the total number of people who had been executed in the rest of the world combined in 2013 (with the exception of China).[42] Clearly the judiciary played a role in the longevity of the Mubarak regime, and it has also played a role in providing a legal justification for the crackdown on secular activists and the attempt to exterminate Islamist activists. But this begs the question: Is the judiciary a tool of the regime or an autonomous actor? And even if it theoretically has the autonomy to break ranks with the regime, would it matter if it did? On both counts I am skeptical. Prior to the 2011 uprising, scholars were divided on the issue of how independent the judiciary was, with some seeing it as an important counterweight to the president because it was formally independent, because activists were not always prosecuted as the regime may have wished, and because protests by lawyers have at times won certain concessions.[43] However, others saw the judiciary as lacking true independence. According to Joshua Stacher, Mubarak was able to subvert the court's power by "selectively applying the court's decisions, manipulating a ruling's implementation, or promulgating parliamentary legislation to counter laws."[44]

For example, after Morsi passed his constitutional declaration in November 2012, a number of lawyers announced that they would boycott the referendum in the following month. Their boycott, however, was ineffective and the referendum proceeded as planned because the Muslim Brotherhood simply found other people to monitor the referendum. The lawyers' boycott of the constitutional referendum cannot be seen as having destabilized Morsi.

In a similar manner, the Ministry of Interior was an important component of the Mubarak regime—indeed, Egypt was often referred to as a police state. But was the Ministry of Interior a tool of the regime, or was it an institution with the ability to act independently? As will be discussed in the following chapters, the police were ordered to defend the Mubarak regime when the mass protests began. Unleashing his police force against protesters was therefore a *regime strategy* of Mubarak. And attacking police stations was a *protest strategy*. In other words, during the first wave of the revolution, the police were less an autonomous actor than a tool used by Mubarak to stay in power. And the people who took to the streets on January 25 and the following days attacked police stations because they saw them as *part of the regime*. After Mubarak was toppled, much of the police force was absent from the streets for the first half of 2011 when the SCAF was in power. Did the fact that the police had largely abandoned their posts destabilize the SCAF? This does not appear to have been the case.

To summarize, it is not clear that the Ministry of Interior or the Ministry of Justice have enough autonomy to withdraw support from the regime, which is why I would see them as components of the regime rather than pillars of the regime with potential autonomy. And even if these ministries are indeed able to hedge their support for the regime in some ways, it does not appear to have as destabilizing an impact as if the military, the business elite, or the United States were to withdraw their support for the regime.

Structure and Strategy

My approach has been inspired by Theda Skocpol's classic work *States and Social Revolutions* and her framework that analyzes the relationship of the elite to the state, the role of the military, and the effect of international pressure. Although the cases Skocpol examined were social revolutions that took place in peasant-based societies and not political revolutions in urbanized societies against modern dictators, I take seriously her insistence that we analyze the level of autonomy of the state from the elite, as opposed to the Marxist assumption that the state merely acts on behalf of the capitalist class.[45] While my focus is primarily on the Egyptian business class and their ability to potentially support either the regime or the opposition, I also take into consideration transnational aid flows from outside Egypt.[46] I have also drawn from Goodwin's *No Other Way Out: States and Revolutionary Movements* and his approach of focusing on the state as the key unit of analysis, in particular levels of repression, bureaucratization, and inclusiveness, which I will discuss further later in the chapter.[47]

In his early work on the French Revolution, Charles Tilly urged scholars to study revolutions as a chain of contentious events.[48] In his later work, he analyzed how variation in regimes affected what he called the "repertoire of contention." Readers familiar with his book *Regimes and Repertoires* will see his influence on my analysis of the relationship between protest strategies and regime strategies during each wave of unrest.[49]

Although I have endeavored to build off the work of these scholars, I have also allowed my own ethnographic observations to shape my arguments. These observations are what have ultimately led me at times to diverge from the comfort zone of eminent scholarship and preexisting explanations. In this way, my ethnography may begin as a descriptive device, but it strives to approach the realm of the analytical.[50] At times I have signposted these ethnographic vignettes as italicized text, and at other times they are included in the text without forewarning.

Goodwin has distinguished between four types of state-centered analyses of revolutions, which he refers to as the state-autonomy, state-capacity, political-opportunity, and state-constructionist approaches.[51] The first of these emphasizes the level of autonomy of state officials from members of the capitalist class

or civil society, while the state-capacity approach examines the material resources of the state and its ability to penetrate society. The state-constructionist
approach looks at how state practices may shape or construct the identities,
ideas, or social ties among actors in society. Finally, the political opportunity
approach emphasizes that state crises may be exploited by opponents of the
regime.

According to a US embassy cable, Mubarak had at least doubled the size of
the internal security apparatus—estimated at 1.4 million strong—compared
to Sadat.[52] From a state-capacity perspective, the Mubarak regime was able to
penetrate the society it ruled. Although there may have been certain parts of
the vast desert wilderness that were not under regular surveillance, between 95
to 99 percent of the population lives along the Nile valley, on less than 5 percent
of the country's territory. It is safe to say that the Egyptian people were, almost
without exception, under the watchful eyes of the state. Furthermore, there
seems to be a general consensus among observers that the political-opportunity
structure in Egypt had not experienced any sort of opening prior to the uprising; if anything, it had become more restrictive. The parliamentary elections
in 2010 resulted in the opposition being expelled from parliament and the NDP
winning 97 percent of the seats. According to Dina Shehata, "the fraudulent
elections of 2010 marked a departure from the limited political pluralism insti-
tuted by Sadat."[53] In what follows I hope to show how the Egyptian case defies
certain expectations of the different state-centered approaches.

In sum, I argue that the Egyptian state relies on four pillars of support: the
elite, the military, the United States, and popular acquiescence. The Egyptian
state can thus be thought of as an expression of the balance of all these social
forces. Analyzing all of them requires "studying up," but also down and side-
ways.[54] However, the state is not a static entity, as each of these four pillars has
agency. I analyze how each of these pillars of the regime responded to the outbreak of mass protests and how the regime itself endeavored to stay in power.
Of crucial importance is not just *whether* each pillar withdrew support from the
regime or not, but *when* it did so. This brings us to the question of timing.

Timing and the Revolutionary Process

Having defined how I combine structure and agency and how I define the
state, I now must also address the issue of time. While Skocpol analyzes the
longer-term structural causes of revolutions, I provide a *micro-periodization*
of both revolutionary and counterrevolutionary processes between the outbreak of mass protests in early 2011 until 2018. I will examine each of the

three antigovernment uprisings as well as the two waves of government crackdowns. Micro-periods have been used to study important historic ruptures, as they can reveal crucial developments that larger-scale models overlook. By honing in on a short period, scholars are able to bring together bigger issues in a new synthesis, which may allow the explanation of structural change.[55]

Precisely because I consider the tactics of activists important, I do not simply register the fact that mass protests erupted, but zoom in on key events during each wave of unrest and describe on a weekly, daily, and at times hourly basis how the protests unfolded, a level of detail that can easily be lost in more sweeping longue durée approaches. In what some consider his seminal essay on the French Revolution, William H. Sewell concentrates on the 12 days between July 12 and July 23, 1789 in order to demonstrate how "the usual articulations between different structures become profoundly dislocated."[56] But in contrast to Sewell and other historians who work on micro-periods, I provide a *real-time ethnography* of the revolutionary events as I witnessed them. Following Victor Turner, Sewell argues that the dislocation of structures results in a liminality or a "betwixt and between." The uncertainty caused by the evaporation of social constraints results in various forms of mass defiance. People no longer know if the person *in* power actually *has* power, to whom they owe allegiance, or whose rules to obey. Aristide Zolberg has referred to these ruptures when "all is possible" as "moments of madness."[57] It is not just the destruction of the old order that constitutes the revolutionary, but the creation, however momentarily and imperfectly, of a new one. Collective defiance leads to collective creativity. Often considered beyond the pale of academic scholarship, it is the elusive, utopian dimension of protests that I also attempt to capture through my ethnography. In other words, while at times activists adopt protest strategies to respond to specific regime strategies, at other times they break out of this macabre dance and create their own forms of struggle—sowing the seeds of a new society. During each wave of revolutionary mobilization I will answer the following questions:

1. When did revolutionary opposition emerge toward each regime? In other words, when did calls to end specific grievances or address certain issues change into demands for the fall of the regime?
2. What other demands were articulated?
3. Which social forces joined the opposition and when?
4. Which social forces remained loyal?
5. To what extent did the business elite, the military, and the United States withdraw their support for the regime—and when?

Here it is important to highlight that I am not attempting to document all forms of social unrest in Egypt during this time period, but rather those groups that demanded the downfall of Mubarak, the military junta, or Morsi. For example, during the second wave I argue that popular support for the SCAF was withdrawn in July 2011 when activists occupied Tahrir for three weeks. During the Battle of Mohamed Mahmoud in November–December 2011, the opposition gained further in strength, momentum, and number of supporters. However, a number of activist groups emerged even prior to November 2011 that began challenging the SCAF's authority. Similarly, although the emergence of Tamarod was an important development during the third uprising against Morsi, protests began even before Tamarod. The issue of timing is important, and it brings us to the politically charged question that gets to the heart of the matter: Was this chain of contentious events in fact a revolution or rather a coup d'état?

Revolutions and Coups

Revolutions and military coups are usually studied as discrete phenomena. Revolutions erupt as a result of mass protests from below, while military coups are top-down seizures of power. Coup-plotters may conspire entirely in darkness, with the public only becoming aware of their intentions when soldiers on tanks emerge from their barracks. By contrast, revolutions are usually preceded by days if not years of civil unrest, and by definition these activities are impossible to conceal from the public.

They purportedly result in very different outcomes. Revolutions with the most far-reaching consequences succeed in changing social structures including class relations. The revolutions in France in 1789, Russia in 1917, and China in 1949 are not the only but perhaps the most prominent examples of what Theda Skocpol termed "social revolutions," involving mass mobilization of the peasantry or working classes.[58] More frequently, such upheavals only result in changes in institutions and are designated as political revolutions. Of all the six major Arab Spring upheavals, the ouster of Zine El Abidine Ben Ali in Tunisia in 2011 may most closely approximate a political revolution because the previous autocratic regime is in the process of being dismantled and replaced by a more representative political system, while class relations remain largely intact.

Military coups, however, are commonly believed to change neither socioeconomic structures nor political institutions but merely to replace one leader with another. And this may even be temporary. A coup attempt is defined as successful if the perpetrators seize and hold power for just seven days.[59] In order for a social revolution to be deemed successful, much more needs to happen. Feudal structures should crumble, land should be redistributed, or some other more significant and lasting transformations should be set in motion. In terms of their political impact, coups are assumed to be inherently antidemocratic. In the language of principal-agent theory, this is because the coup inverts civil-military relations, making the armed forces principals and relegating the ousted politicians to the status of agents.[60] Recently Clayton Thyne and Ozan O. Varol have challenged this assumption. Using case studies of Turkey in 1960, Portugal in 1974, and Egypt in 2011, Varol argues that while all coups have "anti-democratic features," some coups may actually promote democracy if they respond to popular opposition to authoritarian rulers and facilitate free and fair elections.[61] Revolutions, on the contrary, may result in new regimes that can be either more or less democratic than the anciens régimes they replaced.[62]

Given that they can be carried out quickly and with a small number of people, military coups occur much more frequently than social revolutions. According to one count, Bolivia experienced 193 coups between 1825 and 1981. Richard Lachmann claims these turnovers "had virtually no effect on social relations in that country or on the structure and policies of the state."[63] He therefore likens military coups to political neutron bombs: they may kill people, but not institutions.

Because coups are often undertaken by or on behalf of elites, they may be used to thwart popular uprisings from below. For this reason military coups may at times reverse economic policies that threaten either the elite or foreign interests. Examples include the ouster in 1952 of Mohammad Mossadegh, the democratically elected prime minister of Iran, who was toppled by a coup orchestrated by the Central Intelligence Agency (CIA) and MI6 after he nationalized the oil industry. Similarly, President Salvador Allende of Chile was killed during the 1973 military coup that led to the installment of General Augusto Pinochet, who quickly reversed a number of Allende's redistributive economic policies. This has led some scholars to refer to military coups as the harbinger of the counterrevolution or as leading to the "reversal of the process of revolution."[64] Coups that are carried out with the explicit or implicit support of foreign intelligence agencies are widely, but not universally, regarded as inherently antidemocratic.

A third type of regime change combines features of both, and is what Ellen Kay Trimberger termed "revolution from above."[65] Similar to social revolutions, they result in wide-ranging political and economic transformations but, similar to coups, they are led by military officers. In the early 1920s Mustafa Kemal Atatürk oversaw the dissolution of the 600-year-old Ottoman Empire and established the Republic of Turkey. Far-reaching transformations included abolishing the sultanate and caliphate, introducing a new alphabet, and moving the capital from Istanbul to Ankara. In the 1950s, Gamal Abdel Nasser overthrew the monarchy, evicted the British, redistributed land, and nationalized the Suez Canal and other industries. The Free Officers presented themselves as the first Egyptians to rule Egypt since the advent of modernity. Trimberger describes Atatürk and Nasser as "military bureaucrats" who carried out these large-scale transformations with little mass mobilization of the population, in contrast to the Russian and Chinese revolutions.

The scholarly study of these phenomena is largely sequestered into different academic subfields. Even those scholars who take a broad approach to contentious politics, or who work with large n datasets, usually study either revolutions or military coups—but not both. In one of his most ambitious projects, in which he compared various types of revolts and rebellions in Europe between 1492 and 1992, Charles Tilly excluded military coups because, while they may result in a transfer of power and therefore have a revolutionary outcome, they do not take place because of a revolutionary *situation*, which he defines as a deep split in the polity. In other words, coups involve a split within the government, or at least within the military, but not within society as a whole. With a narrower time frame, but a broader geographical focus, Jeff Goodwin studied revolutionary movements in Southeast Asia, Central America, and Eastern Europe between 1945 and 1991. Also focused on the second half of the twentieth century, Sharon Nepstad studied nonviolent revolts against socialist regimes, military regimes, and personal dictators. Erica Chenoweth and Maria J. Stephan compare violent and nonviolent resistance movements between 1900 and 2006, concluding that nonviolent campaigns are more effective in achieving their stated goals. Tilly, Goodwin, Nepstad, and Chenoweth and Stephan all excluded military coups from their large-scale empirical studies of revolutions and antigovernment revolts.

Similarly, those who study military coups often exclude revolutions and popular uprisings from their research. This is because military coups are most commonly defined as originating from within the state apparatus. The perpetrators of coups have been defined variously as belonging to a "segment of the state apparatus" or to the "regular armed troops"; or as members of the "armed forces," the "military or security forces," "small military coalitions," or the "military, security, or police."[66] Most of the large n datasets that have been created on coups or coup attempts explicitly exclude revolutions. Recent examples include Powell and Thyne, who have constructed a dataset that includes 457 coup attempts; 227 of these were successful and 230 were unsuccessful. The authors write that they have "gone to great lengths to assure that coups are not conflated with other forms of anti-regime activity."[67] Another study by Marinov and Goemans was based on a dataset of 249 instances of coups d'état between 1949 and 2004, and it also excludes revolutions.[68] Albrecht's dataset focuses on the Middle East and North Africa and includes 89 coup attempts between 1950 and 2013. Episodes of civil unrest, however destabilizing they may have been, are not included if they did not result in an attempted military intervention.[69]

In sum, revolutions and military coups have been studied separately because they involve different actors with different relationships to the state; arise in dissimilar conditions; involve different processes of mobilization, levels of transparency, and temporalities; and ultimately lead to disparate outcomes. For all of these reasons—and in order to ensure methodological rigor—scholars must choose to study either revolutions or military coups.

Counterrevolutions

If revolutions and military coups have been studied separately, counterrevolutions have received little scholarly treatment at all. The lack of academic research on counterrevolutions is reflected in our nomenclature. In the English language, we have a wide range of terms to refer to revolutions or revolutionary situations: uprising, upheaval, revolt, rebellion, riot, intifada, insurrection, mutiny, and so forth. By contrast, the vocabulary we have at our disposal to describe counterrevolutions is much more limited. A government crackdown or different types of state repression, although often accompanying a counterrevolution, can also occur in the absence of a revolutionary upheaval. Just based on our existing vocabulary, it would seem that there is a wide variety of ways in which people may challenge those in power, but fewer ways in which a government retains its hold on power. And yet, I would argue that the way counterrevolutions proceed are just as varied as the way revolutions are carried out or progress over time. A quick overview of three important works on the counterrevolutions in 1789, 1917, and in the postcolonial period illustrate this point.

In Charles Tilly's classic study of the counterrevolution in France, *The Vendée*, he focused on the regional backlash in the west of France.[70] In the case of the Russian Revolution, it was the appearance of white armies that signaled the counterrevolution had arrived. Leon Trotsky dedicated the entire second volume of *The History of the Russian Revolution* to explaining "The Attempted Counter-Revolution."[71] Subsequent and less partisan treatments of the Russian Revolution have also focused on the triumph of the Red Army over the White Armies. Finally, in an analysis of five former British colonies in Southeast Asia and sub-Saharan Africa, Dan Slater and Nicholas Rush Smith argue that elite parties were critical in reestablishing political order. The counterrevolution in

Egypt, however, took yet another form. It was not a regional backlash as in the case of the Vendée in France, but was orchestrated from Cairo—albeit with help from Riyadh and Abu Dhabi—and swept across the whole country. In contrast to Russia in 1917, but also Bahrain in 2011 when Saudi and Emirati tanks rolled into the small island nation, in Egypt the counterrevolution did not happen because of a foreign military intervention. Finally, the counterrevolution has also not been orchestrated by an elite party. After four years as president of Egypt, Sisi has declined to form a national party similar to the NDP that seemingly served Mubarak so well for the three decades he was in power.

If there was no elite party, no foreign military intervention, and no regional insurrection that tried to overturn the revolution, who then led the counterrevolution in Egypt? How should we even define the counterrevolution, and when did it begin? There were, after all, those who opposed the revolution from the beginning. Already in January and February of 2011, a Facebook group was created that advocated staying home instead of taking to the streets to protest against Mubarak. There was another group called "We are sorry, Mr. President" (*Asfeen ya Rais*). I define the counterrevolution not as the moment when opposition emerged to the revolution, or when violence was unleashed to crush the revolution, but as the moment the old regime regained the upper hand. This did not happen on a single day. The ouster of Morsi on July 3 was an important turning point, but I argue that the tide began to turn in the regime's favor on July 26 with the *tafweed* (authorization) protests and then with the Rabaa and Nahda massacres on August 14. In terms of leadership, in chapters 6 and 7, I show how the counterrevolution was orchestrated by the military establishment and was supported financially by unprecedented financial flows from the Gulf. Instead of Saudi and Emirati tanks entering Egypt as in Bahrain, billions of dollars began entering the Central Bank in Cairo just days after the coup. Despite the inclusion of a few civilian figures in the summer and fall of 2013, there was never any meaningful civilian control over the military after the ouster of Morsi. The United States and EU, while not necessarily always pleased with the counterrevolutionary course of events, did not oppose them either. The United States famously decided it did not have to determine if a coup had happened. And the EU member states, despite some disagreement among themselves, also concluded that it was better not to publicly call it a coup. Furthermore, just as revolutions and social movements occur in waves, I argue that the counterrevolution in Egypt has proceeded until now in two phases: the first under Adly Mansour as interim president, and the second after Sisi was elected president.

In short, I fully agree with Dan Slater and Nicholas Rush Smith, who bemoan the imbalance in the literature and call for this to change: "the birth of a literature on counterrevolution is patently and painfully overdue."[72] It is my hope that this book will make a modest contribution to developing the literature on counterrevolutions as well as military coups and revolutions. I also concur with Jack Goldstone and George Lawson, who have each separately outlined the limitations of the third and fourth generations of revolutionary theory. Goldstone argued for a view of revolution as an "emergent phenomenon":

> Which actors, and how many, cease to support the regime; which leaders and factions come to dominate the revolutionary coalition; which foreign powers seek to intervene, on whose side, and with what effort—all will determine the contours of the revolutionary struggle and its outcome.[73]

Heeding this advice, I developed a framework that seeks to explain who ceased to support the regime, when and how; and who the regime targeted, when and how. In a similar vein, Lawson advocates for moving from an "attributional" approach, which sees revolutions as a collection of attributes, to a "processual ontology," which analyzes revolutions as historically specific *processes* in which the timing of events is crucial.[74] Ultimately, I hope to take a modest step toward building a "fifth generation" of revolutionary theory that takes coups and counterrevolutions as seriously as revolutions.

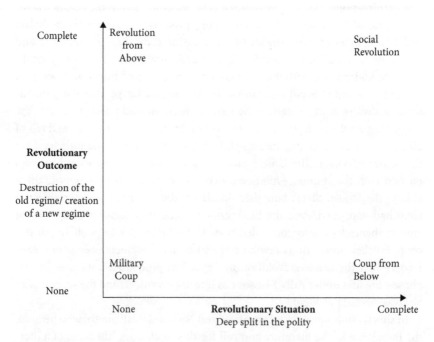

Graph 2.2 Conceptualizing the coup from below.

As will be elaborated in much greater detail throughout the book, I argue that the nature of the counterrevolution in Egypt was determined to a large extent by the nature of the uprising on June 30 and the coup that removed Morsi. I would encourage further research in this area. Despite our lack of an adequate conceptual vocabulary, counterrevolutions are as variegated as revolutions and—I would posit—shaped in a very fundamental way by the nature of the revolutionary upheaval that they seek to crush.

The Myth of Defection in Egypt

Within the literature on revolutions and nonviolent resistance movements, some work has been done on the role of the security forces. During a revolutionary upheaval, a regime's survival often depends on whether it maintains control of the coercive apparatus. Much of this literature is dedicated to understanding why some military commanders remain loyal to the regime while others do not. This is often treated as a dichotomous variable: officers decide to either follow orders or disobey orders; they either defend the regime or defect from it. This involves analyzing the specific moment during a regime crisis when the high command must choose sides, sometimes referred to as the "endgame scenario."[75] Factors that scholars believe influence the outcome of this decision-making process usually include internal variables such as the level of the military's professionalism, patronage, and the ethnic or sectarian composition of the armed forces.[76] As I have argued in previous work, the shortcoming of this particular literature is fourfold. First, a dichotomous variable can account for neither the complex reality of mass uprisings nor the sometimes ambiguous behavior of soldiers. Second, scholars often conflate two issues and assume that, if the armed forces refuse to suppress the opposition, they have effectively *joined* the opposition. Zoltan Barany, for example, argues that during the uprising in Egypt in 2011, the military "sided with the rebels."[77] I contend, however, that this represents a misreading of what happened. After all, just because soldiers do not shoot at someone does not automatically mean they agree with the person whose life they have spared. The notion that the Egyptian military defected from the regime, or joined ranks with the opposition, constitutes *myths of military defection.*[78]

Third, focusing on the specific moment of decision making does not allow us to understand the subsequent trajectory of the uprising.[79] History does not end after a regime collapses. Indeed, the networks that comprised the regime may still be alive and well. And finally, as I will elaborate later, scholars have focused too much on analyzing *internal aspects* of the armed forces rather than their relationship to civil society. My contribution in this area will be to complicate the existing scholarship in several ways. Instead of reducing my analysis of the military to a single decision made during a single moment in time—to shoot or not to shoot—I analyze the complex interactions between the armed forces and the protest movements over a period of eight years (2011–2018). I reveal the high command not as leading or driving the dynamics of the past several years, but as necessarily reactive. Furthermore, the military was not simply reacting to orders given by the president but to the *society* from which the uprising emerged. In order to understand the series of uprisings in Egypt, it is necessary to proceed from the premise that there is a subject-object dialectic at play, rather than assuming that the military commanders—despite yielding considerable power—are always in command.

If one takes a longer historical perspective, however, it becomes clear that Egypt has a checkered history of mass risings demanding some form of popular representation. Juan Cole compared the four great social and political movements since the British occupation of Egypt: the Urabi revolt in 1881–1882, the revolution of 1919, the Free Officers coup in 1952, and the Tahrir uprising in 2011. Demands for a constitution and a national legislature were an important part of the 1882 and 1919 movements, but they were not factors in 1952. He argues that this was because

> the big landlord politicians of the Liberal era had shown themselves corrupt, easily bought by the imperial power, arrogant, and servants of their own narrow class interests. Many Egyptians of the 1950s were in search of a new model of governance more suited to an anti-imperial republic, and the military—coded as servant of the nation and defender against imperial and Israeli aggression—seemed suitable.[80]

Already in 1952, it would seem that Egypt did not fit the transition paradigm. And yet some insights from the transitology literature can be helpful. This expansive academic literature can be divided into two schools that focus either on formal or on substantive democratization. The former refers to elections and the alternating of power, while the latter deals with issues of human rights and the actual exercise of power. Thus, democratization is a historical process that takes place over a period of several years or even decades. While some scholars have developed more complicated models, most would agree that it makes sense to distinguish at least between the initial transition phase away from authoritarianism and a second phase of democratic consolidation.

There is a large scholarly debate on the role of collective actors versus elite actors during transition processes. In *Transitions from Authoritarian Rule*,

Guillermo O'Donnell and Philippe Schmitter explain that they emphasize "elite dispositions, calculations, and pacts" because they "largely determine whether or not an opening will occur at all."[81] Adam Przeworski went further, even claiming that "complete docility and patience on the part of organized workers are needed for a democratic transformation to succeed."[82] These findings were soon challenged by other scholars, such as Nancy Bermeo, who referred to these as "myths of moderation." Dietrich Rueschemeyer, Evelyne Huber Stephens, and John D. Stephens found that it was the working class that most consistently supported democratization, while the landed class was most hostile, with the position of the middle class being the most ambiguous. In a broad study of 17 historical cases and 10 contemporary cases in Western Europe and South America, Ruth Collier inquired into the interaction between working-class pressure and elite actions.[83] By including the elite and the opposition as two of the four pillars in my framework, I also attempt to integrate pressure from below and pressure from above. However, my approach is somewhat different from these, in that I am specifically interested in those activists that were working to topple the three regimes between 2011 and 2013. It is not the labor movement or working-class associations that are at the center of my study of the opposition, but rather any revolutionary activity, regardless of its class origins.[84]

This brings us back to the third pillar of my framework, the military. According to Przeworski: "the institutional framework of civilian control over the military constitutes the *neuralgic point* of democratic consolidation" (emphasis added).[85] Yet, as discussed earlier, the role of the military is still one of the underexamined areas within the literature on transitions. One of the scholars who has recently worked to fill this lacuna is Narcis Serra, who was the minister of defense during Spain's transition period, which is widely hailed as a model for other countries to follow. Serra has outlined seven levels of military intervention in the political system, which are summarized in Figure 2.1. Level 1 represents the highest level of military intervention, in which the military controls political power. In this situation a member of the military is usually president or head of state, and many political posts are occupied by military representatives. In level 2 the military are guardians of national essences—the army considers itself to be above politics and parties and not a branch of the state administration. Finally, level 7 is democratic civil control over the armed forces—the executive defines military policy and the legislature controls the executive and the military.[86]

If we apply this to Egypt we see that under Mubarak, Egypt could be categorized as level 2. With his ousting and the SCAF's assumption of power, Egypt moved to level 1. After Morsi was elected, Egypt moved back to where it was under Mubarak: level 2. But then with Morsi's ouster, Egypt arguably shifted

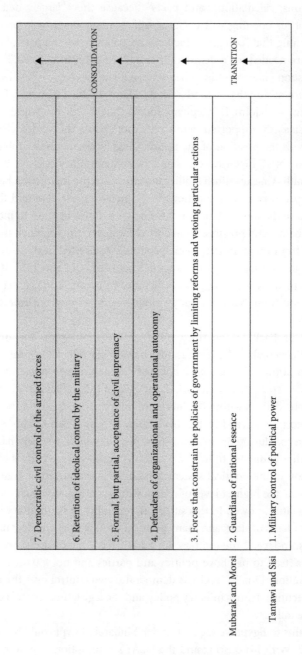

	7. Democratic civil control of the armed forces	6. Retention of ideolical control by the military	5. Formal, but partial, acceptance of civil supremacy	4. Defenders of organizational and operational autonomy	3. Forces that constrain the policies of government by limiting reforms and vetoing particular actions	2. Guardians of national essence	1. Military control of political power	
CONSOLIDATION	←	←			←		←	TRANSITION
Mubarak and Morsi								
Tantawi and Sisi								

Figure 2.1 Stages in the Reduction of Autonomy and Gradual Civil Control over the Military: Applying Narcis Serra's Model to Egypt.

The table is taken from Serra's 2010 book and I have modified it to illustrate the Egyptian case. See: Narcis Serra, *The Military Transition: Democratic Reform of the Armed Forces* (Cambridge: Cambridge University Press, 2010).

back to level 1, the highest level of military control. Officially Mansour, a judge, acted as interim president, but it was clear he was a subsidiary to Sisi, the coup leader and minister of defense, who was then elected president in 2014.

As discussed earlier, much of this scholarship has been preoccupied with the question of how the military can be induced to extricate itself from politics or how to decrease the influence of the men in uniform.[87] And yet in Egypt, the opposite has happened. Perhaps ironically, the revolution that toppled Mubarak with the hope of establishing democracy had the effect of increasing rather than decreasing the power of an undemocratic institution: the military.

Indeed, Egypt has arguably not even begun the first step of transitioning away from authoritarianism. I therefore situate this project within the literature on revolutions, counterrevolutions, and military coups. Some insights, however, will be gleaned from the scholarship on transitions, in particular regarding the role of the armed forces.[88] For example, in his work on the military in Brazil, Al Stepan noted that military coups do not necessarily originate from within the military. He studied all five Brazilian constitutions since 1891 and found that each one had a clause saying that it was the military's responsibility to maintain the correct relationships among the executive, legislative, and judicial branches.[89] He found that in every case, it was civilian politicians and not the military members of the subcommittee who insisted that this clause be inserted. This provided political elites a justification for calling for a military coup. In contrast to Stepan, I am not investigating the constitutional origins of the military's involvement in politics but rather the contradictory relationship between the military and collective actors during a period of intense mass mobilization.

Our existing theoretical toolkit, including the concepts of political or social revolution, military coup, or revolution from above, are all inadequate to explain the upheaval in Egypt between 2011 and 2018. The term Arab Spring erases the non-Arabs who also fought for their rights and recognition, such as the Nubian minority. Mubarak was toppled by a mass uprising in 2011, the Tantawi-led military junta that followed him handed over (some) power after the presidential elections in 2012, and Morsi was ousted in 2013. Popular mobilization played a decisive role in each case. During the first and second waves, the social mobilization threatened the old regime—first headed by Mubarak and then by Tantawi. These were revolutionary antiregime uprisings from below with little to no support from elites or external powers. The social mobilization against Morsi, however, although initially revolutionary in nature when it began in November–December 2012, eventually gained support from powerful forces within the old regime, and led to the military resuming power with the election of Sisi in 2014. However, the social process that led to Morsi's demise was not strictly a military coup. Rather, I argue that his ouster took the form of what I call a *coup from below*: a coup driven by popular mobilization, rather than by a cabal of conspirators within the officer corps, as in 1952. This is not to suggest that this type of coup is "democratic," a normative argument that has been made recently by both partisan commentators and some scholars.[90] The relationship between the mobilized forces and the military is riven with contradictions. In the following chapters I hope to shed light on this paradox.

This analysis attempts to account for these pillars of support upon which each regime relied while in power: the loyalty of the elite, the backing of the military, the acquiescence of the middle and lower classes, and the support of key allies such as the United States.[91] I will analyze the interplay between all of these actors during each wave of unrest, which brings us to the question of regime strategies and protest strategies.

Regime Strategies and Protest Strategies

In addition to illustrating *when* opposition emerged during each wave, I will also offer a detailed analysis of *how* the opposition attempted to overthrow the regime and how it tried to cling to power despite mounting pressure. Each wave was characterized by an at times macabre dance between the regime and the opposition, which involved an interplay of regime strategies and protest strategies.[92] I will show how Mubarak, the SCAF, Morsi, and Sisi have all deployed a similar repertoire of strategies to stay in power, including but not limited to: the use of violence, the denial of use of violence, curfews, state media propaganda, sectarian propaganda, attempts to ban protests, military trials of civilians, torture, and constitutional declarations.

Writing on the Revolutions since 2010

The rumble of mass protests across the Middle East and North Africa since 2010 has led to an equally massive outpouring of academic literature, too vast to be neatly summarized. The first spate of publications on the so-called Arab Spring have provided many valuable insights, with some of the first books in English appearing just months after the toppling of Ben Ali and Mubarak. These early analyses, both academic and journalistic, while useful in some ways, were often quickly overtaken by events.

The second round of more serious scholarly work on the Arab revolutions can be divided into two broad groupings: one that zooms in to focus on a specific issue in a specific country, and another that offers a "God's-eye view" of events in the Arab world as a whole. Examples of the first type of literature on Egypt include research on the role of social media (e.g., Lynch, Nunns, Idle and Souief, Gerbaudo), mourning the martyrs through graffiti (Abaza), the military (Bellin, Barany, Springborg and Clement, Albrecht and Bishara, Albrecht and Ohl, Droz-Vincent, Sayigh, Kandil), the military's economy (AbulMagd, Marshall, Abul Magd and Grawert), the police and attempts at security sector reform (Aclimandos, Ashour), and the role of the United States (Cook, Brownlee, Gardner). A number of authors have offered insightful analyses of specific opposition groups such as April 6 (Cole), the Ultras football fans (Akl, Tarek, Dorsey), trade unions (Alexander, Beinin, El Mahdi), and the Muslim Brotherhood and the Salafis (Wickham, Al Sherif, Kandil, Al-Awadi, Trager).[93] Yet others have focused on specific professions, such as the judiciary (Aziz, Brown, Shalakany, Goldberg), the intelligentsia (Fahmy and Faruqi), or the role of doctors and nurses who provided medical services during the conflict (Hamdy).[94]

Scholars who offered a larger overview of unrest in multiple countries often had to focus on specific issues, such as levels of unemployment, poverty, or other economic grievances. Yet other scholars explained variation across countries through variables such as the existence of oil rents, hereditary rule, the composition of the armed forces, or the degree of alignment with the West.[95]

Finally, a number of case studies of Egypt have appeared, including those by Holger Albrecht, Cherif Bassiouni, Steven Cook, Mohamed El-Bendary, Jeroen Gunning and Ilan Zvi Baron, H. A. Hellyer, Adel Iskandar, Neil Ketchley, Hazem Kandil, Philip Marfleet, Tarek Osman, and Brecht de Smet.[96] There have also been edited volumes by Bahgat Korany and Rabab El-Mahdi, Dan Tschirgi, Walid Kazziha and Sean F. McMahon, and others.[97] Hazem Kandil's *Soldiers, Spies, and Statesmen* provides important historical insights into what he calls "the ruling bloc" and the relationships among the military, the security services, and the political apparatus. As the book was published in 2012, some of his analysis was quickly overtaken by events, or perhaps it foreshadowed what was to come, such as in this passage:

> By the same token, the failure of the democratic activists to recognize the potentially revolutionary role of the army has prevented them from considering a real partnership with the officers. Liberals continued to hold dogmatically to the axiom of civilian control, and leftists saw the military only as a conservative institution in the service of the ruling class—both positions, one must add, were based mostly on theoretical cliches (and unsubstantiated news reports and hearsay) rather than on an accurate analysis of the specific situation and grievances of the military in the Egyptian ruling bloc.[98]

From my vantage point, there is a striking imbalance in the literature. While there is a large outpouring of literature on the period of revolution, there is much less on the period of counterrevolution or what came after the ouster of Morsi. Following Gramsci, Brecht de Smet argues for using the concept of Caesarism to analyze the role of the Egyptian military. He seems to trace the counterrevolution as having begun already in 2011, and he claims that elections and the referenda were "weapons of restoration."[99] To my mind, the first free and fair elections in Egypt's modern history represented a break from previous regime practices. Neil Ketchley's *Egypt in a Time of Revolution* offers a careful and insightful study of protest tactics, including the burning down of police stations in 2011, how protests against Morsi were "elite-facilitated," and the anti-coup protests in 2013. Ketchley provides a useful analysis of how protests by a group called "Students against the Coup" were impacted by repression, but he focuses on the repression of this one type of protest, rather than the full spectrum of state repression against a variety of actors in society, as I will illustrate in chapters 6 and 7. As will become clear later, my analysis of Tamarod differs from Ketchley's in important ways.[100] Eric Trager's book *Arab Fall* offers insights into the Muslim Brotherhood and US policies toward Egypt. He claims that the Brotherhood's participation in elections was not because they believed in elections but saw them as a means to establish sharia law. This (not uncontested) assessment can perhaps explain why he then argues that the postcoup repression was inevitable: "the regime had no choice but to take the battle to the Brotherhood because the fate of Egypt was at stake."[101] Why the regime had to then also "take the battle" to the secular opposition remains unexplained. H. A. Hellyer's *A Revolution Undone* offers a more nuanced understanding of the Brotherhood, and he does touch upon the repression of secular activists, such as the killing of Shaimaa Al-Sabbagh. However, Hellyer maintains that the Rabaa sit-in in 2013 was fundamentally different than the sit-in on Tahrir in 2011: "Rab'a also wasn't a Tahrir-type locus calling for democracy and human rights." . . . The sit-in was about power: the MB had it before the coup, and they wanted it back."[102] While it is true that the sit-ins were different in many ways, to say that Rabaa was not about democracy or human rights misses the point that the Rabaa sit-in was protesting against the removal of a democratically elected president through a coup as well as against egregious human rights violations that included the killing of more than 50 people at the Republican Guards massacre.

A number of scholars including Asef Bayat, John Chalcraft, Joel Beinin, and Dalia Fahmy and Daanish Faruqi attribute the failure of the revolution to the lack of proper revolutionary leadership, the weakness of independent trade unions, or the shortcomings of illiberal liberals.[103] As I argue in chapter 4, one of the more radical demands of the revolution was to end military rule. This was not about reform or incremental change, but a call to fundamentally alter the nature of the state. While this movement may not have had a designated leader, it did have leading activists—many of whom were women.[104]

Finally, a few scholars have begun to analyze how Sisi's regime differs from that of Mubarak. Bruce Rutherford analyzes Egypt's "new authoritarianism" as an attempt to shift from a "provision pact," based on an extensive patronage network under Mubarak, to a "protection pact" under Sisi in which elites back the regime because it protects them from internal and external threats.[105] In chapters 6 and 7, I analyze how the counterrevolution brought about the end of Egypt's democratic interlude and established a more ferociously authoritarian regime under Sisi.

This book represents an attempt to empirically document and theorize both the revolution and the counterrevolution in Egypt. In order to do so, it is necessary to move beyond the study of a single issue, as revolutions are not reducible to single-issue social movements. Furthermore, most of the existing literature, to the extent that it focuses on protests, analyzes the January 25 and June 30 uprisings as the two major periods of protest activity, while neglecting or entirely skipping over the protests that took place during the period of the SCAF. This may be because most analysts would not see the anti-SCAF protests as significant as the other two episodes, yet I contend that they were. In some ways, I suggest, the anti-SCAF protests, or what I call the second wave of the revolution, were the most revolutionary of the three in that they represented a new form of activism in Egypt: antimilitarism. Many of the activist groups that I describe in chapter 4 are not well known outside Egypt, and they were led by women. Regrettably, the role of women in the Egyptian revolution is often only addressed in work that focuses on a single issue, such as those that I mentioned previously. A number of scholars who attempt to explain more than just a single issue, but focus on the revolution writ large, often sideline women.[106] I have attempted to avoid this silencing, although my focus is not on gender per se. My analysis of the three waves of the Egyptian revolution is driven by an attempt to understand if, when, and how key actors withdrew their support from each regime (the business elite, the military, the United States, and popular support). I also cover what I see as two waves of counterrevolution and return to military rule under Mansour and then Sisi. Finally, I propose to analyze the confluence of top-down military interventions and bottom-up revolutionary movements as a *coup from below*. Precisely because the coup emerged from deep within society, albeit with the support of powerful actors from inside the state, I argue that the subsequent crackdown also reached far and wide into society in an attempt to crush any possibility of a fourth antigovernment uprising.

Finally, because we are dealing with *mass uprisings*, they are by definition complex societal phenomena that cannot be reduced to a single actor, issue, or event. Any attempt to explain a revolution requires an approach that can encompass and account for the complexity of radical social change. This is what I hope to offer.

Methodologies and Positionality

As a sociologist specializing in the study of contentious politics and an ABD graduate student at Johns Hopkins University, I was hired in the fall of 2008 to replace the exiled Saad Eddin Ibrahim in the sociology department of the AUC. Ibrahim had been sentenced to two years in prison for "defaming Egypt," and even after being granted bail he was unable to return to Egypt for several years. The department needed someone to teach his classes, including a 300-level social movements course. In the job interview over Skype, I explained my PhD research on the history of opposition movements to the American military presence in Turkey and Germany. So when I was offered the job, I accepted it without having ever set foot in Egypt. I had no idea what I was getting myself into. Since I began work at AUC in September 2008, I have had the privilege of being able to develop and teach courses related to my own research interests in social movements, development, critical security studies, and revolutions in comparative perspective. But more importantly, I have been living in a laboratory of radical social change. Rather than evacuating the country during the uprising, as many did who had the means to do so, I stayed on and witnessed the key events firsthand. Instead of avoiding the sometimes violent confrontations since early 2011, I have often been in the thick of things. I was on the ground in Tahrir Square almost every day of the 18-day uprising that toppled Mubarak in 2011, and I have attended virtually all the major demonstrations since then until Morsi's ouster in July 2013. After his ouster, I attended the Rabaa sit-in of Morsi supporters on August 13, the night before it was besieged by security forces, as well as the Nahda sit-in on the morning of August 14. The assault on the Rabaa and Nahda sit-ins resulted in the largest massacre in modern Egyptian history, with upward of a thousand people killed within twelve hours.[107] In the years after these atrocities, I also witnessed how the political environment became more and more suffocating. Instead of chanting loudly against the regime, people began to whisper or not talk at all. From January 2011 to mid-2013, I saw how academics, students, and journalists poured into Egypt. Many of them were coming for the first time. Some of them were inspired to learn Arabic or to study at AUC because of the revolution, and others just wanted to see Midan Tahrir. By 2014, many scholars who had built their careers studying Egypt were staying away. And many of the activists were imprisoned or fleeing the country. This is undoubtedly one reason why more has been written about the revolution than the counterrevolution. I hope this book will make a modest contribution to correcting this imbalance. In addition to being embedded in Egyptian society through my position at the American University in Cairo, and my own extensive participant observations over the years, I also conducted countless interviews in Cairo, Alexandria, Aswan, Qena, Assiut, Tanta, Mansoura, and other parts of Egypt. By 2016, for security reasons I was not able to travel to Port Said, Ismailia, Suez, and North Sinai, but I interviewed people from those areas in my office in Cairo in 2016 and 2017. I also conducted many interviews with Egyptians living in the diaspora, and with American and European officials or former officials. Furthermore, during the spring of 2012, I carried out an online Arabic-language survey of over 500 Egyptians. While many surveys are conducted with the intention of assessing the popularity of certain politicians, attitudes towards the United States, or the likely outcome of elections, my survey was geared toward understanding what Egyptians believed were the achievements and setbacks of the revolution, one year after the ousting of Mubarak. Second, the survey inquired as to why these achievements and setbacks had occurred, or what were the social forces driving the contradictory dynamics of this period.

I am in the unique position of being both an insider and an outsider. I have been living and working in Egypt since the fall of 2008, and I lived in Cairo during most of the turbulent years that this book attempts to explain. This is not a critique of any authors who have spent less time in Egypt than I have. Many excellent studies of revolution have been written at a geographic or temporal distance. While I still feel incredibly lucky to have borne witness to these events, my rendezvous with history was not always intoxicating. I have often wished I could simply forget or remove myself. Every writer suffers from occasional writer's block or personal distractions, but the events I witnessed were at times traumatic. When a close friend was in prison, I would often be unable to sleep, and then when I did sleep, I had nightmares. When I sat down to write, all I could write was filled with fury and anguish. This is all to say that ethnography has its drawbacks. At one point I almost deleted all the eyewitness-based, ethnographic passages, but I decided against it. I realized that I cannot "un-ethnogrify" my work, even if I wanted to. Many of my personal encounters with the revolution shaped my arguments. In the concluding chapter, I have attempted to summarize how my ethnography informed my analysis. Living the revolution and counterrevolution fundamentally impacted my scholarship, my personal life, and my understanding of what is possible in this world. I would be lying if I said otherwise.

3

الشعب يريد اسقاط النظام
"The People Want to Overthrow
the Regime"

The First Wave against the Mubarak Regime
(January 25–February 11, 2011)

The first wave of the Egyptian revolution lasted a mere 18 days. After Hosni Mubarak had been ousted in short shrift—and before him Zine El Abidine Ben Ali of Tunisia—there was an air of optimism, even inevitability, that other dictatorships would soon come crashing down as well. But as the Arab Spring turned into fall and winter, it became clear that there was nothing inevitable about the collapse of autocratic regimes, making the sudden fall of Mubarak and Ben Ali appear all the more puzzling. Perhaps more than any other uprising that shook the region, the Egyptian case represents not merely a puzzle or paradox but something more akin to a political miracle. After all, the Mubarak regime had held onto power for 30 years, was the foremost US ally in the region, had decades of experience in crushing any and all opposition movements, and had even been seemingly unhindered in its efforts to establish hereditary rule. Contrary to other countries in the region, such as Bahrain and Yemen, which had witnessed large-scale outbursts of antiregime protests in the recent past, Egypt was widely regarded as fundamentally stable. And yet it was here that the regime was suddenly swept away by a mere 18 days of protests. How was this possible?

This chapter will attempt to answer this question by providing an in-depth analysis of those 18 days, from when the mass uprising began on January 25 until Mubarak's ouster on February 11—what I refer to as the "first wave" of the revolution. As discussed at greater length in the previous chapter, the research is guided by two broad theoretical traditions: (1) the structural or state-centered approach to revolutions; and (2) the agency-based or strategic approach. The first part of the chapter employs a structural approach to revolutions. The research will focus on several of Skocpol's key variables for explaining revolutionary outcomes: (1) the role of external pressure on the regime, (2) the role of the military, (3) the autonomy of the state vis-à-vis the capitalist class, and (4) the agency of the middle and lower classes. The second part of the chapter will then delve into an analysis of both revolutionary strategies and regime strategies during the 18 days, which I argue can be divided into three phases. While broad in terms of its attempt to provide an encompassing analysis of state-society relations, in this chapter I provide a micro-periodization of the 18-day insurrection.

Perhaps the most common narrative that has emerged to explain the collapse of the Mubarak regime has celebrated the activism of middle-class youth and their use of social media. On January 24, one day before the protest that activists had planned to take place during the national holiday known as Police Day, *Time* magazine featured an article titled, "Is Egypt about to Have a Facebook Revolution?" Three days later, *Newsweek* ran a story titled, "Inside Egypt's Facebook Revolt." Numerous other examples could be cited here, but the point is that *before* the uprising had even begun, the mainstream media had already anointed Facebook as one of the leading protagonists in the unfolding drama.[1] Even if somewhat tempered in their enthusiasm, a number of scholars have followed suit.[2]

This explanation is problematic for four reasons. First, it overlooks the fact that, for one-third of the uprising, the internet and all forms of social media had been cut off. Indeed, during what many consider the most crucial period of the rebellion, Egypt had been plunged into a regime-mandated cyberspace blackout. Second, it overestimates the actual usage of social media. In November 2011, the Facebook penetration rate in Egypt was estimated to be just 5.5 percent, while Twitter was used by a tiny 0.15 percent of the population.[3] The agency of those who were outside the cybercommunity vanishes in this narrative. Third, activists in Syria, Bahrain, and other countries in the region have also made extensive use of social media in their respective movements but—more than nine years after the outbreak of the uprisings—have not yet toppled their respective dictators. Finally, it also leaves unexamined the role of some of the most powerful institutions in Egyptian society.

My intention is not to dismiss the undeniable importance of social media, but rather to underline the fact that an accounting of the full range of revolutionary strategies is necessary in order to explain the collapse of an entrenched authoritarian regime.

Contrary to other revolutions that were characterized by large coalitions that included dissident elite factions, or members of the armed forces who cooperated with the mass movement to overthrow the regime, I argue that—during the first wave—the revolutionary coalition in Egypt consisted of the middle and lower classes. But this coalition did not have meaningful support of an elite faction, either among the civilian business tycoons or within the higher ranks of the military establishment. Also, contrary to other revolutions, I find little evidence thus far that external pressure was crucial to the ousting of Mubarak. Put simply, there was no dissident elite faction, no conspiracy of junior officers planning a coup, and no one in Washington pulling the strings. Based on preliminary research, it seems that the actions of the business community, the military, and the Obama administration were contradictory due to internal divisions—at times serving to support the mass mobilization and at other times undermining it.

Having identified mass mobilization as crucial to the process of regime collapse, we still need to identify the causal mechanisms that led to the toppling of Mubarak. My second argument about the first wave of the revolution is that, although it only lasted 18 days, it can be divided into three distinct periods, characterized by three different regime strategies, each of which provoked a specific protest tactic or "revolutionary strategy" in response.

The Business Elite

The existence of a dissident elite faction is widely seen as a necessary, if not sufficient, condition for a revolution to succeed.[4] Perhaps one of the earliest examples of this assumption can be found in an oft-cited passage of the *Communist Manifesto*, where Marx and Engels conjure up the possibility of a dissident section of the bourgeoisie joining the "revolutionary class":

> Finally, in times when the class struggle nears the decisive hour, the progress of dissolution going on within the ruling class, . . . a small section of the ruling class cuts itself adrift, and joins the revolutionary class, the class that holds the future in its hands. Just as, therefore, at an earlier period, a section of the nobility went over to the bourgeoisie, so now a portion of the bourgeoisie goes over to the proletariat, and in particular, a portion of the bourgeois ideologists, who have raised themselves to the level of comprehending theoretically the historical movement as a whole.[5]

The notion of potential elite autonomy, however, is more often associated with the classical elite theorists, such as Vilfredo Pareto, Gaetano Mosca, and Robert Michels, rather than Marx or Engels. In his model of "circulation of elites," Pareto envisioned the possibility that elements of the governing class may go over to the side of the governed class and thereby provide the lower class with the leaders it allegedly lacks.[6]

In *States and Social Revolutions*, Skocpol showed that a divided elite is much more vulnerable and hence likely to be overthrown by a revolutionary upheaval than an elite that is unified.[7] Trimberger's notion of "revolution from above" grew out of a fragmentation between economic and political elites. Scholars such as Lachmann have made elite conflict more central to their argument, claiming that popular uprisings are unlikely to even occur without the existence of elite conflict: "Non-elites mobilize when heightened elite conflict creates the opportunities and alliances which can justify the risks of collective action."[8] In his comparison of revolutionary movements in Latin America, Asia, and Eastern Europe, Jeff Goodwin argued that, contrary to orthodox Marxist assumptions, entrenched regimes are not generally overthrown by a single revolutionary class but rather by coalitions of classes.[9]

Egypt seems to defy these expectations in the literature. The final years of the Mubarak regime, and even the outbreak of mass protests in early 2011, did not lead to the formation of a dissident business elite, much less an alliance between a defected elite faction and the masses. To be sure, there were divisions within the ruling National Democratic Party (NDP). This conflict primarily revolved around the issue of succession, with the "new guard" supporting Mubarak's younger son Gamal and the "old guard" favoring less a particular person than the so-called ABG strategy (anything-but-Gamal). However, these were divisions *within* the regime and not the growth of any sort of elite opposition to the regime itself.[10]

To be sure, the divisions within the NDP involved more than just a generational conflict. Hosni Mubarak was a military man, receiving training in the Soviet Union as a pilot in the Egyptian Air Force and then fighting in the 1973 war against Israel. His son Gamal, however, lacked any military career, opting instead to become an investment banker in London.

The rise of Gamal is often associated with the rise of a new generation of businessmen, although the process actually began in the early 1990s before Gamal joined the NDP. There had been a gradual increase in the number of businessmen in the cabinet. In 1970 only 2.4 percent of the Egyptian cabinet were businessmen, and this increased to 14.7 percent by 1981 and to 20 percent by 1990.[11] Concurrent to this was a decline in the number of generals who held minister positions; in recent years only the minister of defense, the minister of military production, and the minister of civilian aviation were held by former military generals, whereas in the 1960s and 1970s the number was much higher.[12]

Mubarak signed an agreement with the International Monetary Fund (IMF) in 1991, which was meant to introduce further liberalization of the Egyptian economy. However, these reforms were met with resistance by those who had an interest in safeguarding the state's role in the economy. Only 91 of 314 state-owned enterprises were privatized, and state-owned banks still constitute around 70 percent of all bank assets. Clearly there were political limits to the privatization project. General Sayed Meshal, former head of the Egyptian Ministry of Military Production, claimed that 85 percent of the Egyptian economy was private during the current period, while others claimed the military's share of the economy was 30 to 45 percent. The National Organization for Military Production manages 16 factories, which produce a large assortment of products ranging from household appliances to olive oil to mineral water. The Egyptian military distributed bread from its own bakeries during the 2008 bread riots. Larger investments include running resorts and hotels and major construction projects, such as building the main highway that connects Cairo to Ain Sokhna.[13] In the 1980s, it was estimated that the military occupied about 128 square kilometers in Cairo, or about *half* of the urban metropolitan area at the time. The development boom in the 1990s contributed to the military's "self-aggrandizing 'enclavization.'"[14]

Gamal Mubarak joined the NDP in 1999, but he did not become a major force until 2002 when he launched the "New Thinking" (*Fikr Gedid*) reform program at the NDP party congress. It was also in 2002 that he and his aides began moving against some of the old guard figures. The first to be marginalized was Deputy Prime Minister and Minister of Agriculture Yousef Wali, just a few weeks prior to the 2002 congress. Other members of the old guard who were not kicked out but allegedly weakened were Kamal el-Shazly and Safwat el-Sherif.[15]

El-Shazly had been the minister for parliamentary affairs and also deputy secretary-general or party whip. He was one of the longest-serving parliamentarians in the world, having been elected in 1964 and serving until his death in November 2010. El-Shazly was a political operative whose knowledge of local politics was thought to be "unparalleled," enabling him to deliver elections. He was replaced by Ahmed Ezz, a close associate of Gamal. While el-Shazly was a political operative who was powerful due to his network of contacts throughout the country, in particular in Upper Egypt, Ezz was a businessman with a monopoly on the steel industry. In some ways the differences between the old guard and the new guard were a matter of style or based on ideas about how to perform politics. In the words of one observer: "Ezz bought people; he didn't know people."[16]

However, these conflicts were not irreconcilable. On the contrary, if the Mubarak regime could incorporate both people with vast political networks and people with vast personal fortunes, all the better. Indeed, the later period of the Mubarak regime was characterized by a growing alliance between the state and the business elite. To name only the most prominent examples: Zoheir Garranah, with major investments in the tourism industry, became minister of tourism; Mohamed Mansour, who ran one of the biggest automobile

Photo 3.1 The 2011 uprising was directed not just against Mubarak, but against his entire regime. From left to right: Farouk Hosny, Youssef Boutros Ghali, Yousef Wali, Ahmed Ezz, Anas el-Fiqqi, Safwat el-Sherif, Fathi Sorour, and Habib el-Adly. Photograph taken by the author on Tahrir Square on February 8, 2011.

dealerships, became minister of transport; Youssef Boutros Ghaly, a senior IMF executive, became minister of finance; Hatem El-Gabaly, the founder of the largest polyclinic in the Middle East, became health minister; the top ex- porter of Egyptian cotton, Amin Abaza, became minister of agriculture; and Rachid Mohamed Rachid, president of Unilever North Africa, Middle East, and Turkey, became trade minister.[17] Did the emergence of these businessmen as political actors result in intraelite trench warfare? This does not seem to have been the case. After Gamal had introduced these key acolytes, "it became more accurate to talk of a power-sharing arrangement within a fragmented party rather than all-out rivalry between old and new guards."[18] Rather than conflict between businessmen and state bureaucrats, the last decade of the Mubarak re- gime was characterized by a growing alliance between the capitalist class and the state, which had become increasingly institutionalized with the so-called businessmen's cabinet of Ahmed Nazif in 2004. Hence the NDP was not divided into hostile camps but instead came to a sort of agreement, with some members of the old guard even switching sides and reinventing themselves as supporters of Gamal, such as Safwat el-Sherif.[19]

But what of the business elite who remained outside the ranks of the NDP? After all, not every businessman could be given a ministerial position and not everyone could become the CEO of a privatized state industry. Hence, at least in theory, there remained the possibility that those capitalists who were excluded from the inner circle may have been disgruntled at having to make their money without the benefit of political rent.

Here again, this does not seem to have been the case. Although well-heeled Egyptians may have been alienated from the regime, and although individual businessmen may have expressed dissatisfaction with certain policies, there is no evidence of the formation of a dissident faction among members of the economic elite. For example, according to records from the oral history archives of the Economic and Business History Research Center at the American University in Cairo, Hussein Sabbour, the president of the Egyptian Businessmen's Association (EBA), expressed anger that insiders such as Ezz benefited from his monopolistic control of the steel industry. And yet these views were not formulated as collective demands as a review of the newsletters of the EBA indicates. According to Sabbour, none of the 500 businessmen who belonged to the EBA donated money to support the occupation of Tahrir.[20] There is scant evidence of any sort of organized dissident capitalist faction, much less any significant pressure on Mubarak to resign.

On the contrary, even those businessmen who were not considered close to Mubarak were willing to sacrifice their own profits in order to appease the regime. All three major cell phone and internet providers in Egypt shut down their service on January 28, 2011, as instructed by Mubarak. The CEOs of these companies include Naguib Sawiris (Mobinil), Hatem Dowidar (Vodafone), and Gamal el-Sadat (Etisalat). They were not known as regime insiders, and yet they were willing to sacrifice their own profits in order to appease the regime. In their defense they have claimed that they had no choice in the matter, and that refusing to shut off service would have been unthinkable. However, the Egyptian Telecommunications Service, which is the landline company in Egypt, was also asked to shut off the landline telephone service but refused to do so.

There are of course many individual businessmen whose political maneuverings pre- and post-Mubarak could be discussed. Naguib Sawiris, due to his prominence, is worthy of some scrutiny. Sawiris, estimated by *Forbes* magazine to be worth $2.5 billion and ranked as the second-richest Egyptian (after his father Onsi), is head of Egypt's largest private-sector company, Orascom, and also a member of the Coptic community. Sawiris declined to become a member of the NDP and established an independent newspaper and satellite television network in 2004 that extensively covered the protests. In an interview in May 2011 he was asked:

Q: You were the first and only high-profile businessman to take part in Egypt's revolution. Why do you think that is?

NAGUIB SAWIRIS: I've always been very critical of the lack of freedom under the old regime and the fact we only had one party we could join if we wanted to be politically active. So I was thrilled to finally see this day come. I had to take action because it's my country and I've always been heavily involved in the past.[21]

And yet his "criticism" was cautious at best, as indicated in interviews he gave *before* the toppling of Mubarak. *Bloomberg Markets* featured him on the cover of their December 2011 magazine, with the title "Billionaire Rebel: Naguib Sawiris Is Pushing for an Egypt That Fulfills the Promise of the Arab Spring." The article claims, "Sawiris risked his corporate empire to support Egypt's revolution."[22] This is questionable, however, not only because he obediently shut off internet and telecommunications service when asked but also because the Sawiris family makes a good deal of their money outside Egypt. The construction arm of the Orascom holding generates $3.8 billion per year, with four-fifths of this stemming from outside Egypt. Orascom is one of the contractors hired by the US government to build military bases in Iraq, Afghanistan, and elsewhere.[23]

Had Sawiris been an outspoken critic of the regime, it is unlikely that he would have acquired one of the largest contracts (Mobinil) in the telecom industry under Mubarak. After the uprising began he maintained a cautious approach, even admonishing the demonstrators to go home after Mubarak gave his first speech when he promised not to run for elections again in the fall. Sawiris was therefore clearly *not* supporting the demand that Mubarak step down immediately, which resounded in the people's chants, "Leave!" (*Erhal*) and "We're not leaving until he leaves."[24] After it was clear that Mubarak would go, Sawiris supported Omar Suleiman, head of the Intelligence Services, as a possible successor to Mubarak. However, the Tahririans saw him as "Mubarak II" as it is believed he oversaw the systematic use of torture and widespread human rights abuses. The office of vice president had been vacant since 1981.[25] On January 29, Mubarak appointed Suleiman as vice president; by January 30, graffiti had been written on the side of army tanks in Tahrir demanding, "No to Mubarak; no to Suleiman" (see Photo 3.2).

In sum, in both the strong and weak version of the argument, divisions among the elite are widely regarded as a necessary, if not self-sufficient, precondition for a revolution to take place. But when the uprising began in Egypt on January 25, this was not the case. On the contrary, the business elite had largely been co-opted. In addition to allowing nonparty members to obtain major contracts, the Mubarak regime had another mechanism to secure the

Photo 3.2 Graffiti on the side of the tank reads "No to Mubarak; No to Suleiman." Omar Suleiman was head of Egypt's General Intelligence, and appointed Vice President by Mubarak on January 29. Photograph taken by the author on Tahrir Square on January 30, 2011.

loyalty of the elite: the transfer of government land into private hands, which was sold for piasters. Whether due to fear of retribution or because they were appeased through sweetheart deals, the selling off of land, or ministerial posi-tions, there is little indication of any sort of organized elite faction that had formed in opposition to the regime. On the contrary, instead of funding the opposition, certain business tycoons are believed to have funded thugs to attack the opposition, such as during the so-called Battle of the Camel on February 2. Ceramics tycoon and former secretary general of the NDP Mohamed Abou El Enein was one of 24 defendants who were accused of conspiring to kill pro-testers by paying thugs to carry out the attack.[26]

The only discernible conflict among the elite was taking place within the re-gime, and it revolved around the question of whether the son (Gamal) should or should not replace the father. The revolutionaries, however, were opposed to the entire apparatus of the regime. One of the more prominent banners on Tahrir during the 18-day uprising featured eight regime figures in addition to Mubarak, including those who the revolutionaries considered part of the re-gime they were aiming to topple: Farouk Hosny (minister of culture), Youssef Boutros Ghali (finance minister), Yousef Wali (minister of agriculture), Ahmed Ezz, Anas el-Fiqqi (minister of information), Safwat el-Sherif (secretary ge-neral of the NDP), Fathi Sorour (speaker of the People's Assembly), and Habib el-Adly (interior minister) (see Photo 3.1). The Egyptian people did not take to the streets because they had perceived any particular elite conflict that they could exploit to their advantage or because of a sudden opening in the political opportunity structure. On the contrary, the regime had become an almost textbook example of what Marx referred to as "a committee for managing the collective affairs of the bourgeoisie."[27]

The Military

The antinomies of the Egyptian military have confounded many.[28] The seemingly contradictory behavior of the military—during the first, second, and third waves of unrest—cannot be fully understood without some reference to its past role in Egyptian society. There is some disagreement among scholars on this point. On the one hand, there are those who argue that, over time, the influence of the Egyptian military has declined as it has "disengaged"[29] from politics or become "professionalized"[30]—or, formulated another way, that the state apparatus has been "demilitarized."[31] At odds with this line of reasoning, Steven Cook maintains that the Egyptian military can best be understood as "ruling but not governing."[32] Yet others argue that, while the military may have lost some of its former influence, the role of the security and intelligence services has been elevated.[33]

Many observers have portrayed the role of the military as generally supportive of the revolution.[34] Those who make this argument usually point out that the military was hostile to Gamal Mubarak and the private economic interests that he represented. In essence, this is another version of the "elite conflict" hypothesis discussed in the previous section. However, according to Zeinab Abul-Magd, "Even when the Gamal Mubarak–controlled cabinet of businessmen accelerated privatization programs between 2004 and 2011, military-owned companies remained untouched."[35] Furthermore, as early as February 3, it was announced that Gamal would not run in the elections that were scheduled for the fall. Therefore even if the military had perceived Gamal to be an existential threat, he had already been removed from the scene a week before his father was toppled. Other observers have attributed the successful ousting of Mubarak to the military's decision "not to shoot" at protesters[36] or the coercive apparatus's "failure to repress."[37] Some scholars argue that Egypt's generals opted to "back the uprising,"[38] or they interpret the military's behavior as a decision "to side with civil resisters."[39]

As someone who witnessed unarmed protesters being shot at by security forces, I argue that it is erroneous to describe the behavior of security forces as nonviolent. On the contrary, during the first week of the uprising, the military stood by the regime and supported the police in their efforts to suppress protests. As described in more detail later in the chapter, it was the military who resupplied the police with ammunition on January 28. Rather than exhibiting a "failure to repress," it would be more accurate to say that the military failed to prevent the violent repression by other branches of the coercive apparatus.[40] First, Mubarak himself had appointed several generals in his cabinet reshuffle in an attempt to secure the loyalty of the military. These included appointing Omar Suleiman as vice president, Ahmad Shafik as prime minister, and Mahmoud Wagdy as interior minister. Second, one week into the revolt, the military declared that it would not use force against the demonstrators.[41] Many observers interpreted this announcement as proof of the military's solidarity with the protesters. However, this decision only came *after* the people had already changed the balance of power in their favor by defeating the hated police force, taking control of public space, and establishing alternative forms of "popular security." A further indication that the military was not acting on behalf of the protesters is that the armed forces did not protect protesters from snipers who were stationed on the rooftops of buildings surrounding Tahrir Square. Moreover, after promises were made that Gamal Mubarak would not succeed his father, the military tried its best to demobilize protesters. These actions included warnings stating that it would enforce the curfew and F-16 flyovers above Tahrir minutes before the curfew began on January 30.[42] Far from leading the revolution, as in the 1950s, the military sought to contain it while seeking to preserve as much of the status quo as possible.

On paper, the Egyptian military is the strongest in the Arab world. It is capable of mobilizing 480,000 soldiers (900,000 including reservists), 3,000 tanks, 550 fighter aircraft, 250 helicopters, and approximately 50 warships.[43] Its strength lies in the sheer number of men it can recruit and the yearly infusions of American military aid, which allow it to purchase state-of-the-art weaponry, such as F-16 fighters and M1A1 tanks.[44] Understanding the military's weakness, however, requires looking beyond the number of men and materiel it has at its command and analyzing the social dimension of the military. The Egyptian military, like the wider Egyptian society, is characterized by enormous gaps between the rich and poor. In 2010, enlisted soldiers earned 125 EGP per month (approximately $20), while the highest ranking generals, it is estimated, earned between 100,000 and 500,000 EGP a month ($16,666–$83,333).[45] Of course, every military is organized around a hierarchical structure with differences in pay scale and prestige. However, many countries try to bridge these differences through a noncommissioned officer (NCO) corps, which is often also a vehicle for mobility within the military. Originally the NCO played this role in the Egyptian military as well; however, the type of social mobility that was possible in the 1950s and 1960s no longer exists. According to one observer, "It has become almost impossible for an underprivileged man or the son of a petit-bourgeois family to be admitted to the Military or Police Academies. Nasser, Sadat and Mubarak would probably not be admitted today."[46]

Outside observers provide confirmation of this assessment. A retired colonel for the US army who was stationed in Egypt for several years has described how these class divisions affect cohesion: "On a typical weekend, officers in units stationed outside Cairo will get in their cars and drive off to their homes, leaving the enlisted men to fend for themselves by trekking across the desert to a highway and flagging down busses or trucks to get to the Cairo rail system." In his rather blunt assessment: "Most Arab officers treat enlisted soldiers like subhumans."[47] These class divisions are not only damaging for morale but could potentially also affect combat capabilities. For example, the same equipment that would be provided to a battalion in the United States would not be distributed to the equivalent unit in the Egyptian army, but only among much higher-ranking officers. He attributed this not to a lack of expertise, as Egyptian officers are provided training for the American equipment they receive, but rather to a lack of trust. This mutual suspicion seemed to go both ways, as the same author commented on the lack of unit cohesion resulting from the fact that "enlisted soldiers simply do not trust their officers."[48] According to one person who was doing his mandatory military service during the first wave of the revolution, the soldiers who were most angry at Mubarak were the majors (ra'id) and lieutenant colonels (moqaddim). Anyone who was a brigadier or above had "too many benefits" and was "bought off." Conversely, the soldiers who were most distrusted by the regime were the reserve officers—people who have received specialized training outside the military. Although they are not full-time military officers, they have to receive permission from the Ministry of Defense to travel abroad until they are 45 years old. According to him, the army distrusts the reserve officers because they are seen as having "a civilian mind."[49]

A US embassy cable from September 23, 2008, described how mid-level officers were "harshly critical" of Defense Minister Tantawi and would openly express their disdain for him by referring to him as "Mubarak's poodle." Many seemed to believe he reached his position only because of unwavering loyalty to Mubarak. The same cable describes how the institution of the military had been in decline, in part due to the fact that the defense minister valued loyalty to the regime more than competence. The military reached its peak of influence in the late 1980s, but after Mubarak removed Defense Minister Abdel Halim Abu Ghazala in 1989, the regime has not allowed any charismatic figure to reach the senior ranks as part of its "coup-proofing."[50]

While in theory, the State Security (Amn ad-Dawla), Central Security (el-Amn el-Markazi), and intelligence service (mukhabarat) were responsible for internal security, in practice the army could also play this role.[51] In Clement

Henry and Robert Springborg's assessment: "The raison d'être of the military was always to support the Mubarak regime, not defend the nation."[52] Is it conceivable that this loyal field marshal known as "Mubarak's poodle" would betray his chief executive? On the contrary, Tantawi's loyalty to Mubarak continued even after the octogenarian had fallen from power. Tantawi was called to testify in the trial of Mubarak in August 2011; in his testimony that was leaked to the public, he protected the former president from accusations that he had ordered the killing of demonstrators.[53]

Chairman of the Joint Chiefs of Staff Mike Mullen praised the Egyptian army during the 18-day uprising for its alleged professionalism and constraint.[54] However, there are numerous indications that the army's position was in fact more dubious. According to Tantawi's official testimony that was leaked to the public, on the evening of January 28, the "Day of Rage," the military was given orders by Mubarak to support the police.

QUESTION: When the events started on January 25 and until February 11, was there any meeting held between you and the former President Hosni Mubarak?

TANTAWI: No direct meetings, but on January 28 when we received orders from the president there was communication between us.

QUESTION: What did the president convey during such meetings?

TANTAWI: Meetings between us were held to know the stance of the armed forces, especially on January 28 when the military was ordered to go down and support the police in fulfilling its duties. There was former planning by the military and this is a drill conducted by the military in case we need to go down with the police. The military goes down to the streets when the police need its help and when they cannot fulfill their duties and when the president orders the head of the military to take such action. The president gave the orders to the head of the military for the forces to go down and protect the important facilities and this is what happened.[55]

So how exactly did the military "support the police," as Tantawi testified they had been ordered to do? The police had been attacking peaceful demonstrators in an attempt to prevent them from reaching Tahrir Square. After hours of street battles, the police had run out of ammunition and now faced tens of thousands of enraged civilians empty-handed. What happened? As Tantawi himself testified, because the police could not "fulfill their duties" the army was ordered to "protect the important facilities." Eyewitnesses claim that the police were resupplied with ammunition by army soldiers driving military jeeps. Some of them also observed soldiers shooting the protesters on January

28. One of my interviewees said he saw a soldier kill approximately 12 people during the night of January 28.[56] It is estimated that over 300 people were killed on that single day, and thousands more wounded.[57] After January 28, enlisted soldiers were deployed throughout Cairo and other cities. A retired major in the Egyptian army has claimed that the Mukhabarat had infiltrated the protests and were assigned the task of informally "surveying" the enlisted soldiers and asking if they would shoot at the demonstrators. These reports then may have contributed to the decision not to use force.[58] After supporting the police in their attempt to crush the uprising during the first week, the army then changed course and issued a statement on January 31 that proclaimed:[59] "To the great people of Egypt, your armed forces, acknowledging the legitimate rights of the people . . . have not and will not use force against the Egyptian people."[60]

However, although the army largely abstained from using force for the remainder of the uprising, it also did not *prevent* violent attacks against the peaceful demonstrators, as became abundantly clear on February 2 during the so-called Battle of the Camel on Tahrir. On this day thugs riding camels and horses stormed onto the square, although it was being guarded by military checkpoints, and assaulted the people. Strangely, the army soldiers, despite being equipped with tanks and Kalashnikovs and stationed at every entrance to Tahrir, were not able to stop the men riding camels and horses from entering the square, where they killed at least 12 people. I had been attending the protests on Tahrir as a participant observer almost every day during the 18-day uprising, and February 2 was the only day that I was not allowed onto Tahrir. I had tried to access the square from the side near the Omar Makram mosque in the afternoon, before the incident had taken place. The soldiers at the checkpoint on that particular day, however, forbade me from entering.[61]

Two of the soldiers I've interviewed have admitted to participating in the uprising without wearing their uniforms, a courageous act considering that, had they been caught, they would have been handled as traitors guilty of high treason. Hence perhaps the most compelling reason for the SCAF to not give orders to shoot at the demonstrators is that they could not be sure the rank-and-file soldiers would follow their orders. Some of the soldiers who occupied Tahrir on the night of January 28–29 even allowed the protesters to spray paint anti-Mubarak and anti-Suleiman slogans on the side of their tanks (see Photo 3.2).

After Mubarak stepped down, the regular army units were moved out of Cairo, and the military police took control over policing demonstrations and maintaining order in the cities, as the military police were generally considered to be more loyal than the rank-and-file in the army.

Photo 3.3 Numerous signs on Tahrir expressed anger about US aid to Egypt.
Photograph taken by the author on Tahrir Square on February 1, 2011.

The United States

Another common assumption in the literature on revolutions is that international pressures can weaken the state apparatus and make it vulnerable to revolution. Jack Goldstone argues that international pressures have always been
an important factor in the development of revolutionary crises, but that they
have become more important with the growth of client relationships between
superpowers and developing states.[62] According to his analysis, neopatrimonial regimes are particularly vulnerable to international pressure. As there is
no mass support base, the temptation to rely on foreign aid increases. Foreign
aid has two benefits for neopatrimonial rulers: it makes them more autonomous from their population and it allows them to secure the loyalty of the
elite through increased patronage. However, too much reliance on foreign aid
may prove fatal, because if foreign support suddenly is withdrawn it makes the
regime vulnerable.[63] He argues that US policy can also increase the vulnerability of dictators as it has often swung back and forth between the contradictory goals of promoting democracy while at the same time also promoting its

own national security interests. "These policy swings precipitated disasters by putting neopatrimonial rulers in an impossible position—if they enacted liberalizing reforms, they undermined the basis of their rule; if they did not enact such reforms, they lost the U.S. aid essential to maintaining the patronage that supported their rule."[64]

In addition to scholars such as Skocpol and Goldstone, other actors, and for other reasons, have also put forth the argument that external powers can be an influential factor during revolutions. Beginning on January 28, the Egyptian state media, under the direction of Anas el-Fiqqi as minister of information, unleashed a xenophobic campaign that blamed foreigners for instigating the turmoil.[65] These attacks came not from ordinary Egyptians but from the highest level in the state bureaucracy: Omar Suleiman, who Mubarak had appointed vice president, and who was believed to have close relations with both the United States and Israel, argued that "foreign influences" were behind the uprising.[66] Foreign journalists in particular were targeted,[67] and on January 30, Al Jazeera had its license revoked and its Cairo bureau office was shut down on the orders of Anas el-Fiqqi.[68] Henceforth regime officials and Egyptian state media spoke incessantly of the *agendat kharegeya* ("foreign agendas"), *qella mondassa* ("subversive minority"), *taraf talet* ("third agent"), and *ayadi khafeya* ("hidden hands").

Who exactly these foreigners were was left unclear. Ironically, and perhaps oblivious to the xenophobic campaign, there were some non-Egyptians who brazenly tried to claim credit for the unrest in Egypt. Just four days after the uprising had begun, neoconservatives such as Elliott Abrams were already trying to score points, with the title of a *Washington Post* article claiming, "Egypt Protests Show George W. Bush Was Right about Freedom in the Arab World."[69] Clearly, the argument about any sort of foreign interference or influence may be politically motivated. The question is, do these arguments—whether of a scholarly or political nature—hold up to empirical scrutiny? The following section will attempt to answer the question: What exactly was the role of the United States during the 18 days between January 25 and February 11?

Egypt has been a major ally of the United States since the late 1970s, when it signed the Camp David Accords. The importance of Egypt to the United States is symbolized by the fact that the American embassy in Cairo is the second-largest in the world—second only to Baghdad. From 1948 to 2011, Egypt received $71.6 billion in foreign aid from the United States, including $1.5 billion annually in military aid since 1987.[70]

Furthermore, in his state of the union address delivered on January 25, 2011, President Barack Obama said: "The United States of America stands with the people of Tunisia, and supports the democratic aspirations of all people."[71] Given this unequivocal support for the democratic uprising in Tunisia, one may have expected a more enthusiastic response to the demonstrations taking place on the same day all over Egypt. And yet, the messages coming out of Washington were contradictory at best, as the brief chronology below indicates.

- January 25: Secretary of State Hillary Clinton said, "Our assessment is that the Egyptian government is stable and is looking for ways to respond to the legitimate needs and interests of the Egyptian people."[72]
- January 27: Vice President Joe Biden gave an interview with *PBS News Hour*. When asked how he would characterize Mubarak, Biden responded that he knew him "fairly well" and that "I would not refer to him as a dictator."[73]
- January 28: White House Press Secretary Robert Gibbs indicated that the Obama administration would "review" the issue of US aid to Egypt after the outbreak of violence.
- January 30: Clinton said there is "no discussion of cutting off any aid" in an interview with Christiane Amanpour on *ABC News*.[74]
- February 1: Mubarak gave a defiant speech, saying he was determined to stay in office until the elections in September, and only conceding that he would not run for president again in the fall. Less than an hour later, Obama called him and, according to White House aides, said: "It is time to present to the people of Egypt its next government." He added, "The future of your country is at stake."[75]
- February 2: Senator Patrick Leahy, Chairman of the Senate Appropriations Subcommittee which oversees foreign aid, says in reference to US aid to Egypt: "That pipeline will be turned off."[76]
- February 3: White House officials were reported to be holding talks with their Egyptian counterparts, which would involve Mubarak resigning immediately, with Omar Suleiman leading a transitional government backed by Lt. Gen. Anan and Field Marshal Tantawi.[77]
- February 4: Frank Wisner, former US ambassador to Egypt who Clinton had chosen to act as US envoy to Egypt during the crisis, spoke to the Munich Security Conference via video link and said: "The president must stay in office to steer those changes through. I therefore believe that President Mubarak's continued leadership is critical; it's his opportunity to write his own legacy."[78]

Why the Obama administration decided the crisis required a special envoy, and dispatched Frank Wisner to Cairo, instead of relying on Margaret Scobey, the US ambassador, is something of a mystery. Wisner was a former US ambassador to Egypt, a retired career diplomat, and had served on the board of trustees at the American University in Cairo for many years. However, he was also employed at Patton Boggs, a New York/Washington law firm, which states that it advises "the Egyptian military, the Egyptian Economic Development Agency, and has handled arbitrations and litigation on the [Mubarak] government's behalf in Europe and the US."[79] The obvious conflict of interest was not lost on observers. This was problematic not only because it was an example of "privatizing" the managing of a state crisis but also because it was unprecedented. According to one observer: "Even in past examples where presidents have sent someone 'respected' or 'close' to a foreign leader in order to lubricate an exit, . . . the envoys in question were not actually paid by the leader they were supposed to squeeze out!"[80] It also raises a more general question: If the Obama administration did in fact want to pressure Mubarak to resign, why did they choose Wisner?

These contradictory messages stemmed to a large extent from divisions within the US government regarding policy toward Egypt. On the one hand were those who represented the traditional foreign policy establishment and who advocated for a cautious approach, including Clinton, Biden, Robert Gates, and Frank Wisner. A second group included Deputy National Security Advisor Denis McDonough; Benjamin Rhodes, who wrote the president's address to the Arab world that he delivered in Cairo in June 2009; and Samantha Power. They all urged Obama to push harder and to side with the street.[81]

While senior officials may have been divided in their approach to Egypt, there is some indication that reducing US aid to Egypt would have received bipartisan support in Congress, whether as a means to reduce the budget deficit or to pressure the Mubarak regime to heed the demands of the protesters. According to a statement made by Senator Leahy on February 2: "There is nobody—Republican or Democrat—in the Senate or I suspect in the House that is going to vote for an aid package to Egypt under these circumstances."[82] Congress was willing to reduce or even cut off aid to Egypt, but the White House did not follow through. Of the various diplomatic tools at its disposal, threatening to cut off $1.5 billion in military aid trumped all others. And yet there is little indication that the United States ever seriously considered playing its hand. Even if Obama, in his private telephone conversation with Mubarak, did urge him to begin a transition process, this was contradicted by what Wisner said in public. As policies emanating out of Washington were contradictory, one cannot credibly argue (based on existing evidence) that pressure from the United States was the decisive factor in weakening the Mubarak regime. In fact, demonstrators on Tahrir were convinced of the opposite: that US aid was propping up Mubarak, not pushing him out (as indicated in Photo 3.3).

The Opposition

Contrary to other revolutions where a faction of the elite or a group of conspirators within the military supported the uprising, or where external pressure was critical in weakening the state, this does not seem to have been the case during the first wave of the revolution. The most substantial and sustained pressure that was brought to bear on the Mubarak regime came from below. The 18-day uprising can be divided into three distinct periods, characterized by three different regime strategies, each of which provoked a specific protest tactic or revolutionary strategy in response. Each regime strategy, depending on the phase of the uprising, included a mix of repression and concessions. These three periods include: (1) January 25–28, characterized by the astonishing resilience of the uprising in the face of massive violence; (2) January 29–February 8, characterized by a situation of "dual power"; and (3) February 9–11, when the regime's normalization strategy was met with a wave of labor strikes that brought down the regime.[83]

Phase 1: January 25–28, Massive Violence and Resilience

The uprising began on Tuesday, January 25, a national holiday that was officially a day of commemoration to honor the police. The mass movement has often been described as leaderless and spontaneous. While this is certainly not entirely incorrect, there were groups such as April 6, the Revolutionary Socialists, We are all Khaled Said, Kefaya, the National Association for Change, the Democratic Front Party, the Society of Muslim Brothers,[84] and others who had been engaging in antiregime activism for years. According to a secret US embassy cable from 2008, an unnamed April 6 activist "alleged that several opposition parties and movements have accepted an unwritten plan for democratic transition by 2011; we are doubtful of this claim." The report went on to describe this plan as "highly unrealistic."[85]

Once they had actually achieved their goals, it would be doubly unfair to the beleaguered activists who had been working tirelessly for years, despite claims that their plans were "crazy" or "unrealistic," to fail to acknowledge their previous efforts. Hence to claim that the uprising was entirely spontaneous would be inaccurate. Indeed, many of the groups mentioned here put significant effort into organizing the demonstration planned for January 25.[86] Their intention was to subvert the original purpose of the holiday and instead to protest police brutality and demand "Bread, Freedom, and Dignity." Asmaa Mahfouz, one of the founders of the April 6 movement, posted a video of herself online on January 18 in which she called upon people to come down and join the protest.

> If you think yourself a man, come with me on 25 January. Whoever says women shouldn't go to protests because they will get beaten, let him have some honor and manhood and come with me on 25 January. Whoever says it is not worth it because there will only be a handful of people, I want to tell him, "You are the reason behind this, and you are a traitor, just like the president or any security cop who beats us in the streets."[87]

The plan was to demonstrate in front of the Ministry of Interior, with the protest beginning at 2 p.m. and disbanding by 5 p.m. As Asmaa explained in her vlog, they wanted to demand "human rights" not "political rights."

On January 22, Dr. Mohamed al-Beltagy, a leading figure within the Muslim Brotherhood, announced in an audio recording that was uploaded on YouTube the participation of the Brotherhood in the demonstrations planned for January 25.[88] However, al-Beltagy's call to participate was not the result of a decision by the Brotherhood leadership that the organization would take part as an organization. On the contrary, there is a general consensus within the literature that the Muslim Brotherhood's participation until January 28 was voluntary. In practice, this means that the decision about whether or not to participate was left to smaller organizational units within the Brotherhood, which could explain why there was Brotherhood participation in some cities but not others.[89] The targeted repression that the Brotherhood faced can also explain the somewhat sporadic nature of their participation in street protests during the first few days.[90]

What had been planned as an afternoon protest extended on into the night. People began to set up an impromptu encampment on Tahrir, but the first tear gas canister was hurled into the sit-in at 12:45 a.m. Ten thousand riot police and 3,000 special forces troops were needed to expel the people from the square.[91] Although the following day was relatively quiet in Cairo, Suez was in flames. Three people had been killed in Suez on January 25 and over a hundred injured.[92] Activists began planning for a "Day of Rage" on Friday, January 28.[93] That was the day that the Tagammu leftists, the Nasserists, and the Muslim Brotherhood decided to join the protests.

In an attempt to forestall the gathering storm, the regime decided to plunge Egypt into a cyberspace darkness: the internet as well as cell phone services were cut off just after midnight on the night of January 27–28. One after the other, the five big internet providers flipped the "kill switch": Telecom Egypt at 12:12 a.m., Raya at 12:13 a.m., Link Egypt at 12:17 a.m., Etisalat at 12:19 a.m., and Internet Egypt at 12:25 a.m.[94] This was unprecedented, and a much more drastic course of action than the internet manipulation that had occurred in Tunisia or even Iran. Outside observers seemed most shocked about the potential economic impact of the blackout.

> Every Egyptian provider, every business, bank, Internet café, website, school, embassy, and government office that relied on the big four Egyptian ISP's for their Internet connectivity is now cut off from the rest of the world. . . . What happens when you disconnect a modern economy and 80,000,000 people from the Internet? What will happen tomorrow, on the streets and in the credit markets? This has never happened before, and the unknowns are piling up.[95]

Despite the limited and reformist nature of the demands, the regime responded to this protest with massive force, including rubber bullets, live ammunition, tear gas, and water cannons, as well as the detention and arrest of peaceful, unarmed protesters.

Foreign embassies in Cairo began to advise their citizens to evacuate, with some countries even offering free flights out of Egypt. Universities and schools were shut down. The American University in Cairo, where I've been employed since 2008, canceled classes and many of the international students and faculty left the country. Embassy personnel, the staff of numerous international organizations including the European Union and United Nations—all abandoned ship.[96] Left behind were some 80 million Egyptians, cut off from telecommunications and the outside world, facing a regime willing to kill its own people.

In addition to the communications blackout, physical barriers were erected as well. Cairo was sealed off from the provinces. Suez was in a lockdown. Within Cairo, in an attempt to prevent the people from assembling on Tahrir, bridges, streets, and metro stops near Tahrir were closed or blocked off. Undeterred, activists called upon people from all over Cairo to march toward downtown and converge there on Tahrir Square.

On the morning of January 28, I took the subway to downtown. I walked to the western side of Tahrir; in order to approach the square from that direction it is necessary to cross either the Qasr al-Nil or 6th of October bridges. These were two of the major arteries and march routes leading to Tahrir. Hundreds of police with armored personnel carriers were stationed along the corniche and on the two bridges in order to prevent people from crossing. At that time, around 1 or 2 p.m., perhaps at most a thousand people were battling against the police who shot at them with water cannons and tear gas. There was so much tear gas in the air that even those of us outside the direct line of fire became dizzy and even temporarily blinded. For maybe two hours we watched from the sidelines as the small crowd inched toward Tahrir, braving a never-ending onslaught of water cannons, tear gas, and gun-wielding security forces. They would gain a meter or two, only to be pushed back. After a while, we decided that they were unlikely to make it across the bridge, so we approached a police officer and asked permission to walk across Tahrir in the other direction. The police, anxious to be rid of us as we were taking pictures and filming, shooed us away.

Tahrir was eerily empty, but blockaded on every side by armored vehicles and security forces. Along the way a woman called out to us and started to walk with us. I had never met her before and didn't immediately recognize her; however, when she explained who she was I realized that I had in fact heard of her. She had been an anchorwoman on the nightly news but had quit her job after tiring of state censorship. Together with two other women she had then formed the Shayfeencom group to monitor the 2005 elections.[97] I was delighted to have met her unexpectedly and we began to talk as we walked across the empty square, when suddenly we noticed that we had been surrounded by about 15 policemen on all sides. I naively thought we only had to explain that we had been given permission to walk across the square by police stationed near the bridge. They began to interrogate us and demanded our IDs. The former anchorwoman simply said, "You know who I am," and tried to continue walking. But the police blocked our path, narrowing in on us and shouting at us. I looked around for someone to help us or a shop to escape into, but everything was closed and the demonstrators were still far from Tahrir. I noticed we were next to a white unmarked vehicle, the kind they use to detain people. The woman shouted "My name is Bothaina Kamel!" as she pushed defiantly forward and grabbed onto a lamppost with her right arm. I instinctively locked my arm around her and the police narrowed in on us even more. She started yelling political slogans such as *"Tahya Masr"* (Long Live Egypt) and *"Kefaya"* (Enough!), both drawing attention to what was happening and attempting to shame them. I was shocked that the police would treat a woman of her stature, who was a well-known media personality, in such a demeaning and degrading way. She was a brave woman, a seasoned activist with years of experience, staring down the regime, and yet I could feel with my arm locked around hers that her whole body was trembling. I made eye contact with the two journalist friends who were with us; they then turned and left. Understandably, they didn't want to be arrested. I said nothing as I clung to her arm, hoping for a miracle. As the harassing continued and the scene became louder, I noticed that people had begun to gather on the balconies and that some were filming us. They too did not dare to leave their apartments or come to our aid. However, by filming us they may have in fact helped us more than had they descended onto the streets and directly confronted the police.

After what seemed like an eternity, the police perhaps realized that there were too many witnesses to be able to detain us, and finally let us go. We "escaped" into an apartment belonging to Pierre Sioufi, whose balcony on the ninth floor directly overlooks Tahrir.[98] Although I was a foreigner and complete stranger, they opened the door and let me in without asking a single question. From there I could see everything. Or so it felt.[99]

For several hours, the situation remained unchanged: the police were in complete control of Tahrir. It seemed as if the police were invincible, and I thought that the various demonstrations taking part across the city would remain isolated from each other. From one of the side streets demonstrators would start throwing things at the police but would then be chased back. Every once in a while we would watch as the police would catch someone and drag them into the white unmarked van we had just been spared from entering. Then somehow, incredibly, a few brave souls darted onto the square from various directions. I thought they were insane. An armored police vehicle careened wildly around the circle, and an old man wearing a long white galabeya appeared from nowhere to stand by himself in front of it. I screamed, watching from the balcony as I panicked that he would be run over. The tank stopped in its tracks and four or five people began attacking it with their bare hands. At some point people tried to run onto the Midan from various directions and the police began marching in military cadence, then running, from one location to the next—the sound of their boots was dreadful against the pavement. Suddenly the positions of the police began to change and the protesters were coming from various directions at the same time—and the police began shooting at them. I saw so many police-men drawing their guns and shooting I lost track of how many—policemen shooting point-blank at their own people—and in broad daylight for eve-ryone to see.

The people were still undeterred. They turned over the white round ves-tibules that police normally sat in at intersections and transformed them into rolling barricades. This way they could move down the street, gaining ground while staying protected behind the moving barricade. They used anything: street signs, cobblestones, ripping signs or pipes off of buildings, anything they could find, to fight for their goal—capturing Tahrir. Twilight was beginning to set in, and I looked out into the direction that we had just come from, the Qasr al-Nil bridge, where just hours before at most a thou-sand people had been fighting a losing battle to cross the bridge. I blinked my eyes, not sure if I could trust them with the billowing tear gas and smoke and dwindling sunlight. There were masses upon masses of people—as far as the eye could see—marching toward Tahrir. It was breathtaking. The people were rising up, and the police were forced to backtrack. For the first time I thought: "This is a revolution."

The fighting continued, but it seemed as if the tide was turning. When a critical mass of people from one direction would surge onto the square, wild celebrations would break out, but not far away vicious battles were still being fought, shots were being fired, and tear gas and riot smoke filled the air. People continued to stream into Pierre's apartment throughout the day and evening. At some point, someone came asking for help to buy medical supplies. I decided to venture out again with a group of about five people to see if we could find a pharmacy that might be open. People on the street would stop me and insisted on showing me the tear gas canisters and bullet cartridges that said "Made in USA." And yet there was not a trace of hostility toward me as a U.S. citizen. A makeshift medical clinic had been set up in a nearby mosque. These clinics led by volunteers not only were crucial in that they saved people's lives, as there were no ambulances in sight or any other sort of provisions for caring for the wounded, but also because they were one of the many initiatives that created a type of "popular security" from below.[100] We returned to Pierre's apartment and, standing on the balcony, saw a huge fire burning not too far away. Someone pointed and said, as if in a rapture, "That is the headquarters of the NDP. That is the Bastille."[101]

Some time after midnight, I ventured out once again with another group of about five people, this time in a different direction, toward the Egyptian Museum. The fact that the police had disappeared from the streets had perhaps emboldened us. However, unbeknownst to us, there were still snipers stationed on the roofs of buildings, including on the roof of the Egyptian Museum.[102] That part of the square was darker and there were throngs of people. I didn't realize it at the time, but one of the people in our group was Khaled Abol Naga, a famous actor. But on that night, as on many others, class or status distinctions seemed to dissolve. Hierarchies were upended.[103] At one point some type of tumult ensued. Then, out of the darkness, I saw a line of tanks moving toward Tahrir—and toward me. What happened next was less a thought process than a visceral reaction. I forgot everything I had been told about how to behave in Egypt. My instincts told me to run. Some people shared my instinct and screamed in panic as they tried to run. But the masses of bodies were so densely packed that it was hard to get anywhere very quickly. Then I noticed that, instead of running *away* from the tanks, others were running *to* the tanks and even climbing up on top of them and cheering wildly while embracing the soldiers. I stopped in bewilderment, again unsure if I could believe my own eyes. The vast majority of academic and journalistic accounts of this day mention only one of these two reactions: those who were running to the tanks and not those who were running away from them in fear. As an eyewitness, however,

Photo 3.4 The moment the police begin to backtrack in the face of oncoming protesters. Photograph taken by the author on Tahrir Square on January 28, 2011.

I can attest that the reaction of the people on Tahrir to the deployment of the military was ambiguous from the very beginning.

Phase Two: January 29–February 7, Dual Power

During the first few days of the uprising, at least 99 police stations were burned down and many prisons and detention centers were broken into, allowing the prisoners to escape.[104] After the people had defeated the despised police force, the regime strategy switched from prevention to intimidation and further violence. This happened undoubtedly in recognition of the fact that their strategies until then had failed: the police had killed over 600 people on a single day,[105] but had failed to deter the rest; the physical barriers had failed in preventing the people from reaching Tahrir; the state media propaganda had failed to brainwash people; and the telecommunications blackout had failed to prevent people from communicating with each other.[106] Hence, a new strategy was needed. First, the regime decided to create a security vacuum. All the police who had not already abandoned their posts were instructed to do so. The jails were emptied and over 23,000 prisoners,[107] including murderers and rapists, were released onto the streets. Meanwhile the telecommunications blackout continued. Hired thugs known as *baltagiya* were used to intimidate protesters as during the Battle of the Camel on February 2. Army soldiers, who were guarding the checkpoints around Tahrir and inexplicably allowed the camel- and horse-riding thugs onto the square, remained passive as seven people were killed in the clashes. State media began a xenophobic campaign, blaming the unrest on foreign instigators in an attempt to delegitimize the protests. A curfew was set sometimes, beginning as early as 3 p.m., in an attempt to keep people off the streets. Many government offices and private businesses were closed.

In addition to these repressive measures, the regime was forced to make a few concessions. After midnight on January 28, Mubarak gave his first speech to the nation, which was the first time he had been summoned by the street. On January 29, Mubarak appointed a vice president for the first time since taking office in 1981, and he also appointed a new prime minister. On January 31, Mubarak reshuffled his cabinet, appointing several army generals in an attempt to secure the loyalty of the military.

In response, the strategy of the activists changed as well. They created proto-state organizations such as the *legan shaabeya* (neighborhood watch groups) to replace the security apparatus, leading to a situation characterized by "dual power." Tahrir was permanently occupied on a 24-hour basis, becoming a "liberated zone" or quasi-utopian community characterized by what Mohammed Bamyeh has called "noble ethics" including "community and solidarity, care for others, respect for the dignity of all."[108] He argues that this emerged "precisely out of the disappearance of government." Qaed Ibrahim Square in Alexandria, Al Arbeen Square in Suez, and other public spaces throughout Egypt were occupied as well.[109] As someone who visited Tahrir regularly during the weeks following January 28, I can attest to the compassion and kindness of the people in contrast to the barbarism of the state. Even during the height of the xenophobic media campaign, when foreigners were being attacked on the street by *baltagiya*, Tahrir itself was a safe haven, virtually free of any sort of discrimination or aggression. As a woman and as a foreigner, I never once experienced any form of sexual harassment or antiforeign sentiment on Tahrir itself during the 18 days. In this context the public and intercommunal praying that took place on Tahrir can be seen not only as a religious ritual but also as a protest tactic to explicitly demonstrate solidarity between Muslims and Christians as well as a living bulwark against the emergence of sectarian tensions.

As many of the businesses were shut down, Tahrir was supplied with food, water, and other necessities by workers in the informal sector.[110] Finally, there was a return to pre-internet forms of media activism as brochures and flyers were distributed by hand. On January 30 by chance I met Hossam Al-Hamalawy, an old friend, well-known blogger, and member of the Revolutionary Socialists, who was, in lieu of blogging, handing out leaflets on Tahrir. People reacquainted themselves with landlines. And they defied the curfew. On February 2, after almost a week of the telecommunications blackout during what I believe was the most critical period of the uprising, internet services were restored.

Phase Three: February 8–February 11, Labor Strikes the State

During this period the regime strategy changed again. And once again, without having access to the former regime officials to confirm this, the new strategies were developed in recognition of the fact that the old strategies had failed. The concessions failed to console people, the Battle of the Camel failed to clear Tahrir, and the curfew and creation of a security vacuum had failed to keep people indoors and off the streets. Instead of killing, arresting, and intimidating the Egyptian people, Mubarak decided to order them to go back to work. If violence couldn't end the uprising, perhaps a normalization strategy would. The curfew continued but was pushed back to 6 or 7 p.m. so that people would be able to go to work, but they were then expected to immediately return home after work rather than take to the streets in protest. In response to this regime strategy, another opposition strategy was required: that of the mass strike. Other protest tactics continued as before: continued defiance of the curfew, continued participation in proto-state organizations, and continued occupation of Tahrir. However, in many ways the locus of the uprising shifted (although to a large extent unnoticed by the media) from Tahrir to the workplaces. It is believed that as many as 20,000 workers participated in strikes on a single day: workers in textile factories, newspapers, government agencies, sanitation, and transportation all demanded economic concessions as well as the ousting of Mubarak. At the Suez Canal, up to 6,000 workers participated in a sit-in. Although the canal itself was never closed—as it was responsible for the second-largest source of foreign revenues after tourism—the threat to its operation was clear.[111]

After 18 days of repression mixed with minor concessions, and following the killing of at least 1,022 civilians at the hands of the security apparatus,[112] a final concession was made on February 11 when Hosni Mubarak, after nearly 30 years, agreed to release his hold on power. His vice president Omar Suleiman also disappeared from public view. The Supreme Council of the Armed Forces (SCAF) assumed power, promising to lead the country in the transition to democracy.

Conclusion

In this chapter I have examined the role of both structure and agency during the first wave of the revolution: the 18-day uprising between January 25 and February 11, 2011. The Mubarak regime represented a set of social relationships that relied on four pillars of support: the loyalty of the elite, the backing of the military, the acquiescence of the middle and lower classes, and the support of key allies such as the United States. Mubarak was able to maintain his hold on power for 30 years because his successful regime strategies involved co-opting the elite, coup-proofing the military, keeping the lid on social unrest through a combination of hard and soft power deterrents, and keeping US military and economic aid flowing. Beginning on January 25, 2011, the first pillar of the Mubarak regime crumbled as people took to the streets en masse and the acquiescence of the middle and lower classes was no longer forthcoming. A week later on January 31, the second pillar began to look unreliable as the military said it would cease using force against the protesters, while also not preventing the use of violence by thugs or *baltagiya*. On February 10 the third pillar represented by the economic elite began to give way. And finally, after Mubarak stepped down on February 11, the US administration officially bid farewell to their former ally. Having single-handedly brought down a dictator who had clung to power for three decades, Egyptians celebrated their victory. One day after Mubarak was ousted, masses of people returned to Tahrir. Many were ecstatic. I took a picture of someone carrying a handwritten sign that read in English and Arabic: "The Egyptian revolutionary youth reached the moon in the Tahrir space shuttle." There was a sense that something even more miraculous than the ousting of a dictator had happened. Aristide Zolberg referred to these moments in time when people believe that "all is possible" as "moments of madness."[113] This belief that "all was possible" did not suddenly end with the ousting of Mubarak on February 11. If anything, his fall from power emboldened many people, and they continued—almost without interruption—to protest for bread, freedom, and social justice. The revolution was not over.

4

يسقط يسقط حكم العسكر
"Down, Down with Military Rule"

The Second Wave against the Military Junta

(February 12, 2011–June 30, 2012)

Introduction

The 30-year rule of Mubarak had been brought to an end by a revolutionary uprising, and a new era was beginning. With Mubarak ousted and the police forces in disarray, a second form of authoritarian rule emerged that was even more militaristic in nature than that of the ousted regime. After Mubarak was deposed, the Supreme Council of the Armed Forces (SCAF) assumed power and dissolved the parliament and the constitution. The SCAF took over the executive and legislative branches of government. A year and a half later, on June 30, 2012, the SCAF handed over (some) power to Mohamed Morsi, the first president of postcolonial Egypt, who had no military background. These 17 months were initially referred to as the "transition period." After all, it was assumed that the revolution was over and a transition to democracy was beginning. However, it would be more precise to call it a period of military rule, as the shadowy institution known as the SCAF emerged from behind the scenes to rule directly. It was under military rule that the second wave of antiregime uprisings began.

The Egyptian military was no longer, to borrow Steven Cook's evocative phrase, "ruling but not governing"—but it was ruling, governing, legislating, judiciating, and controlling the state media along with much more. Their powers were expansive and unchecked, at least not in the institutional sense of checks and balances. Not only that, but the generals and field marshals never bothered even introducing themselves to their subjects, such as providing basic information about who belonged to the SCAF, who was in charge of what, or explaining their decision-making process. Some estimated that 19 generals belonged to the SCAF, others said 25. No one really knew. Activists and researchers took it upon themselves to find out who exactly it was that had assumed something approaching absolute power over them.[1]

Officially the SCAF claimed to want to lead the country in the transition to democracy. Initially, the generals in the SCAF derived most of their legitimacy from the people themselves, as some of the Tahririans chanted "the people and the army are one hand!" while tanks and soldiers were being deployed throughout Egypt back in February 2011. The second wave of the revolution was characterized first and foremost by a power struggle between those who were trying to continue the revolution (*ath-thawra mustamera*) and those who were attempting to salvage the old regime.

Although many observers have claimed that the military "supported" the revolution, it would be more accurate to say that the army never looked favorably on a popular uprising that ousted one of its own. Contrary to the democratic transitions that took place in Eastern Europe and Latin America, where the opposition movements in a number of countries enjoyed formal recognition and seats at the negotiating table, the movement that toppled Mubarak did not have any regular channels of communication with the SCAF. The relationship between the opposition and the interim military government was therefore more confrontational, resembling less a "conversation among gentlemen" than a power struggle carried out on the streets. The SCAF at times called in some of the leading opposition groups such as April 6 for consultation, only to publicly attack them shortly afterward in an attempt to delegitimize them. Members of the Coalition of the Youth of the Revolution met a number of times with Abdel Fattah El-Sisi, who as director of military intelligence was responsible for outreach to the youth.

After being praised by their American benefactors for their professionalism and restraint during the January 25 uprising, the generals adopted a more heavy-handed approach once they were in charge. Military tribunals of civilians became commonplace: over 12,000 civilians were tried in military courts in just eight months,[2] more than during the entire 30-year rule of Mubarak. On March 23, 2011, a law was passed that outlawed demonstrations and labor strikes. The military tortured demonstrators and forcibly conducted virginity tests on detained women.[3] The Maspero massacre of Coptic activists on October 9, 2011, and the Port Said massacre on February 1, 2012, represent the two worst cases of state brutality during the military junta. November then saw the beginning of the "second wave" of the Egyptian Revolution. The five-day uprising in Cairo became known as the "Battle of Mohamed Mahmoud," and clashes at the parliament in December left scores of people dead. Many more had been injured or had lost an eye, as snipers specifically targeted the eyes of the protesters, leaving many partially blind.[4] Members of the Ultras Al-Ahly football club ("Ultras") had played an important role during these clashes in defending the front lines of the battle and carrying the injured on their motorcycles to and from the medical clinics. For most of the transition period, the

Muslim Brotherhood had stayed away from street protests. Indeed, the Muslim Brothers emerged as the closest ally of the SCAF. Instead, street protests were often marked by the organizing capacity of the Ultras. According to one account: "What marks the Ultras is both the will and the capacity to engage the police on something approaching an equal footing—though the logistical capacity to inflict damage is of course not comparable."[5] They were the next target. On February 1, 2012, during a match between Al-Ahly and Al-Masry in Port Said, fighting broke out that resulted in the death of 74 people, with over 1,000 injured.[6] The doors to the stadium had been mysteriously locked, trapping people inside. Many believe that the Maspero massacre was intended to destroy the unity between Muslims and Christians that characterized the mass uprising that ousted Mubarak, while the killings in Port Said were intended to crush the Ultras specifically and the youth movement more generally.[7] It should not be forgotten that the 18-day uprising that ousted Mubarak, while often portrayed as peaceful, resulted in the deaths of 1,022 people, with over 6,500 injured. While Maspero and Port Said were undoubtedly the two worst cases of state brutality while the SCAF was in power, every month witnessed cases of violence and human rights abuses:[8]

- February 2011—military trials of civilians begin
- March 2011—forced virginity tests conducted on female protesters
- April 2011—soldiers protest on Tahrir
- May 2011—Imbaba church attacks, 16 died and 242 injured[9]
- June 2011—assault on martyrs' families and activists in solidarity with them, 590 injured[10]
- July 2011—Battle of Abbasiyya, three-week occupation of Tahrir dispersed[11]
- August 2011—Omar Makram Mosque stormed, demonstrators beaten
- September 2011—Israeli embassy protests, 3 died[12]
- October 2011—Maspero massacre, 27 killed[13]
- November 2011—Second wave of the revolution begins; Battle of Mohamed Mahmoud, 61 killed, 4,455 injured[14]
- December 2011—cabinet clashes, woman trampled by military police "blue bra incident," 26 killed, 1,917 injured[15]
- January 2012—in mid-January Mohamed El-Baradei withdraws from the presidential election saying "Mubarak's regime has not fallen"; on the 25th millions celebrate the one-year anniversary of the revolution all across Egypt
- February 2012—Port Said massacre, 74 killed[16]
- May 2012—Abbasiyya clashes, largest mass arrest since the SCAF assumed power, with over 400 arrested

- June 2012—"soft coup" in which the parliament is dissolved and powers of the president are limited days before the presidential runoff elections

Many activists became convinced that, rather than benevolently guiding the country toward democracy or safeguarding the revolution as they claimed to do, the SCAF was in fact trying to preserve as much of the old regime as possible. The monopoly on power that the former ruling National Democratic Party (NDP) had lost was transferred to the military council. The state media was as deferent toward the SCAF as they had been to Mubarak. And with the police forces in disarray, the military took on some of the functions of the police, in essence enhancing their monopoly of violence. This made the SCAF considerably more dangerous than the remnants of the NDP. A quip by an anonymous activist circulating in social media summed up the predicament quite well: "They have a gun in one hand and the media in the other."

In contrast to the first and third waves of unrest, during the second wave the military itself was the target of popular rage. Instead of celebrating the role of the SCAF in ousting Mubarak, the SCAF was derided as a coterie of septuagenarians, at best out of touch with the youthful revolutionaries, at worst intent on crushing them.[17]

What role did business elites and the United States play during this second wave of mass unrest?

Business Elites

Generally speaking, the behavior of the business community during this time depended on what faction of the bourgeoisie they belonged to. Some of the more "independent" business elites tried to co-opt the revolution, using images from the 18-day uprising in their advertising but not lending any meaningful support to the ongoing forms of mobilization or new activist groups that were created. The less independent business elites with closer ties to the regime came under unprecedented scrutiny—some of them were put on trial, jailed, or fled the country. Hence they were in no position to exert meaningful pressure on the SCAF.

A number of businesses even attempted to squeeze profit out of the revolution's sudden mass appeal. As just one example, Vodafone created a three-minute television advertisement called "Our Power," which suggested that the company supported the uprising that toppled Mubarak. Activists called out the company, not only because of its brazen attempt to gain profit out of the revolution but also because in fact the company had done more to suppress the uprising than support it by shutting down cell phone services. One online comment summed up activists' anger:

> Are you guys seriously planning on leeching something out of this after you cut the phones and internet, after protesters who were being shot at could not call others and warn them about being shot at by snipers because of you? SHAME![18]

The outrage against this attempt at co-optation was so great that Vodafone had to publicly distance itself from the advert. Needless to say, Vodafone did not lend any meaningful financial support to the continued mass mobilization that took place under the SCAF. Neither did any other corporate entity. Although the Battle of Mohamed Mahmoud in late 2011 was an important turning point, as it pressured the SCAF to make a few significant concessions including moving forward the date for presidential elections, there were no commercial billboards celebrating the event. Opposition to the Egyptian military was never commercialized.

Political elites were under even more duress than their economic counterparts. The first wave of arrests of Mubarak's cronies had happened already during the 18-day uprising—Ahmed Ezz, Zoheir Garranah, Rachid Mohamed Rachid, but also Habib el-Adly. It seemed as if the SCAF intended to only prosecute the new guard of the 2004 businessmen's cabinet. Egyptians would joke that the SCAF seemed to think that the purpose of the revolution was to oust not Mubarak but the minister of tourism, Zoheir Garranah, because he wanted to privatize their land.

A second wave of arrests of old regime cronies then occurred in April—Zakaria Azmi, Safwat el-Sherif, Fathi Sorour—but also Mubarak and his two sons, Alaa and Gamal. Mubarak was ousted in February but not prosecuted until April, when a sizable protest demanded he be put on trial. It was arguably only because of the continued pressure from street protests that this second wave of arrests took place. As I showed in the previous chapter, the Tahririans wanted to oust Mubarak's entire regime, not just Mubarak. For the first half of 2011, the primary goal of many of the demonstrations and marches was to expand the gains of the revolution by dismantling the networks of the old regime. In other words, the cronies of the Mubarak clan were under scrutiny as never before. The business community was therefore also under pressure and had no reason to support the ongoing protests and marches. From the perspective of businessmen, the ongoing social unrest was bad for the economy, and it was potentially also bad for anyone who could be suspected of being too close to the former regime. The demand to prosecute the corrupt Mubarak elite was so popular that posters and stickers would be sold in Tahrir featuring a dozen or so of the most hated men either behind bars or hanging from a noose, as in the image here (see Photo 4.1).

During the second half of 2011, activists began to shift their focus away from targeting the business elites and cronies of the regime and toward documenting the SCAF's abuses of power. But even as the youthful revolutionaries' rage shifted from the NDP to the SCAF, or from the civilian to the military wing of the Mubarak regime, the business community still had little reason to support their demands.

The activist groups that I will discuss in the following section made wide-ranging demands regarding the SCAF: they wanted them to be accountable and transparent, they wanted them to stop trying civilians in military tribunals, they wanted them to stop the violence, and, ultimately, they wanted the men in uniform to hand over power to civilians. While many of these activists came

Photo 4.1 From right to left: Youssef Boutros Ghali (minister of finance), Ahmed El-Maghrabi (minister of housing), Ahmed Nazif (prime minister), Gamal Mubarak (son of Hosni Mubarak), Hussein Salem (businessman and Mubarak confidant), Ahmed Ezz (NDP's secretary of organizing), Habib el-Adly (Interior Minister), Safwat el-Sherif (secretary general of NDP), Fathi Sorour (speaker of the People's Assembly), Zakaria Azmi (chief of presidential staff), Mohamed Abou El Enein (businessman and head of Industry and Energy Committee in the People's Assembly), Zoheir Garranah (minister of tourism), and Rachid Mohamed Rachid (minister of trade).

from middle-class backgrounds, I find little evidence that their efforts were supported, much less funded, by the Egyptian business elite.

United States

During the second wave of the revolution, the United States continued to support their longtime ally, the Egyptian armed forces, even as they transformed from the "military-as-institution" to the "military-as-government." Chairman of the Joint Chiefs of Staff Mike Mullen even publicly praised them for their "professionalism" and restraint during the revolution that killed 1,022 civilians.[19] It would have seemed that the relationship was off to a good start.

Indeed, American officials even liked to take at least partial credit for the "restraint" exercised by the Egyptian army. They believed that US military aid to Egypt buys the United States influence, just as they believed that training Egyptian officers in American military academies instills them with democratic values. This narrative is comforting, not to mention self-congratulatory. But does it hold up to empirical scrutiny? Although the events of the second wave— and even more so the third—should have led US officials to question this belief, this does not seem to have been the case.

In May 2011, President Barack Obama spoke about the Arab uprisings to a group of US State Department employees and other invited guests. He vowed to "support the transitions to democracy." Apparently he thought the United States could do this while continuing to fund the military junta that had seized power. To be fair, it seems that US officials strived to be on good terms with all the political actors who had entered the fray. For example, the parliamentary victory of the Islamists "did not lead to panic in Washington."[20]

United States lawmakers, however, did continue to view US-Egyptian relations through the prism of Israeli security. The House Subcommittee on State, Foreign Operations, and Related Programs and the House Foreign Affairs Committee both tried to ensure that US military aid would continue to flow on the condition that Egypt would "fully honor their treaty with Israel." While Obama at least offered verbal support for a transition process, these members of Congress made clear where their priorities were. As Jason Brownlee pointed out: "These were arguments about preventing Egyptian hostility toward Israel, not about fostering democracy."[21]

In a press conference in Cairo on September 28, 2011, Secretary of State Hillary Clinton continued to praise the military, saying, "We also believe that the army has played a very stabilizing, important role during this period."[22] Two weeks later, the Maspero massacre occurred, killing dozens of nonviolent protesters. But even after the outbreak of violence, and the insurrection known as the Battle of Mohamed Mahmoud, there were no strong criticisms to be heard from the Obama administration. In an op-ed in the *New York Times*, Marc Lynch and Steven Cook admonished the Obama administration for its passivity: "The U.S. was virtually silent as dozens of Egyptians died and tons of U.S.-made tear gas bombarded Tahrir Square."[23] Then when US officials did speak, they called for restraint "on all sides." As I pointed out in a short article at the time, the only problem with this argument was that one side was using tanks, rubber bullets, and live ammunition, while the other side jerry-rigged cooking pots into makeshift helmets. Did the White House want protesters to abstain from their homemade self-protection devices?[24]

Despite all the violence and uncertainties of the so-called transitional phase, the Obama administration assured that US military aid continued to flow. While the SCAF gladly pocketed this American money, it regarded any American (or other outside) support for civil society as "foreign interference." According to their logic, foreigners are only allowed to support the Egyptian military, not Egyptian civilians. What this means is that US-funded army soldiers were taking orders from US-trained SCAF generals using US-made tear gas to attack peaceful demonstrators, while the SCAF claimed "foreign elements" were responsible for the unrest.

Despite the continued pro-SCAF rhetoric coming out of Washington, and the pro-SCAF money that continued to flow, the junta did not shy away from picking a fight with the United States. During the first wave, as discussed in the previous chapter, the state-controlled media unleashed a xenophobic campaign, claiming the unrest was the result of foreign interference and speaking incessantly of the "foreign agenda," the "third agent," and mysterious "hidden hands." The xenophobic rhetoric came from the highest levels, including Vice President Omar Suleiman. But these were just words. During the second wave, the anti-American rhetoric became actionable. To the astonishment of Washington, US-funded offices were raided by armed security forces and US citizens were put on trial.[25] Forty-three nongovernmental organization (NGO) workers, including 16 Americans who worked for the National Democratic Institute (NDI) and the International Republican Institute (IRI), including Sam LaHood, the son of US Department of Transportation Secretary Ray LaHood, were ultimately convicted in 2013 of operating illegal organizations and receiving foreign funding.[26] They were initially placed under a travel ban and prevented from leaving the country. Even the highly publicized and politicized arrests of American citizens did not lead to any official threat to reduce or withhold US aid to Egypt.[27] After the travel ban was lifted, all of the US citizens, with the exception of Robert Becker, fled the country rather than stand trial in an Egyptian court.

Why the generals dared to be so brazen is still a matter of some speculation. One answer could be that they knew they could get away with it. In Jason
Brownlee's assessment, the fact that the SCAF had declared they would guarantee the peace treaty with Israel, although the possibility of revoking it was
unlikely, served to buttress their position.[28] Of course, this was not the only
episode of brazenness on the part of the junta. Just three months after army soldiers had shot and killed Coptic protesters in front of Maspero, army generals
attended the Coptic Christmas mass in early January 2012.[29]

In sum, although US officials did slowly change their tone and begin to criticize the SCAF after initially celebrating their role in the first wave of the revolution, they never withdrew any of the material support that the United States
provided to the Egyptian military. In other words, as during the first wave, the
regime's reliance on US aid did not prove fatal—as this aid was never withdrawn. The continuation of military aid was most frequently justified as giving the United States leverage, which it could use to promote democratization.
According to this line of reasoning, curtailing military aid would curtail the
ability of the United States to support reform. But in fact, the opposite happened: the rhetoric of reform and human rights was used to promote militari-
zation, not democratization. Or, as Jason Brownlee puts it, US policies toward
Egypt have resulted in "democracy prevention."[30]

Ironically, the revolution that toppled Mubarak with the hope of establishing democracy had the effect of increasing rather than decreasing the power
of an undemocratic institution: the military. But as the power of the ruling
brass expanded during the "transition," its abuse of power increased as well.
The SCAF became Mubarakism without Mubarak. In fact, the generals were
entrusted with more expansive powers than Mubarak—and yet, paradoxically,
at the height of their powers and influence, they became more vulnerable than
ever before.

Civilians in Egypt were far from being able to determine military policy. They
were not allowed to see the military budget or even to know who belonged to
the SCAF and why.[31] Officially, journalists were not allowed to write about the
military without seeking prior approval, and researchers were not allowed to do
research on the military without obtaining permission. And yet—and here we
come to the second paradox—during the span of just 17 months, civilian activists increased oversight of the military, exposed human rights abuses, forced
certain concessions to be made, unveiled and then scrutinized the military's
economic enterprises, and penetrated the civilian state bureaucracy. In short,
they began to force the military council to increase their transparency and be
accountable to their citizens.

The main challenge to the SCAF's authority did not come from the parliament or from the formation of new political parties. Nor did it come from

the longest and best-organized opposition group in the country, the Muslim Brotherhood. Although business elites may have been displeased with the state of the economy and ongoing unrest, there is little evidence that they exerted pressure on the SCAF to hand over power to civilians or even speed up the transition process. On the contrary, many cronies of the Mubarak regime were under pressure—some were put in jail or on trial, and others fled the country.

The United States continued to provide military aid and even praised the "professionalism" of the Egyptian military despite mounting repression. Instead, the main challenge to the SCAF's authority came from activist groups and workers who staged protests and labor strikes. In addition to describing my survey data, this chapter will also introduce many of the new activist groups that were formed during the second wave, such as No Military Tribunals, Mosireen, Kazeboon, the Ultras, and the campaign to end virginity tests.

The Anti-SCAF Opposition

The Loyal "Opposition": The Parliament and the Brotherhood

For most of the 17 months that Field Marshal Mohamed Hussein Tantawi and his coterie of generals were in power, the parliament and the Muslim Brotherhood showed a great deal of deference to the military council. I therefore do not consider them—because they did not consider themselves—as part of the more radical antimilitarist opposition movements that this chapter is dedicated to understanding.

The parliament, which many believed to be a crucial vehicle for transitioning from an authoritarian to a more democratic system of government, was convened for less than 5 of the 17 months of the transition period. Islamists won 65.74 percent of the seats, including the Muslim Brotherhood's Freedom and Justice Party and the Salafi Nour Party. The remaining seats were divided among other parties, including the Wafd with 7.67% percent and the Social Democratic Party with 3.15 percent. Independents took only 4.52 percent of the seats.

One of the very few MPs who could claim to represent the youth who toppled Mubarak was Ziad El-Elaimy, a young lawyer and human rights activist who belonged to the Social Democratic Party. After the Port Said massacre and soon after the parliament had convened for the first time, El-Elaimy issued a scathing critique of Field Marshal Tantawi by using an Egyptian proverb and referring to him as a "donkey." This led to an outcry among his fellow MPs, who demanded that he be referred to the parliament's ethics committee, even though he had made the statement outside parliament. El-Elaimy offered an apology, but insisted that he was merely trying to make the point that there needed to be a proper investigation of the Port Said football stadium massacre.

Although El-Elaimy apologized, and the Arabic Language Center reportedly said that the expression he had used did not entail offensive language, the campaign against him continued. The SCAF's official website stated: "In our honorable institution [SCAF] we normally don't respond to such quarrels. But what has forced us to respond in this case is the character of the spokesperson." The statement also said, "[W]e must stop and consider his fitness for parliament."[32] In June the military judicial authorities demanded that El-Elaimy's parliamentary immunity be lifted.[33]

Another case is that of Mohamed Abu Hamad, the vice president of the liberal Free Egyptians Party. In a discussion in the parliament regarding the use of birdshot by the police during the clashes on Mohamed Mahmoud Street, the parliamentary speaker Saad El-Katatni, from the Muslim Brotherhood's Freedom and Justice Party, said that he had been told by Interior Minister Mohamed Ibrahim that the police had not used birdshot. El-Katatni's willingness to believe this statement defied logic, as images had gone viral with clear evidence of the use of birdshot. For example, Salma Said, who at the time was 26 years old, sustained injuries to her face and body from birdshot while filming the events as part of her work for the Mosireen collective, which will be discussed later. Abu Hamad held up birdshot canisters and said: "The clashes are between the interior ministry and revolutionaries, but we only spoke to one side and ignored the other. That is not fair."[34] He was booed by other MPs, and one MP even tried to snatch the birdshot canister from his hands. According to Gamal Zahran, professor of political science and former independent MP, the parliament was "combating the few revolutionary youth who won seats."[35]

While a full discussion of the parliament would be outside the scope of this chapter, the El-Elaimy incident illustrates that, instead of functioning as a vehicle to empower the youth who toppled Mubarak, it often operated as a machine to sideline or even silence them. This is perhaps the first reason why many revolutionaries rejected electoral politics. Realizing that they had been excluded from what was supposed to be an institution that represented "the people," in mid-March 2012, 57 groups announced that they would launch the "Revolutionary Youth Parliament" in order to "enhance communication between the youth and the state by presenting united demands to the People's Assembly and the government."[36] The second reason that many rejected electoral politics is because—even if the parliament had been constituted differently—its powers to counterbalance the SCAF were limited. At one point the MPs wanted to pass a resolution of no confidence in the cabinet headed by Kamal Ganzouri, only to be told that they in fact did not have the authority to do so.[37] Third, many activists felt that forming political parties and participating in the electoral process would have entailed accepting the rules of the game, which were dictated by the SCAF. In their reasoning, if the SCAF was illegitimate, then the rules they were establishing were as well. And yet others simply felt that it was morally wrong to vote in the parliamentary elections in November. As many put it at the time, "the blood of the martyrs has not even dried yet," referring to the clashes just days earlier during the Battle of Mohamed Mahmoud.

For many of the same reasons, a number of activists called for boycotting the presidential elections—even before the dissolution of the parliament in mid-June. Instead of seeing the presidential elections as the crowning achievement of the revolution, some of the activists I interviewed have referred to it as a defeat:

> [The SCAF] want the elections to be the final blow to the revolution. To send the message that we are not going to take your shit any longer, we let you play revolutionaries for a while, now get back into your boxes and contain yourself. I think that was their clear and straightforward message. They are not going to tolerate dissent any longer.[38]

In short, the parliament was weak, ineffectual, and short-lived. It was then summarily dissolved by court order on June 14, once again granting the SCAF legislative in addition to executive powers. The events in mid-June, referred to as a soft coup, judicial coup, coup-by-proxy, or coup-within-a-coup, had the effect of expanding the powers of the armed forces while limiting the powers of the president, in addition to dissolving the parliament.[39] The emergency law, abolished just days before, was effectively reinstated as not only police but also soldiers were granted the power to arrest citizens. Instead of relinquishing power or transitioning at the long-awaited end of the "transition period," the generals dug in even further. In many ways these events offered proof that the activists who shunned electoral politics were not merely jaundiced cynics but in fact understood very well that the SCAF was playing according to its own rules, which it made up as it went along.

By this time, even the Muslim Brotherhood had become outraged at the SCAF's behavior. On June 22, 2012, a member of the Brotherhood told me, "We are against the military council who canceled our parliament, who canceled our humanity, and who canceled our dignity."[40] This was, however, at the very end of the transition period. Other groups were much quicker to recognize which way the wind was blowing. The Brotherhood was not leading the opposition to the SCAF, but following. Indeed, the Brotherhood leadership and the military leadership had a common interest in bringing about the demobilization of popular protests.[41] Because in this chapter I am focused on analyzing opposition to the SCAF, I have not included the Muslim Brotherhood as one of the activist groups under consideration. As Anne Alexander has argued, for the first six months after the ouster of Mubarak, the Brotherhood attempted to influence the ongoing street protests primarily through their *absence* from the streets. It was not until July 29, the "Friday of Stability," that the Muslim Brotherhood joined the protests in full force together with the Salafis and other Islamist groups.[42] As Alexander writes:

> During the first six months of the revolution, the Brotherhood's leadership, like its counterparts in 1952, openly proclaimed its support for the post-revolutionary military regime, exhorting striking workers to restart the "wheel of production," and calling on protestors to leave the streets and give the ruling SCAF time to complete its declared mission of overseeing the post-Mubarak political transition.[43]

On May 19, 2011, more than a year before the Brotherhood joined the anti-SCAF opposition after the dissolution of parliament, a young 20-year-old activist named Noor Ayman Noor argued in the *Guardian*:

> To be honest—and I could get in trouble for this, but I don't care—my trust in the military has been falling since February 2nd [the day the army stood by as pro-Mubarak forces attacked protesters in Tahrir square]. Since Mubarak fell thousands have been arrested by the army, tortured, humiliated and given ridiculous prison sentences at military tribunals, and what is catastrophic is not just that these actions are being committed but that the majority of Egyptians are staying quiet about them because they're scared of losing the army. People look at what's happening in Syria and Libya and decide not to speak out because, look what happens when the army doesn't take the side of the people.[44]

Noor was not just speaking for himself. Just four days later, activists declared May 23, 2011 to be a Day to Criticize the SCAF and the #NoSCAF hashtag was created. Thousands of people posted critical comments on this day, effectively breaking the taboo of deference toward the SCAF.[45] And then in January 2012, Issandr El Amrani observed that "for much of the political class and a not inconsequential slice of public opinion, the violence of the early winter has reduced the military's moral authority to a level unseen since its defeat at Israel's hands in 1967."[46]

In the wake of the January 25 Revolution, the SCAF may have thought they would enjoy widespread legitimacy or at least obedience to their rule. They were wrong. The main challenge to the SCAF's authority did not come from the parliament or the formation of new political parties. Nor did it come from the longest and best-organized opposition group in the country, the Muslim

Brotherhood. Instead, the main challenge to the SCAF's authority came from a number of new activist groups such as No Military Tribunals, Mosireen, Kazeboon, the campaign to end virginity tests, and a campaign to boycott army products and demilitarize the state bureaucracy. In confronting the SCAF and the old regime it represented, these groups began to uncover what many believed was perhaps the greatest impediment to democratization in Egypt: the deep state. None of these groups existed prior to the January 25 Revolution. They are all products of this unique period in recent Egyptian history. Although they each work on separate issues, the demand to end military rule is what unites them. These groups were at the forefront of opposition to the SCAF.

I argue that the emergence of these groups represented a new form of activism that was revolutionary in a double sense. First, when the military is the de facto government, demanding that it be toppled becomes a revolutionary act. Here it becomes clear that the type of militarism that Egyptian activists are confronting is quite different from that found in the United States or other societies in which the military is under civilian control. Michael Mann's definition of militarism needs to be modified to be applicable to Egypt. Instead of militarism being "a set of attitudes and social practices which regards war and the preparation for war as a normal and desirable social activity," a better definition would be "a set of attitudes and social practices which regards military dominance in political and economic affairs as a normal and desirable social activity."

This brings us to the second reason why this type of activism is revolutionary. Traditionally, the military has been held in high regard as liberating the country from both colonialism and the monarchy. Gamal Abdel Nasser and his Free Officers, as the founding fathers of modern Egypt, set the country on the path of independence from both Great Britain and the superpower confrontation of the Cold War. The participation of Egyptian soldiers in the First Gulf War in 1990 may have been unpopular, but it did not lead to widespread protests against the Egyptian military. Wars led by the United States, the United Kingdom, or others may have brought people to the streets in protest, but this did not occur in wars led or supported by the Egyptian armed forces. Egypt lacks any meaningful tradition of a peace movement or antimilitarist movement. The new antimilitarist activism in Egypt is therefore revolutionary not only in a political sense—in that it aimed to overthrow the ruling military junta and uproot its sources of legitimacy and power—but also in a cultural sense as it is historically unprecedented.

The antimilitarist activism in Egypt is therefore not comparable with antiwar movements or antibase movements in North America, Europe, or Japan.[47] This is simply because most of these movements are aimed at preventing a war, preventing the spread of nuclear weapons, or preventing the proliferation of overseas military bases. In Egypt, it was about ousting the generals and establishing civilian control of the military. Needless to say, this is a considerably more ambitious goal than ousting Mubarak. The SCAF is not a single person but rather the pinnacle of the most powerful institution in Egyptian society, with tentacles reaching into the economy, the media, the judiciary, civilian parts of the state apparatus, and beyond.

I will discuss these activist groups in the order that they emerged: starting with the No Military Tribunals group, being formed already in February 2011; followed by the campaign against virginity testing beginning in March, the Mosireen collective emerging during the spring and summer, Kazeboon activists forming in the wake of the "second wave" of the revolution in December, and the campaign to boycott army products and demilitarize the state bureaucracy in January 2012.

The empirical evidence is based on a combination of qualitative and quantitative data, consisting of interviews conducted with members of each of the groups discussed here as well as an online Arabic-language survey of over 500 Egyptians. The sample consisted of college-educated Egyptians of all ages, including both activists and nonactivists, with 56.7 percent saying they attended at least one demonstration during the 18-day revolution that ousted Mubarak, while 43.3 percent said they did not take part at all.[48]

No Military Trials

These are not trials; you can't call them trials, they are a total sham. It's unacceptable to call them military trials, it's unacceptable to call them anything else than what they really are: an oppressive tool, the most important tool they are using, to scare people and to terrorize people.[49]

On February 25, 2011, two weeks after Mubarak was ousted, a major demonstration was held on Tahrir called the "Friday of Victory." Demands included calling for Ahmed Shafik to step down; Mubarak had hastily appointed him prime minister just weeks earlier during the uprising. At night, the protest on Tahrir was attacked by army soldiers. One person provides a vivid description of these events:

I returned to Tahrir on the 25th of February, the Friday of Victory. Of course none of our demands had been met and we did not want Ahmed Shafik. At 2 a.m. the army attacked us. About 300 men carrying sticks, batons and electrics beat us for absolutely no reason. . . . They handcuffed me behind my back, all the time swearing at us and shouting that Mubarak is and continues to be the president. The metal wire was cutting into my wrists and when I complained they beat me even more. The commando officer stepped on my back with his boots, kicked my head, and for seconds stood on my neck and I felt I will die. He shouted: "You want Mubarak to leave. He will remain despite all of you."[50]

Most of the people who were arrested on that day were later released. Amr Behairy, however, was not. After his friends inquired as to his whereabouts, they realized that he was being held in prison and subjected to a military trial although he was a civilian who had not broken any law. They decided to begin a campaign to demand the release of Amr, but soon began to realize that this was not an isolated incident.[51] They began to hear of more and more civilians who were being tried in military courts, but no one knew the exact numbers. At first they thought there may be dozens, then hundreds, then thousands. The authorities refused to release any information. The campaign to release Amr turned into a campaign against military trials. They became the first antimilitary group in post-Mubarak Egypt.

After months of organizing, the SCAF finally admitted that over 12,000 civilians were being tried in military courts, more than the number who had been tried in military tribunals during the entire period of Mubarak's rule.[52] Activists believe the number may have been much higher. This means that these civilians had no lawyers, there was no due process, and there was no pretense of a fair trial. Some of the "court cases" were conducted in the kitchen of the Hikstep military prison, not even in a courtroom.[53] Many of those who were tried in military courts were revolutionaries, people who were arrested at demonstrations and protests. According to activists, there was also a clear targeting of the poor.

It's very clear that they want to terrorize this group of people, this faction of society, because they're the most dangerous faction [to SCAF], because they are the largest faction of society and because they have the most to be outraged about; they have the most to revolt about. [The military] wants to put the fear of God in them by making them live with this sense of fear that at any moment they can be taken without due process and without having committed a crime and get thrown in prison, some for 10 years, some for 20 years, and we've seen very harsh sentencing. And I think this is a way to terrorize people and put them back in their containers so that they don't even think about the possibility of demonstrating or protesting or anything like that.[54]

Often the families of those who were arrested were not even informed as to their whereabouts. In one case, after one person had disappeared and not been heard of for over six months, his family assumed that he was dead. They had a funeral for him. His wife dressed in black to mourn the passing of her husband. Then finally they were told that he had been arrested, tried in a military court, and sent to prison, without a lawyer and without even allowing him to notify anyone as to his whereabouts. An activist explained that tanks would some-times scoop up people in poor neighborhoods. She said: "I've heard more than once, 'We have no more men in our village.' It's like a form of kidnapping."[55]

Meanwhile the kingpins of the Mubarak regime were being tried in civilian courts, represented by the best lawyers. The No Military Tribunals' website states: "This is not the freedom that we fought and died for."[56] The group's activities included:

- Providing free legal support to the thousands of people who were being tried in military courts.
- Providing media support.
- Raising awareness about the issue of military tribunals through holding press conferences and uploading videos of testimonies to their website.
- Attempting to establish accountability by demanding that presidential candidates take a position on military trials and recording their statements.

The group began approaching presidential candidates in March 2011, but at the time all of them refused to make any public statement criticizing the military trials. It was not until May 7 that Hisham Bastawisy, a judge and vice president of the Court of Cassation in addition to being nominated by the Tagammu Party as a presidential candidate, agreed to go on record with a statement. Even El-Baradei, one of the most prominent liberal critics and presidential contenders, still refused to make a statement as the issue was still highly controversial.[57]

As the first antimilitary activists in post-Mubarak Egypt, the group walked a fine line between human rights activism and political activism. In June 2011, after major internal discussions, three members of the group met with two SCAF generals, deciding that as human rights activists they would have to resort to any and all methods to help the victims of the military tribunals.[58] In July, when Tahrir was occupied for three weeks, the longest occupation since the uprising that ousted Mubarak, the main demand was to end military trials of civilians. The yellow-and-black logo identifying the group spread both online and as graffiti on the walls throughout Cairo and other cities.

By September 2011, they had created a video of seven presidential candidates who all stated their opposition to military trials of civilians, including

Amr Moussa, Abdel Moneim Aboul Fotouh, Ayman Noor, Hisham Bastawisy, Hazem Abu Ismail, Hamdeen Sabahi, and Bothaina Kamel.[59] Within the span of just a few months, this small group of activists had managed to change the political discourse around the issue of military trials from one of absolute silence to a situation in which presidential candidates from across the political spectrum (liberals, leftists, former regime figures, moderate Islamists, and Salafis) openly stated their opposition to military trials of civilians. I asked a member of the group how they managed this, and if a civilian judiciary could be used to fight the military judicial system. She said: "Nothing legal can help these kids. The pressure is what made it possible."[60]

In the interview I conducted with her, Shahira Abouellail described how she quit her job and had been working full-time on the No Military Tribunals campaign for over a year. When I asked about how they managed to support themselves, she said: "We've all gone broke." Due to the poisoned atmosphere around the whole issue of funding of NGOs, they decided not to accept donations from anyone, even Egyptians.[61] If people want to donate money, they are told to give it to the families of the martyrs. It would seem that the decision to criminally charge powerful foreign-funded organizations like the NDI and the IRI had the (perhaps intended) effect of forcing many Egyptian civil society organizations and social movements to deplete their personal savings before resorting to seeking funding for their activities.

On January 23, just before the one-year anniversary of the uprising that ousted Mubarak, several hundred detainees were released from prison who had been tried in military courts. One of the questions on the survey asked what was the reason for this: 83.1 percent of respondents believed this was due to pressure from street protests, while only 8.1 percent believed this was due to pressure from political parties.

The Campaign to Stop Virginity Tests

If I drop these charges, what happened to me could happen to any girl in Egypt.[62]

On March 8, 2011, less than one month after Mubarak had been deposed, a small group of people gathered on Tahrir to celebrate International Women's Day. My mother was visiting me at the time and we happened to be in the vicinity of Tahrir that afternoon. It was a small gathering that did not even disrupt traffic, and as I didn't see any security forces anywhere nearby, or hear any commotion, I thought it would be safe enough to stop by and say hello. We spent about an hour there, chatting with some of the people I knew. It was a diverse group of both men and women. We later learned that the peaceful pro-testers had been attacked. Some of the women were tortured and taken to a mil-itary prison where they were forced to strip naked and undergo "virginity tests" while soldiers and officers looked on.

The issue did not receive much coverage at the time as many Egyptians de-cided "to trust the military and to avoid questioning its actions."[63] I brought up the issue in the social movements course that I had been teaching at AUC since 2008. Most of the students were somehow sympathetic to the revolution, but of the almost 30 students in the class, only 4 of them believed the story and were convinced that the military had committed a crime. One year later, Samira Ibrahim, one of the women who was subjected to the "virginity tests" and the only one to sue the military for its actions, was named by *Time* magazine as one of the 100 most influential people in the world.[64]

Her story is as grim as it is inspiring. Ibrahim describes what happened to her in the military facility known as C-28, which also includes a detention center:

> I went into a room with a large window, the door was open and soldiers could see you from the other side. I went in with a woman, thought she was going to pat me down, like when they search you in airports, a regular search, but then she told me to take off my clothes. So I just asked her to please close the door and the window. She said no and somebody came in to hit me. So I had to take off all my clothes. Behind the window I could see them laughing. They were joking with each other and laughing that they could see me, both soldiers and officers. They were coming and going, watching. On that day, I truly wished for death. I kept telling myself people get their heart attacks, why don't I just have one and die. . . . Then they took us out and divided us into two groups. . . . I felt envy. Others had died, why couldn't I have died too? . . . They took the girls one by one, I didn't object, didn't talk. Then the woman said, "Lie down for 'sir' to examine you." "Sir" was dressed in army clothes. I took off my pants, they told me to raise my legs. And I . . . a man? Was going to examine me? I was naked, it was like a show, with people watching, all those officers and soldiers. . . . It's just humiliation. They're breaking you. They're breaking you so you don't even think of asking for Egypt's rights.[65]

Another woman who was arrested with her described how for seven hours, almost every five minutes, she was electrocuted with a stun gun. They would sometimes splash water on her to make the shocks more painful. "I begged them. I said, 'You are my brothers. The army and the people are one.' Her tor-mentor replied, "No, the military is above the nation. And you deserve this."[66]

Against all odds, three of the women decided to go public. Although Samira Ibrahim is the most well known, Salwa El Hosseiny was the first woman to speak publicly about what had happened to them, and Rasha Abdel Rahman testified as well.[67] Other women testified but preferred to remain anonymous. The first reaction of the generals was to deny that the virginity tests happened. After continuing in their strategy of denial for more than two months, at the end of May 2011 a senior general admitted in an interview with CNN that in fact the abuse had taken place. He justified the army's actions by saying that the women "were not like your daughter or mine. These were girls who had camped out in tents with male protesters." As if this attempt to slander the victims was not enough, he went on to further justify the abuse as necessary to maintain the honor of the soldiers, saying that the reason for the "tests" was because "[w]e didn't want them to say we had sexually assaulted or raped them, so we wanted to prove that they weren't virgins in the first place."[68]

His statements enraged human rights activists. In a press release, Amnesty International wrote: "This general's implication that only virgins can be victims of rape is a long-discredited sexist attitude and legal absurdity. When determining a case of rape, it is irrelevant whether or not the victim is a virgin."[69] One month later, in June, Major General Abdel Fattah El-Sisi of the SCAF— who would later become minister of defense under Morsi, then a leader of the coup that ousted Morsi, and subsequently elected president in May 2014— discussed the issue with Amnesty International's Secretary General Salil Shetty. Sisi promised that the virginity tests would not be conducted again in the future.[70] One of the questions on the survey asked the respondents why they believe this concession had been made; 74.4 percent of respondents believed it was due to pressure from street protests, while 6.7 percent thought it was due to pressure from political parties and 6.2 percent replied "other."

Then in December 2011, a decision by the Civilian Administrative Court ruled that the virginity tests were illegal. According to Heba Morayef from Human Rights Watch, this was the first time the civilian court had criticized the military for a human rights abuse.[71] This was also important in that it set a judicial precedent, although the civilian court did not have the authority to hold military officers accountable for their actions. After the civilian court's ruling, a spokesman for the Egyptian military said the verdict was moot because such tests are not part of military policy.[72] This was of course in contradiction to previous statements made to CNN and to members of the No Military Tribunals group in which the virginity tests were described as normal procedures.

After a string of victories, a setback occurred in March 2012. Although Samira Ibrahim had filed her case against Tantawi, the head of the SCAF, it was the military prosecutor who specified who was being accused and who would be charged. The military prosecutor determined that only Dr. Ahmed Adel, the army doctor who actually conducted the virginity tests, would stand trial, although he was of course acting on orders received from a higher authority. The military court acquitted Adel—a decision that Amnesty International described as a "travesty of justice" as the military was essentially investigating itself with the judges being serving officers.[73] After this acquittal, the military went on the offensive. At a press conference, Adel implied that the women were prostitutes, while his lawyer referred to Ibrahim as a "criminal."

It is clear that the assaults on women at protests, and the virginity tests in particular, which were conducted after arresting women who were peacefully demonstrating on International Women's Day, constituted attempts to intimidate women and to exclude them from the democratic transition process. Ibrahim has pledged to take her case to an international court of law, saying, "No one violated my honour—it is Egypt's honour that has been violated; I vow to continue the struggle until the end to reclaim our rights."[74] Ibrahim was celebrated not just by *Time* magazine but also by Egyptian activists. Her visage was scrolled across the walls of downtown Cairo, at times towering triumphantly over the army (see Photo 4.2). She became an iconic figure; she dared to speak about the unspeakable.

Photo 4.2 Graffiti of Samira Ibrahim in downtown Cairo. After being subjected to a forced "virginity test" while in detention for a peaceful protest, Ibrahim brought charges against the Egyptian military. She became a symbol of resistance to the SCAF. In 2012 *Time Magazine* named her one of the 100 most influential people in the world. Photograph taken by the author on April 15, 2012 in Cairo.

Mosireen

The very first place [the army] went on January 28, 2011 was Maspero [the state media building]. The armored personnel carriers, the APCs, they secured Maspero first—that was not a good sign. They went to protect the building that had all the lies.[75]

If the No Military Tribunals group primarily took on the corrupt military ju-diciary, Mosireen targeted the corrupt state media. The official state media had been largely discredited by its coverage of the revolution, including showing images of Tahrir that were devoid of people when in fact it was occupied by tens of thousands of protesters. And yet after the ouster of Mubarak, the state media continued in its old ways, substituting unbiased journalism for loyalty to the new (old) regime, the generals in the SCAF. Many of the young revolutionaries felt that even the private media channels, while perhaps taking a more favorable stance toward the January 25 uprising, adopted a "business as usual" attitude toward the post-Mubarak era. For them, the revolution had ended on February 11, and the ongoing strikes, protests, and sit-ins were not an attempt to continue the revolution as activists insisted but were *fi'awi* or sectoral demands that con-tributed to chaos and instability. The demands of women, workers, and Copts were reduced to "special interests." Many of the youth felt that their demands were being misrepresented and that important issues, such as the military trials of civilians, were simply being ignored. In this sense Mosireen grew organically out of the No Military Tribunals group in the spring of 2011 and shared many of their concerns, but Mosireen went on to develop its own unique identity as a collective of media activists. The word "Mosireen" is a play on words combining the Arabic word for Egypt, "*Masr*," and the plural form of persistent or insistent "*Mosir*." In the words of one member of the collective: "We didn't have a televi-sion channel. So we decided to make Tahrir our television."[76]

In July 2011, Tahrir was reoccupied on a permanent 24-hour basis by thou-sands of people for the first time since the ousting of Mubarak. The activists agreed on seven demands, the first one being the end to military trials for civil-ians. Other demands included outlining the "prerogatives of the SCAF"—or a clear delineation of their powers—and not that the SCAF step down.[77] During the sit-in, Mosireen activists organized what they called "Tahrir Cinema," in which they set up a large screen on Tahrir Square in order to make their films available to a wider public. As the majority of Egyptians still did not have reg-ular internet access, this was key in expanding what had been criticized by some as an elite sphere of media activism to a broader public.

The Maspero massacre on October 9, 2011 is significant in several ways. First, it represented one of the worst cases of state brutality since the ousting of

Mubarak, and it was the first massacre to happen under military rule. Second, it is perhaps also the most flagrant example of the biased state media. Instead of reporting on how peaceful Coptic demonstrators, who were merely demanding that their churches be protected, were attacked, run over, and dismembered by armored personnel carriers, the state media reported that armed Copts were attacking soldiers. Not only did they report false information, but they went further and called on "honorable Egyptians" to protect the army, inciting sectarian violence.[78] Some have referred to this horrific incident as an example of how the state media had in fact become even worse than under Mubarak. And it underlines the interconnectedness of the various state institutions. Although Mosireen believes that the state media is essentially a counterrevolutionary force, their goals do not include demanding that specific people resign, such as the head of Maspero, because as they say, "there would be 30,000 people to replace him."[79] Instead, they see the problem as more structural. The activities of the Mosireen collective included:

- Creating a revolutionary media by turning the media toward the revolution.
- Creating an archive of the revolution.
- Creating empowerment by providing training sessions and workshops in video editing, photography, etc. In this way they believe they contribute to creating subjectivities who are able to produce their own narrative about their world.
- Creating accountability by filming violent crackdowns against peaceful protesters and other incidents of human rights abuses.

Within the span of less than a year, Mosireen had trained over 100 people on a pay-as-you-can basis. They also began to spread outside Cairo, have conducted training sessions in Mansoura and Suez, and had plans to offer workshops in six different governorates in the coming year. They have perhaps the largest video archive of the revolution in the world, consisting of over 10,000,000 megabytes of footage. In January 2018, Mosireen launched their archive, calling it "858"—the number of hours of footage they had collected. They described it as an "archive of resistance." One member called it "a defense of the revolution's memory against the regime"; another said it was a way of "advancing the values of the revolution in a time of repression."[80]

Mosireen has documented many cases in which peaceful protesters were attacked, either by soldiers, police, or *baltagiya* (thugs), such as in late April and early May 2012 during the sit-in in front of the Ministry of Defense in Abbasiyya. The protests began when several presidential candidates who were considered frontrunners were suddenly disqualified from the elections, including Hazem Abu Ismail, Ayman Noor, Khairat al-Shater, and Omar Suleiman. Originally the protests were initiated by the supporters of Hazem Abu Ismail, an Islamist lawyer close to the Salafi Front movement.[81] However, the violence with which they were confronted, along with a shared frustration that so many of their candidates had been disqualified in one fell swoop, led activists from across the political spectrum to join the protests in solidarity even as they turned deadly. Mosireen created a short video with footage showing how unidentified assailants attacked the sit-in using tear gas, shotguns, and live ammunition. In the short video clip, one of the demonstrators describes how they found boxes of food that were issued by the military near the location where the attackers launched their assault. A doctor working nearby describes how there were 11 deaths and 25 people who were shot in the eye. The video ends with the statement: "More than a dozen martyrs and tens of wounded in five days of fighting, and the Police and Army, 'Protectors of the nation' idly watched." The SCAF has denied any responsibility for the deaths of the protesters, claiming that the killers were residents of Abbasiyya who were angry about the sit-in and not hired guns.[82]

The Mosireen activists worked under dangerous, even life-threatening conditions. Salma Said, one of the founders of Mosireen, was shot in the face with over 100 bird pellets when she was filming an attack on protesters. She was shot first while she was filming, then she was shot a second time when she fell to the ground, and she was shot again a third time while she was being carried away. She was 26 years old at the time. She has since recovered and continues filming and working full-time in the collective. Clearly these were not merely incidents of stray bullets but attempts to silence these activists.

Despite attempts to stop them, Mosireen has not only carried on, with remarkable "insistence," true to their namesake, but they have succeeded, in particular in their attempts to reach a wider audience. In January 2012 Mosireen became the most-viewed nonprofit YouTube channel in the world, as well as the most viewed nonprofit YouTube channel of all time in Egypt.

I asked one of the members of the collective what he believed was their form of leverage as media activists. In other words, if the ability to strike was one of the main forms of leverage of the working class, what could activists do who work on a volunteer basis and who are not organized in unions or parties that represent large numbers of citizens. He replied that they have spread the notion that the authorities will be filmed: "They cannot do anything in darkness. That is our leverage."[83]

In addition to raising awareness, Mosireen has indeed helped in creating accountability. After the Abbasiyya clashes, Mosireen posted an "open days" calling for people who had witnessed the events to come to their office space and give their testimony on camera. Mosireen activists also recorded testimonies of four of the women who were subjected to virginity tests and made them available online one day before the trial took place.[84] Their videos have been used in other court cases as evidence as well.

Similar to the No Military Tribunals group, Mosireen is mostly composed of middle-class activists, but through their workshops they have trained a number of people belonging to a lower socioeconomic status. Their work represents another, however modest, form of cross-class solidarity in a highly classist society. Secondly, Mosireen activists define themselves as part of a collective. They don't have any individual names connected to their films, and they also generally do not use voiceovers because they don't want to seem to be coming from a position of authority or a single voice. They don't even watermark their videos so that they can be identified as stemming from Mosireen. In this way they are different from other types of media activists, such as Twitter activists who act as individuals tweeting their personal opinions, which may be highly individualistic and fragmented.

Despite their success in a number of areas, members of the collective maintain a sense of modesty and an awareness of their limits. In the words of one member: "Media can be the weapon of the weak. But it can also be a very weak weapon."[85] The effects of creating interdependencies between people who watch the media and those who make the media—of blurring the boundaries between participants and observers—may not yet have reached its full potential, but it is only likely to increase as this type of citizen journalism continues.

In June 2012, just after the dissolution of the parliament, I spoke to another member of the collective and asked her what she made of it—whether she thought the SCAF was acting out of a position of strength or weakness. Her reply was:

> The reason they have to be so brutal and so vulgar is because there is so much resistance, they have every power—and they can't rule in peace. They can't even make people feel safe. Usually dictatorships make people feel safe—there is stability. They don't only feel threatened, but they are threatened. People are taking to the streets, if you crush them they stay home for a while, but they come back. But there are so many people now, where the revolution is the only thing in their life, that is what they live for, and it is very hard to stop them.[86]

Kazeboon

Kazeboon in some ways epitomizes the shift to direct confrontation with the SCAF. In other words, there has been a shift from criticizing or documenting specific human rights abuses, such as military trials or virginity tests, to a more general challenging of the SCAF's authority by attacking their credibility. The group was formed in the wake of the second wave of the revolution—the five-day uprising in November, known as the Battle of Mohamed Mahmoud, and the clashes in December in front of the cabinet building. Of the many cases of violence and abuses of power, one event in particular triggered outrage across Egypt and even internationally. A woman wearing a long black hijab was dragged across Tahrir by several soldiers in broad daylight. Her body was limp and the abaya was either ripped or somehow opened, exposing the upper half of her body. One soldier raised his leg to stomp on her chest. Captured on video, the image of this woman became an iconic symbol of how the revolution was literally being crushed under the boots of security forces. This event sparked what is believed to be the largest women's demonstration in Egypt since 1919, when women came out to protest British colonialism.[87]

The following day, on December 18, Tahrir newspaper featured a front-page headline reading "Kazeboon" or liars next to an image of the "blue bra woman." After this despicable event, Adel Emarah, a member of the SCAF, held a press conference and insisted, despite the fact that the image had gone viral: "The armed forces do not have any procedures involving the use of violence."[88] Emarah went on to complain about the burdens that the army has to shoulder "while having to endure a lot of stress and friction with the public." While the Mosireen collective was expanding, along with their goals and activities, a group of activists decided to adopt their practice but focus their energies on a single goal: to prove that the SCAF consisted of liars. In this sense, the Kazeboon activists had crossed the line from human rights to political activism. Sally Toma, a psychiatrist by training who specialized in working with victims of torture and sexual assault, was one of the cofounders of Kazeboon.[89]

While many of Mosireen's videos document the violence, Kazeboon specifically documents the fact that the SCAF has lied about their use of violence. In order to prove that the generals were deceiving the public and spreading false information, Kazeboon adopted a different style in the short video clips that they made. They would use footage from official SCAF communiqués or from press conferences and then juxtapose the claims they were making—for example, a claim about how soldiers never used violence against protesters juxtaposed with images showing brutal crackdowns.

While Mosireen was becoming established with a large office space in downtown Cairo, Kazeboon grew out of the popular committees of Imbaba and Haram. But Kazeboon never intended to formalize as a group, preferring to remain a loose network, "hard to pin down" or "kids with a projector" as some have described them. According to one Kazeboon activist, they hoped to take Tahrir outside of Tahrir, in other words to decentralize their protests. This is because "it is really easy to control you as long as you are in Tahrir, if you are in the bubble."[90] The idea took off like wildfire: within a matter of weeks screenings were held in Alexandria, Mansoura, Assiut, Aswan, Qalyubia, Suez, and elsewhere. The decentralization strategy was not without risks, however. Kazeboon activists were attacked during screenings on the same day in Alexandria and in the Zamalek neighborhood of Cairo.[91] In perhaps one of their most high-profile and provocative screenings, Kazeboon projected their anti-SCAF videos onto Maspero, the state media building, during the one-year anniversary of the revolution. And on February 11, 2012, the one-year anniversary of the ouster of Mubarak, there was a screening in Abbasiyya in front of the Ministry of Defense.

In the interview I conducted with Amr, a member of Kazeboon, I asked about how effective he thought the group had been. He replied: "Everybody knows that SCAF is corrupt and has to release power, that was the target of Kazeboon, and we reached it."[92] Although Kazeboon stopped their screenings in February 2012, in May 2019, their Facebook page was still updated regularly and they had 1,278,174 followers.

To be clear, the majority of people who took part in these protests against the SCAF did not belong to any of the groups discussed here. And the protests were for the most part not actually organized by these groups, although they may have attended them and called on people to take part. Demonstrations would begin, and no one really knew when they would end. On January 27, for the third consecutive day of protests, I had gathered again with some friends, and we walked with a crowd of people to Maspero. In defiance of the traffic police, the protesters had stopped cars along the corniche and so the whole area in front of the building had been turned into another Tahrir. There was something thrilling about watching Kazeboon's subversive, anti-SCAF videos being projected onto Maspero (see Photo 4.3). They were publicizing everything the state media was trying to cover up. They were projecting the truth, or at least what they believed the truth to be, onto "the building that held all the lies." Despite the mounting repression and violence, during moments like these, it seemed as if the *shabab al thawra*, the revolutionary youth, may still prevail.

With Kazeboon's videos flickering onto Maspero and protesters chanting in the background, we stood and looked over the Nile. I started talking to someone who had joined our group, a friend of a friend. He told me about what he believed, that he believed that they would change the whole "world-system." He actually used that word. He said that he believed in equality, that was one of the main demands. I asked him if he was a socialist. He said: "No, I'm an Egyptian. Lenin and Marx, these people are dead, we will develop new ideas, a new world."

Photo 4.3 Kazeboon projects their anti-SCAF films onto Maspero, the state media building. Photograph taken by the author on January 27, 2012.

Conclusion

The 18-day uprising that toppled Mubarak was followed by a 17-month period of military rule. It now seems clear that the generals seemed to think that they could simply replace Mubarak, purge a few unpopular NDP officials, revise a few articles in the constitution, and tell a revolutionized population to get off the streets and back to work. However, contrary to expectations, the post-Mubarak period was not characterized by demobilization and a return to "normalcy." Nor have elite actors replaced collective actors as the driving force behind the transition, as much of the democratization literature would lead us to expect. The strike wave that had begun on February 8, 2011 continued and expanded under military rule.

Although the Egyptian armed forces maintained a very high degree of political autonomy, activists began the slow process of forcing certain concessions, including initial steps toward establishing accountability and civilian oversight of the military. I argue that these achievements are largely to the credit of the activist networks discussed in this chapter, and not due to pressure from the parliament, newly formed political parties, or other more institutionalized groups. The new activist groups were not supported by the business elite or the United States. And the Muslim Brotherhood was the last to join the opposition to the SCAF, only after they dissolved the parliament.

At the same time, the security forces have engaged in numerous crackdowns against peaceful protesters. In more or less chronological order, the victims of these assaults were: women and the poor with the virginity tests and military trials beginning in the early spring of 2011, Coptic Christians with the Maspero massacre in October, the Ultras and young male revolutionaries in February 2012, the anti-SCAF Salafis at the Abbasiyya crackdown in May, and the Muslim Brotherhood with the dissolution of parliament in mid-June 2012.[93]

The ruling brass crushed—sometimes literally—the youth who started and carried forward the revolution. But they also did not shy away from picking fights with established institutions or even the United States. Three months after the massacre of Coptic Christians at Maspero, the generals attended the Coptic Christmas mass. While pocketing US military aid, US-funded civil society organizations were raided and US citizens put on trial. After the Port Said massacre, where 74 people were killed including Omar Mohsen, an undergraduate student at the AUC, the SCAF accused the AUC of having a plan to divide Egypt.

By including survey data along with data gathered through interviews with activists, I have shown how a larger cross-section of society viewed the period of military rule under Tantawi. Results from the survey indicated that if street protests can take credit for many of the achievements of the transition era, it is the SCAF who was given the blame for the setbacks and defeats (see Graphs 4.1 and 4.2). Responsibility for the setbacks in terms of democratization was unequivocally laid at the feet of the ruling generals in the SCAF. For all 10 categories of setbacks, the SCAF was considered to be more responsible than any other group. For 6 of the 10 categories, more than 50 percent of respondents blamed the SCAF, including violence against protesters (70.2%), the Maspero incident (68.1%), military trials of civilians (94.4%), human rights abuses (64.7%), repression of opposition (73.9%), and increase in prices/decrease in supplies (64.2%). While the activist groups discussed in this chapter have been at the forefront of opposition to the SCAF, it would be wrong to assume that it is just a small band of malcontents who opposed military rule. Egyptians were both empowered through these struggles and suffered unspeakable repression. The zig and the zag of the revolutionary process continued.

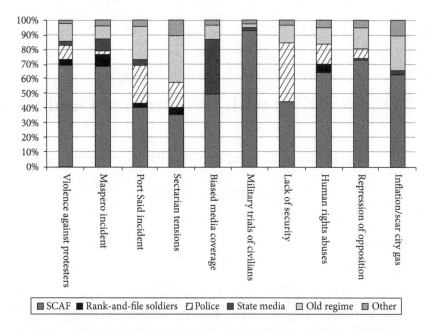

Graph 4.1 Setbacks of the second wave and who is believed to be responsible.

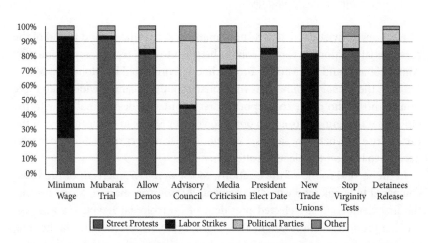

Graph 4.2 Achievements of the second wave and who is believed to be responsible.

5

يسقط يسقط حكم المرشد

"Down, Down with the Supreme Guide"

The Third Wave against the Muslim Brotherhood

(July 1, 2012–July 3, 2013)

The third wave was going to happen—with or without Tamarod. The work on the ground was the work of activists, not of the Mukhabarat. The 2013 wave happened much faster [than in 2011]. But they had their preparations—they were prepared. This time they were not surprised. They knew the wave was coming, so they started planning.[1]

In what one activist decried as a "nightmare scenario," the second round of the presidential elections became a contest between the old regime, represented by Ahmed Shafik, and the Muslim Brotherhood, represented by Mohamed Morsi. Much of the *shabab al thawra* (revolutionary youth) became divided into three camps: those who chose to support Morsi in order to deal a final blow to the old Mubarak regime, those who opted to vote for Shafik in order to prevent the further rise of what they saw as a reactionary Islamist current, and those who decided to boycott the elections altogether.

In the second round of the elections, Morsi won 51.73 percent of the vote,[2] compared to Shafik who won 48.2 percent. By a narrow margin, Morsi became the first democratically elected president of postcolonial Egypt. He was also the first president with no military background to his name. With the holding of relatively free and fair elections and the installation of a new president who had been outside the corridors of power, many believed that Egypt was indeed transitioning away from its authoritarian past. With the social forces that had united in toppling Mubarak now divided into opposing camps, it would seem that the past two years of mass protests and street politics was also coming to an end. The ongoing struggle to determine Egypt's future would move from the streets into the various institutions of government. Power could be both exercised and contested through formal channels. Constitutions and parliaments would matter, not protests and strikes. While not necessarily spelling the end of all forms of demonstrations, it was believed that the period of mass revolutionary mobilizations would be a thing of the past. Now people would finally get off the streets, go home, and allow themselves to be represented.

In terms of his socioeconomic background, Morsi was not unlike Gamal Abdel Nasser, Anwar el-Sadat, or Hosni Mubarak, none of whom were born into upper-class Cairene families. Like them, Morsi also came from humble origins outside the capital, hailing from the small town of Edwa in the Nile Delta. What made him an outsider was the fact that he was a civilian and, of course, his history of affiliation with the Muslim Brotherhood. He had been imprisoned under Mubarak. Morsi was also not the Muslim Brotherhood's first choice. Only after Khairat al-Shater and Mahmoud Ezzat had been disqualified was Morsi trotted out as the Muslim Brotherhood's candidate, earning him the nickname "spare tire." While the powerful military establishment viewed him as an outsider and former prison inmate, even his own Muslim Brotherhood supported him only after other options were not viable. It is therefore perhaps not surprising that, during the short year Morsi was in power, he was not able to muster the necessary resources to truly threaten the old regime. Instead, as I will argue, he did his best to placate both the military and powerful members of the Mubarak regime.

The Muslim Brotherhood had a few heavyweight financial backers, such as Khairat al-Shater. However, as I will demonstrate in the following discussion, Morsi and the Muslim Brotherhood–affiliated businessmen did not want to replace the old business elite. They made no moves to confiscate their assets, freeze their bank accounts, or nationalize private enterprises. They just wanted their share of the pie. For this reason, the old business elite had no real reason to fear them. The relationship between the Muslim Brotherhood and the old business elites was—at least during Morsi's first six months in office—based on mutual interest and cooperation. At worst, the old business elites viewed the Brotherhood-affiliated businessmen with condescension: they were seen as "supermarket owners, not industrialists."[3]

Similarly, Morsi also posed no threat to the powerful security sector. Morsi did not impose security-sector reform on the Ministry of Interior or purge the police—on the contrary, he gave the police better weapons and they became more militarized. He did not take on the Ministry of Defense, but instead displayed great reverence to the Supreme Council of Armed Forces (SCAF). Morsi made no attempt to realign Egypt's pro-US foreign policy, and he honored the Camp David agreement. He kept the Suez Canal open and the border to

Gaza closed. US officials were pleased; they believed that a moderate Muslim Brotherhood government in Egypt could set an example for other countries in the region.

Finally, in an agreement known as the "Fairmont Treaty," the Muslim Brotherhood had agreed on six principles for sharing power with other political forces.[4] The agreement was named after the Fairmont Hotel in Cairo, where the meeting took place, approximately one week before Morsi moved into the presidential palace. In addition to agreeing to share power with other political forces, the "treaty" also affirmed the continuation of street protests, as described by Wael Kandil:

ونؤكد بوضوح استمرار الضغط الشعبى السلمى فى كل أرجاء الجمهورية حتى تتحقق
مطالب الثورة المصرية ومطالب جميع المصريين.

[We affirm clearly the continuation of a peaceful popular pressure in all parts of the republic until the demands of the Egyptian revolution and the demands of all the Egyptians are realized.][5]

In November 2013, a few months after Morsi's ouster, the interim government issued a Protest Law that has been described as more repressive than the assembly law issued by British colonial officers in 1914. The draconian nature of the Protest Law issued by the interim government stands in contrast to the affirmation of peaceful protests in the Fairmont Treaty. In affirming that peaceful protests were necessary as long as the demands of the revolution were not met, the Muslim Brotherhood was careful not to alienate the revolutionary youth. In short, instead of antagonizing the military, the business elite, the United States, or the revolutionary youth, it would seem that Morsi had done his best to placate them.

So why was Morsi overthrown? That is the puzzle that this chapter hopes to explain. In short, I will argue that it was not the military, the business elite, or the United States who first turned against Morsi, but many of the very people who voted him into office. This third wave of mass mobilization was initially galvanized because Morsi failed to deliver on his election promises, and thus he failed to fulfill even the most basic demands of the January 25 uprising. In contrast to the first wave in 2011, however, this wave of street protests in the summer of 2013 was supported by elements within the state, as will be discussed later.

The ousting of President Morsi unleashed a level of violence unprecedented in modern Egyptian history. Those who continued to support Morsi have taken to blaming everything on the resurgent old regime, claiming that they never gave Morsi a chance and plotted his overthrow from his first day in power. In a similar manner, the current opponents of Morsi now prefer to disown the fact that they were his erstwhile collaborators and that they had in fact cooperated with him while he was in office. In December 2013, six months after Morsi's ouster, Egypt's interim government officially declared the Muslim Brotherhood to be a terrorist organization. And yet a sober-eyed analysis would show that the relationship between the Muslim Brotherhood and the feloul—at least during Morsi's first six months in office—was characterized by cooperation, not confrontation.

The Business Elite

During his year in office, Morsi did little to antagonize the old business elite associated with the Mubarak regime. On the contrary, he reached out to them, attempted to cooperate with them, and even appeased them. Morsi's economic policies were largely a continuation of those of the old regime rather than a radical break from them. Stephan Roll wrote about the Freedom and Justice Party (FJP) program and Morsi's presidential election program: "[T]he fundamental economic thrust of both documents exhibited no consequential differences to the policies of the old regime."[6] Morsi did not propose—much less take any concrete steps toward—the establishment of an Islamic economic system.

The markets seemed to like the election results: the Egyptian stock index jumped 6.7 percent after the election of Mohamed Morsi.[7] According to one study, the prices of politically connected firms went up by an additional 2.7 percent relative to nonconnected firms. In other words, the businesses of the old Mubarak elite profited more from the initial announcement of Morsi's election victory than others.[8] Although ironic, this is perhaps not so surprising, given that Morsi's economic policies were largely a continuation of those of the old regime, rather than a radical break from it.

In theory, Morsi could have continued with the same economic policies, but still singled out particularly corrupt members of the old regime for prosecution. Morsi could have demanded the return of stolen assets, such as the 500 million USD that Hussein Salem was allegedly carrying in his suitcase when he fled the country and was apprehended in Dubai.[9] And Morsi could have undertaken a serious initiative to obtain the public wealth that had been squandered through illicit transactions under Mubarak, such as the vast swaths of state land that had been sold off to cronies for a song. Authorities in the United Kingdom and Switzerland had already frozen the accounts of the Mubarak family as well as other oligarchs of the regime—President Morsi simply needed to cooperate with their efforts. After all, this would have been in line with what protesters had been demanding since January 2011: bread, freedom, and social justice. According to a Pew Research Center survey,

Egyptians considered corruption their biggest problem, ranking even ahead of lack of democracy and the economic situation. The intertwining of political and business elites was one of the main issues that fueled popular rage. This is why Egyptians didn't just want to oust Mubarak, but to topple his entire regime. As discussed in chapter 3, the level of cronyism in Egypt was much deeper than in other autocratic regimes. Hamouda Chekir and Ishac Diwan have estimated that the market valuation of political connections was 20 to 23 percent of the value of connected firms, while other countries tended to be in the range of 3–8 percent.[10]

But instead of confronting the most corrupt kingpins of the Mubarak regime, Morsi's government undertook a reconciliation effort that involved trading "cash for innocence."[11] Even prior to coming to office in 2011, the Muslim Brotherhood was allegedly considering the possibility of out-of-court settlements with former regime figures.[12] Then in July 2012, a presidential outreach (Tawasol) committee was created , which was meant to mediate between the private sector and the government. It was also tasked with the responsibility of overseeing reconciliation efforts with the old regime. Hassan Malek was the committee's spokesperson.[13] Finance Minister Morsy Hegazy announced that two bank accounts had been created at the Central Bank in order to receive repatriated funds from former regime officials. By February 2013, those accounts had received LE 69 million by former regime figures who were no longer under investigation. In January 2013, Malek organized a conference at a posh London hotel. From within the black-lacquered walls of the May Fair Hotel's "gorgeously opulent" Danziger meeting room, Malek invited the exiled tycoons to return to Egypt.[14] "Egypt opens its arms to all Egyptians outside Egypt and welcomes all Egyptian investors and businessmen abroad . . . I think the door is now open for all businessmen to come back."[15] This invitation was extended even though 52 percent of Egyptians disapproved of reconciliation with former regime figures, according to a poll by the Cabinet's Information and Decision Support Center in March 2012.[16]

As Roll summarizes: "The established business elite was certainly not regarded as an adversary in this process. On the contrary, the Brotherhood attempted to win over this section of the old elites as a partner in the transformation process."[17] In order to win them over as partners, deals were negotiated. For example, Malek negotiated an agreement with Egypt's largest private company, Orascom Construction Industries (OCI), owned by the Sawiris family, whereby they agreed to pay LE 7 billion ($1 billion US) in back taxes, instead of the LE 14 billion that their tax debt was estimated to be in return for dropping further investigations, which allowed OCI to transfer ownership to a new Dutch company and lift the travel bans on the Sawiris family. This happened at the end of April 2013. In early May, Onsi Sawiris and his eldest son Naguib returned from exile, which was seen as a "sign of reconciliation between Morsi and the opposition business elite."[18]

In March 2012, the Egyptian Business Development Association (EBDA) was formed. It was modeled on the Turkish Independent Industrialists and Businessmen Association (known by its Turkish acronym MÜSIAD). Membership in the FJP or affiliation with the Brotherhood was not necessary. By February 2013, it had about six hundred members, including members of Egypt's Coptic Christian minority. In short, the members of the previously outlawed Muslim Brotherhood were not antagonizing the established business elite. They were extending them an open hand. How did the old business elite respond to this cooperative attitude? For the most part, they reciprocated.

In late August 2012, Morsi led a delegation of 80 businessmen to China. A number of prominent businessmen joined him who were close to the old ruling party of Mubarak, the National Democratic Party (NDP), including Mohamed Farid Khamis, who was a member of the political bureau of the NDP and also a member of parliament. He is chairman of Oriental Weavers Company, a major textile producer and one of the world's largest carpet companies. Other members of the NDP who joined the delegation included: Sherif El-Gabaly, chairman of Polyserve Fertilisers and Chemical Group, who was considered close to Gamal Mubarak; Khaled Abou El-Makarem, chairman of Fibertex; Walid Helal, president of a plastics producing company; and Farid El-Tobgui, chairman of the Bavarian Auto group, which sells BMW cars in Egypt.[19]

In October 2012, there were reports that Khairat al-Shater, considered the second most powerful member of the Muslim Brotherhood, had solicited—and received—the help of Rachid Mohamed Rachid in securing a loan from the emir of Qatar to shore up the Egyptian economy.[20] This raised a few eyebrows given that Rachid was a convicted criminal at the time. Rachid had been trade minister under Mubarak, and he fled the country on February 1, 2011 on a chartered private jet amid the mass protests.[21] Rachid was later charged with corruption and profiteering. In June 2012 he was sentenced in absentia to five years in prison, and in September 2012 he was sentenced to another 15 years.[22] This means that at the time al-Shater solicited his help, Rachid was facing a total of 20 years in prison. An official source close to President Morsi said: "It is not unusual for a head of state to use the capacity of the national entrepreneurs, he [Rachid] was extending a helping hand."[23]

Developing Egypt's moribund economy was supposed to be one of Morsi's goals outlined in his "Renaissance project" (mashru' al-nahda). In order to achieve this, Morsi's government displayed a cooperative attitude toward the entire spectrum of Egyptian entrepreneurs. They cooperated with Christian businessmen and invited them to join EBDA; they cooperated with businessmen of middling rank; and they negotiated favorable deals with some of the wealthiest business families in Egypt, including the Sawiris, to negotiate the payment of back taxes. Perhaps most surprisingly, they even worked with former Mubarak-era tycoons who had been sentenced to 20 years in jail.

In sum, I find little evidence that members of the Muslim Brotherhood were using their newfound power to confront the old business elite, even those with close ties to the Mubarak regime. For the most part, it seems that the businessmen returned the favor—as there is no evidence of economic sabotage on the part of non–Muslim Brotherhood business circles.[24] Historically, it is not unheard of for business elites to resort to more drastic measures to express their displeasure with a new president. For example, in their efforts to weaken Salvador Allende, the Chilean business elites engaged in economic sabotage by attempting to cut off supplies to worker-controlled factories. Allende, however, contrary to Morsi, was engaged in a rather radical overhaul of the country's economy.[25]

Some caveats are in order. It is true that investment was down, but this was true of both foreign and domestic investors.[26] It is also true that some businessmen funded political parties. On April 3, 2011, Naguib Sawiris cofounded the Free Egyptians Party (*Al Masriyyin Al Ahrar*). He is believed to be their primary financial backer. However, the formation of new political parties is a normal part of a transition process, and it provides more evidence of acceptance of the new (erstwhile democratic) "rules of the game" than an attempt to undermine them. Nor am I suggesting that relations between the Muslim Brotherhood and the more established business elite were entirely harmonious. As mentioned earlier, there was a certain amount of condescension toward businessmen with ties to the Brotherhood, as they were derided as "supermarket owners" rather than entrepreneurs. Yehia Hamad, who Morsi had appointed as minister of investment during his cabinet reshuffle in May, was described by a number of my interviewees as unqualified for the position, given that his prior work experience included heading a sales division at Vodafone.[27] But none of this amounted to serious pressure on Morsi to resign or a concerted form of economic sabotage.

Another contentious issue was Morsi's plans for the Suez Canal. However, this was not something new. Even prior to Morsi assuming office, previous Egyptian governments had devised various schemes to develop the Suez Canal. When Morsi took office, he made his own plans that were not identical to those of his predecessors. Although he was careful not to take away any of the military's economic enterprises, he began to make plans for the Suez Canal that allegedly would not have included the military. Perhaps the biggest fear of the business elite was what could have potentially happened had Morsi stayed in power, rather than what had actually transpired during the year he was in power. In the assessment of Robert Springborg: "The Qataris would provide the funding, and then the Muslim Brotherhood would have been setting up the companies, and the military would have been cut out."[28]

To be sure, there was eventually a change in attitude among the business elites—but this was not until *after* the growth of mass mobilization. And even then, the primary way in which the business elite supported the opposition was through media attention and funding for Tamarod, as will be discussed later.[29]

The United States and the Muslim Brotherhood

What role did the United States play during the year that Morsi was in power? In particular, what role, if any, did US officials play in his ouster? A cursory glance at American history indicates that, in the not so distant past, the United States had a hand in the removal of inconvenient leaders, sometimes through the mechanism of military coups. Perhaps the three most well-documented cases include democratically elected leaders in Iran, Guatemala, and Chile: Mohammad Mossadegh in 1952, Jacobo Arbenz in 1954, and Salvador Allende in 1973. All three of them were elected by their own people and toppled by their own generals. And yet their ousters happened—in some cases could have only happened—with the explicit support of the United States. Other less-clandestine forms of regime change include direct military intervention. In 2003 the US-led invasion of Iraq led to the fall from power of Saddam Hussein, and in 2011 the NATO-led intervention in Libya led to the killing of Muammar Qaddafi. For all of these reasons, my theoretical framework of the Egyptian state has been adapted to include the potential influence of the United States. However, being in the possession of structural power is one thing—but using it is something else entirely. Therefore one should not assume that simply because US officials have the potential to wield influence or engage in covert operations that they necessarily do so.

At the time of writing, there is no indication that Morsi's removal was engineered by any branch of the US government. On the contrary, his removal seems to have first confounded US officials, then embarrassed them, and then frustrated them to the point that they eventually (several months later) took the unprecedented step of partially suspending US military aid to Egypt. Perhaps at some point in time some evidence will be unearthed that indicates US complicity in Morsi's removal. For the time being, however, all evidence suggests that the United States had no role in his removal. In fact, the United States had little reason to *want* his removal from power. Contrary to Mossadegh, Arbenz, and Allende, Morsi had done virtually nothing to antagonize US officials. On the contrary, his economic and foreign policies met with their approval.[30]

Both Republicans and Democrats came to accept, if not embrace, the previously outlawed Muslim Brotherhood. In the spring of 2012, a few months before Morsi was elected, a group of Republican lawmakers visited Egypt, including Senator Lindsey Graham from South Carolina. One of the people they visited was Khairat al-Shater, who held no official office but was a leading figure in the Muslim Brotherhood and its primary financier. According to a report in the *New York Times*:

> Mr. Shater assured them of the group's commitments to free-market capitalism, to equality for Egypt's Christian minority and to freedom of association for nonprofit groups, Mr. Graham said. When the senators asked him to publicly clarify the last point in order to help resolve the criminal charges against some nonprofit organizations backed by the United States, the Brotherhood's party released a statement a few hours later, Mr. Graham said, earning the senators' gratitude.[31]

Although it is possible that members of the Muslim Brotherhood were merely courting US officials prior to the presidential election, their generally friendly attitude toward the United States did not change after they took office. And for the most part, the Obama administration seems to have seen the election of Mohamed Morsi as an important milestone in what was still then being called Egypt's democratic transition. From the US perspective, Morsi was the first democratically elected president of Egypt, and they intended to work with him. Their favorable attitude toward Morsi continued even after the outbreak of mass protests in December 2012. On the contrary, it was during these mass protests (discussed in more detail later in the chapter) that a major arms deal was signed with Egypt including the consignment of F-16 fighter jets. While some saw the deal as simply a continuation of the three-decades-long relationship between the Egyptian and American militaries, others believed that the Obama administration was sending a message of support for Morsi. In the words of the retired Egyptian Brigadier General Safwat Al-Zayat:

> [I]t is obvious that the finalisation of the deal on 11 December, which happened to be at the height of the mass demonstrations in Tahrir Square against Morsi, conveyed a political message. Between the lines, Washington was sending a message to three parties. The first was to Morsi and it stated, "We support you. Move ahead." The second was to the army and it said, "We are encouraging this man," meaning Morsi. The third was to the opposition forces and it said the same thing. We need to bear in mind that Morsi had been put to the test during the last [Israeli] war against Gaza and passed with flying colours from the US perspective.[32]

However, by the spring of 2013, as opposition to Morsi gained momentum, it seems that the White House had become concerned enough about the political situation that they sent a special envoy to Egypt, as in 2011. During the uprising against Mubarak, Frank Wisner was selected as special envoy, as discussed in chapter 3. During the uprising against Morsi, a much higher-level career diplomat was selected to mediate the crisis: Deputy Secretary of State William Burns. As in 2011, US officials were divided on how to react to the mass uprising. In May 2013, Ambassador Burns was sent along with Bernadino Leon, the European Union's (EU) Special Representative for the Southern Mediterranean. But in May, the Muslim Brotherhood "wouldn't listen to them."[33] In the week leading up to July 3, Secretary of Defense Hagel spoke at least twice on the phone with his Egyptian counterpart, as well as General Martin Dempsey, the Chairman of the Joint Chiefs of Staff. Although they both warned against a military intervention, this message was apparently "not backed up by any concrete threats, beyond vague warnings that overthrowing Morsi could affect the long-standing military relationship."[34] After the coup, Burns and Leon made another trip to Cairo, and then the military "wouldn't listen to them." The men in uniform simply said they were "done with the Muslim Brotherhood."[35]

The Brotherhood was also apparently not willing to compromise, although Ambassador Burns, the Qatari Foreign Minister Khalid Al Attiya, and the EU Special Envoy Leon all paid a visit to Khairat al-Shater in the Tora prison. For all these reasons, I find no evidence that US officials had withdrawn their support of President Morsi prior to July 3. On the contrary, of the four pillars of the Egyptian state, US support for Morsi was the last to crumble. Once Morsi was ousted, however, the US never demanded that he be reinstated. Therefore I argue that the United States did not play any direct role in his ouster, nor had they even really hedged their support for him prior to July 3, as they had begun to do with Mubarak. However, *after* Morsi was ousted, US actions—and inactions—were important. While US senators John McCain and Lindsey Graham referred to the events of July 3 as a "coup," officials in the Obama administration avoided such terminology. In refusing to call his ouster a "coup," and accepting the new status quo, the Obama administration thereby acquiesced in the military's intervention. However, by postponing the delivery of certain weapons systems, and conducting a review of US military aid to Egypt, the Obama administration signaled their disapproval.[36] There were also limits to their willingness to go along with the military's new line. Despite prodding from Egyptian officials, at the time of writing, neither the United States nor the EU has agreed to officially designate the Muslim Brotherhood as a terrorist organization.[37] Even Saudi Arabia, a staunch supporter of the military regime in

Egypt, delayed designating the Muslim Brotherhood as a terrorist organization until March 2014.[38]

In retrospect, it would seem that one of Morsi's biggest mistakes was that he overestimated the influence of the United States, apparently thinking that having a powerful external ally would be enough to keep him in office. As I discuss briefly later in the chapter, the handmade signs that I personally observed during the mass protests on June 30 indicated that the second most-hated person, after Morsi himself, was US ambassador Anne Patterson. Many of Morsi's opponents were convinced that she was too supportive of the Muslim Brotherhood. This was similar to the first wave against Mubarak in 2011. As discussed in chapter 3, the people on the streets were outraged that the United States was continuing to support Mubarak, not that they had withdrawn their support or conspired to overthrow him.

The Military

Around 5:30 p.m. on July 3, President Morsi was arrested by the head of the Republican Guards. General Abdel Fattah El-Sisi, the minister of defense whom Morsi had appointed less than a year earlier, announced that the president was now under house arrest, that the constitution was suspended, and that new elections would be held. Instead of the SCAF taking power, as in 2011, Chief Justice Adly Mansour from the High Constitutional Court was appointed as interim president. Morsi was taken to an undisclosed location and essentially disappeared from public view. An army spokesman who was questioned as to his whereabouts simply said that Morsi was in "a very safe place."[39] The lack of clarity as to his precise whereabouts was not without reason. After his ouster, Morsi was first held at the Abu Qir naval base near Alexandria, which was under the command of General Osama El-Gendi. When Morsi finally did resurface several months later, he was in a prison facility belonging to the Interior Ministry.[40] In late 2014, leaked audio recordings shed new light on the details of his ouster. The recordings revealed that General Mamdouh Shahin, legal adviser to the SCAF, advised General Abbas Kamel, President Sisi's office manager, that Morsi needed to be moved to a civilian detention facility in order to avoid the collapse of the legal case against Morsi. According to Egyptian law, it is illegal to detain a civilian in a military barracks, which may explain why he was moved to another detention center.[41]

Clearly the military was a key actor in his intervention. But was his ouster therefore a military coup? In order to answer this question, we need to know more than just the technical details of *how* the military intervened, but *when* and *why* the generals decided to remove him from power. Although some analysts point to the decades-long antagonism between the military and the Muslim Brotherhood in order to explain his ouster, this overlooks the fact that there was considerable cooperation between the two factions. Indeed, Morsi did everything he could to please the generals.

As discussed in chapter 2, military coups can take a variety of forms. Despite significant differences, one thing they have in common is a sense of malcontent among the men in uniform. Whether the disgruntlement is widespread throughout the ranks, bordering on a mutinous situation, or limited to a narrow cabal of conspirators, there should be some identifiable sense of unease. After all, they wouldn't take the drastic step of removing the chief executive if they were content with the status quo. Therefore, military coups are usually thought to happen when the armed forces believe that the civilian leadership has done something that is seen as threatening their interests.[42] And yet in Egypt in 2013 this does not appear to have been the case. After all, Morsi had not infringed on any of the military's corporate interests including their autonomy, hierarchical discipline, functional monopoly, security, prestige, or their resource base including a vast economic empire.

Instead of threatening the military's autonomy, if anything Morsi had increased it through the establishment of a National Defense Council and a National Security Council, which allowed military officers to continue to influence politics on a wide range of issues. Instead of besmirching the honor of the armed forces, Morsi gave Tantawi and Sami Anan presidential medals. And instead of infringing upon their resource base, he left the army's businesses untouched and their budget unscrutinized.[43] He allowed them to continue to try civilians in military tribunals, although this was deeply unpopular among the population. And he even gave them certain rights they did not previously have—such as including an amendment in the constitution requiring that the minister of defense be from the military, whereas in the past it was at least possible that this post be filled by a civilian. As Yezid Sayigh argues:

> Six months into the presidency of Mohamed Morsi, Egypt's new constitution has granted the Egyptian Armed Forces (EAF) greater autonomy and a more formal political role than they ever enjoyed under his predecessor, Hosni Mubarak.[44]

In sum, rather than prosecuting the SCAF for the crimes they committed while they were in power or antagonizing the military in any way, Morsi did the opposite: he gave them everything they wanted, and more.

Some have argued that the primary source of antagonism between the military and Morsi was his handling of security issues, in particular in the Sinai.[45] According to this line of reasoning, Morsi allegedly preferred a soft approach that included negotiations, while the military advocated a hard-line approach.[46] Some have even tried to link the attacks in the Sinai to the Muslim Brotherhood. However, there are three problems with these arguments. First, the SCAF pardoned more jihadis than Morsi. According to an investigation by Hossam Bahgat for the independent newspaper *Mada Masr*, Morsi released 27 Islamists during his year in power. The military council released over 800.[47] It was the military council that opened up a political space for jihadist groups to operate in Egypt, not the Muslim Brotherhood. Until now, these jihadist groups have been most active in North Sinai, including one that has pledged allegiance to the Islamic State. Third, militant attacks in the Sinai began in February 2011 and continued through both the SCAF and Morsi. In fact, Morsi removed Field Marshal Tantawi, the minister of defense, and his top deputy, army chief of staff Sami Anan, citing their inability to prevent an attack in the Sinai in August 2012, which resulted in the death of 16 Egyptian security forces. As there was no major backlash after the removal of Tantawi and Anan, it is possible that this was negotiated in advance.[48] As Tantawi and Anan were both septuagenarians when they were replaced, it would be hard to argue that they had been sent into "early" retirement.

Furthermore, the two members of the SCAF were replaced by other members of the SCAF, not by military officers who had been obscure outsiders. Tantawi was replaced by Sisi, the former head of military intelligence who gained notoriety for his defense of the "virginity tests" that had been conducted on female protesters in March 2011. Mohamned Al-Assar became his deputy and General Sedki Sobhy became the new chief of staff.[49]

Given that the military's political and economic interests had been secured, it would strain credulity to claim that they removed Morsi because he had infringed upon their prerogatives. Indeed, quite the opposite was true. Given that Morsi replaced Tantawi with Sisi, merely substituting one SCAF member for another, it would be hard to argue that this was a hostile shake-up of the military council. Given that the SCAF had pardoned more jihadis than Morsi, it would also be unconvincing to claim that they were primarily motivated to remove him because of his allegedly soft approach to dealing with jihadi attacks.

We therefore must consider that the military was acting according to a rather different logic. I argue that it was not Morsi who truly threatened the military but rather the mobilization of the ordinary citizenry. While the exact size and scope of the street protests remains a contentious issue, I argue that it was the revolutionized population who represented a greater threat to the establishment than the meek actions of the chief executive. The military ousted Morsi because, quite simply, this is what the people were demanding. This does not mean, however, that this was an act of benevolence or patriotism. On the contrary—the paradox at the heart of the matter is that the armed forces were subverting civil-military relations by carrying out the demands of ordinary civilian protesters and not following the orders of the civilian commander-in-chief. The military was carrying out the demands of the people at the same time that they were threatened by those very same people as a mobilized force. Because of their ability to further destabilize an already highly volatile situation, it was the people on the streets whom the generals feared, not the president in his palace.

This does not mean that the top brass had never in their wildest dreams conceived of the possibility of giving Morsi the boot. After all, they had just intervened two years earlier. However, Mubarak was a dictator who had clung to power for 30 years, while Morsi was the first democratically elected president of postcolonial Egypt. Ousting a dictator was one thing, but ousting the man who had come to power through free and fair elections was another altogether. As one of my interviewees put it:

> The Military always has a contingency plan. They have a Plan A, a Plan B, and a Plan C etc. Plan A was to cooperate with them, and Plan B was to get rid of them.[50]

The question then becomes: When did they turn to "Plan B"? In order to answer this question, we must turn to the rise of mass mobilization.

The Anti-Morsi Opposition

Given the intensity of the mass uprising on June 30, it is easy to forget that the opposition was initially weak and divided, as discussed briefly at the beginning of the chapter. Much of the *shabab al thawra* (revolutionary youth) was divided into three camps: those who chose to support Morsi in order to deal a final blow to the old Mubarak regime, those who opted to vote for Shafik in order to prevent the further rise of what they saw as a reactionary Islamist current, and those who decided to boycott the elections altogether.

Morsi, despite being elected by a narrow margin, did not go out of his way to reach out to other constituents. For example, he refused to attend any of the ceremonies to inaugurate the new Coptic pope. And in one of his first speeches after becoming president, he referred to the Egyptian people as "my tribe." Although this may have been his attempt to reach across the aisle as it were, it was ridiculed by many as a return to a premodern Gemeinschaft instead of building a new and forward-looking political order. Although brief, Morsi's year in power signaled the creation of yet a third form of rule, this time with a religious flavor influenced by the ideas of the previously outlawed Muslim Brotherhood.

Over the course of the year that Morsi was in office, the opposition gained momentum, especially during what I see as four key turning points.

1. In October 2012, after Morsi's first 100 days in power; there were clashes on October 12 and a large *millioneya* protest.[51]
2. On November 22, 2012 after his Constitutional Declaration.
3. In January 2013, on the two-year anniversary of the revolution, when emergency law was declared in the Canal cities.
4. On April 28, 2013 with the emergence of the Tamarod campaign[52]

The initial weakness of the opposition can be illustrated by two examples. In mid-July, workers at the Mahalla Spinning and Weaving factory staged a sit-in. Prior to the revolution, the textile workers in the industrial town of Mahalla had played a pivotal role in revitalizing the labor movement in Egypt with increasing numbers of strikes beginning in 2006. As discussed earlier, their militancy had inspired the founders of April 6 to name their group after the date the textile workers had chosen to go on strike. But in July 2012, the workers in Mahalla suspended[53] their sit-in after accusations[54] that they were somehow acting as agents of the old regime. Although it would seem preposterous to accuse rank-and-file factory workers of acting on behalf of old regime elites, the workers decided to suspend their sit-in, apparently hoping to "prove" to the Muslim Brotherhood that they were not agents of the *feloul*.[55]

Secondly, a small middle-class group of activists created a website called "Morsi Meter" in order to keep track of how Morsi was fulfilling his election promises.[56] According to Amr Sobhy, a 24-year-old cofounder of the group: "[The site is not about] criticism or advocacy. . . . It's a portal of data. People can use it later, as much as they like, to form whatever opinions they want to hold."[57] Needless to say, the Morsi Meter was not exactly a radical opposition group. It did not aim to even criticize the president, much less plan his overthrow. In fact, it was modeled on a similar group in the United States that was keeping track of how well Obama was upholding his election promises.

October 2011—The First 100 Days

Morsi had promised to accomplish certain things within the first 100 days of being in office. After the first 100 days had passed, the Morsi Meter indicated that the president's achievements have so far been restricted to implementing penalties for fuel smugglers, raising awareness in speeches and through the media about the importance of proper disposal of trash, increasing the value of flour used to make bread, removing road blocks impeding traffic and implementing a reward system for positive performance of police officers.[58]

And yet, according to a poll, 79 percent of Egyptians were still satisfied with his performance, while only 13 percent were not.[59] A little over a month later, the situation would begin to change quite dramatically.

In retrospect, it would be easy to say that Egyptians simply expected too much from their first democratically elected president. After the honeymoon, disillusionment was inevitable. It is true that many had high expectations of Morsi. However, this was not simply because of some far-fetched dreams that emerged out of the Tahrir spirit, which were the result of people who were thirsting for change. But rather, ordinary people expected change because *change had already happened*. Describing the intangible nature of what exactly had transpired—what was different than before—is not easy. Many simply said that the revolution had "broken the fear barrier." As I have argued elsewhere, the encampment on Tahrir was not merely a protest site but developed into a new social experiment, a radical—albeit temporary—break from the past. The everyday praxis on the midan was in some ways more revolutionary than what people demanded from the powers that be.[60] Secondly, Egyptians knew—because of their own historical record—that change was possible and could be implemented from above *and* from below. Zeinab Abul-Magd compares Morsi's first 100 days in power to what Nasser accomplished after his first 100 days:

> In his first 100 days, Nasser turned a military coup that deposed a king and kicked out a colonizer into a social revolution. He responded to the demands of the lower classes and altered the socioeconomic order. The coup took place on 23 July, and on 9 September 1952, the new regime issued the radical land reform Law 178. The code confiscated thousands of acres from the landed aristocracy and distributed them to impoverished peasants. Morsi, in his first 100 days meanwhile, has responded to none of the demands of the lower or middle classes that were put forth during the 25 January Revolution. He has not raised the minimum wage that Tahrir Square loudly cried for, nor has he fulfilled his promise to relieve peasants from debt to state banks (despite the cosmetic erasure of some agricultural loans), or seriously responded to the demands of schoolteachers, doctors, and government employees, among others.[61]

In sum, Egyptians' expectations for genuine change were, considering their past and recent history, not unrealistic.

November 2011—the Constitutional Declaration

While violence against minorities—especially women and Coptic Christians—is not a new phenomenon and it would be wrong to attribute these problems to Morsi, they took on a slightly different form since his election. As discussed in chapter 4, some of the most egregious forms of violence against women and Copts under the SCAF were the forced virginity tests and Maspero massacre. After the election of Morsi, new types of attacks began to take place. Or if they were not entirely new, they became increasingly commonplace: women were targeted during demonstrations on Tahrir, not by army soldiers or police, but by throngs of men who would surround a woman and assault her, sometimes even gang raping her directly on the square. Because the police were entirely unresponsive, activists took it upon themselves to create groups of volunteers who patrolled protests and intervened when an attack took place. These groups included Tahrir Bodyguards, Operation Anti Sexual Harassment (OpAntIsh), and others.[62] In the fall of 2012 sectarian clashes in the area south of Giza escalated to the point that the entire Coptic population of three villages were forced to flee, essentially "cleansing" the area of its Christian minority.[63] While Morsi was certainly not to blame for these escalating forms of violence, he also did not respond to them.

More serious resentment was generated as Morsi stacked his cabinet with Muslim Brotherhood supporters. The cronyism of the Mubarak regime continued under President Morsi, taking the form of the "Brotherhoodization" of the state (*akhwanat ad-dawla*). For all of these reasons, Morsi's actions served to vindicate his critics. But it was Morsi's Constitutional Declaration on November 22 that provoked mass demonstrations. By late 2012, the constitutional crisis was escalating as the constituent committee successively lost non-Islamist members, including important institutions such as Al-Azhar and the Coptic Orthodox Church. As the date approached for two Constitutional Court rulings that were set to declare both the committee and the Shura Council unconstitutional, Morsi made his Constitutional Declaration on November 22 that placed himself above the law until the new constitution was passed. While Morsi argued that his declaration was necessary to protect the revolution, his detractors saw it as his attempt to destroy it.

To the surprise of virtually all outside observers, the protests that erupted spread far beyond the secular, middle-class circles of Cairo or Alexandria. Demonstrations took place in governorates across the country. The working-class city of Mahalla declared itself "independent" of Morsi's Egypt, with other cities soon following suit, while numerous headquarters and offices of the Muslim Brotherhood were set ablaze, reminiscent of the attacks against police stations during the first wave.[64]

On Friday, November 30, I went to the protests on Tahrir, and afterward met with friends who were sitting outside in the Bustan Café. It was one of the cheaper hangouts to drink tea or coffee in downtown Cairo and a place where middle and lower classes would sit side-by-side. Large protests meant large amounts of waste, and in between the plastic chairs and tables trash spilled out onto the ground. In addition to the usual suspects, there was a new person, a friend of a friend whom I hadn't met before. We started chatting, and before long he was expounding on his views of the military and the Muslim Brotherhood. Living in Cairo during those days, one became accustomed to hearing outlandish conspiracy theories and learned to forget them lest they cloud one's mental capacity. But for some reason the ramblings of this particular person lodged itself in my memory, although not because I found what he said particularly plausible. After going on for a while about what he believed to have been the role of the Muslim Brotherhood during the 1967 and 1973 wars, he then fast-forwarded to more recent events. In short, he was convinced that Hamas was the one who burnt down all the police stations in January 2011, and that Egypt was teetering on the brink of a civil war. I began surreptitiously glancing around for another conversation partner among those gathered at the rickety tables, perhaps someone who was less prone to Manichean monologues. After all, the peaceful nature of the mass protests we were witnessing, the signs and symbols of Muslim-Christian unity, and the coalescing of opposition groups across various segments of Egyptian society did not—at least to my mind—resemble a civil war. Then he said he was also 100 percent certain that the military would intervene again. It was the first time I had personally heard anyone say this. Since I knew that some of what he said was inaccurate, it would have been easy to dismiss the idea of a coup, couched as it was amid various and sundry conspiracies and falsehoods. But I was struck by how confident he seemed. Incidentally, his name was Nasser.

Even after the outbreak of mass protests in November, the opposition still felt weak in comparison to the ability of the Muslim Brotherhood to organize and their alleged networks that spanned Egypt's 29 governorates. Rawah Badrawi gave voice to this sense of weakness when she tweeted:

Rawah رواح @RawahBadrawi
0.26% of Egyptians are on twitter & will circulate pics of #tahrir today. #MB working on 20-50 million ppl in the governates for a Yes vote.

Photo 5.1 Mass protests against President Morsi began in November 2012,
months before the emergence of Tamarod. Some of the symbols on display
including the use of the crescent and the cross to represent Muslim-Christian
unity were reminiscent of those used in the protests against Mubarak.
Photograph taken by the author in Cairo on November 27, 2012.

With his Constitutional Declaration, Morsi alienated the judiciary. Egypt's
judges responded by refusing to monitor the referendum, and yet this didn't
stop Morsi from proceeding with the referendum. Indeed, the referendum
passed, with 63.8 percent of voters approving of the new constitution. It was
marred, however, by a low turnout—with only 32.9 percent of eligible voters
taking part.[65] The referendum also revealed a sharp urban/rural divide. Cairo
rejected the new constitution. I spoke with an investment banker at his office
in the well-heeled neighborhood of Dokki. He summed it up perhaps most
bluntly:

> For a thousand years, the ruling class of Egypt came from Cairo or Alexandria.
> And for the past 200 years the ruling class was military—since Mohammad
> Ali, not Nasser. Nasser just brought it to the foreground: 57 percent of Cairo
> voted no to Morsi's constitutional referendum. It was a war against those peas-
> ants who had dreams of becoming the ruling class.[66]

With his constitutional declaration, Morsi had lost the support of many urban residents, including large sections of the educated middle-class. But his base, and the bulk of the population, was still behind him.

January 2013—Canal Zone

The next major turning point occurred during the second anniversary of January 25 and the events in the Canal Zone. Karim Medhat Ennarah argues convincingly that it was the emergence of mass protests that led to the "end of reciprocity" between the Muslim Brotherhood and the security sector. Significantly, the protests that signaled the beginning of the end did not take place in Cairo but in Suez, Port Said, and Ismailia. As argued in the introduction, there was a clear decentering of protests during the third wave. Within Cairo, the epicenter of protest shifted from Tahrir to the presidential palace, located in Heliopolis. But in some ways the center of gravity shifted *away* from Cairo. Morsi's declaration of a state of emergency in the canal cities of Port Said, Suez, and Ismailia succeeded in bringing masses of people onto the streets of all three cities—in defiance of his orders. While the protest events in the Canal Zone received less media attention than the events in Cairo or even Alexandria, historically these cities were fertile ground for revolutionary activity, as evidenced by the anticolonial riots against the British in the middle of the twentieth century.

Morsi's regime strategies displayed remarkable parallels to those of Mubarak and the military junta, including the use of constitutional declarations, emergency laws, and curfews. He seemed to view every challenge to his authority as a security threat. Indeed, Morsi sacked his minister of interior, Ahmad Gamal El-Din, because Morsi believed he did not crack down hard enough on protests during the mass upheaval around the Constitutional Declaration in November and December. Gamal El-Din was replaced by Mohamed Ibrahim, who was happy to oblige and use lethal force against protesters. On the second anniversary of the revolution, at least 75 people were killed during a few days of protests, including 12 in Suez, 11 in Cairo, 2 in Ismailia, 1 in Gharbia, and 49 in clashes in Port Said.[67]

The verdict in the Port Said case sparked further outrage. As discussed in the previous chapter, on February 1, 2012 during a match between Al-Ahly and Al-Masry in Port Said, fighting broke out which that resulted in the death of 79 people, with over 1,000 injured. The doors to the stadium had been mysteriously locked, trapping people inside. Many believed that the killings in Port Said were intended to crush the Ultras specifically and the youth movement more generally.

On January 26 at 10 a.m., a judge convicted 21 residents of Port Said and sentenced them to death.[68] Shockingly, not a single police officer was convicted in the case. A few hours later, gunmen opened fire on police outside the Port Said prison. By the end of the morning, 28 people were dead, including 2 police officers and 26 people who were in the vicinity of the prison. Three days later the death toll had risen to 42.[69] Local prosecutors did not launch an investigation until three days after the incident, and then failed to summon a single police officer for questioning. Sarah Leah Whitson, Middle East director at Human Rights Watch, said about the incident: "A lack of police reform, Mubarak-era laws that effectively give the police a free hand to use lethal force, and the lack of accountability mean we are seeing this kind of excessive response again and again."[70]

Instead of criticizing the police or admitting any wrongdoing, Morsi praised the police and instructed them to respond with "the utmost firmness and strength" to any insecurity and violence. He then declared a 30-day state of emergency in Port Said, Suez, and Ismailia and a nightly curfew from 9 p.m. to 6 a.m. General Ahmed Wasfi, commander of the Second Army and of operations in the Canal, was put in charge of enforcing the curfew and state of emergency. And yet army soldiers openly flouted the curfew and played football with local residents. As Ennarah argues, this sparked an even bigger uproar in the Canal cities, where protest had not subsided since November.

> From January 26th 2013, neither Morsi nor any of his senior aides were able any longer to set foot into Port Said, Ismailia, or Suez. Clashes with the police continued, intermittently, until the verdict issued on the 26th of January was confirmed on the 9th of March. For most of that time, the police was not able to re-deploy in the streets of Port Said and the army—which was welcomed by the Port Saidi population—was rolled out to fill the vacuum. The police remained garrisoned in the police stations, firing indiscriminately at protesters or bystanders approaching the police station. The army thus found itself in an uncomfortable situation, reminiscent of January 28th 2011—received warmly by a population that loathed the police and clashed to death with it, the army was keen on withdrawing and allowing the police to roll back in, a point that General Wasfi emphasised in several interviews ["Thousands March in Egypt's Port Said," 2013]. At that point, the sustainability and the practicality of maintaining an alliance with the Brotherhood was quickly fading away, and many had started speaking already about a military intervention.[71]

It is worth emphasizing that the public anger was not only against Morsi but also, in fact, against the continuation of police brutality (one of the main issues that had sparked the 2011 uprising) and Morsi's inability to do anything about it. Morsi made a few other mistakes that aggravated the armed forces, including statements he made after some Central Security Forces (CSF) soldiers had been kidnapped in the Sinai in May, then a statement he made about Egypt's policy toward Syria in June.[72] However, these statements were not made until *after* protest had already become intractable.

Morsi's unwillingness to engage in any meaningful security-sector reform contributed to his downfall. Not only did he fail to introduce meaningful reforms, he failed to even verbally condemn murderous behavior on the part of the police. He seemed to have forgotten that it was police brutality that sparked the revolution in the first place.[73] By praising the police force as they killed in broad daylight—directly after the police had been acquitted for the Port Said massacre—he made an already tense situation into an explosive one. The Canal Zone was in a permanent state of uproar—and this was even before the emergence of the campaign known as Tamarod, to which we will turn next.

April 2013—Tamarod

On April 1, 2013 a small group of activists met in Khaled el-Balshy's apartment and founded a group called Tamarod, which means "mutiny" or "rebellion" in Arabic. The group wanted to give voice to the rising tide of opposition to President Morsi. Their goal was to collect 15 million signatures demanding early elections—more than the 13 million who voted for him during the second round of presidential elections. They aimed to achieve this ambitious goal by June 30, the one-year anniversary of Morsi's coming to power. Within the theoretical framework of this project, I have argued that Morsi relied on the same four pillars of support that Mubarak and the military council did. The mass protests that erupted in November and December after Morsi's Constitutional Declaration had already signaled that popular support was eroding. The creation of Tamarod announced the emergence of a new form of opposition to President Morsi.

Instead of first creating a Facebook page or mobilizing online, the Tamarod activists decided to try and bridge the digital divide by focusing on organizing in communities. As Adel Iskandar puts it:

> The Islamists' perennial advantage has been their outreach within working class communities across the country and their sophisticated and integrated online platforms. By contrast, much of the non-Islamist revolutionary groups and opposition parties have been notoriously underwhelming in their offline mobilization. . . . [T]his outreach tends to be limited to metropolitan urban areas and produces temporary engagement rather than sustained

organizational loyalty and affiliation. For this reason, with non-Islamist parties having been dealt a blow at every electoral process since the toppling of Mubarak, of which there have been plenty, grassroots outreach strategies have been imperative. Many of these have attempted to marry offline and online components with varying degrees of success.[74]

In addition to overcoming the digital divide, Tamarod asked people not only to sign the petition but also to provide their national identification numbers, which involved publicly registering one's dissent—and also making it possible for the security services to later round up anyone who had signed the petition.

Six of the founding members of Tamarod included Mohamed Abdel Aziz, Mahmoud Badr, Moheb Doss, Waleed El-Masry, Mona Seleem, and Hassan Shaheen.[75] They were all under the age of 35 at the time, and were relatively unknown compared to some of the other activists who had risen to prominence over the years. However, within the span of just a few weeks, these relatively obscure activists would be catapulted into the national media spotlight.

Egypt's previously fractured opposition movement became united around Tamarod. The National Salvation Front had been formed already in November 2012,[76] allegedly on the same day as Morsi's Constitutional Declaration.[77] However, it was not until the spring that it gained momentum. The leaders of the National Salvation Front all endorsed Tamarod, including Mohamed El-Baradei, Amr Moussa, Amr Hamzawy, and Hamdeen Sabahi.[78] Other political parties, including the Free Egyptians Party, the Wafd Party, and the Social Democratic Party, all provided logistical support by allowing Tamarod to use their branch offices across the country. The head of each branch became coordinator of the signature campaign.[79] All trade union federations, both independent and state-run, supported June 30. Mamdouh Hamza—one of the very few businessmen who had supported the first wave of the revolution in January 2011—says that he donated LE 1.5 million to Tamarod (about $215,500 US) and also provided them with an apartment to meet in, although it was allegedly burnt down shortly thereafter.

According to Shadi Malek, one of the cofounders of Tamarod whom I interviewed, Tamarod was not taken seriously by anyone initially. It was not until after they had collected five million signatures that they began to receive attention outside the established opposition circles.[80] Soon, the Tamarod cofounders were making the rounds on virtually every talk show on the private television networks to discuss their campaign. They logged tens if not hundreds of hours of television time. All of the major private media conglomerates, including CBC, ONTV, Hayat, Dream, and others, provided a platform for Tamarod. The powerful media conglomerates never offered this level of media exposure to activists during either the first wave of the revolution against Mubarak or the second wave against the SCAF. Precisely because activists during the first and second waves lacked access to both the state media and the big private media corporations, they had to rely on social media instead. During the third wave, the social media was less decisive because Tamarod had powerful allies in the established media landscape, but also because it relied on more "primitive" forms of outreach: face-to-face communication and photocopied petitions. Egyptian cartoonist Andeel commented, "What we are witnessing today is a defeat of Facebook and Mark Zuckerberg and a thunderous triumph for Xerox."[81]

In addition to the unprecedented level of media support, the Tamarod campaign received support from other powerful segments of Egyptian society. At some point people began to question whether Tamarod was truly a grassroots campaign. Suspicions were aroused for a number of reasons. First, according to a member of the Political Bureau of April 6, they found it odd that Tamarod "only wanted to collect signatures, and didn't have a plan for after that." While the Political Bureau was suspicious, the rank-and-file voted 70 percent in favor of supporting Tamarod, and so they did, eventually supplying Tamarod with approximately two million signed petitions.[82] Even my friends who were sympathetic to Tamarod and hostile to Morsi said they couldn't believe that a grassroots campaign could possibly collect 22 million signatures in two months without the support of state security. It was simply logistically impossible. Some people I spoke to believed that state security agents actively supported Tamarod by distributing petitions and collecting signatures, while others believed they supported Tamarod by providing protection as activists toured the country collecting signatures.[83] In the end, such distinctions may be a matter of splitting hairs. As a blogger who was not part of Tamarod put it: "If state security wasn't trying to stop them, it means they supported them."[84] Second, Tamarod accepted petitions from anyone who was willing to collect them, including from people with ties to Mubarak's old National Democratic Party. Some touted Tamarod's ability to build a crosscutting campaign as one of their strengths, and they welcomed the show of unity after the past two years of disunity and fragmentation among the opposition. Others accused them of "reconciling with the corrupt and dictatorial past."[85] Third, some members of the old regime publicly endorsed Tamarod. In mid-May, former Air Force Commander Ahmed Shafik, who served briefly as Mubarak's last prime minister and then ran against Morsi in the presidential elections, called on his supporters to endorse Tamarod. In response, Tamarod issued a statement, saying:

> We do not require the support of anyone involved in the killing of protesters and revolutionaries. . . . We are against both Morsi and Shafik. We are for the millions that took to the streets during the revolution against the conditions

created by Mubarak and his regime, conditions that were kept in place by an oppressive regime wearing the cloak of religion.[86]

This public rebuffing didn't stop other members of the Mukhabarat from attempting to infiltrate the group—and even to profit from the cultural capital of activists associated with the campaign. Some Tamarod activists had no qualms about cooperating with the security apparatus. In response, during a televised interview one Tamarod activist defended their cooperation with the secret police by saying, "They are Egyptians too."

For example, a former adviser of Omar Suleiman, who had been head of the Mukhabarat under Mubarak, showed up at an event that Tamarod had organized. The adviser approached Ahmed Harara, one of the more prominent activists of the January 25 Revolution. He had been shot in his right eye by a sniper on January 28, during the first wave of the revolution against Mubarak. Then, during the second wave of unrest against the SCAF, he was shot in his left eye on November 19, leaving him entirely blind. He had been included in *Time* magazine's Person of the Year issue in 2011, which featured iconic activists from around the world. After losing his eyesight, he said: "I would rather live blind with dignity than as an oppressed person who can't look others in the eye."[87] Harara had inspired millions of Egyptians and symbolized the tenacity of the revolutionary youth, who were willing to risk life and limb to fight for what they believed in—they rose up against Mubarak and against the military council. Now, entirely blind, Harara was part of the mobilization against Morsi. Suleiman's adviser, knowing that Harrara could not see him, stood next to Harara and had his picture taken: "It was like a slap in the face."[88] This incident illustrates the breadth of support for Tamarod, which ranged from old regime figures, including an adviser of former Vice President Omar Suleiman, to one of the most celebrated activists of the January 25 uprising, Ahmed Harara, who had been blinded in both eyes by regime snipers.

Two police officers who I interviewed said they both joined Tamarod as soon as they heard about it. Given the amount of animosity that still existed between the police and the people, they saw Tamarod as an opportunity to change that. According to a poll around that time, only 35 percent of Egyptians thought positively of the police, while 63 percent thought they were actually doing more harm than good.[89] In the words of one of the officers, the Tamarod campaign was "the last chance for the people and the police to be on the same side. It was a golden chance. It was a life vest."[90] I pressed them, asking whether it was not risky as police officers to join a campaign whose ultimate goal was to unseat the president. He smiled and said, "Obeying orders is also risky."

At the time of writing, there is still no consensus regarding exactly how and when the political composition of Tamarod changed prior to the coup. There are some such as former presidential candidate Khaled Ali, who argued in an interview in May 2014 that Tamarod was initially a "pure youth movement" that was later co-opted.[91] Then there are others who believe that Tamarod emerged from within the deep state and only paraded as a grassroots movement. After the coup, however, it is clear that Tamarod fragmented into different factions, a process I illustrate in detail in the next chapter. A number of Tamarod branches all across Egypt became critical of the interim government under Adly Mansour, or they dissolved altogether to "rejoin the side of the revolution." It was not just the rank and file who broke away from the leadership. A number of the Tamarod cofounders publicly endorsed Sabahi rather than Sisi in the presidential elections in May 2014. However, other factions within Tamarod were more aligned with the regime. When the interim government officially designated the Muslim Brotherhood as a terrorist organization in December 2013, one Tamarod Facebook page praised the decision, although it is impossible to know how many people within Tamarod endorsed this.[92] And in November 2014, after Mubarak was acquitted for his involvement in the deaths of hundreds of Egyptians during mass protests in early 2011, Mohamed Abdel Aziz, one of the leaders of Tamarod, wrote on his Facebook wall: "If Mubarak and the pillars of his regime are innocent, who is the legitimate president now? Isn't it Mubarak?"[93]

What is clear is that by the spring of 2013 lines were already being blurred. Authority was being challenged on multiple fronts. Morsi was still in power—but was he still in control? Apparently sensing that power was slipping out of his hands, Morsi reshuffled 16 of the 28 governors in mid-June. The opposition saw it as an attempt to "Brotherhoodize" the governorates. Mubarak, needless to say, had also appointed loyalists in his quest to stay in power. However, one appointment in particular sparked outrage. As governor of Luxor, Morsi selected Adel Al-Khayat from the Al-Gamaa al-Islamiyya, a group that had masterminded the massacre of 58 tourists in Luxur in 1997. They were also behind the assassination of former President Anwar el-Sadat. The appointment was seen as a reward to their Construction and Development Party, which consistently supported Morsi after he was elected. Although doling out rewards to political allies was not peculiar to Morsi's presidency, it was singular to appoint former terrorists as governors of the cities where they had been involved in terrorist attacks. Mounir Fakhry Abdel-Nour, a former minister of tourism and a secretary-general of the Wafd Party, said, "Choosing Al-Khayat as governor of Luxor shows that Morsi's regime has lost its mind."[94]

Prior to June 30, the police and army began making statements that indicated that their continued support for the president was tenuous at best. In order to underline their neutrality, the Police Club board announced on its Facebook page on Saturday:

"We will not protect political premises or party headquarters. Our role is to secure vital installations and facilities, police stations and prisons." One officer was even more blunt: "[P]eople who were in prison and are now presidents [should note that if even a single officer went to protect a Brotherhood office on Sunday], "I swear to God almighty, he will be shot."[95]

By this time, the police were described as "in more or less open revolt." The armed forces issued a statement that said:

[I]f Sunday's protests were as widespread and prolonged as those that drove Egypt's 2011 uprising, and if serious fighting broke out between Morsi's supporters and his opponents, then the army may regard the protests as a more legitimate representation of the people's will than the elections that brought Morsi to office a year ago—and would step in to facilitate a transition of power to a technocratic caretaker government.[96]

June 30

On the morning of June 30, like so many times over the past two-and-a-half years, I left my apartment on Shagarit El Dor and set out to meet my Egyptian friends, uncertain where the protests that day would lead us. Instead of heading to Tahrir, we met near Ittihadiya in Heliopolis. It was hot and there was no shade along the broad boulevard leading to the presidential palace. One of my friends, Tamer, a documentary filmmaker, wanted me to say something into his camera for a project he was working on. I told him that I had just arrived and felt that I didn't have much to say. After all, nothing had happened yet. He insisted and held the camera in front of my face. So I said that I was there on this day because I disagreed with what US Ambassador Anne Patterson had said. She had discouraged people from protesting, saying she was "deeply skeptical" about "street action." Instead, "Egypt needs stability to get its economic house in order."[97] I thought it was odd that the US ambassador was discouraging Egyptians from exercising their right to freedom of expression. If they couldn't peacefully voice their opinion, or publicly criticize the president they elected to represent them, then what was the point of the past two-and-a-half years? Isn't that what democracy means, and isn't that what US officials claimed they wanted for Egypt?

With each hour that passed, the crowds got bigger and bigger. To my surprise, just based on the handmade signs that people were holding, after Morsi, the second most-hated person was not Mohamed Badie (the Supreme Guide of the Muslim Brotherhood), the billionaire Khairat al-Shater, or some other Brotherhood figure, but US Ambassador Anne Patterson.

Photo 5.2 A screenshot of Al-Nahar TV, a privately-owned Egyptian TV network, covering protests across Egyptian governorates on June 30th, 2013. The locations of protests include Tahrir, Rabaa, Higaz, and Ittihadiya Squares in Cairo, the cities of Mahalla, Suez, and Mansoura in the governorates of Gharbia, Suez, and Dakahliya, respectively, and the governorates of Port Said, Sharkiya, Assiut, and Alexandria. Photograph taken by the author in Cairo on June 30, 2013.

The people on the streets were jubilant. There was a collective effervescence like on February 11, 2011. Morsi gave a speech just as Mubarak did. He seemed to be similarly detached from reality. Instead of acknowledging that there was a full-blown national crisis, he said "legitimacy" 57 times.[98] Like in 2011, the people on the streets became even more exasperated after hearing the president drone on without making any serious concessions. But things were also different. There had been no life-or-death battles with the police as in 2011. Things were largely peaceful. Instead of ignoring the protests, the media showed as many protests as they could fit onto a TV screen (Photo 5.2).

Around 11 p.m. on July 1, General Sisi issued an ultimatum,[99] giving "political forces" 48 hours to "meet the people's demands," otherwise the army would impose a roadmap. This was the first indication that the military may have had its own agenda, although it was not yet entirely clear what that would be. This happened much faster than in 2011. As in 2011, the reactions to the army's ultimatum were not met with unanimous enthusiasm—and yet dissenting or cautious voices were often been swept aside in the deluge of pro-military propaganda that soon followed. For example, Omar Kamel, an activist from the No Military Trials group, tweeted:

Photo 5.3 "Obama supports terrorism" banner on Tahrir Square, just two days prior to the beginning of the protests that led to the ouster of former President Mohamed Morsi. The banner illustrates how opponents of Morsi attempted to equate the fact that the United States recognized the outcome of the first free presidential elections in Egypt's history, which Morsi won, with supporting terrorism. Photograph taken by the author in Cairo on June 28, 2013.

> Message to #MB: You've got 48 hours to pack. Message to Opposition: You've got 48 hours to figure out how to minimize army rule. #Egypt

The next day, on July 2, I met with my friend Mohammed from April 6. We watched Morsi's speech in downtown Cairo from a rooftop bar. He said, "If you put the puzzle pieces together, Tamarod collects signatures. Then one day later the army makes an ultimatum like this. It seems obvious that it is intelligence."

After the speech was over, we left the rooftop bar and walked in the direction of Talat Harb Street, which leads to Tahrir. But Mohammed didn't want to go back to Tahrir. He had had enough of it. The streets were packed and there was a festive atmosphere. But it was different than in 2011. Some people were walking around holding huge posters of General Sisi above their heads. During the mass protests against Mubarak in 2011, I never once saw anyone holding posters of Field Marshal Tantawi in any kind of celebratory fashion, despite the occasional chanting about the army and the people being one hand. As

Table 5.1 Coalition against Morsi on June 30, 2013

Anti-Morsi Coalition						
Radical		Moderate			Conservative	
April 6	Anti-SCAF groups	Tamarod	Independent Liberals	National Salvation Front	Al Azhar, Coptic Church	NDP, old regime	Military, police

discussed in chapter 3, the reactions of the people on Tahrir to the deployment of tanks on January 28 was ambiguous: some ran to them, others ran away from them. But even those who applauded the arrival of the soldiers were celebrating the rank-and-file soldiers, not Tantawi, the minister of defense, or any other member of the SCAF. The personality cult around Sisi was developing while Morsi was still in power.

Mohammed had joined April 6 soon after the ouster of Mubarak, and he had stuck by the organization through the ups and downs of the past two-and-a-half years. Although he was very talented and trilingual, he did not seek the spotlight or use his activism for personal gain. Mohammed was not trying to become a social media hero. He remained unwavering in his beliefs and worked tirelessly for April 6, the organization that he thought best able to achieve them. I admired his loyalty and perseverance. But instead of celebrating this latest incarnation of the Egyptian revolution, he was disgusted. Usually we spoke to each other in English, but sometimes Mohammed digressed into Arabic or French. Gesturing at the scene around us, he made little effort to hide his contempt: "C'est une cirque, c'est une bordelle."

The following day I had plans to meet with another friend for lunch, which meant meeting in the late afternoon. He lived in Heliopolis but worked in a law firm in Zamalek, and so we agreed to meet at Mezaluna on Aziz Osman street just off 26 July. I had met Omar in 2011 through a former graduate student who put me in touch with him, because I was interested in interviewing retired military officers. His grandfather was not just any military officer. His name was Abdul Rahman Farid, and he was one of the last surviving Free Officers. Nasser had chosen him for a very delicate task—arresting Mohamed Naguib, the most senior member and official leader of the Revolutionary Command Council (RCC), and putting him under house arrest. With Naguib sidelined, Nasser became the official leader of the RCC. Omar and I had stayed in touch and we became friends. The café where we met was entirely empty. The curfew was approaching, and people were rushing to get home. I was not so worried, since I lived just a few streets away on Shagarit el Dor, but Omar lived in Heliopolis on the other side of Cairo. Depending on traffic, it could take him anywhere between 30 minutes to two hours to get home. My friend Nawal, a French Morrocan who worked for the French embassy, joined us at the café. Wary of spending that night by herself, she had asked if she could stay over in my guest room. Everyone suspected that something would happen soon, but no one knew exactly what or when. Nawal had to get official permission from the French embassy to spend the night elsewhere, and she had to provide them with my address. Although she was not a diplomat but a staff member who worked on a contractual basis, she was personally escorted to the café by a bodyguard from the embassy. Instead of simply dropping her off out front, the bodyguard actually walked her inside, up the stairs, and right up to the table where we were sitting alone in the otherwise deserted restaurant. Even before Nawal arrived, I was already surprised at how unhurried Omar seemed to be to leave. After all, everyone else was scrambling to get home before the curfew. After she arrived and we had made the usual introductions, we chatted a bit more. Still, Omar sat there, perfectly calm. He lit another cigarette, exchanging pleasantries, as if he had all the time in the world. I asked him if he didn't need to get home, as there would likely be many checkpoints between Zamalek and Heliopolis, and they were threatening to arrest people who were out past the curfew. But he was unworried, even serene. It was more than just the usual self-confidence that appertains to an upper-class background. Everyone else I knew was on edge. Upper-middle-class friends of mine, who previously paid no heed to the curfews, were nervous about getting home on time. The staff of European embassies were being escorted by bodyguards around the safest neighborhoods of Cairo. Perhaps it was just Omar's personality. Or perhaps, as the grandson of a Free Officer, he knew that—come what may—he would have nothing to fear.

An hour or so later, Morsi was arrested.

PART II

COUNTERREVOLUTION AND
THE RETURN TO MILITARY RULE

6

‏#انتخبوا العرص / قاتل CC

"Sisi is a Killer"/"Elect the Pimp"

First Wave of Counterrevolution

(July 4, 2013–June 7, 2014)

First Phase of Counterrevolution: Eradicating the Muslim Brotherhood; Outlawing Street Protests and Any Form of Youth Activism. Targets: oppositional groups with the potential to organize at the national level. Sisi as Minister of Defense, Head of Supreme Council of Armed Forces, Deputy Prime Minister.			
Civil Society/ Target group	*Mode of Repression* In many cases security forces take action prior to legislation being issued to justify the action.		*Outcome or Intended Outcome*
	Security Action	*Legislative Action*	
Muslim Brotherhood	*Massacres July–August 2013 Violent dispersal of Rabaa and Nahda sit-ins. Arrest of leadership Media censorship/taken off air beginning July 3, 2013.*	*Declared a terrorist organization December 2013.[1] Mass death sentences.[2]*	*Eradicate Muslim Brotherhood and Morsi supporters.*

Tamarod	Public warning to demobilize on July 3, same day as coup. Co-optation of some leaders of Tamarod, Fall 2013.	Prevented from forming political party, December 2014.[3]	Neutralize mass movement. Prevent further activity.
April 6	Arrest of leadership and imprisonment (beginning November 2013).[4]	Protest Law November 2013. Declared a banned organization April 2014.[5]	Criminalize April 6. Prevent street protests.
Students	Arrests.[6] Killed inside university campuses. Beginning of academic year postponed. Private security company.	Student union elections canceled nationwide, Spring 2014.	Prevent protests on campus. Prevent normal political activity on campus including student union elections.
Independent Activists	Arrests and imprisonment (beginning November 2013).[7]	Protest Law November 2013.[8]	Prevent street protests. Silence regime critics.
Ultras	Protest Law. Arrests. Cancellation of football league.[9] Preventing fans from attending football matches.[10]		Prevent street protests. Prevent any large public gatherings, even in stadiums.

Civil Society Group/Target Group	Organizational Capacity/Ability to Challenge the Regime in 2013
Muslim Brotherhood (MB)	*Best-organized opposition group in Egypt with networks spanning the country.* *Membership base: estimated at 500,000–750,000.[11]* *El-Sherouk Newspaper cited 861,000 members according to an unknown high-ranking official in the MB.[12]*
Tamarod	*Tamarod branches expanded across Egypt, ability to mobilize millions of people to protest.* *No membership base, but branches all across Egypt.*
April 6	*April 6 expanded to all 27 of Egypt's governorates* *Membership base: roughly 50,000.[13]*
Students	*Student unions at public universities were coordinated at the national level.* *In 2013–2014 there were 2.34 million students at public universities represented by their student unions.[14]*
Independent Activists	*Some prominent activists were influential not because they were heading an organization but because of their outreach in social media, including their number of followers on Twitter or Facebook.* *Some prominent activists with large social media followings included: Alaa Abdel Fattah, Ahmed Douma, Mahienour El-Massry.*
Ultras	*The Ultras, although not usually taking explicit political positions, played a role during the street protests since 2011. The Ultras are characterized by their tight networks, loyalty to their members, and the families of their martyrs. Estimated 20,000–50,000 members across Egypt.[15]*

Timeline of Repression	
June 28, 2013	*Morsi supporters begin sit-ins at Rabaa and Nahda Squares in Cairo, two days before nationwide protests are scheduled to begin.[16]*

Timeline of Repression	
June 30, 2013	Massive protests all across Egypt call for early elections and for Morsi to step down.
July 3, 2013	The military removes Morsi from power and seven Islamist media outlets are taken off the air. On the same day, retired military general makes television statement calling on the anti-Morsi campaign known as Tamarod to demobilize, saying, "Now there is no opposition."
July 8, 2013	Republican Guards Massacre, 95 people killed by security forces. Morsi supporters continue protests, demanding he be reinstated as president of Egypt.[17]
July 26, 2013	Sisi calls for protests to authorize a fight against "terrorists." Manasa Massacre: 109 people killed by security forces near the Memorial of the Unknown Soldier.[18]
August 14, 2013	The largest massacre in recent Egyptian history, with over 900 people killed at Rabaa and Nahda Squares on a single day.[19]
September 2013	Crackdown begins against students, as protests continue on university campuses. The beginning of the academic year is postponed until November or December in public universities all across Egypt.
November/ December 2013	Crackdown begins against secular opposition groups. Protest Law is issued that bans public gatherings of more than 10 people.[20] Arrest of leadership of April 6 and prominent independent activists.
November 2013	Mohamed Reda, a student with no political affiliations, is killed when security forces raid the campus of Cairo University. Both secular and Islamist students stage a march to protest his murder.[21]
December 25, 2013	PM declared MB to be terrorists, verdict issued later. Mass arrests of second tier of MB leadership in all governorates.[22]
January 2014	Three more students killed by security forces on university campuses.[23]

Timeline of Repression	
March 2014	Sisi announces he will resign from the army and run in the presidential elections.[24] Student union elections canceled all across Egypt.
April 28, 2014	Cairo Court of Urgent Matters issues a verdict banning all activities of April 6 in all governorates.[25]
May 2014	Presidential elections; voting has to be extended to a third day due to low turnout.[26] Sisi is declared president with 97% of the votes.[27]

In the 1950s, Gamal Abdel Nasser and his Free Officers Movement redistributed land, nationalized a number of enterprises, evicted the British, and toppled the monarchy. The coup of 1952 precipitated the demise of the old regime, or what Trimberger called a *revolution from above*. By contrast, the upheaval that began in 2011 has led to a reconstitution rather than the removal of the military-backed regime. I have proposed to term this paradoxical historical process a *coup from below*.

As discussed in greater detail in the previous chapters, I have characterized different ideal types of regime change according to two primary variables: (1) whether they arise because of a revolutionary situation (defined as a deep split within society); and (2) whether they result in a revolutionary outcome (defined as the destruction of the old regime and creation of a new one). A revolutionary situation (deep split within society) that leads to a revolutionary outcome (the destruction of the old regime and creation of a new one) is referred to as a *social revolution*. If a revolutionary outcome is brought about without a revolutionary situation (i.e., it is not accompanied by large-scale mass protests), we refer to this as a *revolution from above*. If there is neither a revolutionary situation nor a revolutionary outcome—meaning that the military orchestrates a change of leadership that allows a continuation of the old regime structures in the absence of mass mobilization—we refer to this as a *military coup*. Finally, if the military ousts the leadership in response to a revolutionary situation (mass protests, deep split within the polity) while the regime structures remain in place, I propose to call this a *coup from below*.

In the previous chapter I analyzed the year of Mohamed Morsi (June 2012–June 2013) and the events that culminated in the mass protests beginning June 30, calling for early elections and the removal of Morsi. The current chapter is dedicated to analyzing the outcome of these events during the first year after Morsi's downfall. In brief, I have argued that it was not former President Mohamed Morsi himself—or even the organization of the Muslim Brotherhood—who posed a threat to the military. During the year of Morsi, the Muslim Brotherhood had displayed a willingness to appease the institution of the armed forces, allowing it to maintain and in some cases even expand their economic interests and political prerogatives. On the contrary, it was the ability of civilian activists—both supporters and opponents of Morsi—to destabilize the country through massive protests that threatened the regime's hold on power. In the previous chapter I showed how the ouster of Morsi in 2013 included the mobilization of millions of people across society—taking the form of what I called a "coup from below," in contrast to the "revolution from above" in 1952, when the Free Officers overthrew the monarchy and established a republic. It was therefore these social forces that had to be silenced in the subsequent crackdown. *Precisely because the coup was the culmination of social forces that reached deep and wide into Egyptian society, the crackdown had to reach this extent as well.*

Like the series of revolutionary uprisings, the counterrevolution also proceeded in waves. The period from January 25, 2011 until July 3, 2013 represented a time during which the old regime was in a state of more or less permanent crisis, characterized by continuing street protests and unprecedented challenges to the institution of the armed forces, which represented the core of the Mubarak regime. While the army and its so-called feloul supporters had been trying to reassert themselves for more than two-and-a-half years, it was not until the ouster of Morsi that they were able to stage their comeback. In short, the old regime could begin to reconsolidate itself. I argue that the reconsolidation of military rule has, until now, proceeded in two phases. The three waves of revolutionary uprisings were followed by two waves of counterrevolutionary crackdowns.

The first phase of regime consolidation began with the appearance of a civilian interim government under the leadership of the head of the Supreme Constitutional Court, Adly Mansour. The second phase began when Abdel Fattah El-Sisi became president and the pretense of a civilian façade was dropped. Furthermore, I argue that these two phases were characterized by different forms of state repression. The regime targeted its opponents in different ways, tailoring its crackdown depending on the nature of the challenger. The first phase of regime consolidation targeted those oppositional groups that either had the ability to mobilize street protests or had the ability to organize politically at the national level. Regardless of political orientation, virtually every youth group whose base of supporters spanned multiple governorates across Egypt was targeted for repression: the Muslim Brotherhood, April 6, Tamarod, the Ultras, university students, and independent activists who challenged the Protest Law or had a large following on social media. I argue that it was not necessarily the political position of these groups that the authorities found threatening but simply their potential to organize. The type and intensity of repression varied considerably, as will be discussed further in the following sections of the chapter.

The youth movements that in early 2011 were often described as "unorganized" or "leaderless" had become increasingly organized and emboldened by mid-2013. After the ouster of Mubarak in early 2011, April 6 had dramatically expanded its membership base—jumping from 10 governorates to 27. Even more threatening to the regime, however, was the fact that April 6 had an even wider network of supporters across the country who were not necessarily officially affiliated with the group. In other words, April 6 could potentially mobilize youth across the entire country. The Ultras could claim a membership base estimated at 20,000–50,000 people. The members were primarily young men who came from different class backgrounds. Furthermore, the Ultras were also able to mobilize far more youth than those who officially identified as belonging to the group. Students at public universities were represented by their national student unions. This meant that students had the ability to coordinate their political activities on campuses ranging from Alexandria in the north to Aswan in the south. Independent activists had the ability to spread information or influence opinion through an expansive social media outreach. Finally, Tamarod had built up an impressive network of political activists in a short span of time. Although Tamarod had demanded early elections—and thereby served the interests of the army—there was no guarantee that it would continue to do so.

The first cycle of regime consolidation lasted almost one year, from the ouster of Morsi on July 3, 2013 until Sisi became president of Egypt in June 2014. During this first wave of the counterrevolution, the interim president was Adly Mansour, the former head of the Supreme Constitutional Court. In theory, it was a civilian government. Perhaps even more important than the appointment of Mansour, at least on a symbolic level, was the presence of an array of prominent civilian figures at the press conference on July 3 announcing the ouster of Morsi. Of the 14 people present, half of them were civilians. These included: Pope Tawadros of the Coptic Church, Sheikh Ahmed El-Tayeb of Al-Azhar, Dr. Mohamed El-Baradei, Mahmoud Badr of Tamarod, Mohamed Abdel Aziz of Tamarod, Galal al-Morra (secretary-general of the Salafi al-Nour Party), and writer Sakina Fouaad. They stood side-by-side next to Sisi, not only lending the appearance of civilian support for the military's actions but also signaling that civilian rule may prevail in the end (Photo 6.1). By including Pope Tawadros, El-Baradei, and Fouad (as the sole woman), the military-backed regime perhaps hoped to signal that it would be inclusive and representative of Egypt's diverse population.[28]

During the first wave of regime reconsolidation, Sisi was minister of defense, head of the Supreme Council of Armed Forces, and deputy prime minister. The

Photo 6.1 Civilians include: Mohamed El-Baradei (left, first row); Mahmoud Badr of Tamarod (left, second row); Sheikh Ahmed El-Tayeb of Al-Azhar and Pope Tawadros (right, middle of first row), Galal Al-Morra, secretary general of the Salafi al-Nour Party; writer Sakina Fouad and Mohamed Abdel Aziz of Tamarod (right, from left to right on the second row. Photo by Associated Press.

second wave of regime consolidation began when Sisi was elected president and continues until the present. The crackdown that has ensued since July 3 is extremely wide in scale and scope. The overthrow of Morsi led to the return of a military-backed regime. And yet, both the methods and targets of repression changed from the time during which Sisi was a military commander and when he became president. For this reason I have divided the counterrevolutionary period of regime reconsolidation into two chapters.

Tamarod, one of the leading forces behind the June 30 mobilization, did not call for the military to return to power. The Tamarod petition demanded early elections but not a military coup or even a temporary military intervention. And according to opinion polls, the military had lost popularity by about 34 percent since 2011. Based on representative surveys conducted by Pew Research, support for the military dropped from a high of 89 percent in 2011 to a low of 55 percent in 2014.[29] And yet, the period after June 30 paved the way for the military to return to power. How was this possible? In some ways, the Supreme Council of Armed Forces (SCAF) seemed to have learned from its previous mistakes. Instead of assuming executive power immediately, as happened when Mubarak was toppled on February 11, 2011, executive power was transferred to Mansour as head of the Supreme Constitutional Court. The SCAF also did not issue any communiques like they did while Tantawi was in charge. This made it somewhat more difficult to discern the military's intentions. Rather than parsing their official proclamations, I have endeavored to read their actions, in particular vis-à-vis civil society.

During the first wave of regime reconsolidation under Mansour, there were some attempts to bring in or co-opt members of the secular opposition. El-Baradei accepted the position of vice president,[30] holding this position only for one month. Ziad Bahaa El-Din became deputy prime minister.[31] Kamal Abu Eita, president of the Egyptian Federation of Independent Trade Unions (EFIT) and longtime labor activist and cofounder of the Nasserist Karama Party, was appointed minister of manpower in mid-July.[32] Ragia Omran, Mohamed Abdel Aziz, and Kamal Abbas were offered, and accepted,[33] positions in the National Council of Human Rights.[34] Although perhaps more symbolic than anything else, these appointments were important to give the appearance of a civilian interim government and an independent National Council of Human Rights. The more "liberal" members of the government were all dropped before Sisi took power.[35]

Incorporation of Secular Opposition into the Government under Adly Mansour/Abdel Fattah El-Sisi July 2013–June 2014: First phase of regime reconsolidation			
Name	*Prior oppositional activity*	*Position in the government*	*Time period*
Mohamed El-Baradei	*Head of the opposition movement National Association for Change*	*Vice President*	*July 14–August 14, 2013*
Ziad Bahaa El-Din	*Cofounder of Egyptian Social Democratic Party*	*Deputy Prime Minister*	*July 12, 2013– January 30, 2014*
Kamal Abu Eita	*President of the Egyptian Federation of Independent Trade Unions (EFIT), cofounder of Karama Party*	*Minister of Manpower*	*July 16, 2013– February 24, 2014*
Ahmed El-Borei	*Minister of Manpower in Essam Sharaf's Cabinet[36]*	*Minister of Social Solidarity*	*July 16, 2013– February 24, 2014*

Incorporation of Secular Opposition into the National Council of Human Rights (NCHR) under Adly Mansour July 2013–June 2014: First phase of regime reconsolidation		
Name	*Prior oppositional activity*	*Time period*
Ragia Omran	*Member of Front to Defend Egyptian Protesters, No to Military Trials, and the New Woman Foundation*	*August 2013*
Hossam Bahgat	*Cofounder of Egyptian Initiative for Personal Rights (EIPR)*	*Refusal*[37]
Mohamed Abdel Aziz	*Cofounder of Tamarod, former member of Kefeya*	*September 2013*
Kamal Abbas	*Head of independent Center for Trade Union and Workers' Services (CTUWS)*	*August 2013*[38]

On March 26, 2014, when Sisi announced that he would be running for president, the hashtag "Sisi Is a Pimp" (السيسي العرص) or "Elect the Pimp" (انتخبوا_ العرص) began circulating on social media. By April 2, one week after the start of the online campaign, the hashtag had been used 490 million times.[39] As these protest slogans make clear, opposition to Sisi came from both secular and Islamist camps. Furthermore, even the majority of leaders of the Tamarod movement opposed Sisi's bid for the presidency, as will be elaborated on later in the chapter. With the emergence of widespread opposition to Sisi from various ends of the political spectrum, the stage seemed to have been set for another antiregime uprising, similar to those against Mubarak in 2011, the SCAF in 2012, and Morsi in 2013—which were analyzed in chapters 3, 4, and 5, respectively. Instead, however, the forces of the old regime prevailed, and a fourth revolutionary wave has yet to appear on the horizon. Why?

The return to military rule was accompanied by the repression of any and all forms of activism and the young people of Egypt more generally. There were 41 massacres of civilians by security forces, all carried out after the removal of Morsi and before Sisi became president.[40] It was not just a matter of controlling the coercive apparatus while conducting massacres. Rather, the regime made a calculated decision to apply a specific level and type of repression according to the nature of the challenger. The Muslim Brotherhood suffered the most lethal forms of repression.

Photo 6.2 Picture 2 "Sisi Is a Killer" graffiti in Beheira Governorate. Picture from Google posted on Beheira.net.
"Sisi Is a Killer," digital image, ElBeheira, 2014, accessed August 11, 2017, https://bit.ly/2X7swTk.

The goal of the crackdown was ambitious. The state aimed to fully eradicate the Muslim Brotherhood; to remove it from politics through massacres, mass death sentences, arrests, and asset freezes; and to silence Muslim Brotherhood–affiliated media through censorship. On July 4, the Ministry of Interior issued a statement announcing the closure of the four main Islamist media outlets that were seen as affiliated (Masr 25, ElNas, ElRahma, and AlHafez). Thirty-five broadcasters in Media City were likewise arrested.[41] The Aljazeera Mubasher Masr office was raided, the journalists and staff were arrested, and its broadcast was taken off the air.[42] The Muslim Brotherhood–affiliated print media continued a bit longer. In December 2013 and January 2014 the *Freedom and Justice* and *ElShaab* newspapers were banned, respectively.[43]

However, the crackdown was not limited to the Muslim Brotherhood. Virtually all forms of street protests were criminalized—regardless of political orientation. Many other forms of youth activism were hindered as well. These restrictions included calling on Tamarod to demobilize and cease being the opposition, outlawing public gatherings of more than 10 people, arresting the leadership of April 6 and other independent activists, canceling student union elections at public universities across Egypt, canceling the football league to prevent youth gatherings, declaring April 6 and the Ultras to be banned groups, and declaring the Muslim Brotherhood as a terrorist organization.

Much of the literature on state repression focuses on the so-called repression/mobilization nexus, asking whether repression increases or decreases the number of protests. The results of the empirical case studies are indeterminate. Noting this indeterminacy, a number of scholars have moved away from attempting to quantitatively assess the impact of repression on protest and instead look at its qualitative impacts. Ketchley has examined how anticoup mobilization changed as a result of state repression in the first few months after the ouster of Morsi. He found that anticoup protests moved from large squares to smaller side streets, thereby becoming more mobile and less disruptive. The timing of protest events also shifted; groups decided to stage events in the early morning hours or late at night, often timed according to police shifts. While these insights are important, they are limited to a single group, the Students against the Coup (SAC) (*Tulaab dud el-inkaleb*), and to a relatively short span of time from July until December 2013. By contrast, I examine in this chapter the shifting forms of state repression from the ouster of Morsi in July 2013 until the inauguration of Sisi as president in June 2014. Chapter 8 then covers the period until the summer of 2018—the first five years after the coup. At the time of writing, each wave of crackdown is followed by another fresh crackdown. State repression shows no sign of stopping. It is therefore too early to offer a final assessment of the impact of repression—either on the individual groups that are being targeted or on Egyptian society writ large. My purpose in this chapter is to highlight the patterns of state repression from the ouster of Morsi in July 2013 until the inauguration of Sisi as president in June 2014. I will illustrate how these patterns of repression shifted both over time and in terms of how different actors were targeted in different ways. Secondly, I will show how Tamarod, the movement that emerged with the goal of removing Morsi from power by calling for early elections, has adapted and responded in the aftermath of the coup.

I argue that precisely because the ouster of Morsi took the form of what I call a coup from below or *people's coup*, which encompassed large segments of society, the crackdown had to as well. Secondly, I show it was only a few members of the Tamarod leadership who were truly co-opted into becoming essentially army apparatchiks, such as Mahmoud Badr. Other founding members of Tamarod publicly endorsed Hamdeen Sabahi in the presidential elections in May 2014—and not Sisi—or withdrew from Tamarod. There was an attempt to bring Tamarod "back on track," which was led by Mona Seleem, one of the female cofounders of Tamarod. However, this attempt failed. In the governorates outside Cairo, the Tamarod movements displayed greater criticism of the military-backed regime. As I showed in the previous chapter, Tamarod began as a grassroots social movement, but it was later instrumentalized by the military. Dissenting voices within the small circle of Tamarod founders in Cairo emerged but, rather than publicly challenge Tamarod, they withdrew from the organization. However, some Tamarod branches in the governorates outside Cairo were never instrumentalized, co-opted, or silenced by the regime. On the contrary, the Tamarod branches in Alexandria, Aswan, Port Said, Tanta, Mahalla, and Minya are just a few examples of governorates outside Cairo that publicly criticized either the Tamarod leadership or the military-backed regime directly. Some Tamarod branches announced their dissolution in order to join the side of the revolution. In short, I argue that Tamarod was Janus-faced: a grassroots social movement with broad support, but also a mask behind which counterrevolutionary elements hid. I endeavor to highlight these contradictions in my analysis, and will focus on one or the other depending on what I'm discussing and at what period of time. Ultimately Tamarod faced many of the same challenges that many big tent movements face, including the emergence of divisions within the movement between radicals and moderates and the co-optation of a few key leaders by the regime. As I show, however, the bulk of the Tamarod movement did not endorse the return to military rule.

The Crackdown Begins

Ousting Morsi was easy. Demobilizing millions of Egyptians was much more difficult and much more bloody. This was because the coup emerged from within society—and thus it was the society that had the potential to threaten Sisi. As documented in the previous chapter, the period leading up to July 3 was characterized by large-scale street protests. *After Morsi was removed on July 3, however, the number of protests actually increased as supporters of the Muslim Brotherhood staged protests.* Although these protests were smaller in size, they still were seen as a threat to the regime. Dealing with the continuation of street protests—by both Islamist and secular opposition groups—was a much more difficult task than removing the president.

Although there were a few individuals who appear to have represented alternative voices within the military, such as Ahmed Wasfi and Sami Anan, they seem to have been rather isolated and have since been marginalized from the political scene.[44] In short, Sisi did not have to fear a rival faction within the military, but rather he faced the millions of Egyptians who had shown they had the capacity to bring down a president. This meant that even those groups who supported the coup were potentially a threat to the regime merely because of their organizational abilities—and because the authorities knew that they could not completely control them.

As discussed in chapter 3, the last decade of Mubarak witnessed the growth of a number of secular antiregime opposition groups such as Kefaya, the National Association for Change, April 6, We Are All Khaled Said, and a few independent labor unions. However, while important, none of these groups had a membership base that spanned the entire country. On the contrary, most of these groups were limited to Cairo, Alexandria, and other urban centers such as in the Canal Zone. During the two-and-a-half years after 2011, some of these groups expanded their membership across Egypt.

Demobilizing Tamarod and Arresting the Muslim Brotherhood

After toppling the president, the military's utmost priority—as it was in February 2011—was to demobilize a highly mobilized population. In an interview on CNN, just hours after the military had declared that the elected president was no longer president, retired General Sameh Seif El-Yazal said the following about Tamarod, the anti-Morsi coalition that claimed to have garnered over 20 million signatures:

> We've seen them in the street gathering signatures. Just using a piece of paper and a pen, they really shook the chair of Morsi. But the point is, *now there is no opposition.* Now we have to have one Egyptian identity. The Egyptians have to be in one hand.[45]

Once again, the most immediate goal of the military was to end the ongoing protests. While leading members of the Muslim Brotherhood were free, the military issued a statement against Tamarod in an attempt to neutralize it.

A number of liberal commentators and opposition figures praised the military's behavior and provided direct support to the ouster of Morsi. El-Baradei, for example, who was considered as perhaps the most prominent representative of Egyptian liberalism and who had founded the Al Dostour Party in April 2012, appeared in the press conference next to Sisi announcing that Morsi had been deposed. On July 14, El-Baradei accepted the position of vice president of Egypt. He held the position for just one month until he resigned on August 14, the day of the massacres in Rabaa and Nahda.

In an interview with *Der Spiegel* published on July 8, 2013, El-Baradei insisted that the removal of Morsi was not a coup, that the military was listening to him, and that the number of arrests had been exaggerated. He also related that President Barack Obama and Secretary of State John Kerry had spoken to him. While many of his statements may now appear naïve, it is worth keeping in mind that, at the time of the interview, many leading members of the Muslim Brotherhood had not (yet) been arrested. Whether this was because the military had not yet decided to arrest the entire leadership, because of international pressure, or for some other reason is unclear. Excerpts from the interview with El-Baradei are included in the following section.

Interview with Egyptian Politician El-Baradei, July 8, 2013

"This Was Not a Coup"

El-Baradei: Let me make one thing clear: This was not a coup.[46] More than 20 million people took to the streets because the situation was no longer acceptable. Without Morsi's removal from office, we would have been headed toward a fascist state, or there would have been a civil war. It was a painful decision. It was outside the legal framework, but we had no other choice.

SPIEGEL: No matter how you justify the military's approach, it isn't democratic.

El-Baradei: You cannot apply your high standards to a country burdened with decades of autocratic rule. Our democracy is still in its infancy.

SPIEGEL: Can that justify the fact that hundreds of members of the Muslim Brotherhood are now in custody and the president was placed under house arrest? Many are calling it a witch hunt on the Islamists.

El-Baradei: It cannot come to that, and the military has assured me that there were no arbitrary arrests. For days, I have been demanding that we include the Brotherhood in the process of democratization. No one should be put on trial without a valid reason. Former President Morsi must be treated with dignity. These are the conditions of national reconciliation.

[. . .]

El-Baradei: When I asked the generals, they assured me that many of the reports about arrests are untrue and that the numbers had been greatly exaggerated. They said that when there were arrests, they were made for good reasons, such as illegal weapons possession. And the Islamist TV stations were closed because they were fomenting unrest with their fatwas.

SPIEGEL: Aren't you putting too much trust in the military, given that it has often pursued its own interests in Egypt?

El-Baradei: The military did not force its way into power this time. It has no interest in taking a forward role in politics. The generals are aware that they are historically partly to blame for the disaster in which the country now finds itself. That's why I too don't absolve the army of responsibility.

> SPIEGEL: But does the military listen to you? Aren't you concerned about being misused as a fig leaf?
>
> El-Baradei: It's not a question of blind faith. The next meeting with the generals has already been scheduled, and at least they're listening to me. But the military doesn't get a free pass from me, either. My red line is this: I don't align myself with anyone who ignores tolerance and democracy. And they know that.
>
> SPIEGEL: US President Barack Obama and US Secretary of State John Kerry called you and treated you like the future president.
>
> El-Baradei: Yes, I spoke with both of them extensively and tried to convince them of the need to depose Morsi. But I don't see myself in the role of the future president. I want to use my influence to bring Egyptians together and help them reconcile—as an *eminence grise*, if you will.

Although in this interview El-Baradei stated that he did not see himself in the role of "future president," five days after the interview was published, on July 14, he did accept the position of vice president of Egypt. One month later, on the day of the Rabaa massacre, El-Baradei resigned. He subsequently moved back to Austria and essentially removed himself from public life.

I interviewed El-Baradei at his home in Vienna in October 2016. He had not given many interviews since he resigned as vice president. I thought it best to begin by asking him about the role of the international mediators, rather than questioning him about his own role in the period leading up to the Rabaa massacre. After answering a few questions, he appeared irritated and said that it was a "neocolonial approach" to ask about what foreigners were doing during this period of Egyptian history. So I then asked him directly what exactly he had done as vice president to mediate the crisis during those crucial four weeks between July 14 and August 14, 2013. He admitted to not having met with a single member of the Muslim Brotherhood. He also did not visit the Rabaa or Nahda sit-ins a single time. The international mediators who were working on behalf of the United States and European Union (EU) did, however, visit members of the Muslim Brotherhood who were in prison, such as Khairat al-Shater.

The international mediators included high-ranking diplomats from the United States, Europe, Africa, and the Persian Gulf. Representing the United States was Deputy Secretary of State William Burns, whom Obama selected as special envoy. Representing the EU were first vice president of the European Commission, Baroness Catherine Ashton, and her deputy Bernardino Leon, who at the time was serving as European Union Special Representative (EUSR) to the Southern Mediterranean. Leon not only made prison visits but also visited the Rabaa sit-in many times in an attempt to engage directly with those who were staging the sit-in.[47] Ashton was the first person who was allowed to visit Morsi after he was deposed. The army had been holding him incommunicado; no one knew where he was or even if he was still alive. Ashton's main concern was to be sure that he was in fact still alive and in good health. Until the time of writing, she has not revealed any details about her conversation with him. Deputy Secretary of State Bill Burns also requested permission to visit Morsi, but his request was denied. Burns and his Qatari and Emirati counterparts, however, were permitted to visit al-Shater in the Tora prison. I spoke to Burns in January 2018 in his office at the Carnegie Endowment in Washington, DC, and asked him about their attempts to mediate. Regarding the fact that they were not allowed to visit Morsi, Burns didn't see this as the main problem, as al-Shater was a powerful figure within the Brotherhood, possibly even more so than Morsi. According to Burns, their plan to deescalate the crisis between the Brotherhood and the military was as follows: the three mediators asked al-Shater if the Muslim Brotherhood would agree to decrease the number of people at the Rabaa and Nahda sit-ins, which would then allow the military to go in and remove whatever weapons they claimed were there. Burns recalls that al-Shater appeared in the Tora prison in his flip-flops and prison garb. Al-Shater rejected their suggestion to reduce the number of people at the sit-ins, adding defiantly that he had spent 12 years of his life in prison and was willing to spend 12 more years in prison rather than compromise.[48] Members of the African Union High Level Panel for Egypt, comprising former President Alpha Oumar Konaré of Mali as chair, former President Festus Mogae of Botswana, and former Prime Minister Dileita Mohamed Dileita of Djibouti, were also allowed to visit Morsi for one hour in the undisclosed location where he was being held captive.

In the interview on July 8 with *Der Spiegel*, El-Baradei claimed he wanted to "include the Brotherhood in the process of democratization." However, when he was made vice president and given both authority and responsibility to actually negotiate with the Brotherhood, he did not do so. Vice President El-Baradei did not meet with any member of the Brotherhood even a single time after July 3. El-Baradei's refusal to meet with anyone from the Brotherhood reveals the hollowness of his claims of inclusiveness, and even appears like a form of diplomatic malpractice, especially given the number of American, European, and African diplomats who did meet with Brotherhood leaders. On the contrary, El-Baradei seemed to be more interested in obtaining international support for the coup rather than negotiating a peaceful resolution to the stand-off between the Muslim Brotherhood and the army. However, in fairness, and as I argued before, it is not clear that any of the civilians who had positions in government after July 3 had any real power, including Mohamed El-Baradei, Adly Mansour, Nabil Fahmy, Ziad Bahaa El-Din, and others.

Arrest and Imprisonment of Select Members of the Muslim Brotherhood Leadership under Adly Mansour		
Date of arrest in 2013 (as reported in the media)	Name	Position or Relation to the Muslim Brotherhood
July 3	Mohamed Morsi[49]	President of Egypt
July 3	Saad El-Katatni[50]	President of the Freedom and Justice Party
July 4	Mahdi Akef[51]	The former Supreme Guide of the Brotherhood
July 5	Helmy Al-Gazzar[52]	General Secretary of the Freedom and Justice Party in Giza
July 5	Khairat Al-Shater[53]	Deputy Supreme Guide
August 17	Sherif Heshmat[54]	Secretary of Information of the Freedom and Justice Party in Beheira
August 17	Osama Modather[55]	Member of the Administrative Office of the Brotherhood in Assiut
August 17	Mohamed Abdel Salam[56]	Spokesperson for the Muslim Brotherhood in Luxor
August 20	Mohamed Badie[57]	Supreme Guide
August 29	Mohamed Al-Beltagy[58]	General Secretary of the Freedom and Justice Party
August 30	Fouad Mohamed Zaghloul[59]	General Secretary of the Freedom and Justice Party in Matrouh
September 9	Khaled Hanafy[60]	General Secretary of the Freedom and Justice Party in Cairo
October 30	Essam El-Erian[61]	Member of Guidance Bureau
November 23	Galal Abdel Sadek[62]	Head of the Administrative Office of the Brotherhood
November 30	Samir Osman Khashaba[63]	General Secretary of the Freedom and Justice Party in Assiut

The First Postcoup Massacre of Morsi Supporters Elicits
Condemnation by the AntiMilitarist Opposition

While some leading secular figures such Mohamed El-Baradei or Amr Moussa failed to resolve the crisis, or in some cases even condemn the massacres against the Muslim Brotherhood, the antimilitarist opposition groups did respond. On July 8, just after the dawn prayers, 95 Morsi loyalists were gunned down and 435 were wounded outside the headquarters of the Republican Guard in Cairo.[64] While the Egyptian army claimed that armed men on motorcycle attacked security forces, a weeklong investigation found no evidence for this narrative. Instead, evidence from videos, as well as testimony from medics, local people, and eyewitnesses, shows that security forces launched a coordinated attack on a group of peaceful and unarmed protesters. One of the surviving protesters claimed: "If they'd just wanted to break the sit-in, they could have done it in other ways. But they wanted to kill us."[65]

How did the opposition respond to the military's toppling of Morsi and the subsequent crackdown? A number of op-eds and articles in the Western media have addressed the issue of how so-called liberals could endorse seemingly nonliberal political positions, including the return to military rule. The *Washington Post* asked, "What's the matter with Egyptian liberals?"[66] *The Nation* queried, "What happened to Egypt's liberals after the coup?"[67] Two years later, *The Economist* published an article titled "The Sad State of Egypt's Liberals."[68]

While many liberals failed to defend basic principles of political liberalism, there were a few exceptions. In a televised interview shortly after July 3, Amr Hamzawy referred to the events as a "soft coup" (*enkelab na'em*) because it was supported by popular protests. He also spoke out against arbitrarily imprisoning members of the Muslim Brotherhood.[69] And in an article on July 31, Hamzawy argued that the behavior of liberal opposition figures had led to a crisis of Egyptian liberalism due to their unwillingness to oppose the military's ousting of Morsi earlier that month.[70] Because of his critical statements, he was slapped with a travel ban in January 2014 and accused of insulting the Egyptian judiciary.[71] In October of the same year, his name was removed from the list.[72]

While Hamzawy is well known, the continued criticism of the military by other factions of the secular camp has received less attention. Indeed, the mere existence of an antimilitarist opposition often goes unmentioned in both scholarly and journalistic accounts of Egypt's revolution. Instead of flip-flopping like El-Baradei and other members of the older generation of liberal opposition, many of the youth activists like April 6, No Military Trials, Kazeboon, and others were consistent in their condemnation of the military.

Although some members of the secular opposition did welcome not only the ousting of Morsi but also the subsequent violent crackdown on the Muslim Brotherhood, the more radical antimilitarist opposition groups (discussed in chapter 4) condemned the massacre of Muslim Brotherhood supporters. In other words, many of the secular youth-led activist groups that criticized the military's violence under SCAF rule persisted in their criticism of the military's violence in the first weeks after the ouster of Morsi. However, many of these groups are virtually unknown outside Egypt. Documenting their political positions is important, not only for the purpose of historical accuracy, but also because, as I argue, the nature of the crackdown can only be understood against the backdrop of the social forces that were targeted. The anti-Morsi coalition was not unanimously pro-military. One reason the military-backed regime then moved against the non-Islamist activist groups was precisely because they publicly opposed violent attacks on the Islamists.

The very same day that 95 of Morsi's supporters were killed at the Republican Guards, April 6 issued a statement in Arabic on their Facebook page defending the rights of Morsi's supporters to peacefully protest and demanding an independent investigation. Although April 6 joined the anti-Morsi protests and claims to have collected two million signatures for the Tamarod campaign, the group made clear that this did not entail support for violence against the Muslim Brotherhood, saying, "Spilling any Egyptian blood is haram."[73] On July 31, April 6 issued a statement rejecting the mandate given to the Ministry of Interior to disperse the sit-ins in Rabaa and Nahda, thereby defending the Muslim Brotherhood's right to continue their protests.[74] The Revolutionary Socialists just as quickly condemned the "beastly repression" of the Muslim Brotherhood.[75] On July 11, the No Military Trials group issued a statement, demanding justice for the remaining 1,101 civilians who were still being held in prison and subjected to military courts.[76]

Kazeboon declared that they "viewed the events that started on 25 January 2011 as a revolution and the events of 30 June 2013 as a continuation of that revolution. Kazeboon will continue to counter the regime's narrative when it distorts the facts, irrespective of who is in power."[77] On July 15, Mosireen posted a seven-minute film on their website: *30th of June: Coup or Continuation of the Revolution* The short video begins with the narrator addressing this question and saying:

In one year, Morsi went from being a president trying to monopolize power to a completely powerless one. Military leaders, on the other hand, never really left power.

The video goes on to describe how rehabilitating the army and police will make it easier to crush opposition movements. And finally, it ends by referencing the protests in Brazil, Turkey, Chile, Greece, and Spain.

Regimes are trying to contain revolutionary moments everywhere. June 30 is just one example. This does not mean they will succeed every time.

Secular opposition activists, including April 6, Kazeboon, the No Military Trials group, Mosireen, and the Revolutionary Socialists all issued statements opposing the first postcoup massacre of the Muslim Brotherhood on July 8. At this point, it is at least conceivable that a united front between secularists and Islamists may have been possible. This may have been why the military, after massacring the Muslim Brotherhood, turned to them next.

Minister of Defense Sisi called for Egyptians to come to the streets on Friday, July 26 and give him the authorization or mandate (*tafweed*) to confront "violence and potential terrorism."[78] Essentially, he was asking for permission to conduct further massacres.

I argue that July 26 is the day when the military reasserted itself and began to regain control over the situation. This is when the military began not only to sideline the revolutionary elements of the June 30 uprising but also to marginalize Tamarod. Sisi did not mention the group a single time in his speech. Arguably, July 26 is also the date when Sisi's personal political ambitions became manifest. Sisi was the "new Nasser," speaking directly to and mobilizing people to come to the streets to support his agenda. While Mansour was nominally the interim president of Egypt, it was clear that Sisi was the one in charge. In short, the military intervention may have taken place on July 3, but the return to military rule began on July 26 as Sisi took on an overtly political role. The table below summarizes how eight different political actors, including political parties, trade unions, and activist groups, responded to Sisi's call for an authorization to fight terrorism on July 26.

The Military Returns to Politics

Sisi's Call for Authorization to Fight "Terrorism"—Civil Society Groups Respond

Group	Support July 26 protests: yes or no?	Statement about July 26 protests that Sisi called for to fight terrorism	Reference to July 3 as a coup or revolution?
April 6	no	"To protect the country is your responsibility according to the constitution. Waiting for authorization as a pretext for negligence is a crime, and engaging in violence or breaching liberties under the slogan of fighting terrorism is a bigger crime."[79]	Ahmed Maher said that he didn't call June 30 a coup.[80]
Revolutionary Socialists	no	"We will not give a blank check to commit massacres."[81]	Coup
Tamarod	yes	On their Facebook page Tamarod called on people to go on the streets authorizing Sisi to fight terrorism.[82]	N/A
Popular Alliance	yes	Abdel Ghaffar Shokr, the head of the party, asked the people to go to the streets to authorize Sisi, but warned that this authorization should not lead to unlawful actions.[83]	N/A
Egyptian Trade Union Federation (official federation)	yes	Called on members to protest and participated with a delegation.[84]	Revolution

Group	Support July 26 protests: yes or no?	Statement about July 26 protests that Sisi called for to fight terrorism	Reference to July 3 as a coup or revolution?
Independent Trade Union federation	no	Fatma Ramadan, a member of the executive bureau of the Independent trade union federation, wrote an article asking the workers not to join the protests. She described Sisi's "authorization" to fight terrorism as toxic.[85]	N/A
Egyptian Current	no	They refused to support the July 26 protests, which they described as a personal authorization of power to Sisi, and asked the Egyptian people to respect that all Egyptian blood is sacred.[86]	June 30 was a third revolutionary wave, but refused all attempts of the army to take power.[87]
Strong Egypt Party	no	Ahmed Emam, the party's spokesperson, refused to participate in the July 26 protests, saying that the party was concerned it might lead to civil war.[88]	June 30 was a revolution but July 3 is a coup.[89]

N/A indicates that while individual members of the group may have taken a position on whether July 3 was a coup or revolution, the organization did not issue an official statement on the matter.

The Rabaa Massacre: Egypt's Tiananmen Square

Despite the deadly attacks against Morsi supporters during July and the first half of August, the sit-ins at the Rabaa and Nahda squares continued. This was perhaps because the Muslim Brotherhood seemed to believe that they could restore Morsi to the presidency through protests. I visited the Rabaa sit-in on August 13, the night before it was besieged by security forces, and the Nahda sit-in on August 14, in the midst of the largest massacre in postcolonial Egyptian history. The Rabaa sit-in was larger than that on Tahrir Square, both in terms of the physical space that was occupied and in terms of its duration, lasting 47 days compared to the 18-day uprising centered around Tahrir in 2011. On August

16, I published a short article about my visit to Rabaa and Nahda. Many journalists and photographers risked their lives documenting the atrocities. Some who witnessed the massacre did not live to tell about it, and others were imprisoned. Mahmoud Abu Zeid, a young photojournalist known as Shawkan, was arrested on August 14 for taking photographs at Rabaa.[90] He spent more than five years in prison, before he was finally released in March 2019.[91] On that day, as on many other days, I was lucky. Of course, assistant professors are not supposed to be in the business of covering breaking news. More than anything, it was the beating drums of state propaganda that described all participants in the Rabaa and Nahda sit-ins as members of the Muslim Brotherhood—and therefore terrorists—that compelled me to write something, at least as a personal testimony. Published just two days after the massacre, I believe my piece may have been one of the first articles published by an academic about the massacre. My former AUC colleague, Emad Shahin, also published an article just days after the Rabaa massacre. He was later sentenced to death in a mass trial.[92]

I decided to include my article here because it reflects my relatively unfiltered and immediate reactions to both the sit-ins and the massacre. I cite the figure of "over 600" being killed on a single day, but we now know that the figure is upward of 932,[93] and possibly a thousand that were killed on August 14. Otherwise, and despite the fact that this piece was written very quickly, I have no writer's remorse. I believe my arguments are as valid now as they were when this was published, two days after the massacre.

Before the Bloodletting: A Tour of the Rabaa Sit-In

I visited the Rabaa Al-Adawiya sit-in the night before security forces besieged it. The atmosphere was relaxed. Children jumped on trampolines. Men were playing soccer. A woman wearing a black niqab embraced me when I told her in Arabic that I lived in Cairo. There was no sense of impending doom.

The exception was the entrance, where people kneeled at a makeshift shrine, stones in a circle on the sidewalk. They kissed the blood on the pavement of those who had been killed in the previous two massacres, fellow supporters of deposed President Mohamed Morsi. Wednesday was the third. With over 600 dead, and more than 56 churches,[94] monasteries and Christian schools attacked, it was the single most violent day in recent Egyptian history.

Together with a journalist friend, I had signed up for the Rabaa Tour, an outreach initiative launched about ten days earlier. We were met by Mohamed and Aisha, who spent the next several hours showing us around the huge encampment. According to our guides, they had approximately one visitor per day. Presumably, we were their last guests.

The sit-in was huge, sprawling over several kilometers. It had grown into a miniature city, considerably larger in terms of physical space than the sit-in on Tahrir Square.

State officials, the media, as well as a number of liberal commentators, have framed their battle against the Muslim Brotherhood as a war on "terrorism." The sit-in has been described as "violent and armed." For a variety of reasons, I was skeptical.

First of all, holding a sit-in is not exactly the tactic of choice of a terrorist organization. I'm not aware of Al-Qaeda ever having staged a sit-in. They tend to prefer taking more drastic measures, such as kidnapping people, hijacking airplanes, car bombings, etc. Holding sit-ins are, however, a relatively common tactic of non-violent social movements.

Second, state media had also claimed that armed Coptic Christians were attacking army soldiers on October 9, 2011. That turned out to be false. In reality, the Maspero massacre resulted in the deaths of 26 unarmed civilians, most of them Copts.[95]

Finally, social movements do not necessarily have strict membership criteria. Even those who claim leadership of a movement may never know how many people or who exactly "belongs" to a movement due to differing levels of engagement. Some people may dedicate their entire life to a movement, others may only show up occasionally at a demonstration. If there is no membership, there is no such thing as excluding members for bad behavior. This is what makes social movements harder to grasp and more difficult to study than political parties. So while some participants of the Rabaa sit-in may have engaged in violence, this does not necessarily mean that all other participants supported this. The same is true of the Tahrir sit-ins.

To be sure, some elements of the Muslim Brotherhood have engaged in acts of violence. However, not everyone at the Rabaa sit-in belonged to the Muslim Brotherhood.

In fact, not a single one of my interlocutors at Rabaa were members of the Brotherhood. Maissa, a housewife who has been living in France for 13 years, said that before she started coming to the sit-in she didn't even know anyone from the Freedom and Justice Party, an organizing force behind the demonstration. Aisha, a young college student studying international relations in New Hampshire, told me that she was not there for Morsi, but for her principles. "If you get elected by the ballot box, you have to leave by the ballot box." If Mohamed El-Baradei had been president, and had been removed by a military intervention, she claimed, she would be defending him instead of Morsi. Mohamed, a 27-year-old marketing instructor at the American University in Cairo, was also not a member of the Brotherhood. He even referred to Morsi as a "loser." He said that he wasn't insisting that Morsi be re-instated. What was it then that they wanted? Why had they been camping out there for 45 days, enduring bullets, tear gas, and the August sun. As if he were pleading for his life, he said, "We just want people to know we are peaceful. We are not terrorists."

The hundreds, possibly thousands, of signs that had been hung up all over the sit-in, also did not give much indication of nefarious terroristic intent. One large banner read: "The People Want the Return of President" in Arabic, English, and French. Another said: "Democracy versus Coup." And another: "We Refused Military Coup in Egypt." Then there was a series of signs that said "Veterinarians for Morsi," "Teachers for Morsi," "Liberals for Morsi," and so on. And my personal favorite: "The Army Threw Away My Vote."

Despite threats that the sit-in would be cleared, on Tuesday evening the protesters showed no signs of leaving. In addition to the tents, one of our guides proudly pointed out how wooden structures consisting of three levels had been erected. It was as if they were about to build a three-story home. I had never seen anything like this attempted during the various encampments in Tahrir Square. The protesters were determined to stay. In fact, they seemed to be quite happy there. Maissa, the housewife who lives in Paris, said the Rabaa sit-in was "the best 37 days of her life."

I woke up Wednesday morning to the news that the sit-ins were being attacked. Upon hearing that it was impossible to gain access to Rabaa, I went immediately to the middle-class neighborhood of Mohandessin. This is where many of the protesters from the Nahda sit-in had escaped. Blood was on the pavement and gunshots whistled through the air. At least seven barricades had been erected along Batal Ahmed Abdel Aziz Street. A Central Security Forces vehicle was overturned and on fire. As the shooting intensified, a group of bearded men to my right began chanting, "Allah Akhbar." To my left was a clean-shaven man visiting from London. I asked if he had voted for Morsi. After hesitating, he admitted that he did not vote at all in the presidential elections. He said that he had come to the protest, not to defend Morsi, but because he didn't want his country to return to military rule. "Sixty years of military rule was enough."

Back home on Wednesday evening, I called Mohamed, the marketing instructor at the American University in Cairo. He had been shot in the stomach during the siege on Rabaa. He said he was "lucky," and that he would be okay.

In defending the bloodletting, Ahmed Ali, the spokesman for the Ministry of Defense, said, "When dealing with terrorism, the consideration of civil and human rights are not applicable." Calling people like Maissa the housewife, Aisha the student, and Mohamed the marketing instructor terrorists is not only inaccurate, it is dangerous. Shooting at them is the logical consequence. Even over the phone, I could hear the pain in Mohamed's voice: "We will tell our grandchildren about this day, if we have the chance to live some more."

Who exactly within the security apparatus ordered the massacre we may never know. El-Baradei told me in the interview that he was in regular contact with Sisi during the four weeks he was vice president, and that he believes that Sisi did not intend for the dispersal to be as violent as it was. Chuck Hagel, former US Secretary of Defense, reportedly spoke with Sisi by phone after the massacre. "He said that he was sorry, so sorry," Hagel remembered. "He said he wished it hadn't come to this. This was never something he wanted, or his country wanted."[96] And yet, the massacre was orchestrated and overseen by Sisi.

What role did the Egyptian army play in the Rabaa massacre? The killing was done by the Central Security Forces and Special Forces, in close cooperation with the Egyptian Armed Forces. The Rabaa massacre occurred at the intersection of Nasr and Tayaran streets, which is flanked by an army base on one side and a Ministry of Defense building on the other. The army opened its base to snipers, who shot at protesters from the rooftop. Army helicopters provided air cover while soldiers drove bulldozers that allowed gunmen to move toward protesters. Soldiers were also stationed at the exits and entrances to the sit-in. The entire operation was overseen by Sisi, who at the time was minister of defense, general commander of the armed forces, chair of the SCAF, and deputy prime minister for security affairs.[97]

Defections and Dissenting Voices within Tamarod Leadership

After the Rabaa massacre, Mona Seleem, one of the cofounders of Tamarod, drafted a Statement of Principles. The purpose of the statement was to bring Tamarod back on track—this included condemning Rabaa and rejecting military rule. The statement referred to June 30 as a "popular revolutionary wave" and declared Tamarod's support for the "road map" that Sisi announced. However, the statement also called for a fact-finding committee and investigation into what happened in the dispersal of the Rabaa sit-in. Finally, the statement also declared that "no one is above law even if he is accomplishing a mission in a critical time" and that Tamarod wanted to prevent the "return of the repressive state."[98] The statement never saw the light of day.

Seleem then confronted Mahmoud Badr personally on September 30, 2013. They were longtime friends and had attended many protests together over the years. She again asked him to distance himself from the military. However, he refused. Although he had attended protests and chanted against military rule in the past, she could not convince him to publicly criticize the military's actions after Rabaa. He had become a different person. The next day, on October 1, 2013, she left Tamarod permanently. She was not the only founding member of Tamarod who became critical of the military's actions at Rabaa. Moheb Doss and Waleed El-Masry also disagreed with what they perceived as the opportunism of Mahmoud Badr, Hassan Shaheen, and Mohamed Abdel Aziz. These dissenting voices, however, were largely drowned out by that of Badr, who had risen to prominence, especially in the pro-state media, in part because of his willingness to cooperate with the state apparatus. Seleem withdrew from Tamarod without explanation and never published the statement. A little over a month later, in November 2013, Doss and others held a press conference at the Syndicate of Commerce, demanding that certain members of Tamarod should be investigated for corruption.[99] They then joined the protests on Talaat Harb Square, which were against the Protest Law—a key piece of legislation in the reconsolidation of the old regime. In the spring of 2014, however, two other founding members of Tamarod, Hassan Shaheen and Mohamed Abdel Aziz, essentially defected from Tamarod by publicly endorsing Hamdeen Sabahi in the presidential elections and not Sisi.

Defections and Dissenting Voices within Tamarod Outside Cairo

Seleem, one of the few female cofounders of Tamarod, was also the first one within the small circle of Tamarod leaders who began to oppose the military's crackdown and insisted that Tamarod should continue advocating for the demands of the January 25 Revolution. However, her dissenting voice was silenced and she withdrew. Many of the Tamarod branches outside Cairo were not silenced. The table below lists some of the critical campaigns that emerged within Tamarod branches all across Egypt. Outside the capital, Tamarod activists were less co-opted and less under the control of the state.

Tamarod Outside Cairo and the Emergence of Opposition to Sisi	
Governorate	Campaign critical of the military-backed regime or dissolution of Tamarod branch to "rejoin the side of the revolution."
Alexandria	*Already in May 2013 Tamarod split into two branches, one in favor and another against the regime.*[100]
Aswan	*Campaign in February 2014 against Sisi running for president.*[101]

Tamarod Outside Cairo and the Emergence of Opposition to Sisi	
Port Said	*Campaign criticizing Rabaa and Nahda massacres. Support for left-wing candidate Khaled Ali as president.*[102]
Minya	*Campaign "Wake up Mr President before the people turn on you" in September 2016.*[103]
Tanta	*Ahmed El Gammal, one of the leaders of Tamarod in Tanta, issued a critical statement.*[104]
Assiut	*The coordinator of the Assiut branch was summoned by security officials soon after June 30, and the Tamarod branch in Assiut essentially disappeared.*[105]
Mahalla	*Dr. Mohamed Awad, the Tamarod coordinator from Mahalla, was offered a position in the Ministry of Health, but refused as he did not want to support the new regime.*
Ismailia	*In November 2013 the admins of the Tamarod Ismailia Facebook page announced they were dissolving the movement, deleting the page, and rejoining the side of the revolution.*[106]
Matrouh	*In November 2013 the admins of the Tamarod Matrouh Facebook page announced they were dissolving the movement, deleting the page, and rejoining the side of the revolution.*[107]
Kafr El Sheikh	*In November 2013 the admins of the Tamarod Kafr El Sheikh Facebook page announced they were dissolving the movement, deleting the page, and rejoining the side of the revolution.*[108]

Furthermore, in November 2013 the Tamarod offices in Alexandria, Ismailia, and Suez all accused the Cairo branch of Tamarod of being traitors and spies. In short, Tamarod—the group most responsible for bringing about the fall of Morsi—had now turned against Sisi. As Ketchley has shown, Tamarod was elite-facilitated. However, as I have outlined here, it was never entirely under the control of those elites.[109] On the contrary, Tamarod was confronted with the same dilemmas and internal divisions that many grassroots social movements face. Some Tamarod supporters were co-opted by elite actors, but many more were not.

The Protest Law and Crackdown against April 6

The regime had unleashed a massive and unprecedented level of violence against the Muslim Brotherhood, culminating in the Rabaa and Nahda sit-ins. After issuing a warning that Tamarod should demobilize, the regime then successfully co-opted a few of the key leaders of Tamarod, in particular Badr. Other activist networks among the secular opposition remained intact. The regime turned against them next. This included targeting the very same people who had demanded and brought about the downfall of Morsi. If the ouster of Morsi had been a military coup, or a "popularly backed" military coup, the military would have treated the activists who supported the coup as allies rather than enemies. I have argued, however, that Morsi's ouster was a coup from below or a people's coup. This meant that the erstwhile allies of the military were treated as enemies. In other words, the military viewed any mobilization within society— even by those who supported the removal of Morsi—as a potential threat to their authority. This necessitated a crackdown that was unprecedented in the level of ferocity in modern Egyptian history.

The Muslim Brotherhood represented a threat to the regime because they had won a majority of the seats in parliament and had also won the presidential elections. The secular opposition did not control any institutions of government. However, they had displayed an uncanny ability to stage massive demonstrations to unseat those in power. They are also the ones who spearheaded protests and gave birth to new activist groups that specifically challenged the SCAF, which was led by Field Marshal Tantawi. Finally, many of these groups had expanded their networks, growing in terms of both their membership base and confidence in their ability to challenge the regime. This is why they too threatened the military and needed to be brought to heel. To repress them, the state opted for a different strategy.[110]

The Protest Law seems to have been their weapon of choice. Issued in November 2013, this law gave the Interior Ministry the right to ban public gatherings of more than 10 people. This draconian law was clearly an attempt to curtail any further street protests—which, as I have argued throughout the book, had been the most effective means of challenging all three successive governments under Mubarak, the SCAF, and Morsi. The new military-backed regime under Mansour aimed to take away the most effective tool of nonstate actors: their ability to gather in public and protest.

The Protest Law was the centerpiece of authoritarian legislation passed under Mansour. After Sisi became president, the crackdown expanded from activists to the civil society at large. As will be discussed in the next chapter, this period was accompanied by further repressive laws, including the NGO Law, the

Terrorism Law, the Military Courts Law, an amendment to the Penal Code, and a new draft Trade Unions Law and Labor Law.[111]

In retrospect, it almost appears like a trap: a court issues an order banning protests; activists come out to protest the Protest Law; and then they are easily rounded up, arrested, and given prison sentences ranging from three years to life in prison. Some of the leading secular activists and human rights defenders who were arrested under the Protest Law in late November or early December 2013 included Ahmed Maher, Mohamed Adel, Ahmed Douma, and Alaa Abdel Fattah.[112]

In short order, virtually the entire leadership of April 6 was arrested. The fortunes of April 6 are illustrative of the roller-coaster known as "the revolution." In early 2011, April 6 was not only celebrated by the many Egyptians who took part in the revolution but also by those who were treated with aplomb by the SCAF. Sisi himself, as a representative of the SCAF, met with Ahmed Maher and other members of April 6. For a fleeting moment in time, the revolutionary youth were treated as dignitaries to be respected. At the same time, however, the state spied on them. According to members of the political bureau of April 6, the youth movement had suffered from infiltration by informants (*amngeya*), especially after 2011. After the ouster of Mubarak, the April 6 movement expanded into all of Egypt's 27 governorates.[113] Perhaps as a normal corollary of such rapid expansion, the movement also divided into two wings over internal disagreements about when to hold elections. One wing called themselves the "Democratic Front" because they wanted elections to be held earlier, while the other wing was referred to as the "Ahmed Maher Front" because they wanted to allow more time for new members to be brought into the organization before holding elections.

Soon April 6 fell afoul of the SCAF. In July 2011 the SCAF issued Declaration #69 in which they declared that April 6 was an enemy of the state.[114] Sisi held meetings with Maher and other leading members of April 6. In these private meetings, Sisi allegedly told Maher that not all members of the SCAF agreed with the decision to declare April 6 an enemy of the state.[115] Whether there were genuine differences within the SCAF regarding April 6, or Sisi was just trying to play the "good cop" in order to maintain open channels of communication with leading members of April 6, may be impossible to discern. What is clear, however, is that this strategy backfired as the group witnessed a surge in membership immediately after the SCAF attempted to criminalize them. Despite infiltration by *amngeya* and internal divisions, April 6 kept going strong. According to a member of the political bureau, this attempt to ban April 6 failed because "the revolution was still happening."[116] After the ouster of Morsi, however, the previously failed attempts at state repression could be successfully implemented.

In March 2011, the SCAF issued a decree that attempted to ban protests and strikes, but it could not be implemented, as activists continued to call for *millioneya* and people continued to heed their call.[117] In other words, in 2011, the attempt to ban protests simply could not be implemented. The attempt to criminalize April 6 backfired and only made the group more popular among the youth.

In the aftermath of the ouster of Morsi, however, both of these tactics of repression could be implemented with a vengeance. The Protest Law was no longer an impotent decree but was harshly enforced. It became very difficult, if not impossible, to stage large street protests. Even small protests often ended either in deadly violence or in the arrest of activists. Then in April 2014 the April 6 youth movement was—this time successfully—declared a banned organization, accused of espionage and defaming Egypt's image abroad. The types of state repression that were impossible in 2011 could be carried out with gusto by 2013 and 2014.

Finally, there were a number of members of April 6 who were killed, including Ahmed Mansour,[118] Gaber Salah "Gika,"[119] Abul Hassan Ibrahim,[120] and Ahmed Al Masry.[121] However, according to a leading April 6 activist, they were not specifically targeted as members of April 6 but were simply "in the wrong place at the wrong time." By contrast, the state explicitly targeted members of the Muslim Brotherhood in the massacres at Rabaa, Nahda, the Republican Guards, and elsewhere.

However, the youth movement had survived despite all this during the tumultuous period from January 2011 until November 2013. During the first year after the ouster of Morsi, the state changed its strategies of repression. The arrest of its leadership and then banning of the organization dealt a severe blow to the ability of April 6 to continue to mobilize.

In an interview in December 2016, a member of the political bureau said that he believed their best period was under Morsi. This was not because they had no problems. In the spring of 2013, Maher had been arrested and was held for a day in detention. His comrades in April 6 protested his arrest and he was quickly released. This was quite an accomplishment. Not only was Maher released but also, as he remarked, "We managed to protest in front of President Morsi's house, and then we went home. No one was arrested."[122]

When Maher was released from prison in January 2017, he was released on probation for another three years. When I met him a few months after that, he was required to report to the police station every day at 6 p.m., where he was kept overnight until 6 a.m. In other words, he was really only half-free. During the day he could enjoy some freedom, but at night he had to return to his prison cell.

Other Secular Opposition Groups and Independent Activists

It was not only April 6 that was targeted by the Protest Law. A number of other leading activists and human rights defenders who belonged to an assortment of political parties or opposition groups were also arrested under Mansour. These included Ahmed Douma, a member of the Egyptian Popular Current; Alaa Abdel Fattah and Sanaa Seif, both members of the No Military Trials group; Yara Sallam, a lawyer and researcher at EIPR; Hany El-Gamal, a member of the Dostour Party; and Mahienour El-Massry, a lawyer and former member of the Revolutionary Socialists. Many were arrested around the same time, in late November or early December 2013. Some of them were arrested at protests, while others were arrested from their homes.

A number of the antimilitarist opposition groups that were discussed in chapter 4 and earlier in this chapter had already ceased their activities. For example, Kazeboon had not actively organized film screenings since late 2011. The No Military Trials group continued to work, albeit on a smaller scale. Mosireen also continued to work. However, as protests declined in size and the public space became increasingly closed to any form of activism, there were fewer and fewer protests—or any public events really—for the Mosireen activists to film. The We are all Khaled Said Facebook page stopped posting on July 3, 2013—the very same day Morsi was ousted.

Arrest and Imprisonment of Select Secular Activists and Human Rights Defenders because of Protest Law		
Date of arrest	Name	Political affiliation
November 28, 2013	Alaa Abdel Fattah[123]	Independent activist, member of No Military Trials Group
November 30, 2013	Ahmed Maher[124]	Founding member of April 6
December 2, 2013	Loay El Kahwagi[125]	Independent activist
December 20, 2013	Ahmed Douma[126]	Member of Egyptian Popular Current
December 28, 2013	Ayat Hamada	Member of the Revolution Road Coalition

January 25, 2014	Khaled El-Sayed[127]	Former Revolutionary Socialist and member of the Justice and Freedom Youth movement
April 12, 2014	Mahienour El-Massry[128]	Lawyer, former member of the Revolutionary Socialists, independent activist
June 21, 2014	Yara Sallam[129]	Lawyer and Researcher at Egyptian Initiative for Personal Rights
June 21, 2014	Sanaa Seif[130]	Member of No Military Trials Group
November 26, 2014	Hany El-Gamal[131]	El Dostor Party

As Table 6.1 illustrates, during the first wave of the counterrevolution, the moderate and radical wing of the anti-Morsi coalition, consisting of liberals, April 6, independent activists, and Tamarod, had been eliminated from the political scene. During the second wave of the counterrevolution, cracks began to emerge even within the conservative wing of the anti-Morsi coalition.

University Students

In contrast to the other groups discussed here, university students do not necessarily share a common set of political beliefs. They do, however, by virtue of their age alone, represent the youth of Egypt—who were overrepresented in the mass protests that brought down Mubarak in 2011.[132] As university students, they are also the most well-educated demographic. Furthermore, the gathering together in public of any group of 10 people or more was prohibited by the November 2013 Protest Law, making the normal operation of universities, where thousands of young people meet on a daily basis during the academic year, a potentially subversive endeavor. The fear of student gatherings was illustrated by the fact that the beginning of the academic year was postponed in the fall of 2013 in all universities across Egypt until September 21.[133] Al-Azhar University was not reopened until October 20.[134] The spring of the academic

Table 6.1 Repression of parts of the anti-Morsi coalition during first wave of the counterrevolution

Anti-Morsi Coalition						
Radical		Moderate			Conservative	
April 6[X]	Anti-SCAF groups[X]	Independent Leftists[X]	Tamarod[X]	Independent Liberals[X]	National Salvation Front	Al Azhar, Coptic Church	NDP, old regime	Military, police

X indicates that these groups had been arrested or targeted by state repression year 2013–2014 was postponed from February 8 to March 8, 2014 for Al-Azhar university.[135]

And then, one day before the beginning of the fall semester, Gaber Nassar, the president of Cairo University, announced that the student dormitories would remain closed, apparently out of concerns that students could organize themselves in the dormitories outside the supervision of faculty, staff, or campus security officers. Closing the dormitories would mean that students from outside Cairo would not be able to begin the academic year unless they could afford other accommodations outside the university.

Public universities—like many institutions and aspects of political life in Egypt—are highly centralized and governed by the same bylaws. The minister of higher education has the ability to intervene in many aspects of university life, including postponing the beginning of the academic year all across the country, subjecting student groups to the same bylaws and regulations, and overseeing and postponing or even entirely canceling student union elections. The centralized nature of public universities made it relatively easy for the state to suppress student political activity on campuses throughout Egypt. According to a university bylaw from 1979, students are not allowed to organize in political parties on campus. However, it was common practice for student groups to form unofficial ties to political parties off campus. This was why administrative decisions by the university presidents were issued to ban political parties from working on campus.[136] During the first year after the ouster of Morsi, from July 2013 until June 2014, students were targeted in an attempt to prevent protests on campus and student union elections. As I will describe in the next chapter, after Sisi was elected, the regime strategy expanded beyond its focus on students to target outspoken faculty members and intellectuals. The regime also passed laws that allowed Sisi to appoint loyalists in the highest positions of leadership in public universities all across the land.

Between January 2011 and June 2013, university campuses were relatively protected. Students could stage sit-ins or protests on their campuses and not fear for their safety. The flourishing of student political activity spread across both public and private universities. In September 2012, students protested at the AUC, at the German University in Cairo, and at Nile University. In order to protest rising tuition fees, students at AUC escalated their tactics and blockaded all gates—preventing students, faculty, and staff from entering campus.

Also, student union elections represented an opportunity for students to vote and run for office. The elections of March 2013 were described by Mohamed Saad, who was vice president of the Student Union at the Faculty of Economic and Political Sciences at Cairo University, as "maybe the greatest elections ever held in history of universities in Egypt."[137] This was because of the high level of participation among students and the official participation of political movements from across the political spectrum.

This vibrant campus life changed after the coup—in particular in public universities. State repression targeted students from different political backgrounds. A group called "Students against the Coup" was formed during the sit-in at Rabaa in order to protest the ouster of Morsi.[138] Prior to July 2013, there had been Muslim Brotherhood student groups at various universities. However, after the coup, the link between the leadership of the Muslim Brotherhood and the student groups was lost. For this reason, Students against the Coup (SAC) organized themselves independently, without any political or financial ties to the leadership of the Muslim Brotherhood.[139] The group was most active at Cairo University, Ain Shams, and Al-Azhar.

As it became increasingly dangerous to hold protests on public squares, students opted instead to hold sit-ins and marches inside their university campuses. Security forces followed them. On November 28, 2013 Mohamed Reda, a student with no political affiliation, was shot and killed at Cairo University by security forces.[140] A number of student activists described this event as a turning point, as it led to large protests by both secular and Islamist students. A few days after his death, on December 1, students rallied, with tens of thousands protesting—in defiance of the Protest Law passed just a week earlier.[141] However, the majority stayed inside the confines of Cairo University—only SAC left the campus and headed to Tahrir. Even Gaber Nassar, the president of Cairo University, took part in the demonstrations. This show of solidarity did not, however, lead to any concessions on the part of the state. In January 2014, three more students were killed by security forces inside their campuses.[142] Internal divisions between the various student groups also persisted. Students affiliated with April 6 and the Revolutionary Socialists wanted the SAC to give up some of their demands and mottos regarding Rabaa and the ouster of President Morsi. This attempt at unifying the student movement failed, however.

In March 2014, student union elections were canceled all across Egypt. State repression not only targeted the students who were protesting the ouster of Morsi but also *prevented normal student activity*, such as the holding of student union elections. According to a report by the Association for Freedom of Thought and Expression (AFTE), there were 1,181 students detained, 21 students killed, and 65 students referred to military trials between 2013 and 2014. As Graph 6.1 makes clear, the vast number of arrests happened during the academic year 2013–2014—in other words, during the first year of regime consolidation under Mansour.

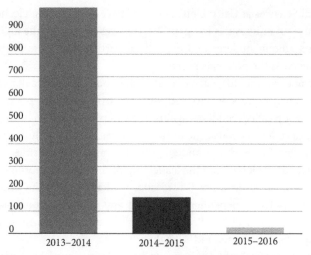

Source: Association for Freedom of Thought and Expression By Mai Shams El-Din

Graph 6.1 Arrests of students.

Although the number of arrests dropped in the subsequent two years, the number of students who are imprisoned is still considerable—so much so that some student activists have dedicated themselves to pressuring the university to ensure that students are allowed to study and take their exams while in prison. In Tanta University, one young student said that so many of his friends had been arrested that he feared that if they languished in prison without being able to take their exams, their whole future would be ruined.[143]

Then in June 2014, very soon after Sisi was elected president, he introduced a law that allowed him to directly appoint university presidents and deans, as will be discussed in the following chapter.

The United States Determines There Is No Need to Make a Determination if the Ouster of Morsi Was a "Coup"

As I argued in the previous chapter, there were indications that the authorities in Egypt wanted to call the presidential elections in favor of Ahmed Shafik in 2012. The US demand to respect the outcome of the elections, the first free and fair elections in Egypt's history, may have contributed to the decision to call the elections in favor of the candidate who had in fact won: Mohamed Morsi. Once Morsi had been removed from power, however, the United States almost immediately accommodated itself to the new reality. There is no indication that US officials had withdrawn their support for President Morsi prior to July 3. On the contrary, of the four pillars of the Egyptian state, US support for Morsi was the last to crumble. Therefore, I argue that the United States did not play any direct role in Morsi's ouster, nor had they even really hedged their support for him prior to July 3 as they had begun to do with Mubarak. However, *after* Morsi was ousted, US actions—and inactions—were important. While US senators John McCain and Lindsey Graham referred to the events of July 3 as a "coup," officials in the Obama administration avoided such terminology. According to a former member of the State Department's Policy Planning Staff, the word "coup" was even avoided in internal US government documents.[144] Secretary of State John Kerry went so far as to claim that the Egyptian generals were "restoring democracy" when they removed the first freely elected president. "The military was asked to intervene by millions and millions of people," Kerry said, and furthermore "the military did not take over, to the best of our judgement, so far."[145] The remarks were made during a visit to Pakistan, a country that had experienced four military coups since the 1950s. However, in my interviews with US officials who served in the Obama administration at the time, they would often voluntarily describe the removal of Morsi as a "coup" without any prompting. A few have even published articles or books in which they refer to his removal as a coup.

In his memoir *The Back Channel* William Burns, who served as Deputy Secretary of State from July 2011–2014, wrote: "The military's actions clearly fit the classic definition of a coup, notwithstanding the considerable popular support for Sisi's decision."[146] Why then did the Obama administration refuse to call it that? Burns argued that cutting off aid, as required by law, would reduce the leverage that the United States had with Egypt and potentially alienate a chunk of the population that enthusiastically supported Morsi's removal. It would appear that one reason the United States declined to call the removal a "coup" was its alleged popularity with the Egyptian people. As I have documented, what was actually popular were the mass protests and the demand for early elections, which is what the Tamarod petition called for, not a military intervention or return to military rule. The popularity of the Egyptian military had in fact declined significantly since 2011. As illustrated in the table earlier in the chapter, a number of the Egyptian activist groups and political parties that took part in the protests distinguished between the events of June 30, which they described as a revolutionary wave, and those of July 3, which they saw as a coup. In other words, the size of the mass protests, and perhaps also the fact that Sisi announced Morsi's removal while surrounded by both military and civilian leaders, persuaded American officials that this was not a coup or at least not to label it as such. On the surface at least, it did not look like a military coup.

What I have argued, however, is that this is precisely why we need to expand our conceptual vocabulary to account for different types of military coups. Just as we are capable of distinguishing among different kinds of revolutions, we need to be able to distinguish among different types of coups. I suggest that the removal of Morsi is best understood as a coup from below: one that emerged from within civil society rather than the military apparatus and unleashed massive street protests, thereby toppling Morsi, but potentially also threatening the organs of the state concerned with law and order who wanted to ensure that the protests ended quickly so as not to spiral out of control.

What had a bigger impact on the United States' thinking and policy toward Egypt was not the coup itself but the subsequent massacres. It was not until October 2013, after the Rabaa/Nahda massacres, that the United States suspended four big-ticket weapons systems—Apache attack helicopters, F-16 fighter jets, M1A1 Abrams battle tank kits, and Harpoon missiles—pending "credible progress" toward some form of democratization. In his memoir *The Back Channel*, Burns wrote: "Lawyers and those of us pretending to be lawyers edited and reedited formulas we thought could finesse the problem. Finally, we split the difference. . . . Looking back, we should have simply given a straight answer, called the coup a coup, and then worked with Congress to avoid the blunt tool of complete aid suspension. . . . Instead, to make clear his displeasure with the coup that wasn't a coup, and the subsequent steps Sisi took against the Muslim Brotherhood, the president suspended shipment of certain weapons systems, including F-16s and M1A1 tanks, which were never essential to Egypt's main security priority—fighting a growing Islamist insurgency in the Sinai."[147]

American official or member of Congress	Reference to 2013 removal of Morsi as a coup
John McCain, Senator [R-AZ] and member of Senate Foreign Relations Committee Lindsey Graham, Senator [R-SC] and member of Senate Foreign Relations Committee	"[T]he circumstances of [Morsi's] removal was a coup. This was a transition of power not by the ballot box."[148]
Howard Berman, congressman [D-CA], 1983–2013	"[T]he executive branch gets to decide whether it's a coup or not. Under the plain meaning rule, there was a coup."[149]

American official or member of Congress	Reference to 2013 removal of Morsi as a coup
Patrick Leahy, Senator [D-VT]	"[O]ur law is clear: U.S. aid is cut off when a democratically elected government is deposed by military coup or decree."[150]
William Burns, Deputy Secretary of State, 2011–2014	"[B]y any objective measure it was a coup."[151]
Andrew Miller, Director for Egypt and Israel Military Issues at the National Security Council, 2014–2017	"Sisi, who as defense minister led the 2013 coup."[152]
Amy Hawthorne, State Department official who focused on Egypt, 2011–2012	"Sisi, who as defense minister led the 2013 coup"[153]

The recent literature on military coups has highlighted that there is some variation among coups that happened during the Cold War and after. As Oisin Tansey has shown, in the post–Cold War era, coups were more likely to be followed by elections within a few years than coups that took place during the Cold War. This has led some scholars including Ozan Varol to argue that coups could potentially lead to democratization or at least to cause a rupture by introducing elections into what were previously authoritarian regimes.[154]

In refusing to call his ouster a "coup," and accepting the new status quo, the Obama administration thereby acquiesced in the military's intervention. However, there were also limits to their willingness to go along with the military's new line. Despite prodding from Egyptian officials, at the time of writing, neither the United States nor the EU has agreed to officially designate the Muslim Brotherhood as a terrorist organization.[155] In contrast to his predecessor Tantawi, Sisi had spent a year studying at the US Army War College in Pennsylvania, where he wrote a 12-page thesis on "Democracy in the Middle East." Because of this, one might have expected that US military officers would have established closer ties with Sisi than Tantawi, and that Sisi would have been better versed in American notions about civilian control of the military. The Pentagon likes to claim that their training programs help forge closer ties between US and Egyptian officers, and even help to instill democratic values in foreign officers who work in authoritarian countries. Clearly, Sisi's yearlong stint at the US Army War College did little of either.

The United States provides training not only to the Egyptian military but also to the Egyptian police. As part of a project that lasted from 2007 until 2013, the INL provided training to 550 Egyptian law enforcement officials. The website of the State Department's International Narcotics and Law Enforcement Affairs (INL) claims they were introduced to "modern principles of community policing." Even during the month of the coup, in July 2013, INL sponsored a study tour for 10 Egyptian police officers who were affiliated with the Violence against Women unit in the Ministry of Interior.[156]

International Actors in Egypt in the Summer of 2013

During the summer of 2013, the United States, the European Union, the African Union, the United Arab Emirates (UAE), and Qatar all sent high-level envoys to Egypt in an attempt to mediate the crisis. Despite their concerted efforts, these international mediators failed to prevent the Rabaa and Nahda massacres. Why?

1. The United States had sent a respected, high-level foreign service officer, William Burns, the Deputy Secretary of State, to help mediate the crisis. Together with Bernardino Leon, EUSR to the Southern Mediterranean, he visited Khairat al-Shater in the Tora prison in an attempt to find a peaceful resolution to the standoff between the Muslim Brotherhood and the interim government. However, it is not clear that all branches of the US government were sending the same message. Hagel and Kerry were not equally emphatic as President Obama in delivering the message. Prior to the coup, there were warnings, but no real threat of sanctions if the military would intervene. The review of US military aid to Egypt began in October 2013 after both the coup and the series of massacres. Although some aid was withheld, it was too little, too late.

2. Despite internal disagreement within the 28 member states of the EU, the EU had decided that the removal of Morsi was not a coup. Catherine Ashton was the first non-Egyptian allowed to visit Morsi after he was deposed. Her main concern was to assure that he was still

alive and in good health. In line with the position of US officials, she did not publicly call for Morsi to be reinstated.

3. The African Union (AU) suspended Egypt after the ouster of Morsi. The AU High-Level Panel for Egypt was led by former Malian President Alpha Oumar Konare, who insisted that the suspension was not meant "to punish Egypt" but was part of the AU's procedures. The AU delegation was allowed to visit Morsi but offered little criticism.

4. The UAE and Saudi Arabia began pouring money into Egypt within days of Morsi's ouster. Although the UAE was taking part in negotiations to resolve the crisis between the military and the Muslim Brotherhood, they were financially backing the interim government.

Sisi Is Elected President and an Undercover Agent Blows His Own Cover

The elections in May 2014 were a spectacle to behold. They were also a turning point, both for Sisi and the police state, as I witnessed myself in Dokki.

In May 2014, presidential elections took place between Abdel Fattah El-Sisi and Hamdeen Sabahi. Some of my friends joked that Egyptians could now choose between a Nasserist or a Nasserist. The outcome of the election was a foregone conclusion. In an op-ed published on May 5, I claimed: "In less than a month, May 26–27, Field Marshal Abdel Fattah El-Sisi will be installed as president of Egypt, and it will be called an election."[157] Still, I thought it would be interesting to see what would happen. I attended the polling station where Hamdeen Sabahi cast his vote in the middle-class neighborhood of Dokki. There was a long row of television cameras pointed straight at the entrance to the polling station, representing both the Egyptian and international media. With so many journalists and foreigners milling around, I did not think I would attract any particular attention. However, a plainclothes security officer began interrogating me and the Egyptian journalist who I was with. Although one would have thought that the regime would welcome journalists specifically covering the district where Sabahi was casting his vote—the fact that Sisi had someone to run against him was after all what was necessary in order to make the spectacle look like an election. But for whatever reason this particular security agent thought it would be better if my friend and I were not there. He began inquiring about who we were, where we were from, and what we were doing. We told him we were there for the elections, like everyone else. He told us we should leave. When we did not vanish as he wished, he decided he had to up his intimidation tactics and bluntly told us that he was working for the Mukhabarat. While I was accustomed to easily identifiable Mukhabarat lurking around Cairo, this was the first time one had openly identified himself as such. It was quite bizarre—equal parts disturbing and ridiculous. After all, he had just blown his cover. It was a sign that the security agencies had fully regained whatever confidence they had lost, but were not necessarily deploying their regained strength to their best advantage.

Why this particular security agent wanted to scare us into leaving the polling station we will never know. Perhaps it was due to the much lower turnout than expected. Voting had to be extended for a third day because so few people came out to vote. In a further attempt to encourage people to vote, Tuesday was suddenly declared a public holiday. However, voters still stayed away. Watching TV with a friend in the evening, we laughed as media personalities like Lamis Al-Hadidi and Amr Diab screamed into their cameras in an attempt to boost the number of voters: "Fein el shaab??" (Where are the people??) "A'yzeen eh??" (What do you want??)."[158] Ahmed Abdallah, a member of April 6, explained: "The Egyptian people have realised that whoever comes to power by tanks will not leave through elections—so they are boycotting it."[159] Sisi officially won 97 percent of the vote.

The Obama administration apparently viewed the election of Sisi as an indication that Egypt's democratic transition was back on track. In his remarks in late July 2013 cited earlier, Kerry had pointed out that the military had not taken over "so far." When that happened with the election of Sisi, instead of withholding or hedging US support, Kerry promised Apaches. On June 22, 2014, in a joint press conference with the Egyptian foreign minister, Kerry stated: "We will work that out, and I am confident that we will be able to ultimately get the full amount of aid for precisely the reasons that I describe—because it is strategic and it is important for us to be able to work together. . . . I am confident . . . that the Apaches will come and that they will come very, very soon."[160]

Hours after Kerry left Cairo, a court sentenced three AlJazeera journalists to jail. Peter Greste and Mohamed Fahmy received 7 years; Baher Mohamed received 10 years.[161] While the timing of the court decision may be coincidental, it is hard not to see how the failure of the Obama administration to designate the removal of Morsi as a coup, and their embrace of the military general who removed him, was at least partially responsible for the regime's continuing crackdown.

The election of Sisi represents another opportunity to revisit Tamarod. As I have argued in the previous chapter and earlier in this chapter, Tamarod emerged as a grassroots movement to unseat Morsi—it was not, as some have suggested, purely an artifact of the deep state. Furthermore, Tamarod did not explicitly endorse the coup or even a temporary military intervention. During the first year after the ouster of Morsi, the military began to reassert itself. Mahmoud Badr, one of the cofounders of Tamarod, supported Sisi, but many of the other founding members of Tamarod publicly endorsed Hamdeen Sabahi, rather than Sisi, as indicated in the table below.

Leader of Tamarod	Endorsement during presidential elections in May 2014 (public or private)	Subsequent political activity
Mahmoud Badr	Sisi (public)[162]	Attempted to turn Tamarod into a political party in December 2014, but his application was rejected.
Mohamed Abdel Aziz	Hamdeen Sabahi (public)	Appointed to the National Council on Human Rights in September 2013.
Hassan Shaheen	Hamdeen Sabahi (public)	Supported Sabahi's campaign for president, then later joined the Popular Current Party.
Mona Seleem	Hamdeen Sabahi (public)[163]	Withdrew from Tamarod on October 1, 2013.
Moheb Doss	Hamdeen Sabahi	Arrested on January 6, 2014 and held for approximately 70 days, accused of belonging to the pro-revolution activist group "Januarians."
Waleed El-Masry	Hamdeen Sabahi	Arrested on January 2, 2017 while taking part in a protest against the transfer of the Tiran and Sanafir islands to Saudi Arabia. He was subsequently released.

A Coup from Below

Was Tamarod a grassroots movement or product of the deep state? Because Morsi was overthrown, and eventually replaced by the military, a number of observers have concluded that the movement to oust Morsi must have been the product of the military's machinations or some other actor within the shadowy network known as the "deep state." I argue, however, that Tamarod was neither created nor took orders from state actors but was in fact a social movement with a broad social base that included both revolutionary and counterrevolutionary actors prior to July 3. Afterwards, Tamarod fragmented along those same lines, with only a few key figures co-opted by the state. Only one of the leaders publicly endorsed Sisi in the presidential elections, while many more endorsed Sabahi. I summarize my arguments again below:

- To assume that the millions of Egyptians who protested on June 30 were acting on behalf of or as puppets controlled by the deep state is to deny them their agency. As I witnessed myself on June 30, the vast majority of people who were protesting had handmade signs or banners. They were often even handwritten rather than computer-printed. The mobilization of millions or even just tens of thousands of people is impossible to control entirely from the top-down.
- In the spring of 2013, Tamarod spread across Egypt quickly. However, in the governorates outside Cairo, branches of Tamarod were established in a haphazard manner, suggesting that this was the work of local activists rather than coordinated from above.
- Serious divisions emerged within Tamarod between those who favored the military and those who were more critical of the state. For example, in Alexandria the divisions emerged in May 2013. These types of divisions are typical of social movements, especially during the period when social movements expand. Such political divisions are less likely to emerge, and much less likely to become public in secretive networks characteristic of the deep state.
- On July 3, the very same day of the ouster of Morsi, the military was already signaling to Tamarod that they needed to demobilize and that now "there is no opposition." If Tamarod had been controlled by the state, it could have easily been demobilized or controlled after June 30. However, this did not happen. Instead, after July 3, Tamarod split further into different factions.

- In the presidential elections in May 2014, the majority of leaders of Tamarod did not endorse Sisi. Instead, Hassan Shaheen, Mohamed Abdel Aziz, Moheb Doss, and Mona Seleem publicly endorsed the Nasserist candidate Sabahi in the presidential elections in May 2014 rather than Sisi, the former minister of defense who ousted Morsi.
- Some Tamarod branches began to criticize Sisi and the military, including those in Alexandria, Aswan, Port Said, and Minya. Tamarod branches in Ismailia, Matrouh, and Kafr Sheikh were dissolved in November 2013 to join the side of the revolution.

Conclusion

In this chapter I've made three main arguments. First, I showed *how* the interim government under Mansour/Sisi paved the way for the military to return to power. In short, I demonstrated how the old regime reconsolidated itself. Second, I explained *why* and *when* each opposition group was targeted. Without claiming to open up the black box of regime intentions, I illustrate the *broad pattern of the crackdown*. Finally, I argue that the unleashing of an unprecedented level of state repression led to a *process of fragmentation* within Tamarod. While two key leaders in Cairo (Badr and Abdel Aziz) took the side of the new interim administration under Mansour, many more Tamarod leaders in the governorates all across Egypt became critical of the military. Many of the existing analyses of Tamarod end with the coup on July 3. However, by following their subsequent activities in the year following the coup, it becomes clear that, while they supported the removal of Morsi, the majority of Tamarod branches across Egypt did *not* endorse the massacres against the Muslim Brotherhood. Nor did they unequivocally support the return to military rule.

Regime Reconsolidation: A Civilian President and Civilian Prime Minister, but No Civilian Control of the Armed Forces

The civilian interim government installed after July 3, headed by Adly Mansour, paved the way for the military to return to power. While finalizing this manuscript in 2019, a number of Egyptians I interviewed about the period of Mansour would jokingly congratulate me on even remembering his name. Some activists described him as "cute." Others felt sorry for him because he was the interim president who—if he was remembered at all— would be known for presiding over the bloodiest period of modern Egyptian history. Were there any protest slogans about Mansour? No one, including myself, could recall having heard one. He was a civilian fig leaf. But he was not the only one.

There was also Prime Minister Hazem el-Beblawi. Prior to the Rabaa massacre, there was a meeting between Beblawi and a few leaders of the human rights organizations about the issue of dispersing the sit-ins. The head of one of these nongovernmental organizations (NGOs) asked Beblawi whether Sisi would consult him or seek his permission before security forces would move against the sit-ins. And although Beblawi was prime minister, he was not insulted by the question. At least, according to the NGO representative, he did not appear outwardly embarrassed, and responded by saying: "I asked him [Sisi] to inform me."[164] Even with a civilian interim president and a civilian prime minister, there was no civilian control over the armed forces of Egypt.

Furthermore, a few prominent so-called liberals were incorporated in the government of Mansour—albeit only temporarily. These included Mohamed El-Baradei as vice president, Ziad Bahaa El-Din as deputy prime minister, and Kamal Abu Eita as minister of manpower. In short, there was even a façade of liberalism on top of the civilian façade. However, all three of them were either dropped or quit prior to Sisi's election in June 2014. Even while they were in office, it is not clear they had any noticeable impact on the government. They were certainly not able to prevent any of the numerous violent crackdowns and massacres of civilians. As discussed earlier in the chapter, even El-Baradei, who claimed he did not want to exclude the Muslim Brotherhood from politics, did not personally meet with even one member of the Brotherhood while he was vice president.

Pattern and Timing of the First Wave of Counterrevolution

Eradicate the Muslim Brotherhood and Imprison the Secular Activists

The crackdown began by attempting to eradicate the Muslim Brotherhood through massacres unprecedented in scale in modern Egyptian history. Security forces killed over 900 Morsi supporters in cold-blooded confrontations. Other minions of the state worked to ensure that the Brotherhood's ideas could no longer be disseminated through blatant media censorship, including taking Islamist and Brotherhood-related channels off the air and stopping the publication of their newspapers. By December, the government officially declared the Muslim Brotherhood to be a terrorist organization. Even before this, however, the crackdown had already spread to the secular opposition, including those who supported the ouster of Morsi. The regime swiftly moved to targeting virtually every single opposition group—whether secular or Islamist.

In short, the timing of the crackdown first targeted Islamists, then the secular opposition. Why would the regime move against the secular opposition— including those who supported the ouster of Morsi? They had not won many seats in parliament, they did not control any government ministries, and they were not busy staging *millioneya* protests in the fall of 2013. I have argued that, during this first wave of regime reconsolidation, the authorities saw *any* group that had even the potential ability to mobilize across governorates—regardless of their political orientation—as a threat. This included secular opposition groups like April 6, independent activists with no organizational structure behind them but a large outreach on social media, apolitical groups such as the Ultras, university students, and even Tamarod. All of these groups had developed both formal and informal networks that spanned numerous governorates across the country; I argue this is the primary reason they were targeted. Even in the absence of long-established mass political parties, the regime felt threatened by the informal networks of solidarity that spanned the country. Perhaps ironically, the behavior of the regime in 2013–2014 confirmed the findings of my online survey in 2012. The majority of respondents believed that it was street protests that led to concessions being made—not political parties or other forms of pressure.

In order to reconsolidate itself, the regime had to liquidate not only the Muslim Brotherhood but also any group that could potentially challenge it in the future. The military did not remove Morsi so that it could establish a democratic or even a semidemocratic system where at least some (non-Brotherhood) political parties could compete for power. The army generals removed Morsi in order to reassert full control over the political system in Egypt. They knew they had to first regain control of the streets. This meant putting an end to the large street protests and sit-ins that had characterized the period of revolution from January 2011 until mid-2013. For a few months, students at both public and private universities maintained university campuses as spaces where protests could continue. However, the regime then moved to destroy these safe havens of nonviolent protests by regaining control of university campuses. A number of students were killed while peacefully protesting on their campuses.

The regime then began issuing draconian legislation. This included passage of the Protest Law, which allowed the regime to not only target continuing Brotherhood protests such as the SAC but also allowed the targeting of secular opposition. Many leading figures of both Islamist and secular opposition groups were arrested and imprisoned. Having arrested their leadership, the regime then moved toward criminalizing the opposition groups entirely—apparently in an attempt to banish them from any political activity and reassert the old regime's monopoly on politics. In December 2013, the Muslim Brotherhood was declared a terrorist organization. And in the spring of 2014, April 6 and the Ultras were declared banned groups.

While April 6 was the most prominent secular opposition youth movement, the Ultras were not officially a political group at all. The Ultras did, however, have the ability to mobilize their supporters across multiple governorates, and they had a history of openly taunting the police and other security forces. Hence both groups were banned. Students at public universities were also not necessarily aligned with any particular political group. However, the student movement was still seen as a potential threat for three reasons: (1) students had maintained university campuses as a safe place to protest; (2) they were organized nationwide through the student union; and (3) after the killing of Reda in November 2013, Islamist and secular students protested together in a rare (for the time) show of solidarity. The national student union was not banned, as was April 6 and the Ultras, but student union elections were canceled in 2014 all across Egypt. Killing students inside their universities destroyed the sense of security students once had. The university campus was no longer a safe haven.

The Political Fragmentation of Tamarod: How a Tool of the Regime Turned against the Regime

During the period of Mansour, many Tamarod branches in the governorates outside Cairo became critical of the military. The fact that Tamarod fragmented and shifted its political focus to becoming critical of the military is another indication that it was a grassroots social movement and not a puppet controlled by the deep state. In fact, only two members of Tamarod seem to have been "rewarded" or co-opted by the state: Badr and Abdel Aziz were offered positions in the NCHR. By contrast, Tamarod branches in Alexandria, Aswan, Port Said, Minya, Tanta, and Mahalla began campaigns that were in some way critical of the military. The branches in Ismailia, Matrouh, and Kafr El Sheikh announced that they were dissolving the movement and "rejoining the side of the revolution." Finally, a number of the founding members and leaders of Tamarod publicly endorsed Sabahi for president—not Sisi.

The ouster of Morsi took place because of the mobilization of millions of civilians and was therefore a coup from below or people's coup. Thus the crackdown targeted the people as well, not a rival faction within the military. It was the mass mobilization that had the potential to truly threaten the regime—perhaps even more than the Muslim Brotherhood itself—and this is what the crackdown aimed to stop. During the first phase of regime reconsolidation, protest activity first increased and then dropped off after passage of the Protest Law in November 2013.

This is the subject of the next chapter, to which we now turn.

Other Cases of Coups from Below?

In the year following the removal of President Morsi in Egypt, Thailand and Burkina Faso witnessed a similar confluence of events: mass protests by civilians that led to the removal of the president, a senior military officer taking power, and the instigation of a large-scale crackdown. Rather than "siding with the opposition" or representing a "democratic coup," the military oppressed the opposition, including those who supported the removal of the president, and prevented any further democratization. Turkey in 2016 saw a similar pattern, but the attempted removal of President Recep Tayyip Erdoğan was derailed and the coup attempt failed. A crackdown followed nonetheless, including purges of thousands of civilians and military officers. In what follows I will briefly discuss these three cases in a schematic way in order to draw out their similarities and differences to the Egyptian case.

Thailand 2014

Beginning in November 2013, Thailand witnessed large protests that were organized by the People's Democratic Reform Committee (PDRC) and led by Suthep Thaugsuban. These protests featured public calls for the removal of Prime Minister Yingluck Shinawatra, who had been democratically elected. During this period of political crisis and prolonged protests, which lasted approximately six months, the commander-in-chief of the Royal Thai Army, Prayut Chan-o-cha, claimed that the military was "neutral" and would not stage a coup. However, when Prime Minister Shinawatra was then ousted on May 7, 2014, General Prayut was immediately installed as prime minister. Broadly speaking, the political divide in Thailand is between a Bangkok elite and a movement led by the Shinawatras who have their power base in rural areas. The coup was immediately followed by a wave of repression. On May 20, martial law was declared. On the same day, Suthep Thaugsuban and other leaders of the

PDRC were jailed, although they led the protests that removed the prime minister. In other words, similar to Egypt, the military targeted not only their opponents but also those who were their erstwhile allies: the very people who supported the coup. A curfew was imposed and political gatherings were banned. Even political discussions or any criticism of the government were outlawed. Every Friday evening Prayut would address the Thai people in what he called "Returning Happiness to the People" speeches that were broadcast on national television. In 2018, four years after the coup, the police still regularly blocked protests from taking place. In February 2018, about 400 activists took part in an antigovernment protest; 50 of them were charged with sedition.[165]

Burkina Faso 2014

The Burkinabé Uprising began in October 2014, just a few months after the tumultuous events in Thailand that led to the ouster of the prime minister. In Burkina Faso, the movement was directed at the removal of President Blaise Compaoré, who had been in office for 27 years. It was organized by several groups including Balai Citoyen, a grassroots protest organization, and the Movement of the People for Progress (MPP), a political party that had been founded in January 2014. These were both civilian-led organizations. One of the cofounders of Balai Citoyen was the rapper Serge Bambara, and the founder of the Movement of the People for Progress (MPP) was Roch Marc Christian Kabore. On October 30, the parliament and the CDP party headquarters were set on fire. The following day, Compaoré resigned and army chief general Honore Traore took over. The removal of Compaoré was followed by a brief period of military rule, first under General Traore and then under Lieutenant Colonel Isaac Zida. Its brevity was due in part to pressure from the African Union. As in the case of Egypt, the African Union sent a delegation to Burkina Faso after the coup, stressing the importance of civilian rule. Michel Kafando became head of the transitional government, but his government was still under the influence of the military. The crackdown in Burkina Faso does not appear to have been as severe as in Egypt and Thailand, but in May 2015, Burkina Faso's Higher Council for Communication declared a three-month ban on live political broadcasts. In September 2015, there was an attempted coup aimed at removing both interim leaders, Zida and Kafando. During the coup attempt, the music studio of rapper Serge Bambara (who founded Balai Citoyen) was burnt down. The coup attempt was led by members of the Regiment of Presidential Security (RSP) and briefly installed General Gilbert Diendéré, who had been an aide to Compaoré. After a few days, interim President Kafando was reinstated and elections were held in November 2015. Roch Marc Christian Kabore ran as a candidate from the MPP. He was elected in the first round of voting, making him the first president of Burkina Faso without ties to the military. In contrast to Egypt and Thailand, in Burkina Faso the period of military rule was limited and, despite a second coup attempt, at the time of writing a civilian president remains in power. However, a 2018 report by Human Rights Watch, "By Day We Fear the Army, by Night the Jihadists," documents violations committed by the security forces and heavy-handed tactics they have used in response to the increased presence of armed Islamist groups in Burkina Faso.[166]

Turkey 2016

Like Egypt, Thailand, and Burkina Faso, the Republic of Turkey has had a long history of coups d'état that resulted in the removal of the chief executive. In July 2016, however, the attempted coup failed. This is not the only reason it does not fit the pattern of a coup from below. To be sure, Turkey had also witnessed a growing wave of protests against Erdoğan, with the Gezi Park protests often seen as a turning point. However, the Gezi protests took place in the summer of 2013, or three full years prior to the coup attempt, and were not characterized by public calls for Erdogan to step down or for the military to intervene. By contrast, in Egypt, Thailand, and Burkina Faso, the protests immediately preceded the coups and did include public calls for the president to step down or be removed. In Turkey, the coup plotters organized themselves secretly and did not disclose their intentions to the public. Instead of supporting the removal of Erdogan, civilian protesters in Turkey opposed the coup and risked their lives confronting the conspirators. Over 260 people were killed in clashes between civilians and security forces during the coup attempt. After thwarting the attempted putsch and regaining full control, Erdogan immediately declared a state of emergency. A large crackdown ensued that led to thousands of people being purged from the military and police. At the time of writing in summer 2019, or three years after the coup attempt, the government crackdown continues and targets both security officers and civilians. For these reasons, the coup attempt in Turkey in July 2016 does not fit the pattern of a coup from below: there were no public calls by civilians for the military to intervene, nor were there large protests demanding the ouster of Erdogan immediately prior to the coup attempt.[167]

Coups from Below					
	Public calls for removal of president by civilians	Large protests demanding removal of president by civilians immediately prior to ouster	Military removes president (successful coup)	Senior military officer assumes power within one year of ouster	Large-scale crackdown against civilians
Egypt 2013	Yes	Yes	Yes	Yes	Yes
Burkina Faso 2014	Yes	Yes	Yes	Yes	Yes
Thailand 2014	Yes	Yes	Yes	Yes	Yes
Turkey 2016	No	No	No	No	Yes

7

#تيران_وصنافير_مصرية
"Tiran and Sanafir are Egyptian!"

Second Wave of Counterrevolution: Sisi as President

(June 8, 2014–July 2018)

Second Phase of Counterrevolution *Attacking Civil Society and Criminalizing NGOs, Academia, Independent Media, and Minorities* *June 2014–June 2018*			
Civil Society *Target group*	*Mode of Repression* *In many cases security forces take action prior to legislation being issued to justify the action.*		*Outcome or Intended Outcome*
	Security Action	*Legislative Action*	
Nongovernmental Organizations (NGOs) • *Human rights organizations* • *Women's Rights Initiatives* • *Charities*	*Raids by armed security forces (beginning December 2011)* *Ban on receiving foreign funding* *Seizure of assets* *Arrests* *Imprisonment* *Travel ban* *Forced closure (both temporary and permanent)*	*NGO Law ratified by Sisi May 2017*	• *Eradicate independent civil society* • *Prevent human rights violations from being documented* • *Starve NGOs of funds necessary for work* • *Prevent NGOs from educating the public about women's rights*

Media • Television • Newspapers • Online news sites	State pressure to cancel widely viewed news and satire programs • Bassem Youssef, May 2014 • Yosri Fouda, September 2014 • Reem Maged, May 2015 Three AlJazeera journalists sentenced to prison terms of 7–10 years (June 2014) Storming of Journalists' Syndicate (May 2016) Blocking of more than 496 online news sites (beginning May 2017)	Media Laws ratified by Sisi on December 24, 2016, January 1, 2017, and September 1, 2018	• Intimidate independent journalists • Silence regime critics
Academia • University Leadership • Researchers	Sisi gives himself power to appoint university presidents and deans University presidents given power to expel students from public universities for no reason—male students then must serve in the military for three years Murder of Giulio Regeni Denial of entry to Egypt and deportation of foreign researchers	Law to appoint presidents and deans of universities, June 2014 Court issues death sentence for AUC professor Emad Shahin, May 2015	• Ensure that university leadership is friendly to the regime • Prevent student political activity on campus • Prevent research from being conducted on certain topics
Minority Groups • Nubian minority	Arrest and imprisonment of two dozen Nubians who were holding a peaceful rally and demanding constitutional rights (September 2017)	Use of Protest Law and NGO Law against Nubians	• Prevent Nubians from obtaining land rights guaranteed in the 2014 constitution

Timeline of Repression

Sisi as President: June 2014–July 2018

June 2014	Sisi reintroduces law giving himself power to appoint university presidents and deans directly. Bassem Youssef announces end of program. The director and a board member of the Cairo Institute for Human Rights Studies (CIHRS) receive death threats.
July 2014	Ultimatum given to NGOs: announcement in Al Ahram that every nonregistered NGO had to register by November 2014, otherwise they will be considered illegal entities.
September 2014	Yosri Fouda goes off-air. Ministry of Social Solidarity sets a deadline for NGOs to register by November 10, 2014 otherwise they will be considered illegal entities. Defamation campaign in the state-backed media against many NGOs, in particular human rights organizations.
November 2014	EIPR begins closure of branch offices in Luxor.
January 24, 2015	Shaimaa Al-Sabbagh shot dead by security forces in downtown Cairo while laying flowers for martyrs of revolution.
April 11, 2015	Mohamed Soltan, a dual US-Egyptian citizen, is sentenced to life imprisonment after 21 months in prison, much of which he spent on a hunger strike. Soltan is accused of supporting the Muslim Brotherhood. His father, Salah Soltan, was a senior member of the Brotherhood, but Mohamed had never joined the group.
May 2015	AUC professor Emad Shahin is sentenced to death in absentia during a mass trial. He is accused of espionage and undermining Egypt's national security, although no evidence is ever provided. After relinquishing his Egyptian citizenship, Mohamed Soltan is released from prison after almost two years. He is flown back to the United States in a wheelchair.

December 2015	*Townhouse and Rawabet Theater raided and shut down.*
January 25, 2016	*Giulio Regeni disappears; his body is found later in a ditch with signs of torture.*
November 2016	*Parliament passes draft NGO Law widely described as most draconian NGO Law ever.*
December 2016	*Egyptian Center for Economic and Social Rights closes branch office in Alexandria.*
January 2017	*Hisham Mubarak Law Center closes office in Aswan after 20 years.*
February 9, 2017	*Forced closure of the El Nadeem Center, which specializes in providing help to victims of torture.*
April 3, 2017	*President Trump welcomes President Sisi to the White House, and says, "I just want to let everybody know, in case there was any doubt, that we are very much behind President Sisi." This is the first visit of an Egyptian president to the White House since Mubarak visited Obama in August 2009.*
April 9, 2017	*Declaration of State of Emergency.*
May 21, 2017	*In his first foreign visit since taking office, President Trump meets President Sisi in Riyadh, Saudi Arabia and praises Sisi for doing a "tremendous job."*
May 23, 2017	*Security forces detain Khaled Ali, founder of Bread and Freedom Party and Egyptian Center for Economic and Social Rights; a case is brought against him that may prevent him from running in presidential elections in spring 2018.*
May 24, 2017	*Egyptian authorities blocked 21 news sites and websites of human rights groups on a single day.*
May 29, 2017	*After almost 6 months delay, President Sisi ratifies the controversial NGO Law that increases the government's control over civil society; noncompliance with the law can be penalized with up to 5 years in prison.*

June 2017	Blocking of online news sites continues, over 107 blocked including Mada Masr, HuffPost Arabic, AlJazeera, Daily News Egypt, Borsa News, etc.
September 3, 2017	Two dozen members of Egypt's Nubian minority are imprisoned in Aswan for a peaceful rally that demanded implementation of constitutional rights of the Nubian minority. Over 400 websites blocked.
September 21, 2017	Meeting between Trump and Sisi. Trump describes the relationship as "very, very good" and says about Sisi, "we appreciate everything that you've done." Media censorship continues; at least 496 websites are blocked.
September 22, 2017	At a concert, one of the few types of public gatherings still permitted in Egypt, several youth flew a rainbow flag. They were arrested for "promoting sexual deviancy." Public prosecutors said the young men would be forced to undergo anal exams to determine whether they were homosexual.
November 15, 2017	Nubian detainees in Aswan are released from prison after the death of Gamal Sorour, former head of the Nubian Association in France, who died of medical neglect while inside his prison cell. They are not, however, acquitted.
November 18, 2017	Award-winning human rights lawyer Mahienour El-Massry is taken into pretrial detention, charged with taking part in a protest over the transfer of the Tiran and Sanafir islands to Saudi Arabia. This is the third time she has been imprisoned since 2011.
November/ December 2017	Former Air Force General Ahmed Shafik announces that he wants to run against Sisi in the presidential elections in the spring, but that the UAE is preventing him from returning to Egypt. He is then deported from the UAE back to Egypt. After being detained for 24 hours upon arrival in Cairo, he reappears in public and withdraws his candidacy. Ahmed Konsowa, a colonel in the Egyptian army, announces his intention to run in the presidential elections against Sisi. He is sentenced to six years in prison.

January 2018	*Vice President Pence visits Cairo; he is the highest-ranking US official to visit Egypt since Obama visited Egypt in 2010. Sami Anan, former chief of staff of the army and former Deputy chief of the SCAF under Tantawi, announces that he intends to run against Sisi in the presidential elections. He is arrested.*
February 2018	*After all serious challengers to Sisi have been arrested or withdrawn, Moussa Mostafa Moussa, head of the Ghad Party, emerges as the only candidate who is permitted to challenge Sisi in the presidential elections. Moussa had previously publicly supported Sisi's second term.*
March 26–28, 2018	*Presidential elections, turnout is estimated at around 40%.*
April 1, 2018	*One day before Sisi is announced the winner in the elections, a coordinated defamation campaign is launched in the state-controlled media that targets the Nubian minority and my research in Egypt. At least seven media outlets mention trips I made to Nubian resettlement villages in February 2017. Nubian human rights defenders are accused of internationalizing the Nubian issue and tarnishing Egypt's reputation and Sisi's success in the elections.*
April 2, 2018	*Sisi is elected with 97% of the vote, according to official returns. President Trump congratulates Sisi on the phone. The White House issued a statement saying: "The two leaders affirmed the strategic partnership between the United States and Egypt."*

Inching toward Totalitarianism: Sisi as President

On July 3, 2013, Morsi was removed after civilian protesters had flooded the streets of Egypt. An interim government was created with a civilian interim president (Adly Mansour), a civilian vice president (Mohamed El-Baradei), and a civilian prime minister (Hazem el-Beblawi). With Sisi's "election" in May 2014, the pretense of civilian rule was dropped. In this chapter, I show how Sisi's promotion within the state apparatus from minister of defense to president led to a change in the level and type of state repression—and inaugurated the second wave of the counterrevolution.

During the period of Mansour, the regime's first priority was to target activists who were engaged in mobilizing for street protests, as well as other youth groups that had the ability to organize across multiple governorates. After becoming president, Sisi then moved against civil society, including nongovernmental organizations (NGOs), charities, cultural initiatives, the media, researchers, and the leadership of public universities. These are organizations that traditionally played no role in mobilizing for street protests. Some of these organizations were engaged in charity or developmental work and avoided any engagement in political activity. Others were silent or even condoned the regime's actions during the first wave of the counterrevolution. It is therefore perhaps ironic that they became victims themselves during the second wave. Why, then, did the regime deem them threatening? I argue that during this period the mere fact of independence from the regime was enough to prompt suspicion. The state attempted to curtail any independent activity, whether it be on the part of cultural initiatives, charities, media, or researchers. During the first wave, the regime had attempted to include certain liberal figures in the government, many of whom resigned within a few months, as discussed in the previous chapter. During the second wave, the regime became less inclusive while its crackdown on civil society expanded. Finally, the authorities continued the targeting of activists, including relatively small groups that mobilized at the local as opposed to the national level.

The attempt to bring civil society under the full control of the state is an attempt to create a regime that does not just have a firm grip on the government but also aims to totally control society all the way down—in short, a totalitarian regime. This is quite different than the period under Mubarak, when Egypt was at times described as a "hybrid regime" that combined both democratic and authoritarian features.[1] Over the years, a vibrant civil society had emerged that featured human rights organizations, feminist organizations, cultural initiatives, and a media landscape that had space for opposition newspapers and bloggers who took pleasure in blasting the regime on a variety of issues. In other words, while the top of the regime was controlled by a dictator who managed to cling to power for 30 years, below this there was an impressive array of initiatives outside the purview of the state—what Gramsci called "civil society."[2]

Since Sisi has become president, I argue that the hybrid nature of the regime is undergoing a transformation. During Sisi's first four-year term, the regime has been steadily incorporating elements of totalitarianism into its authoritarian core, while democratic aspects are increasingly difficult to discern. This is not just about returning to the pre-2011 status quo ante. It is rather an attempt to fundamentally alter the nature of state-society relations in Egypt.

Sadat and Mubarak wanted to be seen as allowing a limited form of democ-ratization or partial liberalization. Mubarak allowed civil society organizations to flourish, expanding to some 48,000 NGOs. Egyptians are accustomed to hav-ing independent newspapers, social media, NGOs, and opposition parties. Sisi seems to believe that this limited liberalization was a mistake.[3] It is not clear yet, however, that civil society will simply forfeit the ground it has gained. This is different than the situation in Libya, where Qaddafi did not allow for the growth of independent civil society to the extent that happened in Egypt, or in Saudi Arabia where political parties have been banned since the founding of the kingdom.

Compared to the period of Mansour, Sisi's presidency has—until now—witnessed fewer massacres of protesters. That is in part because there have been fewer protests—or at least, fewer large-scale protests or *millioneya*. Under Mansour, the regime developed the ability to prevent large-scale mo-bilization of street protests. The regime of Sisi is trying to control society to a much greater extent: censoring independent media; obstructing academic research; and preventing human rights groups, arts and culture initiatives, and even charities from doing their work. In short, the crackdown is not just about tightening the regime's grip over civil society but attempting to pre-vent it from operating altogether. It is not yet clear whether this will succeed. However, it illustrates that the regime is attempting to move toward a more totalitarian system.

Although the targets of state repression changed from Mansour to Sisi, there is a common pattern in terms of which branch of the state apparatus took the initiative in executing repression. In both periods, it was almost invariably the security forces who took the lead in carrying out arrests, raids, or killings and only later that the parliament passed legislation justifying the actions. Timing matters, because it can help us to understand, or at least make an educated guess, as to who is the driving force behind the crackdown.

As minister of defense and head of the Supreme Council of Armed Forces (SCAF), Sisi oversaw the largest massacres in postcolonial Egyptian history. Perhaps it is for this reason that as soon as he became president, he immedi-ately moved to shut down Egypt's human rights organizations. A number of my informants believe that, already back in the early days of the uprising in 2011— when Sisi was still an obscure member of the SCAF—it was Sisi himself who was handling the human rights and activist files. Even as a junior member of the SCAF, it was Sisi who was the one who took part in the raid at the Hisham Mubarak Law Center in early February 2011.[4] It was also Sisi who met person-ally with April 6 and other leading activists in early 2011. And then it was Sisi who, as minister of defense, oversaw the Rabaa and Nahda massacres.

Innovations in State Repression under Sisi

How does one measure repression? A number of human rights organizations both inside and outside Egypt have documented cases of torture, forced disappearance, death in detention, political assassinations, and other types of human rights violations. These kinds of quantitative measurements can show whether state repression increases or decreases, which can allow for comparisons over time and also between countries. This is one of the reasons why, according to Sally Engle Merry, "quantification is seductive." This is because "it organizes and simplifies knowledge, facilitating decision making in the absence of more detailed, contextual information."[5]

Quantitative assessments also, however, have their drawbacks. Especially in opaque, authoritarian regimes, it is difficult to conduct this kind of research, or sometimes even to get access to the country. A delegation from Human Rights Watch was denied entry to Egypt after publishing their report on the Rabaa massacre. In contrast to a number of other repressive countries in the region, the government of Egypt does not allow any international organizations access to their prisons.

The Political Terror Scale (PTS) is one example of an attempt to quantitatively measure how state repression varies from year to year. The PTS counts state-sanctioned killings, torture, disappearances, and political imprisonment from 1976 until the present across a wide range of countries.[6] This index can be useful to illustrate change over time. For example, if from one year to the next the number of political prisoners increases, the regime would seem to be more repressive. If, on the contrary, political prisoners are released, and prison cells are emptied, then the regime is presumably less repressive. What if, however, a state engages in entirely new forms of repression that they never engaged in before? If something happens for the first time in 2017, which never happened before—or perhaps was never documented before—then it becomes impossible to compare across time. Instead, a new category of state repression would need to be created. A quantitative approach cannot capture entirely new forms of repression. At times a quantitative approach cannot even adequately measure those categories that it does claim to cover.

Instead of offering a quantitative analysis, I offer a qualitative assessment by highlighting new forms of repression. In the two chapters covering the period of counterrevolution, I highlight how there were a number of incidents that were unprecedented in recent Egyptian history. In short, Sisi's regime is not just *more* repressive than Mubarak's or any of his predecessors, but it is repressive in *different ways* (see Fig. 7.1).

Protest Law

↓

Closure of streets and public squares to protest

Media Law

↓

Closure or censorship of independent media

NGO Law

↓

Closure of NGOs

Labor Law and Trade Unions Law

↓

Closure of independent unions

Figure 7.1 The restriction of Egypt's civil society in one simple diagram.

After Sisi became president, there were a number of "firsts" in terms of state repression. In the following brief section, I list forms of state repression that were unprecedented in modern Egypt.

- The first time a foreign academic was murdered because of his research: January/February 2016. Before Sisi, foreign researchers would often be denied research permits or denied entry to Egypt, but Giulio Regeni was the first foreign researcher to be disappeared and then tortured to death.[7]
- The first time American citizens were sentenced to life imprisonment in Egypt on fabricated charges. Mohamed Soltan was eventually released in 2015 after 22 months in prison; Aya Hegazy was released in 2017 after three years in prison.[8]
- The first time the Journalists' Syndicate was stormed by police since it was established in 1941: May 2016.[9]
- The first time that more than 500 websites were blocked, including news sites and NGO websites: beginning May 2017.[10]
- The first time that leaders of human rights organizations received death threats: summer of 2014.[11]
- The first time an Egyptian human rights organization relocated its headquarters outside of Egypt: December 2014. The Cairo Institute of Human Rights Studies (CIHRS) was founded in 1993 and had been in operation for 20 years.

- The first time virtually the entire leadership of the human rights community in Egypt have been subjected to asset freezes or travel bans.[12]
- The first time dozens of Nubians were imprisoned for a peaceful rally demanding rights that are enshrined in the Egyptian Constitution: September 2017.[13]
- The first attempt to criminalize homosexuality, with jail time up to five years. Anyone who promotes the acceptance of homosexuality or who attends a gathering or even music concert where members of the LGBTQ community are present could also be sentenced to up to three years in prison: October 2017.[14]

The Subjugation of Civil Society

During the first wave of the counterrevolution, the regime had managed to put an end to, or at least forestall, the continuation of large street protests that had characterized the period between January 25, 2011, and August 14, 2013. The time of the *millioneya* was over, at least for the time being. The protests that did take place were smaller in size and located in side streets or isolated areas far from government buildings. This meant that the protests received less media attention, had less impact, and were generally less threatening for the regime. Of course, there were still smaller protests that continued to take place. For example, in 2015 and 2016 Nubian activists in Upper Egypt organized a caravan to their ancestral homelands to demand the right to return to the lands from which they had been displaced because of the building of dams along the Nile. They also organized a protest that took place inside the Abu Simbel temple when it was filled with tourists. These protests, however, were novel forms of contention in that they did not involve people marching along a street or staging a sit-in on a public square.[15] It is perhaps for this reason that the regime had not yet developed a strategy in response. When a small group of Nubian activists staged a more conventional street protest in Aswan in September 2017, they were promptly arrested and imprisoned.[16] This incident and the subsequent incitement in the state-controlled media against members of the Nubian minority, and my research in Upper Egypt, launched just one day before Sisi was "reelected," will be discussed in more detail later in the chapter.

Having killed thousands of Morsi supporters, arrested or issued arrest warrants for at least 37,000 people for violating the Protest Law, imprisoned the leadership of many leading activist organizations, returned a military officer to the presidential palace, and ended massive street protests, the regime could have perhaps felt secure in having eliminated its opponents.[17] The military had reasserted itself and was seemingly in firm control. However, instead it continued and even expanded its crackdown. During this second wave of the counterrevolution, the regime moved against civil society at large.

Because this period is not over yet—Sisi is still president at the time of writing—this chapter should be read as an epilogue or tentative assessment of an ongoing phenomenon. Still, I will attempt to present my argument with the same systematic approach as in previous chapters.

I will proceed by showing how Sisi's regime has targeted *NGOs,* including human rights organizations, arts and cultural initiatives, and charities; *the media,* including television, newspapers, and online news sites; *academia,* from top-level university administrators including presidents and deans all the way down to researchers including PhD and MA students; and *minority groups,* including the *Nubian minority* and the *LGBTQ community.* Finally, in the few months leading up to the presidential elections in the spring of 2018, Sisi's regime turned against a few key *members of the old Mubarak regime,* including Ahmed Shafik and Sami Anan, who had declared their intention to challenge him in the elections. This chapter is meant to be an overview of how the regime is proceeding to silence civil society—it is not an exhaustive accounting of every incident of state repression, but rather intends to show the breadth and patterns of the crackdown. I will first analyze the crackdown on NGOs, then on the media and academia, and finally on the Nubian and LGBTQ minorities. Finally, I will touch upon what may be rifts within the military establishment based on the events surrounding the arrest and imprisonment of Shafik and Anan.

Conducting Research on the Crackdown

In the summer of 2016 I was awarded a grant that allowed me to hire five young researchers. For the first time in my life, I was able to assemble a team of researchers to help me. It was a small grant, but I felt like I had won the lottery. I advertised the positions as involving research on the impact of the NGO Law on civil society. Youth unemployment was around 30 percent.[18] Over 90 people applied for the five positions. Many of those who applied had worked in NGOs previously, but had been laid off as NGOs were struggling to survive or secure funding.

By coincidence, around the same time as I got the grant, Mahienour El-Massry was released from prison. Along with many other young Egyptians, she had been convicted of violating the Protest Law. I went through my emails and found that I still had an email exchange between us from 2009. We met back then, before the revolution, because she had translated for me when I attended an event by the Revolutionary Socialists. I still remembered sitting in the back of the crowded room as she whispered in my ear near-perfect simultaneous translation. I had emailed her thanking her for the free translation, and invited her to dinner the next time she was in Cairo. That never happened. With the revolution, Mahienour rose to prominence as one of the most well-known activists on the secular left. She had been to prison twice. I doubted she would even remember me, but I sent her an email anyway and asked if she'd like to apply for one of the research positions. To my surprise, she replied and said yes.

I asked the American University in Cairo (AUC) for an office in the downtown campus that we could use as our work space and to conduct interviews. The NGOs and other associations that were still operating in Cairo were almost all located in or near downtown. Asking someone to commute an hour or more out to Tagammu Khamis, where AUC's new campus was located, was unreasonable. I was told there were no available offices at the downtown campus—but I knew that wasn't true. After convincing the janitors to open the empty rooms, sending pictures of those empty rooms to the AUC administration, and three months of negotiations, we were finally given a room in the Hill House of AUC's Tahrir campus. It was the old Center for Arabic Study Abroad (CASA) office. The Arabic-language program had been suspended because foreign students had basically stopped coming to Egypt. Rather than allowing it to continue to collect dust, AUC finally agreed we might as well use it. I also had to argue with the administration in order to be able to hire Mahienour as part of my team. The human resources office asked me if she was the one who had had "political problems" and said it might not be possible to hire her as she had spent time in prison. It was a misdemeanor and the Protest Law she had been sentenced under was issued by the British colonial authorities in Egypt in the early twentieth century—and was still in effect. No matter. I knew many young Egyptians who had risked their lives fighting for a better future for their country. I didn't think it right that their futures should be ruined because of it. In the end, I found another way to hire everyone I wanted—four women and one man—through another branch of the university administration.

Despite all these hurdles, I thought we at least had a fighting chance. Because of the NGO Law, a number of the prominent NGOs that had been conducting research had to cease their activities. The Egyptian Initiative for Personal Rights (EIPR) had closed its entire field research division. But we were not subject to the NGO Law; we were part of a university. Since we did not have an office outside the AUC campus, I hoped security forces would be unlikely to raid our office. Since we didn't have a website, they couldn't block our website. We finally had an office to work in, my team were all issued contracts and armed with AUC identity cards, I received Institutional Review Board (IRB) approval for the research project, and I had the resources to pay their salaries and for us to travel as a team throughout Egypt. I did not receive any salary myself, but just one course release *from my 3-3 teaching load. We decided to call ourselves the State Repression and Civil Society Research Group. We were ready to go. Miracles could still happen— even in Sisi's Egypt.*

Nongovernmental Organizations: Eradicating Independent Civil Society

Human Rights Organizations

After having attempted to eradicate the Muslim Brotherhood and silence secular activists through criminalizing street protests, arresting scores of activists, and banning youth groups like April 6 and the Ultras, the regime set its sights on Egypt's vast civil society: some 48,000 NGOs.[19] It didn't seem to matter whether the NGOs were particularly critical of the regime, whether they documented human rights abuses, or if they were charities performing humanitarian work like helping street children.[20] What seemed to bother Sisi and his minions was the entire notion of independence from the state—in other words, the fact that they were *non*-governmental organizations.

The harshest repression was reserved for the most outspoken human rights organizations. The Cairo Institute for Human Rights Studies (CIHRS) has acted as an umbrella organization and attempted to coordinate the human rights movement, not just in Egypt but in the Arab world ever since it was founded in 1993. Around two weeks after Sisi's inauguration as president, Bahey El-Din Hassan, CIHRS director, received a death threat. He was warned that it would be best to leave the country, as he may otherwise face the same fate as Mansour El-Kikhia, a former Libyan minister of foreign affairs, who became a dissident and was abducted in Egypt and later handed over to Qaddafi in Libya, where he was executed.[21] Moataz Al-Fogairy, who is a board member of CIHRS, also received a death threat during the summer of 2014.[22] He had been in Brussels, and when he returned to Cairo, he found a paper on the windshield of his car that read, "You are going to die today." What made the threat even more ominous was that his car was in the parking lot of the building where he lived in a heavily guarded compound.[23]

Within about a month of Sisi becoming president, an ultimatum was issued requiring all NGOs to register under the new NGO law by July 2014,[24] otherwise they would be considered "illegal entities." It also required any organizations performing "NGO-like" activities to register. Some human rights organizations were registered as limited liability companies—but they also had to register in order to avoid being shut down.[25]

The CIHRS, one of the oldest human rights organizations in Egypt, decided to move its regional office to Tunisia.[26] The Cairo office remained in Egypt and was headed by Mohamed Zaree. In October 2017, Zaree was awarded the Martin Ennals Laureate, having been selected by a jury of 10 global human rights organizations.[27] He was unable to receive the award in person, however, as he was banned from leaving Egypt. After the 2011 uprising, several of the largest Cairo-based human rights organizations, like EIPR, the Egyptian Center for Economic and Social Rights (ECESR), and the Hisham Mubarak Law Center, had established regional branch offices in Alexandria, Aswan, and Luxor. Beginning in 2014, the human rights organizations shrank again in a very real sense, closing their offices in the governorates outside Cairo. By the time the parliament issued the draft NGO Law in November 2016, large parts of Egypt no longer had any independent human rights groups.[28]

Virtually the entire leadership of the Egyptian human rights community has been targeted with travel bans, asset freezes, or summons for informal questioning and arrests. Azza Soliman, founder of the Center for Egyptian Women's Legal Assistance (CEWLA), was arrested on December 7, 2016.[29] Prior to the arrest, her assets were frozen when she tried to travel to Jordan in November. As part of its trials against NGOs,[30] the Cairo Criminal Court has also frozen the assets of a number of organizations' directors, including Hossam Bahgat of EIPR, Gamal Eid of the Arab Network for Human Rights Information (ANHRI), Bahey El-Din Hassan of CIHRS, and Mohamed Lotfy, director of the Egyptian Commission for Rights and Freedoms (ECRF). The list goes on. While authorities have often targeted high-profile figures, many of the rank-and-file members of the human rights community have lost their jobs, as frozen assets mean many organizations have had to downsize or close down. At its peak, the EIPR employed about 80 people across the country but now includes about 30 full-time employees.

While CIHRS, EIPR, Nazra, and the Hisham Mubarak Law Center are known for their advocacy and outspoken attitude, the regime has been cracking down on a whole array of NGOs, not just those that are outspoken. Ironically, even reformist NGOs that only advocate for the state to uphold its own laws face harassment from state officials. For example, even small initiatives in Upper Egypt that advocate for upholding the existing laws against underage marriage face harassment.[31] It is not just a matter of merely silencing the critical or outspoken NGOs.

The Egyptian authorities have often claimed that they merely want all NGOs to register, and if they do so, they will not face any problems. However, even NGOs that were legally registered have faced problems. The Egyptian Democratic Academy tried to register in September 2014 and the government approved their registration, but then they were put under a travel ban in

November 2014. They then even received their registration number in January 2015.[32] Clearly, the crackdown is not just an attempt to persuade NGOs to legally register nor is it about filling legal loopholes.

Instead, Sisi seems to want to eradicate any notion of independence from the government by turning all NGOs into governmental nongovernmental organizations (G-NGOs or GONGOS). The scope of the state's project is quite vast, as Egypt is estimated to have around 48,000 NGOs. Just like Nasser nationalized the Suez Canal, Sisi seems to want to "nationalize" civil society. However, civil society is not an inanimate object, but a dense network of social relations that cannot so easily be brought under the control of the state. By attempting to tame Egypt's unruly associational life, President Sisi is not just trying to return Egypt to the pre-2011 status quo but is inching toward a much more authoritarian system.

Governorates outside the capital have suffered more because the human rights community is smaller and more vulnerable. In the governorate of Beheira, the Ministry of Social Solidarity closed down 75 NGOs and 121 child care centers, allegedly due to links to the Muslim Brotherhood. The media proclaimed that this governorate was "free of any associations which receive foreign funding."[33]

Arrests or imprisonment of opposition figures may bolster their reputation by garnering sympathy among those who would not have otherwise been sympathetic to their cause. In other words, arresting and imprisoning the opposition may at times backfire. Instead of tarnishing the reputation of opposition figures, the regime may unintentionally make them more popular by imprisoning them. The accusation of being spies or the drying up of funds is more difficult to respond to—and therefore perhaps even more pernicious. This accusation is particularly damaging as many of the founding members of the human rights organizations were leftists, including Communists and Nasserists. One of the more prominent figures in the human rights movement was Ahmed Seif El-Islam, who had belonged to an underground organization called Al-Matraqa that had split off from the Egyptian Communist Party. In the words of his widow, Laila Soueif, who is a math professor at Cairo University and an important figure in Egypt's opposition in her own right, the split happened because "they were disillusioned by the party's reformism, including its renunciation of armed struggle."[34] In 1999, Seif later went on to found the Hisham Mubarak Law Center, a law firm that worked in the field of human rights litigation. To be accused of taking funds from the West is then hard to respond to, especially if one's own political orientation was based on a firm rejection of Western meddling in Egypt.

As documented in the previous chapter, massive human rights abuses were committed, and in some cases they were directly overseen by Sisi while he was minister of defense. After becoming president, Sisi moved to ensure that the human rights organizations were crippled and starved of the funds they need to survive. Even those human rights organizations that did not sign public statements condemning the Rabaa massacre or other massacres against the Muslim Brotherhood have been targeted. And even those organizations that were meek or "played it safe," or perhaps sided with the regime because they genuinely preferred military rule to the Brotherhood, are facing severe restrictions. So it is not just a matter of "punishing" those human rights organizations that were critical of the regime or that tried to hold it accountable.

Charities: The Three-Year Imprisonment of Aya Hegazy, a US Citizen and Founder of a Charity

Although exact numbers are hard to verify, it is estimated that in the first two years after the coup, over 1,133 Muslim Brotherhood–affiliated charities were shut down.[35] However, even non–Muslim Brotherhood charities have been caught up in the crackdown. One prominent case is Aya Hegazy, an Egyptian American charity worker who spent almost three years in prison under fabricated charges. In 2012, she had established a charity called Belady that was engaged in garbage removal in poor neighborhoods and helping street children. In most contexts this would be considered a form of social work rather than activism. Nevertheless, she and her husband Mohamed Hassanein were arrested in May 2014,[36] shortly before the election of Sisi. They were accused of human trafficking and child abuse. The pro-government media publicized their case as "proof" that civil society associations were part of a foreign conspiracy against Egypt. Although they were never charged with receiving foreign funding, this was a prominent theme in the Egyptian media. The accusations were as absurd as they were dangerous, given that the services they were providing (garbage removal and mentoring street children) were sorely needed. One headline in *El Watan* read: "Arrest of American and Her Husband Who Run 'Fake' Society to Train Street Children to Fight and Attack Police" (Photo 7.1).[37]

The fact that Aya and some of the kids she worked with had once visited the AUC was used as "evidence" against them in court. Their arrest was a harbinger of what was to come: in contrast to Mubarak, who allowed space for charities and even human rights organizations to operate, Sisi views any civil society organization—even the most benign—with deep suspicion and hostility.

In the past, foreigners or dual nationals may have been treated with greater leniency than Egyptians. The imprisonment of Aya Hegazy, Mohamed Soltan, and other American citizens indicates that this is no longer the case. Aya

Photo 7.1 *El Watan* Newspaper, May 4, 2014: "Arrest of American and Her Husband Who Run 'Fake' Society to Train Street Children to Fight and Attack Police."

believes that her American citizenship worked to her disadvantage. If she were not an American citizen, she believes the regime would have targeted her in the "normal" way it targets NGOs: through denial of funds, forced closure, raids by security officers, or other forms of harassment. Ironically, the apolitical service provision–oriented nature of her work may also have been what got them in trouble. "It makes them look bad," Aya said. "We're a small NGO. If we can remove garbage, why can't the government do it?"[38]

The way Aya and her husband were treated in prison also was an indication of how the government wanted to politicize the case—and how both Aya's American citizenship and her gender were used against her. She and her husband Mohamed Hassanein were kept in separate cells and also interrogated separately. While in detention, the police pressured Mohamed to say that his wife Aya was a spy. When he refused, they tried to cajole him by saying that they had been married for a year already prior to their arrest, and yet they did not have any children. If he would betray his wife by offering a false testimony that she was a spy, they told him, he would be released from prison. He could then remarry another woman who would bear him children. These treacherous and misogynistic tactics failed, as Mohamed refused to lie about his wife.[39]

In September 2016 Don Beyer, Aya's representative from Virginia, held a press conference at the US Capitol to raise awareness about her imprisonment. Former Secretary of State Hillary Clinton then brought up the issue with President Sisi. Secretary of State John Kerry, United Nations (UN) Ambassador

Samantha Power, and the leadership of the Senate Foreign Relations Committee, including Senators Tim Kaine, Ben Cardin, Marco Rubio, and Bob Corker, among others, also raised the issue.[40]

After high-level intervention by US officials, Aya, her husband Mohamed, and the codefendants in the case were all acquitted. While the Obama administration also worked to release Aya, it was not until April 2017, and after Trump described Sisi as a "fantastic guy," that she was released, along with her husband and four of their coworkers.[41] Upon their release from prison, Aya and Mohamed were essentially forced to leave Egypt and were escorted to the airport, where they boarded a plane for the United States. After returning to the United States, President Trump invited her to meet him in the White House. In an interview, Aya revealed that Trump did not seem to realize she had been arrested and kept in prison for three years under Sisi—not Morsi.[42]

In November 2017, Aya and Mohamed received the Leaders for Democracy Award from the Project on Middle East Democracy (POMED). In her acceptance speech, Aya said that when she was taken into custody, the prison guards told her she would be hung or, if she was lucky, given a life sentence. At the awards ceremony, surrounded by people who were dressed in formal evening attire, Aya was wearing the same white prison gown that she wore on the day she was set free.

The crackdown against charity workers like Aya and Mohamed is even more shocking if we compare their case with the infamous Iran hostage crisis when 52 American diplomats were held hostage in the US embassy in Tehran following the 1979 revolution. They were held for one year and 79 days. By comparison, Aya and Mohamed and their coworkers were held for three years inside a prison cell—more than twice as long—although Aya had no connection to the US government other than her citizenship.

The "Sisification of the Media"

While independent journalists had been struggling for years under Mubarak, the assault on the media escalated after the election of President Sisi. Immediately after the ouster of Morsi in July 2013, a number of Islamist channels were taken off the air and the newspapers affiliated to the Muslim Brotherhood ceased publishing in December 2013.[43] With the election of Sisi, the witch-hunt expanded from journalists suspected of supporting the Muslim Brotherhood to prominent non-Islamist or independent journalists and media personalities.[44] These efforts include a terrorism law passed in August 2015 that allows journalists to only report the "official" version of terrorist attacks, and a media law passed by the parliament in December 2016 that increases government control over the media.[45] Reporters without Borders described this as a "Sisification of the Media."[46]

Television

This unprecedented level of media censorship was not limited to Islamist channels or small, independent media outlets, but it targeted three of the most prominent television personalities, including Bassem Youssef, Yosri Fouda, and Reem Maged. Youssef's late-night satire show *ElBernameg* had become the most-watched television show in the Arab world, with an estimated 40 million viewers every week—in a country with 91.5 million people.[47] His popularity extended far beyond Egypt, with *Time* magazine describing him as "the Arab World's most important political humorist."[48] Youssef was not only referred to as "the Jon Stewart of Egypt," he was even asked if he would replace Jon Stewart after the latter resigned from the Daily Show.

Youssef had been an outspoken critic of the Muslim Brotherhood, calling them "Nazis" in a tweet on the day of the coup.[49] Yet a few days before Sisi became president, Youssef announced that he was canceling his show. In September, Yosri Fouda's news program *Akher Kalam* was canceled.[50] Reem Maged gained a reputation as a critical voice under the SCAF, and her television program garnered a wide following. In the spring of 2011, Maged invited blogger and journalist Hossam Al-Hamalawy onto her program and he railed against the abuses of the SCAF. They were both subsequently summoned for interrogation.[51] After being off the air since mid-2013, when her show *Baladna bil Masry* was canceled, Maged began a new program in May 2015 that focused on women's issues. It lasted only for two episodes before it too was canceled.[52] Within the first year of Sisi becoming president, three of the most prominent and outspoken media personalities were either canceled entirely or were no longer broadcasting in Egypt.

Even after Youssef's show was canceled, censorship against him continued. In the spring of 2017, students at the AUC had organized a film screening of the documentary *Tickling Giants*. Youssef was invited to Skype in after the film screening for a Q&A with the students. However, the whole event was canceled. The dean at AUC who was responsible for canceling the event was a US citizen, who justified his decision to cancel the event because the student who organized it was "just a 17-year-old" and AUC had apparently received phone calls from state security. The dean believed that, by canceling the event, he was protecting the young student, but he also expressed fear that the government could cut off water and electricity to AUC's campus.[53]

Storming of Journalists' Syndicate and Blocking of News Sites

In August 2015, three newspapers were shredded at Al-Ahram print house and their printing and distribution was stopped. These were the *AlMasryoun*, *Al-Sabah*, and *Sout El-Omma* newspapers.[54] On May 1, 2016 the Journalists' Syndicate was stormed by police for the first time since it was founded 75 years earlier. Two journalists were arrested—Amr Badr and Mahmoud El Sakka—and accused of "spreading false news, inciting the public, and plotting to overthrow the regime."[55]

In December 2016, the parliament approved two draft laws. The media regulators' law was approved on December 19 and the media law on December 27. In an interview Yehia Qalash, head of the Egyptian Journalists' Syndicate, described the laws as an "entrenched inclination toward domination by the executive power branch."[56] The law stipulated the formation of a Supreme Press Council, whose chairman would be personally selected by President Sisi.

Then in May and June 2017, at least 496 online news sites were blocked, including *Mada Masr*, arguably Egypt's leading independent news site.[57] Co-founded by Lina Attalah, *The Guardian* described *Mada Masr* as "the news outlet that's keeping press freedom alive in Egypt."[58] Other news sites that were blocked were *AlJazeera*, *HuffPost Arabic*, *Daily News Egypt*, and *Borsa News* (the latter focuses mainly on business issues). Other websites that were blocked included a human rights organization based in the Sinai that reported on human rights abuses in the Sinai peninsula.

The blocking of over 400 news sites began just three days after President Sisi met with President Trump and King Salman in Riyadh in May 2017. The "glowing orb" in Riyadh seems to have inaugurated another escalation of government repression in Egypt. In the World Press Freedom Index for 2017, Egypt was ranked near the bottom: 161 out of 180 countries.[59] And Egypt is the third-largest jailer of journalists in the world, just behind Turkey and China.[60]

Academia

University Leadership

In June 2014, shortly after being elected president, Sisi reintroduced a law that gave himself the power, as president of Egypt, to appoint presidents and deans of universities throughout his realm. After the ouster of Mubarak, student protests had pressured the SCAF to introduce legislation that allowed faculty to elect university leadership. Furthermore, university presidents were given additional powers over students, which they did not have in the past. University presidents were also given the right to expel students permanently from public universities, without needing to provide further justification. In the past, expelling a student required a lengthy procedure and clear justification. Now students could be expelled quickly and permanently from all public universities in Egypt. Expelling a student was one way to ruin the future of young people who could not afford to pay tuition at AUC or other private universities. Without a university degree, the chances of finding any middle-class employment were highly unlikely. For male students, being expelled meant being sent immediately to the military, where they would have to serve for three years.

Clearly, the regime had tightened its grip on public universities. However, private universities such as AUC were also not immune to state intervention and were seemingly unable to protect their own faculty or affiliated researchers. Beginning in January 2014, two AUC professors were targeted. Emad Shahin, professor of public policy, was charged with espionage and conspiring with foreign entities to undermine Egypt's national security. Amr Hamzawy, professor of practice, was charged with insulting the judiciary after questioning a court ruling. Both had criticized the crackdown after the coup. Nathan Brown, political science professor at George Washington University, described the charges against both Hamzawy and Shahin as laughable. Of the charges against Shahin he wrote: "I would sooner believe that Vice President Biden is a member of the Symbionese Liberation Army than I would give credence to the charges against Emad."[61]

By this point I had become alarmed that now colleagues of mine at AUC were being singled out by the regime. I had received a fellowship at Brown University beginning in September 2013. After the incident with Emad Shahin in early 2014 I started to think I should try to stay away for another year. I applied for a fellowship at Harvard. Quite to my surprise, I was awarded the fellowship. However, AUC would not allow me to extend my unpaid leave for a second year. In order to go up for tenure, I was told I would have to prove I was "committed" to AUC and make a decision: either give up the Harvard fellowship and return to AUC, or accept the fellowship but give up my job just as I was about to go up for tenure. I knew that many of my friends had already left Egypt, or were planning to leave. My mother begged me not to go back to Egypt. My parents had always supported me in whatever I did, although they had become increasingly worried about the situation in Egypt. But this time was different. Even after I had made up my mind, and turned down the fellowship, my mother pleaded with me to stay in the United States until the very minute I left for the airport. Standing on the driveway in the early morning, she asked me one last time to stay.

I returned to an Egypt which was emptying. My friends, my colleagues at AUC, journalists, students studying Arabic—everyone was leaving. Or so it felt. A month after I returned, my mother had a stroke. As a result of the stroke, she went blind in one eye. Of course, the timing could be a coincidence. But it was hard not to regret. Ultimately, I had decided to go back because I had lived through the revolution, and I wanted to see where things were going. I had no idea how bad it would get.

In May 2015, my colleague Emad Shahin was sentenced to death along with over 107 other people at the same time. As there was no legal terminology for such an outrageous breach of justice, people called it a "mass death sentence." Two of the people sentenced to death were in fact already dead, and a third had been in jail for over 19 years.[62] Despite the glaring travesty of issuing a mass death sentence in a kangaroo court against one of their own faculty members, AUC remained silent.[63] Fortunately, Professor Shahin was outside the country, and thus was sentenced in absentia. He never returned to AUC. At the time of writing, he still resides outside Egypt and has been able to continue his career in exile. Giulio Regeni, however, was not so lucky.

Researchers: The Disappearance and Murder of Giulio Regeni

At the end of January 2016 I met with a friend at a cafe in downtown Cairo. After chatting for a while, he told me, almost in passing, that a friend of his named Giulio was missing. He was a PhD student at Cambridge University, but currently living in Cairo to conduct research on trade unions for his dissertation. A few days ago, Giulio had gone out to meet a friend of his, but never showed up. I asked if I could do anything, but he said no. They hadn't gone public yet because they were hesitant to cause a stir. Maybe he would turn up soon. Or, he said, "maybe he is dead." I went back home. A few days later the hashtags #WhereisGiulio started appearing on Twitter. My friend told me they didn't want to say "Free Giulio" because that would make it sound like he was in prison or somehow detained, and they didn't want to jump to that conclusion. Maybe he was just missing. Or maybe he would be released from wherever they were holding him. I told a few of my journalist friends in the United States and Europe about the case. If they were interested to write about it, I could help. All we knew at that point was that a young Italian PhD student named Giulio Regeni was missing in Cairo. They were journalists who had all previously lived in Cairo, but had left. One of them told me, "I can't write a story every time someone gets arrested in Egypt." She had a point. Just in the first eight months after the ouster of Morsi, more than 40,000 people had been arrested.[64]

The friends of Giulio were extremely cautious. As foreigners conducting research in Egypt under Sisi, you had to be cautious. Foreigners had been blamed for the revolution since the early days of 2011. Then when Mubarak was ousted, the revolution was suddenly (and rightly) attributed to the Egyptian people. In the celebratory billboards, commercials, and posters that popped up, there was no mention of this being the work of *khawaga* (foreigners). But now that the revolution was being crushed, once again, foreigners were to blame. About a week later, Giulio's body was found in a ditch. He had been tortured to death, and then dumped by the side of the road.

If the death sentence for Emad Shahin was alarming for many of us, the disappearance and murder of Giulio Regeni was truly horrifying—and not just for the small community of foreigners or academics in Egypt. On the two-year anniversary of his murder, the Italian prosecutor officially announced that Giulio had been murdered specifically because of his research.[65] Of course we had suspected this all along, but some people had speculated that perhaps the authorities just wanted to scare him, or torture him a bit, but not actually kill him. In other words, some people thought his murder was a "mistake." Or, on the contrary, perhaps his murder was intentional and happened under the jurisdiction of a branch of the security apparatus that wanted to cause a scandal and embarrass Sisi. Then, there was yet another line of speculation that Sisi's own son Mahmoud, who was an officer in the General Intelligence, may have been involved in Giulio's murder.[66] Until today, the Egyptian authorities refuse to admit any guilt and many questions remain unanswered. It is clear, however, that the Egyptian security forces themselves promote xenophobia. As Heba Morayef pointed out:

> This didn't happen in a vacuum. . . . It came after three years of almost constant rising xenophobic propaganda, fed by the security services, encouraging citizens' arrests of foreigners, and so on. . . . There are so many people in the Egyptian security forces that talk about this foreign conspiracy, that more and more people start to believe it. This is how a deeply paranoid police state operates.[67]

Over the years, I had dealt with cases of both Egyptian and foreign students being arrested or imprisoned, as well as faculty members being denied entry to Egypt. In the fall of 2011 Marie Duboc, a French citizen, was hired as a tenure-track assistant professor in my department. Since she had just had a baby, she was on maternity leave in the fall and would begin teaching in January. That fall, she flew to Cairo with her infant child to visit her husband, who was also employed at AUC in a different department. Although she had a contract with AUC and should have received a residency permit, the authorities at the airport refused to let her in, even on a tourist visa, to see her husband. Marie and her infant child were forced to wait in the airport until they were put on a flight back to France.

There were other cases where friends of mine who were conducting research in Egypt were denied entry to the country and a few times when AUC students had been detained. This was the first time, however, that a foreigner was murdered in Egypt because of his research. A memorial service for Giulio was held at AUC. There was a silent vigil on the campus. A large banner hanging above the campus read, "Giulio's Murder Is Not an Isolated Incident. The AUC Bubble Will Not Protect You." [68]

About a year after his murder, Egyptian state television aired a video of Giulio Regeni that had been recorded a few weeks before he disappeared. The video was secretly recorded by the head of the street vendors' union, Mohamed Abdallah. In the video, Abdallah repeatedly asked Giulio for money, which he said he needed to pay for his wife's cancer operation. Giulio replied in Arabic: "Mohamed, I cannot use the money because it is not my money. I cannot use it like that because I am an academic. I cannot tell the institution in Britain in the application that I want to use the money for personal reasons."[69]

Instead, Giulio offered to help Abdallah apply for a grant to support union activities but said that the money could not be used for personal reasons. Abdallah later confirmed that he reported Giulio to the police, believing him to be a spy.

The way the video was edited, it was clear that an attempt was being made to connect foreign researchers to the issue of foreign funding as part of an alleged foreign conspiracy against Egypt. The assault on researchers, NGOs, and the media was interconnected. Some of the very people who Giulio was trying to help were, apparently, the ones who betrayed him.

When I began directing the research project in the summer and fall of 2016, the murder of Giulio Regeni was still being investigated. The incident provoked anger and fear but also aroused defiance among the academic community in Egypt. Some came to the conclusion that it was no longer safe to do research in Egypt; others believed it was more necessary than ever. Most academics I knew living in Egypt tended to take a position somewhere in-between: if you avoided certain sensitive topics, and took certain precautions, you should be okay. I thought the topic of the NGO law was sufficiently "safe": we were not conducting research on the labor movement or any other social movement, or the Muslim Brotherhood, or any other Islamist groups, or issues of sexuality, or the military, or the police, or Egypt's foreign relations, or poverty, or unemployment, or the state of the economy, or the old Mubarak regime, etc.

The NGO law was openly discussed in the Egyptian media, occasionally also in the foreign media. It didn't seem like a taboo subject. The Egyptians whom I had assembled as part of my team agreed with me. All of them had experience working in NGOs in the past. AUC had approved the grant that supported the project, approved the hiring of my team, approved our travel throughout Egypt, and had given me IRB approval. I gave strict instructions to my team to not publicize anything about the project, anywhere. The idea was to not just have a low profile but to have no profile whatsoever. The environment we faced was one of pervasive surveillance and an increasing sense of suffocation. At the same time, the people we contacted to interview were almost without exception willing, even eager, to speak to us. In particular, many people in the governorates outside the capital told us they felt overlooked and ignored, and they were keen to tell us their story. They welcomed us with warmth and gratitude.

Field Research in Upper Egypt: "Tell Sisi Mahienour is in Aswan"

On January 2, 2017 we set off on our trip to Upper Egypt. We boarded the 8 a.m. train heading south. Before the train had even left the station a plainclothes security officer walked up to me and asked me where I was going. I told him Assiut. I assumed he had singled me out because I was easily identifiable as a foreigner, although it was not unheard of for foreigners to travel by train. Some Egyptian trains even have entirely separate compartments for Egyptians and non-Egyptians.

I had traveled around Egypt many times using public transportation, and was more worried that Mahienour would be recognized. Once we arrived in Assiut, we checked into a small and entirely empty hotel boat on the Nile. It was cold and damp, but the good thing was that we were literally the only guests in the entire hotel. And the manager of the hotel was a friend of a friend. We wouldn't have to worry about too many people noticing us. But every time we would leave or return to the hotel, the security guards would ask us if wanted a security escort—because I'm a foreigner. We simply refused and so they let us walk around the town, which a friend and native of Assiut, who happened to be back visiting, found shocking.

In the 1990s, Assiut had nearly fallen under the control of the Gamaat Islamiyya. This terrorist organization had many followers at the University of Assiut, where they were able to hang up a large banner on the campus that proclaimed their political goals.

The hotel guards became irritated with us, and they asked again if we wanted a security escort. Mahienour again said no. Then the security guards complained to the manager of the hotel about why they weren't asking me, the foreigner, if I wanted a security escort, and why the Egyptian tour guide was answering for me. We realized that the security guards apparently thought Mahienour El-Massry, who in some circles is a household name and celebrated as a prominent human rights lawyer, was not recognized by these security guards in Assiut.

However, among human rights defenders and activists in Upper Egypt, Mahienour was welcomed like a rockstar. In Qena, we visited a law firm that had just opened six months earlier. They claimed to be the first independent human rights lawyers in the entire governorate of Qena. They had a picture of Mahienour hanging on the wall of the kitchen, and they somehow found out that her birthday was three days later. So one of them snuck out while we were interviewing them and brought back a birthday cake for her—three days early.

We had agreed ahead of time that we would not publish anything about our trip on social media and would try to be as low-profile as possible. The problem, however, was that—instead of being encountered with suspicion—virtually everyone we met was very friendly and happy to meet us. Many of them seemed to marvel at the fact that a group from AUC was traveling to rural parts of Upper Egypt. And almost everyone wanted to have their pictures taken with us. Even if we asked them not to post the pictures online, this invariably happened. When we arrived in Aswan, on the very first evening of our stay word had already gotten out that we were there. Someone tweeted: "Tell Sisi Mahienour is in Aswan, maybe he won't come."

We had arranged a meeting with a number of Nubian activists including Mohamed Azmy, who was president of the General Nubian Union and founder of NubaTube,[70] the first and only YouTube channel to promote the Nubian language. Instead of meeting in a café or coworking space, we met him at night on a boat that was covered on all sides, in the middle of the Nile, far from the traffic and people on the corniche. A Nubian friend of ours had advised us this was the safest option.

The United States and Sisi

The escalation of the crackdown in 2016 and 2017 did not go unnoticed in the United States. In mid-November 2016, the parliament passed an NGO Law that essentially criminalized normal NGO activity,[71] prompting a number of organizations to immediately shut down. Two weeks later, Senators John McCain and Lindsey Graham issued a strongly worded statement: "We urge President Sisi to reject this legislation and uphold Egypt's constitutional commitment to freedom of association and assembly."[72] After a six-month delay, and a few days after a meeting in Riyadh among President Trump, Sisi, and King Salman of Saudi Arabia, Sisi ratified the draft law.

Trump seems to have further emboldened Sisi. On Tuesday, May 23, Khaled Ali was detained.[73] He is one of Egypt's most prominent rights lawyers who dared to suggest he may run against Sisi in the presidential elections scheduled for the spring of 2018. On Wednesday, just one day later, 21 online media sites were blocked.[74] These included Mada Masr, arguably Egypt's top independent news site, as well as AlJazeera, Mekameleen, Masr El Arabia, and others. Also on Wednesday, Mohamed Zaree, director of the Egypt office of the Cairo Institute for Human Rights Studies and a finalist for the prestigious Martin Ennals Award for Human Rights Defenders, was interrogated.[75] He had been banned from traveling for over a year and was accused of harming Egypt's national security with his human rights advocacy.

In sum, within the span of 48 hours, the regime detained arguably the most prominent opposition figure in Egypt and potential presidential challenger, interrogated the director of Egypt's oldest independent human rights organization, and carried out the most sweeping media censorship since Sisi took office three years before. This all happened just a few days after President Trump placed his hands on that glowing orb in Riyadh in the company of President Sisi and King Salman. Sitting next to Sisi in Riyadh, Trump heaped praise on the Egyptian autocrat: "We have a fantastic relationship . . . and we appreciate what you're doing.[76]

After the Rabaa massacre, the United States began a review of US military aid to Egypt and withheld some of the aid package, while Saudi Arabia and the United Arab Emirates (UAE) were pouring money into Egypt. Under Obama, the United States acted as a kind of counterweight to the Gulf. Even if the withholding of some US aid could not offset the billions of dollars that were pouring in from the Gulf, the US position at least showed that the Obama administration was not happy with the direction things were going. After the election of Trump, the United States no longer acted as a countervailing force, but on the contrary, President Trump appeared to be in agreement with the authoritarian leaders in Egypt and Saudi Arabia. This was perhaps best symbolized by the image of King Salman, Sisi, and Trump holding their hands over a glowing orb in Riyadh.

Financial Flows from the Gulf to Egypt

As discussed in the previous chapter, the ouster of former President Morsi and subsequent massacres of his supporters illustrated that Sisi's one-year stint at the US Army War College in Pennsylvania failed to instill an appreciation for human rights or civilian control of the armed forces, values the US military claims to impart through its International Military Education and Training programs. In theory, US military aid to Egypt is another form of leverage that the United States could use—either through establishing conditionalities for receiving the aid or through withholding the aid or delivery of equipment. If education was ineffective, perhaps financial sanctions would work. The Obama administration's decision to withhold some aid to Egypt was cause for consternation in Cairo, but it did not seem to restrain the interim government under Mansour or Sisi from engaging in further repression. However, American aid money was dwarfed by financial flows coming from the Gulf. The three tables below illustrate the dramatic changes in aid flows to Egypt since mid-2013. Graph 7.1 compares aid to Egypt from the UAE, Saudi Arabia, Kuwait, Qatar, and the United States from January 1, 2013 until July 3, 2013 (the day of Morsi's ouster), compared to the period beginning the day after the coup until the end of the year.

Graph 7.2 compares aid flows to Egypt over a longer period of time, from 2005 until 2015, from the UAE, Saudi Arabia, Kuwait, Qatar, the United States, and the EU. Here it becomes clear that the increase in aid from the Gulf was so dramatic that the minor dip in American aid may have hardly been felt.

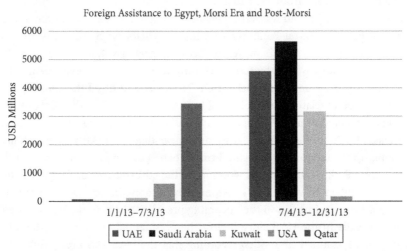

Foreign Assistance to Egypt, Morsi Era and Post-Morsi

Sources: AidData.org, Central Bank of Egypt, OECD.stat Table DAC2a, Congressional Research Service, Tracking Underreported Financial Flows, ForeignAssistance.gov, United Arab Emirates Ministry of Foreign Affairs and International Cooperation

Graph 7.1 Foreign Assistance to Egypt in 2013, before and after the ouster of Morsi.

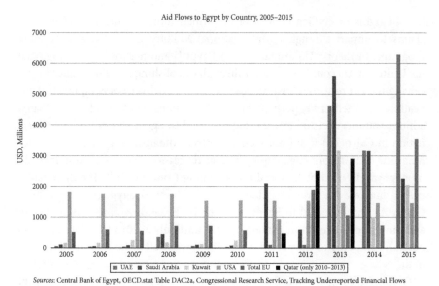

Aid Flows to Egypt by Country, 2005–2015

Sources: Central Bank of Egypt, OECD.stat Table DAC2a, Congressional Research Service, Tracking Underreported Financial Flows

Graph 7.2 Aid flows to Egypt.

Finally, Graph 7.3 covers aid only from the UAE to Egypt but over a much longer span of time, from 1971 to 2015. Here again, it becomes clear how dramatic the increase in aid was, especially beginning in 2013. Hisham Ramez, the head of Egypt's Central Bank, traveled to Abu Dhabi on the night of July 7, 2013, just days after Morsi's ouster, to "seek financial assistance."[77] Even if US aid to Egypt was dwarfed by money coming from the Gulf, Egypt seemed to still care about its image in Washington. To this end, it hired the Glover Park Group, a public relations and lobbying firm. In October 2013, the Glover Park Group registered as a foreign agent on behalf of Egypt. In leaked emails from Ambassador Yousef Al Otaiba, it became clear that the UAE was essentially picking up the tab for the lobbying firm on behalf of Egypt.[78] As of July 2017, the Glover Park Group was still working for the governments of Egypt and the UAE. Finally, in November 2017 Ahmed Shafik announced from Dubai that he would run against Sisi in the upcoming presidential elections. He had been living in exile in the UAE since he lost the presidential elections to Morsi in 2012. Shafik claimed in a video recording that the UAE was preventing him from returning to Egypt. Soon after this, he was summarily deported back to Egypt. Upon resurfacing after being incommunicado for the first 24 hours after his arrival in Egypt, Shafik announced that he had changed his mind. This episode is yet another indication that the UAE was not necessarily supporting the regime as an apparatus but Sisi himself. Clearly, the UAE wanted to prevent

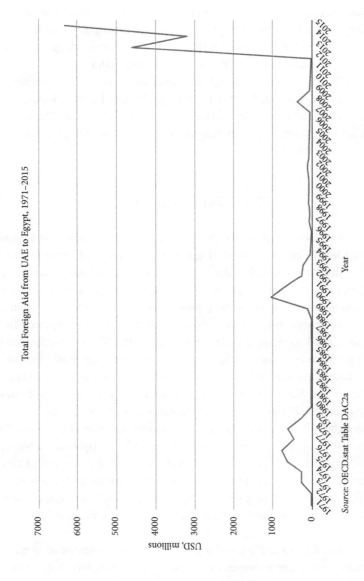

Graph 7.3 Total foreign aid from UAE to Egypt, 1971–2015.

any serious challenger for Sisi to emerge prior to the presidential elections in March 2018. This makes Emirati aid quite different from American aid, which is geared toward supporting whoever is in power as long as certain policies are maintained. Should this level of financial and political support continue, it may be necessary to include the UAE as a pillar of the Egyptian regime. For the time being, however, aid from the Gulf appears more as an emergency crutch, or as a personal favor to Sisi, than as an enduring form of support for the government of Egypt comparable to the aid provided by the United States.

Graph 7.3 was generated using the total *gross* flows ("Development Assistance" and "Other Official Flows") from the UAE to Egypt as reported by the Organisation for Economic Co-operation and Development. The annual numbers are slightly different according to the UAE Ministry of Foreign Affairs, but none of them deviated further than $20 million US.

The Nubian Minority

After the removal of Morsi in July 2013, a new constitution was written. Amr Moussa headed the constitution-writing process. As described in the previous chapter, the first six months after the coup witnessed the inclusion of a number of liberal figures including Mohamed El-Baradei, Ahmed El-Borei, Ziad Bahaa El Din, and others. A member of a prominent human rights organization described this first six months as a "honeymoon period" as it appeared that the regime wanted to create a united front against the Muslim Brotherhood. By offering several positions to a few high-profile liberals, the appearance of a civilian interim government was created. In a similar fashion, by including a few new articles in the constitution, one could have the impression that the new 2014 Constitution represented an improvement over the previous one.

Nubian rights advocates, including Haggag Oddoul and Fatma Emam, saw the constitution-writing process as an opportunity to push for the rights of the Nubian minority.[79] In a remarkable concession, and as a result of the efforts of Oddoul and Emam, and their entire committee, Egypt's 2014 constitution acknowledged some of the Nubians' historic grievances, in particular their forced displacement because of the building of dams along the Nile. Article 236 stipulates:

The state shall develop and implement a plan for the comprehensive economic and urban development of border and underprivileged areas, including Upper Egypt, Sinai, Matrouh, and Nubia. This is to be achieved by the participation of the residents of these areas in the development projects and the priority in bene-fitting from them, taking into account the cultural and environmental patterns of the local community, within ten years from the date that this constitution comes into effect, in the manner organized by law. The state works on developing and implementing projects to bring back the residents of Nubia to their original areas and develop them within 10 years in the manner organized by law.[80]

With this article, one of the Nubians' longstanding demands became ensconced in the constitution in Article 236. Nubians no longer needed to plead or implore the Egyptian government to allow them to return to their traditional homelands; they had a right to return. The first wave of the counterrevolution may therefore have appeared like a victory for the Nubian minority. During the second wave of the counterrevolution, however, it became increasingly clear that their rights existed more on paper than in reality. Since becoming president, Sisi has issued a number of decrees that make the possibility of return more and more unlikely. This includes Presidential Decree 444, which designates a 125-kilometer-wide swath of land along the border with Sudan as a military zone. Any territory designated as a military zone is off-limits, hence Nubians will not be able to return there. By contrast, the militarized zone along the border with Gaza is just 5 kilometers in width, which has caused many to speculate that Decree 444 is less about securing the border than it is about preventing Nubians from settling there.

In response to what they saw as a betrayal of their constitutional rights, Nubians have attempted to exert pressure through peaceful protests. In November 2016, this included staging a caravan that traveled along the Aswan-Abu Simbel Highway.[81] In February, protests were staged inside the Abu Simbel Temple when it was filled with international tourists. These two protests—the caravan and the demonstration inside the temple—were novel and represented innovations in the repertoire of contention in postrevolutionary Egypt. More importantly, they allowed the Nubians to evade the draconian Protest Law.

In the spring of 2017, I was teaching a class on borders, wars, and displacement at AUC. I had invited a Kurd from Turkey to speak to my class, via Zoom, about the Kurdish struggle and their long history of displacement. I decided to invite a group of four Nubians to speak about the history of Nubian displacement in Egypt. Fatma Emam had gotten sick and was unable to come, but Mohamed Azmy, the president of the General Nubian Union and founder of NubaTube, along with two other Nubian researchers, spoke to my class for over an hour at the downtown campus. I wasn't sure how much my students knew or how interested they would be. To my surprise, I learned later that none of my Egyptian students had ever seen maps of Nubian villages before. And none of them had ever seen a book in the Nubian language.[82] But, because of this presentation, many of the students were eager to learn more. By the end of the semester, many of the students had elected to write their final papers or other assignments about Nubia.

Throughout the spring of 2017 my team and I continued to make field visits to Mansoura, Tanta, and Mahalla. We also had a trip planned in May to the Canal

Zone cities of Suez, Port Said, and Ismailia. But that month there was an escalation of the crackdown that coincided with Sisi's ratification of the NGO Law. We had already arranged interviews with around 30 people, but when we heard that some of the very people we wanted to meet had been arrested, we canceled our trip at the last minute. That summer I stayed in Egypt through the hottest months. In June, my team and I returned to Aswan. In contrast to many of the other cities we had visited for our research, Aswan was a tourist destination. The Egyptian tourism industry actually encourages tourists to visit the ancient sites and colorful Nubian villages around Aswan. By bringing a group of five people to Aswan, I was doing exactly what the beleaguered tourism industry wanted and needed. We had booked a Nubian house in a remote location on an island away from the city center. It was idyllic, with few distractions, so that we could focus on our work and also be unnoticed. But when we arrived, the water and air conditioning were not working. It was about 100 degrees Fahrenheit, and after two days, we moved to one of the big hotels where the showers and air conditioning were functioning. We conducted a few more interviews and wrote up drafts of our papers.

On August 26, 2017, I left Egypt to begin a fellowship at the Wilson Center. I had a small farewell gathering at the Windsor Hotel in downtown Cairo, then left to go to the airport with three suitcases. None of my suitcases arrived at Dulles International Airport, but I did.

On September 3, 2017,[83] during the Muslim Eid holiday, about two dozen peaceful protesters were arrested and imprisoned in Aswan. Two of those arrested included Mohamed Azmy, the former president of the General Nubian Union in Egypt, and Gamal Sorour, the former president of the General Nubian Union in France. After staging several innovative protests, they had decided to hold another new kind of protest, which they called a "singing march" or "tambourine march" (مسيرة الدفوف) along the corniche. While playing traditional Nubian tambourine instruments and singing Nubian songs, they defied both the Protest Law and the suppression of the Nubian language. They were met by tanks and Central Security Forces that had been deployed from as far away as Qena, a four-hour drive from Aswan.

The 24 peaceful protesters were thrown into the Shellal camp run by Egypt's Central Security Forces. They were all put in the same cell and were not even given beds to sleep on. Egypt's prisons were already overcrowded. Their arrest coincided with the publication of two reports documenting torture in Egyptian prisons. Two days after their imprisonment, on September 5, Human Rights Watch issued a report arguing that Egypt's torture epidemic may constitute a "crime against humanity."[84] The UN Committee Against Torture came to the "inescapable conclusion that torture is a systematic practice in Egypt."[85] One of the detainees in the Shellal prison was Gamal Sorour; he had been the former president of the General Nubian Union in France. He was known for his philanthropy and peaceful activism. He was diabetic and needed to take medicine on a regular basis. Lacking proper medication, Sorour fell into a diabetic coma multiple times. The other detainees demanded that the prison authorities call an ambulance, but they refused to transfer him to a hospital until it was too late. Sorour died inside the prison cell. On November 15, the detainees were released, but not acquitted.

I was both horrified to learn what had happened inside the prison, and incredibly relieved the surviving detainees were now free.

But then, two-and-a-half days later, on November 18, Mahienour El-Massry was arrested and detained.[86] She was accused of taking part in a peaceful protest against the transfer of the Tiran and Sanafir islands to Saudi Arabia. The happiness I felt for Azmy being released was immediately replaced by a new wave of despair.

Writing a book over a period of seven years is always fraught with challenges, all the more so if one's own life is inextricably entwined with the story. Fearing for friends who are in prison is a crushing psychological burden that was hard to bear. Around Christmas 2017 I had a nightmare that Mahie was tortured in prison while she was being held in pretrial detention. Then a few days later came the verdict: a two-year prison sentence. It felt as if things could not get any darker. I could not contact her. I wrote a letter and gave it to a friend who wanted to hand-deliver it to Mahie in court. She traveled from Cairo to Alexandria to attend the court session, but then she was not allowed inside the courtroom. Mahie probably never saw my letter. It was difficult to contact any friends in Egypt—even ones who were not in prison. Skype and WhatsApp calls were either blocked or didn't work most of the time. The VPNs that people used to access blocked websites were also blocked. Calling someone on their cell phone was risky.

I had hoped that being away from Egypt for nine months would give me time to focus on writing and research. Instead of a period of respite from the suffocation and surveillance, things only got worse. A few years earlier, it felt like the whole world was celebrating the young people of Egypt who overthrew a dictator and tried to set their country on a path towards democracy. Now some of those very same people were languishing in prison—and no one cared. I was furious at how the entire issue of the Nubian minority was systematically ignored. I was outraged that women were being marginalized from the political scene in Egypt and erased from the history of the revolution—although women like Mahienour were such important protagonists in the ongoing saga and had sacrificed so much. It was her third time in prison. In trying to raise awareness about the imprisonment of Azmy and Mahienour, about the marginalization of Nubians and women of any background, I felt like I was confronted with the combined racism and sexism of Egypt and the United States.

Mohamed Azmy was in prison for two-and-a-half months, from September 3 until November 15. Then two days after he was released,[87] Mahienour El-Massry was detained on November 18. On December 30 she was sentenced to two years in prison.[88] *But then on January 13, the verdict was overturned in an appeal. On January 14, the day Mahienour was released, I realized I had been a fellow at the Wilson Center for 131 days, but there were only 2 of those days (on November 16 and 17) when none of my close friends in Egypt was in prison. Every other day someone I knew was serving time in Sisi's prison system.*

I was drained and yet on overdrive at the same time. My anger gave me adrenaline, but once the adrenaline dropped off, I was left physically and emotionally exhausted. I had experienced burnout before, but this was a type of exhaustion that I had never felt before. And then I met Aya Hegazy and her husband, Mohamed Hassanein, who each spent three years in prison in Egypt. That amount of time—three years in prison—is almost incomprehensible. Three years. It is to hard comprehend how they survived and how they found the strength to continue their work today.

Presidential "Elections" in March 2018

Sisi's Purge of Potential Candidates

In this chapter I have focused on the targeting of civil society actors during Sisi's first four years as president. The presidential elections in March 2018 offered a glimpse into what appear to be changes on the side of the regime. What was remarkable was both the number of challengers who emerged from within the ranks of the armed forces and how Sisi proceeded to eliminate them one by one. To be fair, rigging elections and eliminating political rivals is not a particularly new strategy in the repertoire of autocrats. Elections under Mubarak were not free or fair, although he did allow Ayman Noor, a genuine opposition candidate, to run against him in the presidential elections in 2005. Soon after the elections were over, Noor was summarily arrested. By contrast, President Abdel Fattah El-Sisi eliminated his challengers even before the elections, ensuring he had no serious contenders. Former Prime Minister Ahmed Shafik was placed under house arrest. Former head of the Joint Chiefs of Staff Sami Anan and Colonel Ahmed Konsowa were imprisoned, as if they were renegade activists or common criminals and not members of Egypt's military establishment. Mohamed Anwar el-Sadat, the nephew of former President Anwar el-Sadat, withdrew from the race on January 15, citing concerns for the safety of his campaign staff.

I had suggested we do an event at the Wilson Center about the presidential elections in Egypt. It took some persuading because it was clear that the outcome of the elections was a foregone conclusion. Aaron David Miller, the director of the Middle East Program, agreed to do a Ground Truth Briefing, which is a live phone conversation with a few people, usually at least one of whom calls in from the Middle East. Aaron wanted to be sure that we had a balanced group of speakers. I reached out to Mohamed Anwar el-Sadat, and he agreed to do it. Nathan Brown also agreed to take part. Aaron and I reached out to about six or seven former Mubarak diplomats and others who were not critics of the current government because we wanted people to hear that perspective as well. But no one agreed to take part. In our conversation on April 4, Sadat, who was calling in from Cairo, said:

> There is no space anymore for fear. People have to understand that the constitution is clear; the president has only two terms. He has to step down and we will have to see another president.[89]

Sisi had just begun his second term, and Sadat was already warning about the possibility of extending for a third term, in violation of the constitution. At the event at the Wilson Center, I was the third speaker, and I used the opportunity to discuss a defamation campaign that had been launched in the state-controlled media, just one day before Sisi was announced the victor.

Campaign in the State-Controlled Media against the Nubian Minority—and My Research

On April 1, just one day before Sisi was announced the victor in the presidential elections, the state-controlled media launched a coordinated campaign against Nubian human rights defenders—and my research in Egypt. At least 10 articles appeared on the same day with the same content, presumably copied and pasted directly from a report by intelligence agencies. Six articles and a talk show host mentioned me as a professor at AUC and mentioned research trips I had made to Nubian resettlement villages. Some of the articles featured the photographs and names of the presidents of the General Nubian Union in Austria and Egypt, as well as Wafaa Ashry, a Nubian woman who had run for parliament. They were described in derogatory language as "Nubian elements," although they are Egyptian citizens. They were accused of trying to internationalize the Nubian issue and thereby tarnish Egypt's reputation and Sisi's success in the elections. Talk show host Tamer Abdel Moneim, in a segment where he claimed to reveal "the secrets of the meddlers," described a research trip I made to Nasr El Nuba, a village where Nubians were forced to relocate at the time of Gamal Abdel Nasser. What was startling to me is that I had made this trip back in February 2017. The Mukhabarat—or whoever was behind the campaign—had waited until April 2018 to launch this wave of incitement, presumably so that it would coincide with the presidential elections and an upcoming court date for the tambourine march in Aswan.

The concerted media campaign illustrated the regime's willingness to use both racism against Egypt's Nubian minority and xenophobia against foreigners. It was all for the purpose of discrediting peaceful dissent. The Nubian minority poses no real threat to the regime and is merely asking for the implementation of an article that is *already* in the Egyptian Constitution. Why then does the regime—which successfully eliminated all political rivals and returned Sisi to the presidency with allegedly 97 percent of the vote—need to target a small minority? Why do they need to concoct absurd allegations that the Nubian minority and the Muslim Brotherhood— and me—were engaging in "wars of fourth generation against Egypt"? Some of the articles claimed I had visited villages where I had never even been. In reality, I had only visited one Nubian resettlement village, accompanied by one woman, where we met another woman. But three women chatting in a village was apparently not scandalous or conspiratorial enough, so it had to be embellished with lies and falsehoods. See Box with excerpts from some of the articles in the state-controlled media. The accusations were absurd, but also dangerous, given their attempts to make a link to the Muslim Brotherhood which Egypt had declared a terrorist organization. My research had nothing to do with the Muslim Brotherhood. Although every aspect of my research project was fully approved by AUC and conducted in accordance with Egyptian law—there was no law against visiting a village— university officials decided to not make any public statement to defend or clarify my work. At this point I had dedicated almost ten years of my life to working at the American University in Cairo.

"Bahlul of Nuba Exposes the Ikhwan Plot to Agitate Wars of Fourth Generation against Egypt." *Horreyati*, April 1, 2018

"بهلول النوبة يفضح مخطط الإخوان للتحريض ضد مصر بحروب الجيل الرابع"

Excerpt from this article:

- وأضافت المصادر أن النوبي محمد عزمي محمد، قام باصطحاب الأمريكية إيمي هيويستن دكتورة بالجامعة الأمريكية بالقاهرة- لزيارة قرى توشكى وبالنة والسيالة، بمركز نصر النوبة بأسوان وإجراء مسح اجتماعي حول العمل العام للجمعيات والمؤسسات الأهلية ولقاءها ببعض العناصر النوبية وأبرزهم وفاء عبد القوي وشهرتها وفاء عشري.

[The sources added that the Nubian Mohamed Azmy Mohamed accompanied the American Amy Austin, a doctor at the American University in Cairo, to visit the villages of Toshka, Balana and Salalah, Nasr El Nuba Center in Aswan and conduct a social survey on the general work of associations

and NGOs, where they met Nubian elements, notably Wafa Abdul Qawi and
is known as Wafaa Ashry.]

"Suspicious Elements Spread Lies Abroad against the Nation." *Masress*, April
1, 2018.

"عناصر مشبوهة تروج الأكاذيب عالمياً. . ضد الوطن"

"Details of the Attempts of 'Terrorist' to Use Mercenaries to Trade in the
Nubian Case." *Rose al Youssef*, April 1, 2018

تفاصيل محاولات "ارهابية" استخدام مرتزقة التمويل للمتاجرة بـ"النوبة"

"Muslim Brotherhood Starts Provoking against Egyptian State with Nuba
Card." *Ahram Gate*, April 1, 2018.

"الأخوان" تبدأ التحريض ضد الدولة المصرية بورقة النوبة"

Photo 7.2   "Tamer Abdel Moneim Reveals the Secrets of the Meddlers in
Internationalizing the Nubian Case."

AlAssemaTV

"تامر عبد المنعم يكشف اسرار وكواليس المتلاعبين في قضية تدويل النوبة"

Conclusion: What Sisi Has Repressed until Now

During the first wave of the counterrevolution, which I described in the previous chapter, I made three main arguments: about the nature of the regime, about the targeting of the opposition, and about the fragmentation of Tamarod. Regarding the nature of the regime, I highlighted how, despite a civilian interim president, civilian vice president, and civilian prime minister, there was no real civilian control of the armed forces. In its war on the opposition, the regime carried out numerous massacres of the Muslim Brotherhood in the summer of 2013. By the fall of 2013, the regime turned its focus to imprisoning the secular opposition. Finally, I showed how Tamarod, which had been critical in mobilizing for the removal of Morsi, did not unequivocally support the return to military rule. In fact, many of the leaders of Tamarod publicly supported Sabahi for president and not Sisi.

This chapter covers what I have described as the second wave of the counterrevolution. Here I have also made three overarching claims about time, law, and geography. The timing of events matters because *when* something happened could help us understand *why* it happened or *who* was driving the agenda. *How* the regime went about implementing its agenda also mattered; there was a shift from the use of bullets to the use of laws. Was this milder approach due to international pressure? Or was it because, through laws, it is possible to reach into the far corners of the vast desert country? Bullets only go so far. If the first wave of the counterrevolution was the most bloody period in modern Egyptian history, during the second wave the regime turned increasingly to the use of laws to imprison and silence its opponents. If we look at the entire period as a whole (the first and second waves of the counterrevolution), we see that in many cases security forces took action *prior* to legislation being issued to justify the action. Nongovernmental organizations were raided *before* the NGO Law was ratified, the Muslim Brotherhood was massacred *before* it was declared a terrorist organization, and prominent media figures were forced off the air, and newspapers were shut down, *before* the media law was ratified.

Second, in the summer of 2013, the vast majority of the massacres against the Muslim Brotherhood took place in Cairo. It appeared as if the governorates outside Cairo were spared the most brutal period of the counterrevolution. During the second wave, however, the counterrevolution clearly spread to the entire country as NGOs and initiatives all across the country were targeted. While much of the reporting on the NGO crackdown has focused on the organizations based in Cairo, the research project that I directed has documented how small NGOs and initiatives all across the country have suffered. From

Alexandria in the north to Aswan in the south, no organization was too small, or too removed from the capital, to be spared.

Third, this phase of the counterrevolution targeted even organizations and people who supported the first wave of the counterrevolution. The second wave targeted even small, local activist groups that did not have networks spanning the whole country and would seem to pose no threat to the regime. Finally, during this period, the regime targeted foreigners, including American and European citizens, in ways that differed from the raids of international organizations under the SCAF. In 2011, the US citizens who were caught up in the infamous NGO trial were allowed to leave the country. Aya Hegazy and Mohamed Soltan, both American citizens, were not so lucky. Soltan spent almost two years in prison, where he underwent a surgical operation on his arm without any anesthesia. Hegazy spent three years in prison before the fabricated charges were finally dropped. Giulio Regeni, a 28-year-old PhD student, did not make it out of Egypt alive. The overall pattern of the counterrevolution is summarized below.

Overall Pattern of the Counterrevolution

First and Second Waves of Regime Reconsolidation after the Ouster of Morsi

First Phase under Adly Mansour as President/Sisi as Minister of Defense

> *Targets of state repression:* Muslim Brotherhood and all secular youth or oppositional groups that had the ability to organize at the national level.
> *Objectives of state repression:* The regime regains control of the streets, university campuses, and its monopoly on politics.
> *Features:* The bloodiest period of modern Egyptian history, including the Rabaa and Nahda massacres orchestrated by the military and security forces, but under a nominally civilian interim government.

Second Phase under Abdel Fattah El-Sisi as President

> *Targets of state repression:* Civil society associations including cultural initiatives, human rights organizations, women's organizations, charities, independent media, university leadership, researchers, and smaller activist groups who organized at the local level including the Nubian minority.

Objectives of state repression: criminalizing normal NGO activity, criminalizing research, banning independent media, and bringing civil society under the control of the state.

Features: With the election of Sisi, there is a shift to less lethal forms of repression on the Egyptian mainland, although violence continues including the Air Defense Stadium massacre. The insurgency in the Sinai escalates. State repression becomes more totalitarian in tendency, with an attempt to shut down independent civil society.

8

Conclusion

Waves of Revolution and Counterrevolution

The last few years in Egypt have been characterized by a cycle of riotous uprisings followed by severe crackdowns. Raw power, rather than the parliament or other institutions of government, has been deployed to resolve fundamental issues of politics. Instead of a democratic transition, Egypt has witnessed three waves of revolutionary uprisings, two military interventions, and two waves of counterrevolution and regime reconsolidation. Because revolutions usually emerge from within society, while coups originate from within the state apparatus, the study of these two phenomena has resulted in distinct bodies of literature. I have attempted to think together the bottom-up nature of revolutionary uprisings and the top-down nature of military interventions. Drawing inspiration from a range of theoretical schools of revolution studies, including the state-centered, mass mobilization, Marxist, and international approaches, I have created a new framework for analyzing the Egyptian state and its relationship to society. This framework incorporates four pillars that both prop up and can potentially press upon whoever is in power: the business elite, the military, the United States, and the multiheaded opposition. I have linked a structural analysis with an emphasis on agency, including both regime strategies and protest strategies. Instead of analyzing historical precedents or the longer-term origins of the antiregime explosion, I have provided a micro-periodization of the process from the beginning of revolutionary mobilization in January 2011 until mid-2018, by which time President Abdel Fattah El-Sisi had survived his first term in office and reestablished the military-backed regime through levels of violence and repression that were unheard of under Mubarak. The coup in July 2013 and the Rabaa massacre in August signaled the beginning of the first wave of the counterrevolution when the utmost priority was to end any form of popular mobilization, regardless of whether Islamist or secular in nature, and to regain control of the streets and university campuses. The second wave of the counterrevolution began with the election of Sisi as president and an assault on civil society at large, including organizations that played no role in mobilizing for street protests or challenging the regime. This included banning hundreds of independent news sites and forcing shutdowns of many NGOs, charities, and local initiatives or starving them of the funds they needed to work. If the first wave of the counterrevolution focused on targeting activists, the second wave of the counterrevolution targeted virtually anyone who worked in civil society. While Mubarak had allowed tens of thousands of independent NGOs to operate, and perfected the art of simply ignoring certain kinds of protests he deemed unworthy of attention, Sisi viewed any form of independent civil society associations with suspicion. In this concluding chapter I will first discuss my empirical findings and then my conceptual contribution.

In summary, I have argued that the Egyptian revolution has played out in three mass uprisings: against the Mubarak regime, against the military junta, and against Morsi's government. The revolutionary nature of each upheaval is that each wave went *beyond* the demand to oust the ruler at the pinnacle of the regime and represented opposition to three distinct forms of authoritarian rule: the autocratic Mubarak regime and the police state that protected it, the unelected military junta that seized power after the toppling of Mubarak, and the religious authoritarianism of the Muslim Brotherhood.

On the surface, the three governments had little in common, and they had come to power through very different means. Mubarak had managed to stay in office for almost 30 years through a series of questionable electoral procedures. The Supreme Council of Armed Forces (SCAF)—although entirely unelected—was an interim government composed of the top brass of the armed forces who claimed to want to lead the country in the transition to democracy. Finally, Morsi was the first democratically elected president in Egypt, with no military background to his name, who represented the previously outlawed Muslim Brotherhood. And yet, each regime used remarkably similar tactics to stay in power: by attempting, albeit with varying degrees of success, to co-opt the elite, coup-proof the military, and ensure a steady flow of US military aid.

The strategies of co-opting the elite and coup-proofing the military continued under Adly Mansour and Sisi; the reliance on foreign aid continued as well, but the donor countries became more diversified. Egypt began receiving billions of dollars in aid from Saudi Arabia and the United Arab Emirates (UAE) even before the United States began its review of US military aid to Egypt in October 2013 in response to the Rabaa massacre. Furthermore, each government saw popular mobilization not as an expression of a vibrant civil society or a normal part of a transition process but as an existential threat. Therefore each ruler attempted to ban, severely restrict, and then violently quash street protests.

The first wave of revolutionary upheaval aimed to oust Mubarak, but it also represented an assault on the police state. The second wave demanded that the SCAF hand over power to civilians and confronted the entrenched power of militarism. In other words, the first two waves represented a demand for democratic, civilian rule—and thereby also an attack on two of the most powerful institutions of the autocratic state. Finally, the police and the military saw the rise of opposition to Morsi as a golden opportunity. Instead of using violence to crush protests, the police and army explicitly supported the Tamarod campaign that collected signatures throughout the country to demand early elections. Both private and state media invited the Tamarod activists to appear on talk shows and publicize their views extensively. This level of media exposure was never offered to activists during the first or second waves, hence the widespread reliance on social media.

During the first and second waves, the police were generally hostile to the civilians who took part in massive street protests as they were actively involved in arresting or killing them. The army was, at best, ambivalent: if the army used less violence than the police, they also did not *prevent* the use of violence by the police or thugs. For example, army soldiers sat idly in their tanks surrounding Tahrir Square when men on camel and horseback charged past them, killing a dozen protesters on February 2, 2011. The business elite only very belatedly offered their support to the activists, if at all. These dynamics changed dramatically during the third rising. During the final wave of upheaval against Morsi, the grassroots activists had the support of the most powerful institutions of the Egyptian state and capitalist class. What began as a grassroots campaign to demand early elections evolved into a coup from below.

The role of the United States exhibits a certain continuity throughout this period. During each uprising, the United States was not the first but rather one of the last actors to withdraw support from the regime. There is also continuity in terms of the role of activists: it was the withdrawal of popular support that signaled the beginning of the end for each regime. Each wave began as activists on the ground succeeded in mobilizing increasing segments of the population for protests, labor strikes, sit-ins, marches, and other forms of street politics. Furthermore, my unique survey data allowed me to compare the power of institutionalized versus noninstitutionalized forms of politics in winning concessions from the SCAF during the second wave. In sum, while each revolutionary upheaval was inaugurated by the appearance of mass mobilization, each of the three waves was brought to a close as the United States withdrew support from the regime and gave its blessing to the handover of power.

This book has attempted to make an empirical, theoretical, and methodological contribution to the literature on Arab revolutions. My empirical contribution has been fourfold: (1) to systematically compare the three waves of the revolution followed by two waves of counterrevolution; (2) to analyze the role of key actors during each of these waves (the military, the business elite, the United States, and the opposition); (3) to introduce the new activist groups that have emerged and document their changing repertoire of protest tactics; and (4) to provide a *micro-periodization of the revolutionary process itself.* I show *how* and *when* each pillar of the regime withdrew support from the respective ruler during each wave or, on the contrary, remained loyal. Theoretically, I expand upon existing notions of the state as a social relation in order to understand the networks that exist between state and society in Egypt and how they constitute the changing pillars of the Mubarak, military, and Morsi regimes. This has allowed me to explain the paradoxical confluence of military intervention from above and revolutionary mobilization from below.

Three Waves of the Egyptian Revolution: Regime Pillars and Regime Collapse

First Uprising against Mubarak				
Pillar of support for the regime[1]	Popular acquiescence	Military	United States	Business elite
Date at which support was publicly withdrawn	Jan 25, 2011	Jan 31, 2011	Feb 2, 2011	Feb 10, 2011

Second Uprising against the Military Junta				
Pillar of support for the regime	Popular acquiescence	Business elite	Military (rank-and-file)	United States
Date at which support was publicly withdrawn	July 2011	No withdrawal of support	No withdrawal of support	No withdrawal of support

Third Uprising against the Muslim Brotherhood				
Pillar of support for the regime	Popular acquiescence	Military (rank-and-file)	Business elite	United States
Date at which support was publicly withdrawn	November–December 2012	February–March 2013 Canal Zone July 3, 2013 Cairo	April 2013	July 4, 2013

How Ethnography Shaped the Argument

As I have outlined before, I have included ethnographic vignettes throughout the book, not just for the sake of adding color or in an attempt to spice up the narrative but because my ethnographic observations and experiences were critical in developing a number of my key arguments.

1. On January 28, 2011, I saw how people turned over police vestibules and created rolling barricades, which allowed them to encroach on Tahrir despite security forces firing at them. I saw how other people, who may have been afraid to confront the police directly, filmed Bothaina Kamel and me from balconies as the police interrogated us on Tahrir. I suspected this was the main reason the police decided to let us go rather than arrest us, as they had been threatening to do.

2. Also on January 28, I saw the first line of tanks that deployed to Tahrir and I saw the immediate, unfiltered reactions of protesters: some people cheered the soldiers, but others screamed and ran away. I knew that the initial reaction of the protesters to the soldiers was ambiguous—the protesters did not all welcome the soldiers or believe that they would protect them. I knew that the slogan "the army and the people are one hand" was not a statement of fact but an appeal to rank-and-file soldiers to take the side of the protesters instead of the regime.

3. During the 18-day uprising, I was only prevented from visiting Tahrir on one day: the day of the so-called Battle of the Camel. On that day, prior to the attack, the soldiers turned me away. A few hours later, the

assault happened, which left about 13 people dead. If soldiers sitting in tanks wanted to protect protesters, or side with the revolution, then why did they allow men on camels and horses to kill peaceful demonstrators? Although I had no hard evidence, I began to suspect that the soldiers may have even known the attack would happen, which is why they did not want outside observers like myself to witness it. I began to doubt both the scholarly narrative about the Egyptian army defecting from the regime and the narrative from Washington about the alleged professionalism of the Egyptian military.

4. I saw the large gulf between state propaganda, which tried to blame foreigners for the revolution, and the protesters on Midan Tahrir, who simply did not believe it. Instead, they wanted to show me the tear gas cartridges that were labeled "made in USA."

5. From 2011 to 2012 I saw the rise of small activist groups that were opposed to the SCAF. Many of them were largely ignored by scholars or not taken seriously as fringe groups. I began to realize how unprecedented this type of antimilitarist opposition was in Egypt. I saw how these groups acted, what tactics they adopted, what arguments they made, and the impact they had on the ground.

6. I saw the spread of different forms of activism and how even everyday life outside of demonstrations could turn into an act of protest. I saw how my friends would interrupt their dinners at downtown restaurants to chant in unison against the SCAF. I saw how people's confidence grew and how their anger increased—they truly believed they could bring about the fall of military rule.

7. I experienced the cascading events as a continuous cycle of shock, trauma, numbness, and normalization repeated over and over again for many years. As just one example: on October 10, 2011, one day after the Maspero massacre, I had to go to work. I had to teach and give a midterm exam in my Intro to Sociology class at AUC. I considered postponing the exam, but decided against it. Standing in front of the class, I said as much as I knew was accurate about the massacre, and as much as I could muster. Perhaps I was in a state of shock, or disbelief. I decided it was better to wait until things became more clear to have a longer discussion. Many students did not even know what had happened, and did not seem eager to discuss it. Or perhaps they just wanted to go forward with the exam. I began to feel a twinge of guilt—was I normalizing the violence by going to work as if it was just another normal day?

8. I saw how people were suddenly doing things they had never done before—how things that were unimaginable under Mubarak were

suddenly possible. Bothaina Kamel, the first woman to run for president in Egypt's history, invited me to come with her on one of her campaign trips to Upper Egypt. I saw how she was welcomed warmly in small villages around Luxor. I saw how she would meet with the local people and listen to their problems. Although none of the pundits seriously believed that a woman could win the presidential elections, I saw how the villagers—both women and men—did take her seriously. Many of them seemed to be genuinely happy, even honored, that she had traveled all the way from Cairo to meet with them.

9. I saw how the state attempted to erase or rewrite the history of the revolution, and how each year my students at AUC knew less and less about major events of the revolution. I had been hired in 2008; one of the courses I was hired to teach was on social movements and revolutions. Every semester, I would update the syllabus to take into account the latest trajectories of the Arab revolutions. But every semester, I had to go back and explain things that in previous years needed no explanation.

10. I saw the harmful effects of centralization. Even in 2017, more than six years after the overthrow of Mubarak, there were still in some sectors only tenuous connections between activists from Upper Egypt and those from Cairo or Alexandria. I had invited NGO representatives from both Cairo and the governorates outside Cairo to a workshop at AUC. One person from Qena told us, "Thank you for thinking we are important."

11. I attended the Rabaa sit-in on August 13, 2013, which turned out to be the last day of its existence. I saw how people were building three-story structures to live in as if they were planning to stay there for a long time. I spoke to people at the Rabaa sit-in who did not belong to the Muslim Brotherhood or did not even vote for Morsi but were protesting the coup. The state propaganda called them all terrorists. The next day, more than 900 people were massacred.

12. I saw the dreams and ambitions of activists change over time. I interviewed Ahmed Maher, the cofounder of April 6, back in 2011–2012 and then again in 2017, just a few months after he was released from prison but still under surveillance. Instead of protesting the regime, he was thinking about pursuing a master's degree. But it was hard for him to have a normal job or study because he had to spend every night in prison from 6 p.m. till 6 a.m.

13. I saw how a single sentence from an American president or ambassador could set off a whole chain of events in Egypt. Immediately after the "glowing orb" meeting of Trump, Sisi, and King Salman in

Riyadh in May 2017, there was an escalation of the crackdown, including the blocking of websites and a wave of arrests of activists that forced us to cancel our trip to the Canal Zone. Although I could never prove that there was a connection, I was quite sure it was not a coincidence.

14. I saw how paranoia and propaganda could destroy people's minds. I listened incredulously as a university instructor with a PhD told me that the Muslim Brotherhood controlled the economy of Germany. I didn't know whether to laugh or cry.

15. In 2011, there were so many people flocking to Egypt to see Midan Tahrir that my colleague Mona Abaza referred to them as "academic tourists." By 2014, many scholars who had built their careers studying Egypt were staying away. I felt the emptying of Egypt. Virtually anyone who could get out of the country, did.

16. I was appalled at the ignorance of American and European political affairs officers who worked at embassies in Cairo: the American who referred to the Camp David Accords as having started in the "1960s," the German who had not read the bilateral agreement between Germany and Egypt, and the Romanian who thought the number of websites that had been blocked was around "40" when by that time it was well over 100.

17. I felt the closure of civil society as a form of suffocation. The closing of public spaces affected everyone, not just people who worked at NGOs or charities. People began to fear meeting in public or being seen with activists. We met Nubian activists in Aswan on a boat at night that was covered on all sides. After traveling across many governorates, I realized that the crackdown was impacting the entire country, although most of the media reporting about the NGO crackdown only focused on Cairo.

18. I saw how the revolution seemed to both break down but also reinforce structures of patriarchy and Arab nationalism. I suspected this was one reason the counterrevolution could triumph.

19. Between 2011 and 2013 I saw so many protests I lost track. I saw so many clashes and violent episodes I also lost track. Many protests and massacres have been captured in photographs and videos. But after 2014, I saw how the regime's strategy changed—and how it was something you couldn't capture on film. Instead of spewing bullets, the regime spewed laws. But laws were something you couldn't see or witness. Repression had become invisible but omnipresent.

20. I saw how the Mukhabarat increased in confidence, especially after 2014. I witnessed how one agent blew his own cover in an attempt to scare me. I saw how another agent pulled his chair literally right up to our table at a café in downtown Cairo so he could hear the conversation I was having with two other people. I saw how the Mukhabarat were actively spying on people at the annual Middle East Studies Association conference in the fall of 2017 which was held in Washington DC. Sisi's repressive apparatus was now active on American soil.

The Military

The uprisings in Egypt have triggered some comparisons to be made between the revolutions in 1952–1956 and 2011–2018, especially regarding the continuity of military rule and the importance of the Free Officers and the SCAF in both.[2] I have argued, however, that there are at least three major differences between the Free Officers and the SCAF; these include differing class backgrounds, foreign patrons, and their agency in the upheavals between 1952–1956 and 2011–2018. Whereas Nasser and his conspirators were junior-ranking officers and represented the middle classes, the SCAF was composed of high-ranking generals. It was their relative autonomy from the elite classes that allowed the Free Officers to carry out wide-ranging reforms, thus bringing about a revolution from above. Their position regarding their patrons in the West—namely the United Kingdom and the United States—has also changed over time. In the 1950s the largest overseas British military base in the world was located along the Suez Canal, where approximately 80,000 British troops were stationed. In addition to ousting King Farouk, one of the main objectives of the Free Officers was to rid Egypt of British rule after 74 years of occupation. In October 1952 an agreement was reached to withdraw British troops, which by then were concentrated mainly in the Canal Zone. The final evacuation occurred in June 1956; during the same month Nasser was confirmed as president of the republic. The SCAF, on the contrary, maintained a seemingly unshakable alliance with the United States from the signing of the Camp David Accords up until the fall of Mubarak. Relations with the United States began to sour, however, especially after the Obama administration partially suspended US military aid to Egypt following the July 3 ouster of Morsi. In response, Egypt began upgrading its relations with Saudi Arabia, the UAE, and Russia. If Egypt's previous reorientations are any indication of things to come, US officials may have a few surprises in store for them. As discussed briefly above, the withdrawal of British troops in 1956 signaled the long-awaited end of the British colonial period. Nasser's subsequent Arab Socialist project was assisted by the Soviet Union, a relationship that was meant to repudiate any and all inklings of the colonial past. But the 20,000 Soviet advisers who settled in Egypt soon became another malodorous elephant in the room. And in 1972, they too were expelled, marking a dramatic rupture in Egypt's security relations with Russia. This is not to suggest that a similarly abrupt expulsion of American troops is in the offing. Given that Egypt never agreed to a large-scale deployment of US military personnel on Egyptian soil, there are no large brigades of US soldiers who could be sent packing. Instead, the Egyptian media blusters against American civilians residing in Egypt. Anti-American rhetoric took a particularly virulent form, especially as the old regime reasserted itself with the ousting of Morsi. For example, on a television debate that aired on January 13, 2014, between former Egyptian MP Mostafa Bakry and retired general Mohsen Hefzy, both claimed to know that there was an American conspiracy to assassinate Sisi. In response, they claimed this would lead to a "revolution of massacring Americans in the streets."

MOSTAFA Bakry: What frightens me, 'Imad, and I say this openly, is that there is a plot to assassinate Sisi, and the security forces know this full well. This plot is being concocted not only in Egypt, but also abroad. [. . .]

TV host [Tharwat Al-Kharbawy]: In such a case, there would be a third revolution.

MOSTAFA Bakry: Yes, but this time around, it will be a revolution of massacring Americans in the streets. No one will let the Americans escape. When the Egyptian people roars, it will have no enemies other than Obama, the Americans, and their lackeys.

Let anyone dare lay a finger on General Sisi. . . . All the Egyptians will brandish their weapons then, and we will slaughter the traitors and the criminals in their homes. [. . .]

TV host: I won't ask you for your sources, but are you sure of what you are saying?

MOSTAFA Bakry: Absolutely!

FORMER Egyptian General Mohsen Hefzy: It's a plot. I'm 100% sure.[3]

Although anti-American sentiment is not a new appearance on the Egyptian scene, such rhetoric does stand in contrast to Mubarak's years in power when, according to Samer Soliman, the regime was obsessed with its image abroad, in particular in the United States. In Soliman's assessment, Mubarak tolerated a certain level of dissent, but cracked down especially on those who tried to jeopardize Egypt's foreign aid.[4] For this reason Saad Eddin Ibrahim, who tried to lobby the US Congress to suspend US aid to Egypt, was sentenced to two years in jail in 2008.

As discussed previously, the legitimacy of the Egyptian military stems to a large degree from its anticolonial heritage as well as from the fact that it claims to be the last barrier defending Egypt from foreign domination. At the same time, however, the Egyptian military is the greatest recipient of foreign aid. Cognizant of Egypt's geostrategic significance, the high command has made good on its ability to shift from one foreign patron to the next.

The harsher-than-usual tone toward the United States may in part be explained by the Egyptian military's current reorientation towards the Gulf. After expelling the British in the 1950s and the Russians in the 1970s, perhaps now—lacking any sizable US military presence that could be expelled— the call for "a revolution of massacring Americans in the streets" is the current variation on a past theme. The exact amount of Gulf aid flowing into Egypt is less transparent than American aid; however, a series of leaked recordings have lent credence to the belief that the Gulf states have been providing direct financial support to the Egyptian military.[5] For example, in a recording between Abdel Fattah El-Sisi and his chief of staff Abbas Kamel, a voice that is believed to belong to Sisi demands that Saudi Arabia should pay $10 billion directly into the coffers of the Egyptian army, circumventing the Central Bank. Another recording refers to a bank account that belongs to Tamarod, the allegedly grassroots campaign to topple Morsi. The voice goes on to give instructions to take 200,000 Egyptian pounds from that account, specifying that it should be taken from the money that was deposited by the UAE.[6]

The reliance on foreign patrons is directly related to the agency of the Egyptian military in the power struggles of the 1950s and today. The role of the Egyptian military in both upheavals was fundamentally different. Whereas the 1952 revolution was led by the Free Officers, the leading protagonist in the 2011 uprising, and the first pillar of support to be withdrawn from the Mubarak regime, was the civilian opposition.

From Coup to Revolution from Above: 1952–1956	
Winter 1951–1952	Nationalist Egyptian police begin protecting attacks by resistance (Fedaayeen) on British colonial authorities in Cairo, Alexandria, and Suez Canal Zone.
January 1952	Cairo Fire: Free Officer cells initiate riots that lead to arson; many buildings that were symbols of British rule were burnt down in Cairo.

July 23, 1952	Around 80 junior officers remove King Farouk from power. Anwar el-Sadat, a member of the Free Officers, reads message on the radio that provides justification for what they call the "Blessed Movement." Royalist officers were arrested and the Free Officers secured support of the Muslim Brothers and Communists.
August 1952	Workers strikes in Kafr el-Dawar; two workers executed.
September 9, 1952	Agrarian Reform Law: European-owned property was seized, land redistribution announced.
December 9, 1952	The Revolutionary Command Council (RCC) announces that the 1923 Constitution is dissolved.
January 16, 1953	RCC dissolved all political parties. The events previously referred to as a "Blessed Movement" from now on are called a "Revolution."
March 3, 1956	Women granted right to vote for the first time in Egyptian history.
June 18, 1956	Nasser raised Egyptian flag over Canal Zone and announced complete evacuation of British troops.

From Revolution to Coup from Below: 2011–2018	
January 2011	Civilian activists plan to subvert the national holiday to honor the police for their role in ousting the British in the 1950s, and instead protest against police brutality and the corruption of the 30-year Mubarak dictatorship. After 18 days, Mubarak steps down and the senior officers in the SCAF take over, promising to lead the country in the transition to democracy.
October 2011	Maspero massacre: army soldiers kill dozens of Coptic Christians who were peacefully demanding that their churches be protected.
November/ December 2011	Second wave of revolution begins with mass protests against the SCAF during the Battle of Mohamed Mahmoud. Muslim Brotherhood largely stays away from protests.

From Revolution to Coup from Below: 2011–2018	
June 2012	Mohamed Morsi from the Muslim Brotherhood is elected; he is the first civilian president in the history of postcolonial Egypt. The military and the business elite appear willing to cooperate with him, at least for the first six months he is in power. The United States believes a transition to democracy is underway.
November 2012	Morsi issues a Constitutional Declaration. Civilians organize large protests against Morsi. The National Salvation Front (NSF) is formed in opposition to Morsi; leaders of the NSF include Amr Moussa, Hamdeen Sabahi, and Mohamed El-Baradei.
Spring 2013	Tamarod is formed by civilian activists. They begin to collect signatures to demand early elections—not a military coup. The leaders of Tamarod belonged to the new generation of activists, much younger than the leaders of the NSF.
July 2013	Minister of Defense Sisi removes Morsi from power. An interim government is created with civilians who appear to have no control over the armed forces. Massacres of pro-Morsi protesters begin within days of his ouster.
August 2013	Rabaa and Nahda massacres: over 900 people killed on a single day, making it the largest mass killing in postcolonial Egyptian history.
November 2013	Protest Law is passed. The regime begins arresting and imprisoning tens of thousands of political prisoners, in particular anyone belonging to a group that has the ability to mobilize for street protests.
May 2014	Turnout for the presidential elections is so low that voting is extended for a third day. Sisi is elected president.
June 2014–June 2018	Having ended large street protests, the regime moves to silence independent civil society including NGOs, charities, the media, universities, and minority groups including the Nubian minority and the LGBTQ community.

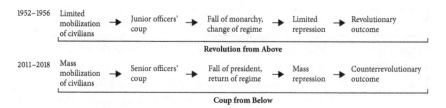

Graph 8.1 Revolution from above and coup from below.

In contrast to other scholars, I have argued that the Egyptian military never defected from the regime. Instead, the military was forced to *respond* to the demands of the protesters to remove Mubarak. By removing Mubarak, the military hoped to preserve as much of the regime—and their privileged position within it—as possible. The military elites and civilian protesters agreed that Mubarak had to go and that his son Gamal Mubarak should not replace him. Beyond this, their goals diverged dramatically. This became clear already in the days and weeks after February 11, 2011. Throughout the remainder of 2011 and early 2012, the role of the military continued to be more reactive than proactive. The generals were usually summoned to act by the street. When protests would escalate, the SCAF would sometimes call the youth activists in for a dialogue, and at other times they would order arrests, torture, or use of lethal force against them. In 2013, the Egyptian military *facilitated* the campaign known as Tamarod and *instigated* mass mobilization on July 26, when coup leader Abdel Fattah El-Sisi called for nationwide protests to give the military a mandate to face "violence and terrorism." The removal of Morsi was not, however, a "democratic coup d'état." The notion of a "democratic coup" is as flawed as the idea that the military defected from the regime. The military used mass mobilization at the same time as they were potentially threatened by it.

How can we explain this contradictory behavior? We must first do away with dichotomous variables that have been used to analyze the behavior of the military during mass uprisings. Instead of merely asking whether the military used violence, scholars should also analyze if they *permitted* the use of violence by other members of the coercive apparatus. Instead of focusing on the so-called "end-game," I have analyzed the longer-term trajectory of the uprising between January 2011 and July 2018. And instead of focusing on the military's internal characteristics, I have attempted to analyze the Egyptian military's relation to society, to the regime, and to foreign patrons. In sum, it's not a question of variables that led the military to repress or not, once and for all, but rather a question about the decisions that the SCAF took in an ongoing contentious dialogue with protesters, the business elite, and the United States about *whether, how, whom,* and *how much* to repress *many, many times over the course of the eight-year-long power struggle.* The so-called end-game that analysts have dissected in an attempt to understand military behavior is but a fleeting moment in time. After it passes, the networks of the old regime may still be largely intact. At least in Egypt, the end-game never ended.

Before 2011, there were generally two perspectives on the Egyptian military. On the one hand were those who believed that the men in uniform had largely disengaged from politics. Scholars of this persuasion believed this was either because the generals had more or less willingly agreed to retire from politics in return for overseeing a vast economic empire, or that they had (perhaps less willingly) been marginalized as the Ministry of Interior became more important. On the other hand were those who believed that the military continued to exercise significant influence but that they were not in the business of governing directly—in Steven Cook's apt phrase, the military was "ruling but not governing." Recent history has disavowed both assumptions. At the time of writing, the Egyptian military is currently ruling, governing, legislating, wielding significant influence over the judiciary, and overseeing massive repression of civilian activists from secularists to Islamists in addition to managing a large economic empire.

In short, scholars have underestimated the power of the Egyptian military—and misinterpreted military behavior. If we truly believe the Egyptian army defected from the Mubarak regime, we could conceivably imagine that the military may have an interest in transitioning to democracy, as they consistently claimed. If we believe that the Egyptian army was "professional," as Admiral Mike Mullen claimed, we would have reason to believe that they would refrain from using violence against protesters. If we believe that the removal of Morsi was a "democratic coup d'état," we could believe that the Egyptian army was "restoring democracy" as Secretary John Kerry claimed. Instead, I have argued that the military was guilty of permitting violence by other branches of the coercive apparatus—and then engaged in massive levels of violence in the summer of 2013. Thus, I argue that the military was the biggest impediment to democracy.

Furthermore, in comparing the period when Tantawi ruled as head of the SCAF and the current period in which Sisi is in charge, there has clearly been a centralization of power. In other words, the armed forces not only obstructed the transition to democracy but also seemingly concentrated power within their own ranks of the upper echelons of the military. Under Tantawi, it was common for other members of the SCAF to speak in public, such as Sami Anan, Sedki Sobhy, Mamdouh Shahin, Mohammed Al-Assar, and others. After Sisi was elected president, it has become rare to hear other generals speaking in public. Sisi has declined to create a ruling party, so there is not even an institutional framework within which power could be dispersed or tasks could be divided

among committees. Power seems to be concentrated in fewer hands than at any
other time in postcolonial Egypt.

Following Perlmutter, it would seem that the praetorian state has shifted from
an arbitrator-type army to a ruler-type army. Under Tantawi, the SCAF ruled
as an arbitrator—it was an interim government that lacked a coherent political
agenda or ambitions to rule indefinitely, even if they did extend their period in
power. With Sisi as president, the military's political ambitions are self-evident.
In the absence of a parliament, over 300 laws were promulgated. Once the parliament was convened, with close to no members who openly identify as the
opposition and those who did, such as Mohamed Anwar el-Sadat, unceremo-
niously removed from parliament, the decrees were quickly rubber-stamped.

In short, it would seem that the current state of affairs in Egypt exhibits a
twist on Marx and Tocqueville's writings about the outcomes of revolutions.
Marx famously believed that revolutions empower a new social class—the
bourgeoisie after the French Revolution and, he hoped, the working class after
a possible socialist revolution. Tocqueville, on the other hand, believed that
the French Revolution had empowered not so much a new class but rather a
stronger state apparatus. In Egypt, the revolution has not strengthened the state
apparatus as a whole. In many ways, the state has been weakened. According
to the World Bank's Worldwide Governance Indicators, Egypt's regulatory capacity has decreased from a 43 percent ranking in 2007 to 26 percent in 2013.
Government effectiveness in Egypt has declined from a ranking of 46 percent
in 2003 to 19 percent in 2013. Finally, rule of law has declined from a ranking of
50 percent to 34 percent in 2013. In Egypt, if many parts of the state apparatus
have been weakened, the military has been ascendant. Thus, the military has
been empowered as a social class.

The Military and Mass Mobilization		
	Relation to protests	Involvement in violence
First wave against Mubarak	Passive. Military responded to protests.	Military provided support to police, refilled police with ammunition. Military allowed violent thugs to attack peaceful protests (e.g., Battle of the Camel).
Second wave against SCAF	Reactive. Military itself is the target of protests.	Military became more directly involved in violent crackdowns (Maspero massacre and cabinet clashes).

Third wave against Morsi	Active. Active both in facilitating protests against Morsi, and then in overseeing crackdown against his supporters.	Before ouster of Morsi, military allowed protests to take place.[7] After his ouster, military oversaw biggest mass killing of civilians in modern Egyptian history (Rabaa and Nahda massacres).

Business Elite

The economic policies of the final years of the Mubarak regime, the interim military government led by Tantawi, and Morsi's administration were more similar than different. Perhaps for this reason, Egypt's elite businessmen exhibited a willingness to obey whichever political master was in charge—and an unwillingness to join or make major long-term investments in the opposition groups. Although in theory, those businessmen who were not close to the regime, who were excluded from sweetheart deals, and who had to pursue profit without the benefit of political proximity to the regime could have been displeased with the level of corruption and thrown their lot in with the opposition, this does not seem to have happened. Especially during the first and second waves of the revolution, some crony capitalists were themselves the target of popular rage.

After the outbreak of mass protests in early 2011, the two government ministers perhaps most responsible for Egypt's economic policies fled the country like fugitives. On February 1, Rachid Mohamed Rachid, minister of trade and investment, fled to Dubai. On February 11, just before Mubarak stepped down, Minister of Finance Youssef Boutros Ghali traveled to Lebanon and then took up residence in London. Even before they had escaped the country, Hussein Salem, a business tycoon known as the "Father of Sharm el Sheikh," fled to Spain on February 1. He was allegedly carrying large sums of cash in his suitcase. Like bank robbers fleeing the scene of a crime, government ministers and crony capitalists took the money and ran. Others, including Ahmed Ezz, Egypt's "most despised billionaire," had their assets frozen and were prevented from leaving the country, even while Mubarak was still in power.[8] During those 18 days, capital flight was so endemic that ATMs across Cairo ran out of cash. The AUC had to dispense emergency money to its employees who had not left the country. During the first six months following Mubarak's ouster, the elite continued to take their money out of the country, and Egypt's foreign reserves dropped precipitously. In the face of the mass uprising, the elite, it seems, feared for their lives—or at least for their bank accounts.

By contrast, in 2013, instead of transferring their wealth outside Egypt, money was pouring into the country to fund the alleged grassroots movement known as Tamarod. As discussed above, in a leaked recording dating from June 2013, Abbas Kamel, Sisi's chief of staff, asks Sisi's then deputy Sedki Sobhy to withdraw money from Tamarod's bank account. "Sir, we will need 200 [thousand Egyptian pounds] tomorrow from Tamarod's account, you know, the part from the UAE, which they transferred."[9] Although Tamarod seems to have been supported primarily by military and intelligence officers as well as influxes of cash from the Gulf, it was also supported by Egyptian businessmen such as Mohamed El Amin, the owner of the CBC cable network.[10] Beginning in July 2013, it was the Brotherhood who began to flee the country. What role did business elites play in each of the three waves? Under Mubarak, the elites were co-opted because they knew they could be easily replaced. Prior to the first wave of the revolution in 2011, and as argued in chapter 3, elite opposition was mainly confined to conflicts *within* the regime. There was no significant opposition to the regime itself from the business community. Furthermore, the conflicts within the regime were not irreconcilable and revolved mainly around the question of whether Gamal Mubarak should replace his father or not. The later phase of the Mubarak regime was characterized by a growing alliance between the state and the business elite, as evidenced by the number of businessmen in the cabinet. And yet even those businessmen who were excluded from the inner circle, or who had reason to be disgruntled by regime favorites such as Ahmed Ezz and his monopoly on the steel industry, had not formed any kind of organized opposition against crony capitalists, much less against the regime. Indeed, even those businessmen who were not close to the regime were willing to sacrifice their own profits to appease Mubarak. When Mubarak instructed cell phone companies and internet providers to shut down their service on January 28, they complied even though it cut into their profits. By and large, the business class displayed a remarkable amount of fealty toward Mubarak. There were a few exceptions, such as Mamdouh Hamzah, who openly admitted to purchasing supplies that were used in the occupation of Tahrir, such as blankets, tents, and food. Naguib Sawiris, ranked as the second-wealthiest citizen in Egypt, created and largely funded an opposition media outlet, *Al Masry Al Youm*, whose coverage of the mass protests provided an alternative to the state-controlled media. However, after the outbreak of massive civil disturbances in early 2011, Sawiris admonished protesters to go home after Mubarak gave his first speech and promised not to run for elections again in the fall.

During the second wave of the revolution, the behavior of business elites depended on their relationship to the regime. Those business elites with closer ties to the regime either fled the country if they had not done so already, or maintained a low profile. This is largely because, during the first half of 2011, demonstrations continued and indeed even gained momentum after Mubarak had stepped down. Many of the demands were aimed at expanding the gains of the revolution by prosecuting cronies and dismantling the networks of the old regime. The more "independent" businessmen stayed in the country, and indeed some even attempted to co-opt the revolution, for example by using images from the 18-day uprising in their advertising. As discussed in chapter 4, Vodafone created a three-minute advertisement called "Our Power," which suggested that the company supported the uprising that toppled Mubarak. Activists were furious because the company had done more to suppress the uprising than support it by shutting down cell phone services. The outrage against this attempt at co-optation was so great that Vodafone had to publicly distance itself from the advert. Unsurprisingly, Vodafone did not financially support any of the continued mass mobilization that took place under the SCAF, and neither did any other corporate entity. Although the Battle of Mohamed Mahmoud in late 2011 was an important turning point, as it pressured the SCAF to make a few significant concessions including moving forward the date for presidential elections, corporations shied away from celebrating the event in their advertising. Opposition to the Egyptian military was never commercialized.

After Mubarak was ousted, April 6 became perhaps the most prominent youth group in Egypt. Some of their leaders such as Ahmed Maher and Asmaa Mahfouz—who had previously been relatively unknown figures both inside and outside Egypt—were catapulted into the limelight as revolutionary activists. Young people flocked to join April 6 and regional offices sprang up in different governorates. This allowed April 6 to expand its network across the country, but the businessmen stayed away.

One exception, perhaps, is the renegade businessman Mamdouh Hamza, who allowed April 6 to use one of his apartments located in downtown Cairo as a meeting space and for other activities.[11] However, disagreements emerged in 2011 as April 6 split into two wings. There were also disagreements between April 6 and Hamza that escalated in 2012 during the presidential elections. During the first round of elections, April 6 had not backed any of the candidates. However, during the second round between Ahmed Shafik and Mohamed Morsi, which as described in chapter 5 involved choosing between the old regime and the Muslim Brotherhood, April 6 called its members to vote for Morsi. After doing so, Hamza withdrew any remaining support he had been providing and asked the activists to vacate his apartment. According to a member of the April 6 political bureau, they have received no other support from any members of the business community.

The more radical groups that emerged in opposition to the SCAF, such as Askar Kazeboon, Mosireen, No Military Trials, and the campaign against virginity tests, likewise did not receive any financial support from the business community. These groups were largely begun by middle-class youth who either had time or had modest financial resources and could therefore sustain their activities until, according to one of the leaders of the No Military Trials campaign, they all "went broke."

During the second half of 2011 many activists shifted their focus from demanding that the cronies of the Mubarak regime be brought to justice to documenting the SCAF's abuses of power, especially after the Maspero massacre in October 2011. But even after activists' rage shifted from businessmen to military men, the business community had little reason to support their demands.

After Morsi was elected, the business community for the most part (again) switched loyalty to the political leadership. Some allegedly even pleaded for forgiveness for their past sins of fealty toward the Mubarak regime. One prominent businessman described himself as a Muslim Brother "to the marrow of my bones."[12] The businesses of politically connected firms benefited more from Morsi's election than others. Morsi's policies were a continuation of the old regime rather than a radical break from it. He did not raise taxes or engage in any major redistribution of wealth, another indication that the Egyptian case does not fit Acemoglu and Robinson's framework that suggests that coups take place in order to thwart the threat of redistribution.[13] Morsi's leniency toward the business elite is perhaps even surprising, given that the level of cronyism in Egypt was deeper than in other autocratic regimes (market valuation of political connections was 20–23% of the value of connected firms; other countries tend to be in the range of 3–8%). Instead of confronting the most corrupt figures of the old regime, a committee was created called "Tawasol" to mediate and reconcile with the old regime.

In order to develop Egypt's moribund economy, Morsi cooperated with the entire spectrum of Egyptian entrepreneurs. They did not confront the old business elite, even those with close ties to the Mubarak regime. Businesses did not turn against Morsi until the Tamarod campaign was underway and already well-funded by money flowing from the Gulf. The Brumairian moment of the Egyptian bourgeoisie had arrived: the military seized the opportunity to intervene.[14] However, I have argued that it is unlikely the traditionally risk-averse bourgeoisie would have taken this chance if there had not been mass mobilization. The Brotherhood did not truly threaten the old Mubarak bourgeoisie or the military. If there had not been massive pressure from below, they might have tolerated his rule.

As Figure 8.1 indicates, Egypt's wealthiest citizens made substantial gains in their share of wealth between 2011 and 2014, despite all the complaining about the state of the Egyptian economy. In 2010, the year before the revolution

Wealth Share of Egypt's 1% (Top Percentile) 2000–2014														
2000	2001	2002	2003	2004	2005	2006	2007	2008	2009	2010	2011	2012	2013	2014
32.3	33.0	33.7	34.5	35.3	36.1	36.9	37.7	38.7	40.3	42.0	43.7	45.6	46.5	48.5

Wealth Share of Egypt's Richest 10% (Top Decile) 2000–2014														
2000	2001	2002	2003	2004	2005	2006	2007	2008	2009	2010	2011	2012	2013	2014
61.0	61.5	62.1	62.7	63.4	64.1	64.7	65.3	66.1	67.3	68.6	69.8	71.2	71.8	73.3

Figure 8.1 Wealth share of Egypt.

began, Egypt's top 1 percent enjoyed 42 percent of their country's wealth. By 2014, their share of the wealth had increased to 48.5 percent. By comparison, the top 1 percent of the American population in 2014 enjoyed 38.4 percent of the wealth.[15] Despite their enormous share of Egypt's wealth, which has only increased during the course of the revolution, I find little evidence that the bourgeoisie used their resources to support the three waves of popular mobilization. After Sisi became elected president, he did call upon the business elite to support the state itself, creating the Tahya Masr fund. However, donations from Egyptian businessmen were dwarfed by the much larger sums flowing from the Gulf.

The United States

In the past, the Egyptian regime was obsessed with its image abroad, particularly in the United States, because of its reliance on foreign aid. As Samer Soliman has pointed out, Mubarak displayed a certain amount of tolerance for dissent except toward those who tried to jeopardize US aid to Egypt. Saad Eddin Ibrahim was sentenced to two years in jail in 2008 for his attempts to lobby the US Congress to end its military aid to Egypt.[16]

As discussed at length in earlier chapters, I have included the United States as a pillar of the Egyptian state due to its structural power: it has the strongest military in the world; it has a history of regime change, in particular in the Middle East; and it has a built-in ability to influence the Egyptian armed forces through training programs and the second-largest military aid package in the world. The United States participated in the NATO intervention in Libya, which was decisive in the toppling of Qaddafi, and has contributed to propping up the Al Khalifas in Bahrain. And yet, US actions alone were not decisive in changing any of the three heads of state in Egypt. Mubarak, Tantawi, and Morsi were not toppled because officials in Washington or undercover operatives in Cairo pulled the strings. Obama did tell Mubarak in early February 2011 that "the time for change had come"—but he never would have made that phone call if masses of ordinary Egyptians were not filling the streets and public squares all across the country.

The United States may have overwhelming structural power, but this doesn't mean that it always uses this power. I have therefore endeavored to dissect US actions and what US officials actually did or said, rather than make assumptions based on what, in theory, they could have done. The contradictory and at times even incoherent approach of the Obama administration toward Egypt is primarily due to four reasons. First, unlike Libya, Egypt is a major non-NATO ally of the United States. Qaddafi was a pariah, but Mubarak was an ally, a friend of the United States. Even after mass protests erupted against Mubarak in January 2011, Vice President Joe Biden said of Mubarak, "I would not refer to him as a dictator" as discussed in chapter 3. However, unlike Bahrain (also a major non-NATO ally of the United States), Egypt does not host any significant US military installations such as the headquarters of the Fifth Fleet. Bahrain has hosted a US Navy presence continually since 1947, while Nasser did not agree to the establishment of any US military installations. Third, while US officials may view Bahrain through the prism of military facilities, in Egypt US officials tend to care more about the continuation of certain policies rather than the continuation of a certain person in office or the continued forward deployment of US troops and facilities. One reason the US position toward Mubarak could shift relatively quickly was because his ouster would not entail the loss of any US military bases.

Finally, the Obama administration was divided during key moments, especially in 2011 and 2013. These divisions led to contradictory messages. In early February 2011, Obama told Mubarak that a transition needed to happen "now" but Frank Wisner, the special envoy to Egypt, advocated publicly for Mubarak to stay in power until the fall—at least eight more months. And in 2013, although special envoy Bill Burns seemed to deliver the message that President Obama intended (don't do a coup), Kerry and Hagel did not. In conversations with Sisi, Hagel told him: "I will never tell you how to run your government or run your country."[17] That's not only a different message than Obama intended, but a message that suggests it could even be Sisi's business—he was still minister of defense at the time—to run the country. Ambassador Patterson and Secretary

Kerry were also not exactly on message. David Kirkpatrick summed up what appear to be four different messages from four different American officials in the crucial days and weeks prior to the coup in 2013: "Obama was trying to help Morsi. Patterson was warning the Muslim Brotherhood. Kerry had given up on Morsi. Hagel was reassuring Sisi."[18] I asked a high-ranking Obama official if, in retrospect, these different messages were a problem. He said he wouldn't call it "insubordination."[19] I asked another former member of the National Security Council why the US government was so incapable of coordinating its policies toward Egypt. He said that for the Department of Defense "it was institutional," while for the State Department "it was personal."[20] The Department of Defense valued their institutional relationship with the Egyptian military. Kerry valued personal relationships, and he thought Morsi was "the dumbest cluck I ever met."[21]

After the coup, the United States did signal that it was displeased with the course of events, but it took a "wait and see attitude." They wanted to give Sisi the benefit of the doubt.[22] It was not until October, after the massacres in August, that Obama ordered a review of US military aid to Egypt and withheld some equipment. Obama never invited Sisi to the White House, agreeing to only meet him in New York in October 2014. But by that point, it was too late. Clearly, the Obama administration had a rather incoherent approach to the crisis in Egypt, which resulted in numerous contradictory statements. This would not be the first time that US officials were unable to formulate a coherent policy toward an allied country in the throes of revolutionary upheaval. In 1976 President Jimmy Carter emphasized human rights as part of his campaign for president, and he even threatened to weaken US support for the shah. But in December 1977, Carter gave his infamous New Year's toast in which he pronounced: "Iran, because of the great leadership of the Shah, is an island of stability in one of the more troubled areas of the world." According to the assessment of one of the leading scholars on the Iranian revolution, the previous threat to withdraw US support for the shah "never materialized."[23] Carter's cabinet was divided over how to respond to the revolutionary movement in Iran. Because of this divisiveness within the Carter administration, the US ambassador in Tehran repeatedly told the shah he had "no instructions" from Washington.[24]

In her case studies of the French, Russian, and Chinese revolutions, Skocpol found that external pressure contributed to the weakening of the anciens régimes. In his analysis of revolutions in modern dictatorships, Goldstone also found that foreign patrons could weaken autocratic regimes if their previous support was suddenly withdrawn. But contrary to tsarist

Russia and Manchu China, Egypt had not recently fought a war, much less suffered any devastating defeat that would have destabilized the regime. Also contrary to Libya and Bahrain, where external pressure was key to ousting one dictator and propping up another, it does not seem that external pressure was decisive in the case of Egypt. As policies emanating out of Washington were contradictory, one cannot credibly argue (based on the existing evidence) that pressure from the United States in any way was decisive in weakening the Mubarak regime, the military junta, or Morsi's administration. The United States' actions were only really decisive *after the fact*. It was only after each handover of power that the United States, in accepting the new status quo, influenced the outcome of events. The US officials were important in condoning or acquiescing in the overthrow of Mubarak and Morsi, but they did not engineer the ouster of either. In fact, in order to acquiesce in the overthrow of Morsi, the State Department famously determined that it did not have to make a determination as to whether his ouster constituted a coup. No American or EU officials ever advocated for Morsi to be reinstated. The US position was that they would not "turn back the clock" once Morsi was removed from office.[25] In her meeting with Morsi, Catherine Ashton conveyed the message to him that "it was over" and that the Muslim Brotherhood should accept reality. The African Union, by contrast, expelled Egypt. In theory, it would have been possible for the Obama administration to follow the example of the African Union and take a more principled stance. But this never happened. If both scholars and policymakers recognize that military coups can take a variety of forms, including what I propose to call a "coup from below," this may make it possible for aid to be suspended in the future should there be a similar confluence of bottom-up mobilization and top-down intervention in Egypt or elsewhere.

After Trump was elected, Washington's tune changed entirely. The thinly disguised disapproval of Obama turned into an embrace of Egypt's postcoup autocratic regime. In contrast to Obama, President Trump welcomed Sisi to the White House. He also heaped praise upon his Egyptian counterpart, describing him as a "fantastic guy." Beyond the symbolism of the official meetings and the rhetoric, however, there are some important underlying continuities between the Obama and Trump administrations. Until the time of writing, both declined to list the Muslim Brotherhood as a terrorist organization despite pressure from the Egyptian government.

A certain degree of internal division also continued regarding the issue of making US aid to Egypt conditional. Under the Obama administration, a review of US military aid began in October 2013 and continued until March 2015. Despite Trump's enthusiastic rhetoric, his first secretary of state took a more critical approach. In August 2017, Secretary of State Rex Tillerson withheld $195 million in foreign military financing, or 15 percent of Egypt's total US military aid, citing concerns over Cairo's relationship with North Korea as well as the deteriorating human rights environment. One year later, and despite no improvement in the human rights situation, Secretary Mike Pompeo quietly released the aid without offering any justification for doing so.

In sum, despite vastly different rhetoric from the Obama and Trump administrations, they have both been characterized by internal divisions over US policy toward Egypt. Under Obama, the Samantha Power/Ben Rhodes camp wanted to withhold aid, while the John Kerry/Chuck Hagel camp advocated for restoring aid. Both camps agreed, however, that whatever they did, Egyptian officials were unlikely to change their behavior. This, apparently, is what ultimately convinced Obama to restore aid in March 2015. Even under Trump similar divisions continued: Tillerson withheld 15 percent of US military aid in 2017, but then his successor Pompeo restored it in 2018.

The Saudis and the Emiratis

While American officials were internally divided about what to do in Egypt, Saudi and Emirati officials were resolutely united, especially in 2013. Both Saudi Arabia and the UAE viewed Morsi and the Muslim Brotherhood as an existential threat to their own governments. In coordination with Sisi, the Saudis and Emiratis led the counterrevolution against Egypt's first democratically elected president. At the time, it appeared as if Saudi Arabia was taking the lead, but as I highlighted in the previous chapter, it seems clear now that the Emiratis were in fact the driving force. The Emirates and Saudi Arabia had offered bribes to a few (not all) of the Tamarod activists prior to the coup. Then, within days after Morsi was ousted, they began pouring money into Egypt's Central Bank. In the weeks after the coup and before the Rabaa massacre, the Emiratis were working feverishly to undermine efforts by the United States and the EU to mediate and find a peaceful resolution to the conflict. During the uprising in 2011, Wisner served as special envoy to mediate the crisis. But during the crisis in 2013, Obama selected as envoy none other than Deputy Secretary of State William Burns, a high-ranking and widely respected career diplomat. Burns made numerous trips to Egypt and was also attempting to coordinate American efforts with his EU counterparts, Catherine Ashton and Bernardino Leon. However, his efforts were obstructed by the UAE. After several trips to Cairo, Burns finally canceled another upcoming trip because Sheikh Abdullah bin Zayed Al Nahyan (known as ABZ) was allegedly telling the Egyptians not to listen to him. In the words of one former official familiar with the negotiations, Burns realized he was going to be "put in the hallway" and so there was no point in making another trip. Leon, who was negotiating in earnest on behalf of the EU and who had visited the Rabaa sit-in numerous times, was offered a lucrative job as director general of the Emirates Diplomatic Academy. Even several years after the coup, the UAE has been picking up the tab for Egypt's public relations firm in Washington, DC. And finally, when Sisi faced opposition from Ahmed Shafik and Sami Anan in the 2018 presidential elections, the Emirates placed Shafik under house arrest. The UAE then deported Shafik back to Egypt, whereupon he withdrew from the race. The Emiratis were clearly invested in Sisi personally and would not tolerate the emergence of opposition to him, even if his challengers were other former military generals and not Islamists.

Although many American officials continue to hold fast in the belief that the United States has very little leverage over Egypt, two former political prisoners believe otherwise. Mohamed Soltan spent 22 months in prison and was released under Obama. Aya Hegazy spent three years in prison and was released under Trump. Upon their release, they were both essentially deported from Egypt, although they hold Egyptian citizenship, and they both currently reside in the Washington, DC area. Through their respective organizations, Soltan's Freedom Initiative and Hegazy's Belady Foundation, they continue to advocate for the release of political prisoners in Egypt.

The Opposition

In sum, during the first three waves of antiregime uprisings, the United States, the Egyptian military, and the business elite were for the most part reacting to events rather than proactively shaping them as they pleased. If the most powerful players, whether domestically or internationally, were not determining the trajectory of the upheaval—then who was? I have endeavored to avoid simplistic answers that point to a single actor but instead analyzed the interaction among four pillars of society: the business elite, the military, the United States, and the revolutionary opposition. I have contended, however, that each of the three waves of the revolution was driven forward by a radical antisystemic opposition. The first wave targeted both the Mubarak regime and the police state. The second wave was directed against military rule and gave rise to the unprecedented growth of antimilitaristic movements. And finally, the third wave was an uprising against the Muslim Brotherhood. Some of the anti-Morsi activists took issue with the religious fundamentalism that Morsi was believed to espouse, while others rose up against him because they felt he had betrayed the revolution. Finally, another set of Morsi's opponents were acting less out of idealism than opportunism. Contrary to the first and second waves, members of the old regime joined the third wave, seeing it as an opportunity to reassert themselves after the battering they had taken during the first two mass risings.

The members of the old regime are more or less identifiable. But who were the revolutionaries? The 2011 uprising disavowed many of the classic theories of revolution as formulated by Marx, Lenin, or Gramsci as it was not led by the working class, by a vanguard party, or by organic intellectuals. Instead, the revolutionaries resembled a multiheaded Hydra and included both working and middle classes, women and men, young and old, Nubians, Arabs, Christians, Muslims, nonbelievers, secularists and the devout, seasoned activists and ordinary people. As they were all guilty of taking part in the revolution, they were all targeted in the counterrevolution.

The high command responded to the popular will during the uprisings in 2011 and again in 2013. However, they did so not out of patriotism, as their spokesmen claim, but rather because the popular mobilization represented a threat to the status quo, indeed to themselves: the ruling brass. During the first week of the uprising in 2011, the military stood by the Mubarak regime and supported the police in their efforts to suppress protests. Rather than exhibiting a "failure to repress," as some scholars have argued,[26] it would be more accurate to say that the military enabled the violent repression by other branches of the coercive apparatus. One week into the revolt, the military switched sides and declared that it would not use force against the demonstrators. This decision only came *after* the people had already changed the balance of power in their favor by defeating the hated police force, taking control of public space, and establishing alternative forms of "popular security." Far from causing the revolution, the military belatedly acknowledged it, while seeking to preserve as much of the status quo as possible.

During the second wave, the SCAF made a calculated decision to allow for the freedom to create political parties. In contrast, other aspects of freedom of association were still heavily restricted—and remain so today. Successive governments delayed any serious discussion of the freedom of unionization draft law, and they continue to propose heavily restrictive draft legislation for the organization of NGOs.[27] The SCAF did not seem to fear the formation of political parties or the convening of the parliament. In fact, they even admitted to a roomful of foreign journalists that the parliament would not be able to do anything against the will of the people, as discussed in chapter 3. The generals did, however, feel threatened by the ongoing mass protests and labor strikes and by the increasing oversight exercised by NGOs and other civil society organizations. This can in part explain why the counterrevolution targeted any groups with the ability to mobilize for protests, independent labor unions, and NGOs.

Furthermore, the military was not just responding to orders from their commanding officers but also reacting to society. During the first and third waves, this included the ousting of presidents—first Mubarak and then Morsi. During the second wave, the SCAF also responded to a number of demands emanating from society, which usually took the form of concessions. Although the SCAF seemed intent on protecting Mubarak and his family from prosecution, he was eventually put on trial after mass protests in April. Although the SCAF attempted to ban protests, they were unable to enforce their own ban. The date for presidential elections was moved forward after the Battle of Mohamed Mahmoud. And after a campaign against the practice of conducting "virginity tests" on female detainees, the SCAF eventually promised not to continue the practice.[28] Finally, new trade unions were allowed to form independent of the state-run federation, and a number of political detainees were released. As my survey data has shown, during the year-and-a-half that the Tantawi-led SCAF was in power, street protests were more effective in gaining concessions from the military junta than any other form of pressure.

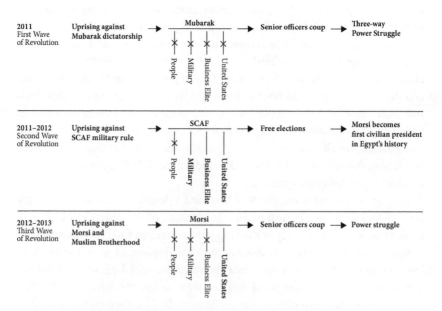

Graph 8.2 Uprising against Mubarak Dictatorship/SCAF/Morsi.

Note: An "x" denotes that the pillar of support was withdrawn.

Furthermore, in terms of the setbacks that occurred during this time—including the continued use of violence against protesters, the Maspero massacre, repression of the opposition, human rights abuses, and military trials of civilians, survey respondents blamed the SCAF more than any other institution, including the previously despised police force, the state media, or the old regime.

Regime Strategies and Protest Strategies

The revolution was not propelled forward by a self-contained logic, ideology, or according to foreordained stages, as earlier scholars and agitators have suggested. Instead, I have shown that it was driven by the need to forestall, co-opt, and defeat the popular movements from below. The dialectic of revolution and reaction became a macabre dance of protest and repression. This entailed, on the part of the regime, the unleashing of violence on a scale unprecedented in modern Egyptian history. While this violence intimidated some, it emboldened others. During the phase of revolutionary upheaval, from 2011 to 2013 when the balance of power was still in their favor, activists responded to the violence in myriad ways, including through the formation of popular committees to provide a kind of "security from below," sometimes through public screenings of videos that documented the violence and at other times through counter-violence or attacks on state institutions such as police stations. Many protest strategies were developed directly in response to actions by the government, as the table below indicates. When the regime tried to close Tahrir, protesters occupied Tahrir. When the regime shut down the internet, activists resorted to handing out flyers and brochures by hand. When the regime neglected to provide medical services, doctors and nurses organized field hospitals. When lies were spread in the state media, activists used the social media. When the regime tried to stifle workers' demands with the state-run federation, workers created independent unions. And when the regime attempted to ban protests, people simply continued to protest. However, during the third wave, the old regime reasserted itself by appropriating the strategy of activists and calling for mass street protests. *The state resorted to the repertoire of those who sought to overthrow it.* The state made contention; called for mass protests; and then made war against the Muslim Brothers, massacring their followers at Rabaa and Nahda and then, after killing them, declaring them terrorists. The state infiltrated and transformed the popular mobilization against Morsi into a mobilization for war against the Muslim Brotherhood and any other oppositional movements. This is the one regime strategy to which activists had no appropriate response.

Regime Strategies and Protest Strategies, 2011–2013

Regime strategies	Protest strategies	First Wave		Second Wave		Third Wave	
		Regime	Protest	Regime	Protest	Regime	Protest
Use of violence by police, thugs, military, snipers	Self-protection, counterattacks	x	x	x	x	x	x
Denial of use of violence	Public screenings, video	x		x	x	x	x
Security vacuum	Self-protection, creation of popular committees	x	x		x		x
Closure of Tahrir and other public squares	Occupation of Tahrir and other public squares	x	x		x		x
Curfew	Defiance of curfew	x	x	x	x	x	x
Cyberspace blackout	Pre-internet activism	x	x				
State media	Social media	x	x	x	x	x	x
Normalization strategy	Labor strikes in formal sector; informal sector continues to work	x	x				
Lack of medical services	Field hospitals	x	x	x	x	x	x
Sectarian propaganda	Public praying	x	x				

		First Wave		Second Wave		Third Wave	
State-run federation	Independent unions	x	x		x		x
Ban on protests and strikes and other repressive legislation	Protests and strikes			x	x		
Crackdown on NGOs	Continuation of NGO work			x	x		x
Virginity Tests	End virginity tests campaign			x	x		
Military trials of civilians	End military trials campaign			x	x		x
Military given power to arrest	Legal challenges					x	x
Protest dispersal weapons: tear gas, bird shot, live ammunition	Public screenings and spread of images	x	x	x	x	x	x

At times, however, activists would break out of this macabre dance of protest strategies that countered specific regime strategies. Sometimes—either out of a creative process or out of necessity—they would create new forms of struggle, new ways of relating to one another. According to my observations, this most often happened during moments of crisis. At several critical junctures during the course of these eight years, people no longer knew if the person *in* power actually *had* power, to whom they owed allegiance, or whose rules to obey. Aristide Zolberg has referred to these ruptures when "all is possible" as "moments of madness."[29] It is not just the destruction of the old order that constitutes the revolutionary, but the creation, however momentarily and imperfectly, of a new one. Collective defiance leads to collective creativity. Often considered beyond the pale of academic scholarship, it is the elusive, utopian dimension of protests that I also attempted to capture through my ethnography.[30] In other words, while at times activists adopted protest strategies to respond to specific regime strategies, at other times they broke out of this macabre dance and created their own forms of struggle, which contained the seeds of a new society. These bursts of collective creativity, although they escape the logic of tit-for-tat and are not necessarily a response to anything in particular that the powers-that-be have done, often provoke repression nevertheless.

Rather than present the unfolding events in Egypt as being the result of the spread of democratization, I have argued here that the dynamics can be traced to the actions of powerful actors to subdue the Egyptian people. The so-called Arab Spring, at least in its Egyptian formation, has led to the spread of repression—not democracy. The majority of Egyptians, in contrast to their counterparts in Libya, Syria, or Yemen, did not take up arms. They have no coercive apparatus to deploy and few institutions to represent them. Structurally speaking, they are weak. But they have heaping amounts of agency. They have succeeded in instigating three mass uprisings, but not in achieving a new democratic order. They specialize in disorder and upsetting the structures of power, not in creating new ones.

How can all of this inform our theoretical approach to revolutions and counterrevolutions? The Egyptian case in some ways defies the expectations of the various state-centered approaches to revolution. For example, scholars working within the state-capacity approach have documented how revolutionary guerrilla movements have often emerged in peripheral areas that are not thoroughly penetrated by the state. And yet in Egypt, the uprising was strongest in urban centers characterized by a heavy police presence. In terms of the political opportunity structure of Egypt, it had by most accounts become more closed in the months leading up to the start of the uprising and not more open. Furthermore, prior to January 25, 2011, the young revolutionaries had no real allies among the business elite or high command of the military and no support from any external powers. From a state-constructionist perspective, it may be possible to argue that the Mubarak regime did engender protest through its arbitrary violence. However, to suggest that the barbarism of the state "constructed" the quasi-utopian nature of the liberated zones would be a hard case to make. Of the four state-centered approaches to revolution, the state autonomy perspective seems to be the most convincing. A state that is able to violate the interests of the elite and make concessions to the masses in order to preserve itself stands a better chance of surviving than one which lacks this autonomy. As I hope to have demonstrated, the Mubarak regime was characterized by a deepening alliance between the capitalist class and the state. And yet, Mubarak was able to order the shutting down of telecommunications, which cut into the profits of these companies; he was able to reshuffle his cabinet; he was able to throw a few of his cronies under the bus; he was even able to sacrifice the political career of his own son, who represented the interests of neoliberal elites, hoping these concessions would allow him to cling to power. And yet he still succumbed to the revolution. In order to explain this, we must turn to the agency of the Egyptian people.

I have argued that the confluence of mass uprising, coup, and return to military rule/resurrection of the old regime may be understood as a *coup from below*, in contradistinction to a *revolution from above*, characterized by limited mass protests, followed by a coup and then a change of regime. This concept refers to the dual nature of civil-military relations: the relationship between the armed forces and the regime, as well as the relationship between the armed forces and the citizenry. In Egypt, the military has been described as critical in ousting both Mubarak and Morsi and thereby having the autonomy to defect from the civilian leadership. I have argued that many of the early analyses about January 25 created "myths of military defection," and that it is incorrect to describe the actions of the military as constituting defection from the regime. The second part of the concept refers to the military's equally contradictory relationship with the mobilized population, as the armed forces responded to (some of) their demands while also engaging in fierce repression. The nature of the coup determined the nature of the crackdown. The coup led by the people turned into a counterrevolution that targeted many of those very same people.

The third wave of protests represented an even more confounding confluence of bottom-up protest and top-down military intervention. The ouster of Morsi was not simply a popularly supported coup but a coup in which the deep state used activists' most effective weapon—mass mobilization—against them. During the third wave, the state itself called for antiregime mobilization, rather than attempting to restrict it or crush it, as during the first and second waves of the uprising. The Ministry of Defense and Ministry of Interior facilitated the grassroots campaign known as Tamarod, which was crucial in galvanizing support for the June 30 protests. Then on July 26—as if he was mobilizing the citizenry for war—Abdel Fattah El-Sisi called for a mandate to fight "terrorism," although the Muslim Brotherhood had not (yet) been officially designated as terrorists.

For a country that had experienced more protests than any other country in the world in 2011, this was an ignominious turn of events. In order to deter protests, the regime had resorted to a variety of tactics over the course of two-and-a-half years, including conducting sexual assaults referred to as "virginity tests" on detained women, placing civilians on military trials, running over Coptic Christians with armored personnel carriers, and carrying out massacres in football stadiums during a harmless match between rival teams. But in order to crush the oldest and best-organized opposition movement in the country—and topple the incumbent president—it resorted to a new tactic. The regime's strategy became a protest strategy. Extant members of the old Mubarak regime resorted to the very tactics that had been used to topple Mubarak, and the

Rabaa massacre followed. Because the military relied on mass mobilization to oust Morsi—precisely because it was a coup from below—the regime knew they would have to be accountable to the people later on. Unless, by carrying out a slaughter of civilians that exceeded in scope that of the Tiananmen Massacre in China, it would be possible to kill their opponents, silence any surviving critics, and demobilize a highly mobilized population. Because the ouster of Morsi relied on social forces outside the scope of the military who may later demand further concessions or accountability, or even threaten the post-Morsi government, these same social forces had to be crushed.

Six years after the coup, the crackdown continues and shows no signs of stopping. At the time of writing, the counterrevolution has lasted more than twice as long as the period of revolutionary upheaval, and yet we lack the same level of empirical research on this period. A rich theoretical literature on counterrevolutions has yet to be born. By documenting in detail what I see as two waves of counterrevolution, each with their own distinct types and targets of state repression, and offering an explanation for the timing and pattern of the crackdown, I hope at least to have thrown a few seeds into the desert.

Appendix

The Military Responds to Mass Mobilization—Evidence from Survey Data

In order to document the contradictory relationship between the military and mass mobilization, I conducted an online Arabic-language survey of over 560 Egyptians in the spring of 2012. As discussed in chapter 4, the period of military rule was characterized by continuing mass protests as well as continuing state repression. In some ways it seemed that the old pattern of interaction between the state and the opposition was continuing, but in other ways much had changed. Paradoxically, the Supreme Council of Armed Forces (SCAF) was both omnipotent and yet unable to enforce some of its own decrees, such as the ban on demonstrations. At times the SCAF engaged in harsh crackdowns on protesters and at other times backtracked or made concessions. The election of the parliament was hailed as a milestone by some, but it was derided by many revolutionary youth. What did Egyptians think had been the most important accomplishments one year after the ousting of Mubarak? What did they see as the major setbacks? What did they hope for the future? In order to answer these and other questions, I conducted a survey. The sample included college-educated Egyptians of all ages, including both activists and nonactivists, with 56.7 percent saying they attended at least one demonstration during the 18-day revolution that ousted Mubarak, while 43.3 percent said they did not take part at all. Contrary to other surveys, which try to predict the future, the purpose of this poll was to try to make sense of the past.

The survey consisted of about 35 questions, some open-ended and others closed-ended. The full results of the survey cannot be summarized here. But I will point to one interesting finding. Based on input from a focus group of Egyptian citizens, the survey listed what were considered to be nine important achievements. Participants then had to choose what type of social pressure they believe led to this accomplishment—pressure from street protests, labor strikes, political parties, or other. Please refer to Graphs A.1 and A.2.

As Graph A.1 demonstrates, pressure from labor strikes was considered to be decisive in leading to the promise to raise the minimum wage and the creation of independent trade unions. For all of the seven other achievements, pressure from street protests was considered to be the most decisive.

- The decision to put Mubarak on trial:
  - 89.3 percent of respondents believe this was due to pressure from street protests.
  - Only 4.6 percent believe this was due to pressure from political parties.
- The decision to release civilians who had been detained for political reasons:
  - 83.1 percent believe this was due to pressure from street protests.
  - Only 8.1 percent believe this was due to pressure from political parties.

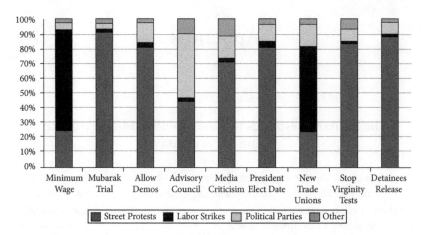

Graph A.1 Achievements during the second wave and who is believed to be responsible.

- Moving forward the date of presidential elections/handing over power to civilians:
  - 80.6 percent of respondents believe this was due to pressure from street protests.
  - Only 11 percent believe this was due to pressure from political parties.

Just how substantial these concessions are, or whether certain promises will indeed be upheld, cannot be ascertained by this survey. Nevertheless, these results are interesting as they question some of the assumptions in the literature on democratization, which generally sees the formation of political parties as the most important factor in transitioning away from authoritarianism.

If street protests can take credit for the achievements of the transition period, it is the SCAF who was given the blame for the setbacks and defeats. Responsibility for the setbacks in terms of democratization was unequivocally laid at the feet of the ruling generals in the SCAF. This is again significant, especially as the survey was conducted before the dissolution of parliament and power grab by the military earlier that month. For all 10 categories of setbacks, the SCAF was considered to be more responsible than any other group.

For 6 of the 10 categories, more than 50 percent of respondents blamed the SCAF. These included: violence against protesters (70.2%), the Maspero incident (68.1%), military trials (94.4%), human rights abuses (64.7%), repression of opposition (73.9%), and increase in prices/decrease in supplies (64.2%).

Given that the transition period witnessed both achievements and setbacks raises the question of how responsive Egyptians believe the ruling generals have been to their demands.

The survey found that 70.5 percent of respondents believe that the SCAF is not responsive to the Egyptian people at all, while only 0.5 percent believe the SCAF is completely responsive to the Egyptian people. The standing of the military council as an institution had decreased significantly among both activists and nonactivists (Graph A.3).

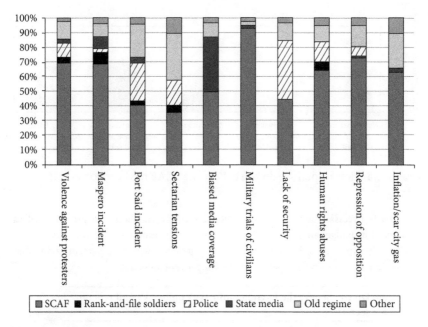

Graph A.2 Setbacks during the second wave and who is believed to be responsible.

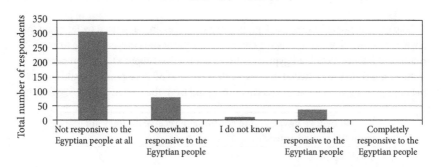

Graph A.3 How responsive do you believe the SCAF has been to the Egyptian people?

What may be more surprising is that 83.3 percent of those surveyed believe the SCAF is either completely or somewhat responsive to the United States. Only 0.2 percent believe the SCAF is not responsive to the United States at all (Graph A.4).

Related to the issue of accountability is that of budget transparency. Until now the military's budget has not been subjected to civilian oversight. The SCAF has maintained

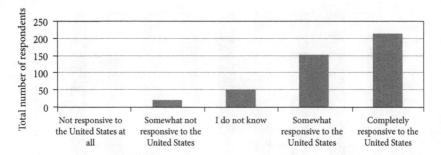

Graph A.4 How responsive do you believe the SCAF has been to the US?

that this is necessary for reasons of national security and hopes to prevent civilian scrutiny of its budget after the handover of power. But respondents to the survey overwhelmingly expressed a desire to increase transparency, with 81.2 percent saying that they believe the military's budget should no longer remain secret.

Do you believe the Egyptian military's budget should remain secret?		
Total responses	441	
Yes	83	18.8%
No	358	81.2%

Like most national armies, the Egyptian armed forces are supported by Egyptian taxpayers. Another channel of support comes from American taxpayers in the form of US military aid. Since 1979 the Egyptian military has received about $1.5 billion per year in military aid from the United States. Two-thirds (66.9%) of all respondents said that they believe Egypt should no longer receive military aid from the United States.

Do you believe Egypt should continue to receive military aid from the United States?		
Total responses	441	
Yes	146	33.1%
No	295	66.9%

Respondents were then asked to explain in an open-ended question why they supported or rejected the continuation of US military aid to Egypt. The two main arguments for supporting the continuation of aid were because "Egypt needs the aid" and "Egypt earned it." The two main reasons for rejecting US military aid were because it is "humiliating/shameful" and because "it gives the US power over Egypt."

It would be wrong to interpret this as simply a matter of anti-Americanism. Surveys that merely try to gauge whether people's perceptions of the United States are positive or negative are often unable to explain the reasons behind these sentiments. Evidence from this survey sheds light on what may be driving the resentment.

Key Findings

There are six clear results from this section of the larger survey.

(1) Survey respondents clearly believe that the achievements of the transition period happened as a result of pressure from street protests and labor strikes, while the role of political parties was negligible.

(2) More than the old regime, the police, or the state media, survey respondents blame the SCAF for the setbacks of the transition period, especially concerning the use of violence against protesters, military trials of civilians, and other human rights abuses.

(3) The standing of the military has seen a sharp decline, with 70.5 percent of respondents believing that the SCAF is not at all responsive to the Egyptian people.

(4) The overwhelming majority of respondents (83.3%) believe that the SCAF is either completely or somewhat responsive to the United States.

(5) Two-thirds of respondents (66.9%) believe that Egypt should no longer receive military aid from the United States.

(6) And finally, the majority of respondents (81.2%) believe that Egypt's military budget should no longer remain secret.

Notes

Chapter 1

1. My own ethnographic vignettes are at times italicized and set apart from the chapter, as this passage. At other times, when I felt that the ethnography flowed naturally with the narrative of the chapter, they are included in the body of the text and are not italicized.
2. See an overview of the first four of these uprisings by Juan Cole, "Egypt's Modern Revolutions and the Fall of Mubarak," in *The New Middle East: Protest and Revolution in the Arab World*, ed. Fawaz A. Gerges (Cambridge: Cambridge University Press, 2014), 60–79. See also John Chalcraft, *Popular Politics in the Making of the Modern Middle East* (Cambridge: Cambridge University Press, 2016).
3. Jeff Goodwin, *No Other Way Out* (Cambridge [u.a.]: Cambridge University Press, 2001), 3; Eric John Hobsbawm, *The Age of Revolution 1789–1800* (London: Weidenfeld & Nicolson, 1962).
4. Mark N. Katz, *Revolutions and Revolutionary Waves* (New York: St. Martin's Press, 1999), 26.
5. Charles Tilly, *From Mobilization to Revolution* (Reading, MA: Addison-Wesley, 1978); Theda Skocpol, *States and Social Revolutions: A Comparative Analysis of France, Russia, and China* (Cambridge: Cambridge University Press, 1979); John Foran, *Theorizing Revolutions* (London and New York: Routledge, 1997); Goodwin, *No Other Way Out*; Jack A. Goldstone, *States, Parties, and Social Movements* (New York: Cambridge University Press, 2003); Eric Selbin, *Revolution, Rebellion, Resistance* (London: Zed, 2010).
6. Theda Skocpol, "Rentier State and Shi'a Islam in the Iranian Revolution," *Theory and Society* 11, no. 3 (1982).
7. See John Waterbury and Gamal Abdel Nasser, *The Egypt of Nasser and Sadat* (Princeton, NJ: Princeton University Press, 1983). Waterbury argues that the pre-1952 bourgeoisie was indeed uprooted and that the Nasserist state had eliminated the preexisting dominant classes, creating a state bourgeoisie that operated with a great deal of autonomy. Beinin and Lockman, however, see a good deal of continuity in class relations. See Joel Beinin and Zachary Lockman, *Workers on the Nile: Nationalism, Communism, Islam and the Egyptian Working Class, 1882–1954* (Princeton, NJ: Princeton University, 1987).
8. Ellen Kay Trimberger, *Revolution from Above: Military Bureaucrats and Development in Japan, Turkey, Egypt, and Peru* (New Brunswick, NJ: Transaction Books, 1978).
9. Michael Herb, *All in the Family* (Albany: State University of New York Press, 1999); Joseph Kostiner, *Middle East Monarchies* (Boulder, CO: Lynne Rienner, 2000); Ellen Lust-Okar, "Divided They Rule: The Management and Manipulation of Political Opposition," *Comparative Politics* 36, no. 2 (2004): 159; Oliver Schlumberger,

Debating Arab Authoritarianism (Johanneshov: TPB, 2007); Holger Albrecht, *Contentious Politics in the Middle East* (Gainesville: University Press of Florida, 2010); Bassam Haddad, "Syria's Stalemate: The Limits of Regime Resilience," *Middle East Policy* 19, no. 1 (2012): 85–95; Eva Bellin, "Reconsidering the Robustness of Authoritarianism in the Middle East: Lessons from the Arab Spring," *Comparative Politics* 44, no. 2 (2012): 127–149.

10. According to Weber, "Sultanism tends to arise whenever traditional domination develops an administration and a military force which are purely instruments of the master." See Max Weber, *Economy and Society* (Berkeley: University of California Press, 1978).

11. See "Infographics," Tahrir Institute for Middle East Policy, accessed October 14, 2017, https://timep.org/esw/infographics/; Robert Kagan and Michele Dunne, "Obama Embraces the Nixon Doctrine in Egypt," *Washington Post*, April 3, 2015, accessed October 14, 2017, https://wapo.st/2TNrBVI.

12. Data is from Wikithawra, https://wikithawra.wordpress.com/2013/09/03/rabiadis-peral14aug/.

Chapter 2

1. For state theorists in the Marxist tradition, who see the state as the institutional accretion of past class struggles, class relationships are primary. See Bob Jessop, *State Theory: Putting the Capitalist State in Its Place* (Oxford: Wiley, 2013); but also Peter B. Evans and Dietrich Rüschemeyer, *Bringing the State Back In* (Cambridge: Cambridge University Press, 2010).

2. Nazih N. M. Ayubi, *Over-Stating the Arab State* (London: I. B. Tauris, 1995).

3. Khaled Fahmy, *All the Pasha's Men: Mehmed Ali, His Army and the Making of Modern Egypt* (Cairo: American University in Cairo Press, 1997); Juan Ricardo Cole, *Napoleon's Egypt: Invading the Middle East* (New York: Palgrave Macmillan, 2008).

4. Roger Owen, *The Rise and Fall of Arab Presidents for Life* (Cambridge, MA: Harvard University Press, 2012).

5. Max Weber, *Economy and Society*.

6. Samer Soliman, *The Autumn of Dictatorship: Fiscal Crisis and Political Change in Egypt under Mubarak* (Stanford, CA: Stanford University Press, 2011), 24.

7. For a discussion of the distinction between state and regime, see Robert M. Fishman, "Rethinking State and Regime: Southern Europe's Transition to Democracy," *World Politics* 42, no. 3 (April 1990), accessed August 12, 2017, https://ntrda.me/2RZcWoM. See also Dan Slater, *Ordering Power: Contentious Politics and Authoritarian Leviathans in Southeast Asia* (Cambridge: Cambridge University Press, 2011); Dan Slater and Sofia Fenner, "State Power and Staying Power: Infrastructural Mechanisms and Authoritarian Durability," *Journal of International Affairs* 65, no. 1 (2011): 15–29, http://www.jstor.org/stable/24388179.

8. An extreme type of exclusive authoritarian regime is a form that Weber termed "sultanism" or "sultanistic dictatorships." In such regimes power is concentrated

in the hands of the ruler, who is essentially detached from the people he governs, hovering above society and exercising power, unchecked by other institutions or even wealthy elites. See Weber, *Economy and Society*; Juan J. Linz and Alfred Stepan, *Problems of Democratic Transition and Consolidation: Southern Europe, South America, and Post-Communist Europe* (Baltimore, MD: Johns Hopkins University Press, 1998); For a more recent discussion see Robert Springborg, "Arab Militaries," in *The Arab Uprisings Explained: New Contentious Politics in the Middle East*, ed. Marc Lynch (New York: Columbia University Press, 2014), 142–159.

9. Soliman, *The Autumn of Dictatorship*, 25.

10. Waterbury and Nasser, *The Egypt of Nasser and Sadat*; Robert Springborg, *Mubarak's Egypt: Fragmentation of the Political Order* (Boulder, CO: Westview Press,1989); Eberhard Kienle, *A Grand Delusion: Democracy and Economic Reform in Egypt* (London: I. B. Tauris, 2001); Lisa Blaydes, *Elections and Distributive Politics in Mubarak's Egypt* (Cambridge: Cambridge University Press, 2011).

11. Blaydes, *Elections and Distributive Politics*, 6.

12. Joshua Stacher, *Adaptable Autocrats: Regime Power in Egypt and Syria* (Cairo: American University in Cairo Press, 2012), 52.

13. Stacher, *Adaptable Autocrats*, 78.

14. Soliman, *The Autumn of Dictatorship*, 26.

15. Beinin, *Workers and Thieves: Labor Movements and Popular Uprisings in Tunisia and Egypt* (Stanford, CA: Stanford Briefs, 2016); Saskia Brechenmacher, *Civil Society under Assault: Repression and Responses in Russia, Egypt, and Ethiopia*, report, Carnegie Endowment for International Peace, Washington, D, accessed February 10, 2018, https:// bit.ly/ 2qAFOK1.; Maha M. Abdelrahman, *Civil Society Exposed: The Politics of NGOs in Egypt* (London: Tauris Academic, 2004); Hala AlSayed, "ثقوب تعوق العمل الخيري" [Holes impeding charity work], AlAhram, October 29, 2016, accessed February 13, 2019, http:// www.ahram.org.eg/ NewsPrint/ 558304.aspx. [Translation provided by author].

16. Jason Brownlee, *Democracy Prevention: The Politics of the U.S.-Egyptian Alliance* (New York: Cambridge University Press, 2012); Oisín Tansey, *The International Politics of Authoritarian Rule* (Oxford: Oxford University Press, 2016).

17. Steven Levitsky and Lucan A. Way, *Competitive Authoritarianism: Hybrid Regimes after the Cold War* (New York: Cambridge University Press, 2010).

18. Brownlee, *Democracy Prevention*, 6.

19. Rami Raouf, comment on "Egypt: Timeline of Communication Shutdown during the Revolution," مدونة رامي رؤوف (Rami Raouf's blog), June 9, 2011, accessed February 13, 2019, https://bit.ly/2TLlq4x. [Translation provided by author].

20. A full accounting of the various ministries that comprise the vast Egyptian bureaucracy and their degree of loyalty to Mubarak is outside the scope of this project. To cite just one example, however, all of the members of the Supreme Constitutional Court had been designated by Mubarak. Its president had been chosen by Mubarak to prepare a dynastic transmission of power to his son, Gamal Mubarak.

21. Neil Ketchley, *Egypt in a Time of Revolution: Contentious Politics and the Arab Spring* (Cambridge, UK: Cambridge University Press, 2017).

278 NOTES

22. John Sfakianakis, "The Whales of the Nile: Networks, Businessmen, and Bureaucrats during the Era of Privatization in Egypt," in *Networks of Privilege in the Middle East: The Politics of Economic Reform Revisited*, ed. Steven Heydemann (New York: Palgrave Macmillan, 2004), 77–100.

23. Stephan Roll, "Egypt's Business Elite after Mubarak: A Powerful Player between Generals and Brotherhood," report, German Institute for International and Security Affairs, September 2013, accessed February 11, 2018, https://bit.ly/2BARtgK

24. Joshua Stacher, *Adaptable Autocrats*.

25. Bessan Kassab, "Tahya Masr: How Sisi Bypassed Auditing a Multi-Billion Pound Fund," Mada Masr, April 6, 2016, Accessed February 8, 2018, https://bit.ly/2SJ0sWZ.

26. The influence of the military in politics is often referred to in the English-language academic literature as "autonomy." It is therefore not uncommon to discuss the "level of autonomy" of the military vis-à-vis the state. However, this creates the impression (and may indeed be based on the assumption) that the military is a separate branch of government, akin to the role of the Department of Defense in the United States. In Egypt, however, the military has at times acted as the governing power. If the military *is* the state, it is meaningless to discuss the level of the military's autonomy from the state. Alfred Stepan's distinction between the "military-as-institution" and the "military-as-government" is useful in this regard.

27. At least since the early 1990s American defense officials had been trying to convince their Egyptian counterparts to downsize their force and to discard their remaining Eastern-bloc equipment in favor of weapons systems built in the United States. At the time they were unwilling to downsize their force, however, because they did not want "to add several hundred thousand individuals with military training and experience to the unemployment lines." See Stephen H. Gotowicki, "The Role of the Egyptian Military in Domestic Society," Foreign Military Studies Office Publications, 1997, accessed August 12, 2017, https://bit.ly/2Eayew4.

28. Pierre Razoux, "What to Expect of the Egyptian Army?," technical paper, February 14, 2011, accessed February 20, 2017, http://www.ndc.nato.int/news/news.php?icode=244.

29. Elke Grawert and Zeinab Abul-Magd, *Businessmen in Arms: How the Military and Other Armed Groups Profit in the MENA Region* (Lanham: Rowman & Littlefield, 2016); Zeinab Abul-Magd, *Militarizing the Nation: The Army, Business, and Revolution in Egypt* (New York: Columbia University Press, 2017).

30. Alvin Z. Rubinstein, *Red Star on the Nile: The Soviet-Egyptian Influence Relationship since the June War* (Princeton, NJ: Princeton University Press, 1977); Craig Daigle, *The Limits of Détente: The United States, the Soviet Union, and the Arab-Israeli Conflict, 1969–1973* (New Haven, CT: Yale University Press, 2012).

31. Brownlee, *Democracy Prevention*.

32. Hillel Frisch, "Guns and Butter in the Egyptian army," *Middle East Review of International Affairs* 5, no. 2 (June 2001): 1–12.

33. Moheb Zaki, *Civil Society and Democratization in Egypt, 1981–1994* (Cairo: Ibn Khaldoun Center, 1995).

34. Soliman, *The Autumn of Dictatorship*.

35. Stacher, *Adaptable Autocrats*, 66ff.

36. "Remarks at the American University in Cairo," US Department of State, June 20, 2005, accessed February 14, 2019, https://bit.ly/2AEDlCo.

37. Carrie Rosefsky Wickham, *Muslim Brotherhood: Evolution of an Islamist Movement* (Princeton, NJ: Princeton University Press, 2013); Jamil Hilal and Katja Hermann, eds., "Mapping of the Arab Left: Contemporary Leftist Politics in the Arab East," publication, March 2014, accessed February 10, 2016, https://www.rosalux.de/publikation/id/7637/.

38. Goodwin, *No Other Way Out*, 10–11.

39. Several scholars attribute what they see as the failure of the Egyptian revolution to the lack of proper revolutionary leadership; see for example John Chalcraft's *Popular Politics* (2016) and Asef Bayat, *Revolution without Revolutionaries: Making Sense of the Arab Spring* (Stanford, CA: Stanford University Press, 2017).

40. Although by no means an exhaustive list, some of the classic works on revolutions prior to the Arab uprisings include: Tilly, *From Mobilization to Revolution*; Skocpol, *States and Social Revolutions*; John Foran, *Theorizing Revolutions*; Misagh Parsa, *States, Ideologies, and Social Revolutions: A Comparative Analysis of Iran, Nicaragua, and the Philippines* (Cambridge: Cambridge University Press, 2000); Goodwin, *No Other Way Out*; Goldstone, *States, Parties, and Social Movements.*; Charles Kurzman, *The Unthinkable Revolution in Iran* (Cambridge, MA: Harvard University Press, 2004); and Selbin, *Revolution, Rebellion, Resistance.*

41. Maher Abdel Sabour, "إحالة أوراق ٥٢٩ متهما للمفتي وبراءة ١٦ آخرين في أحداث عنف المنيا" "عقب فض رابعة والنهضة" [Transferring the papers of 529 defendants to the Mufti and acquitting 16 others in the Minya Case], AlSherouk News, March 24, 2014, accessed February 14, 2019, https://bit.ly/2DGvMMg. [Translation provided by author]. Said Nafei and Tereza Kamel, "قاضي إعدام المنيا يحيل ٦٨٣ «إخوانيًا» جديدا بينهم «بديع» للمفتي" [The Minya judge refers 683 new Muslim Brotherhood defendants including Badei to the Mufti], AlSherouk News, April 28, 2014, accessed February 14, 2019, https://bit.ly/2N5D0xQ. [Translation provided by author].

42. Amy Austin Holmes, "In Egypt, Industrial Scale Death Decrees," Providencejournal.com, May 5, 2014, accessed August 11, 2017, https://bit.ly/2E6tY0H.

43. See Mona El-Ghobashy, "Constitutionalist Contention in Contemporary Egypt," *American Behavioral Scientist* 51, no. 11 (2008): 1590–1610. Nathan Brown describes how dissident judges gained the upper hand in the Judges Club around 2005, but after the regime responded with "harassment, character assassination, stonewalling" and some pay raises, less confrontational judges eventually regained control. See: Nathan Brown, "Egypt's Judges in a Revolutionary Age," Carnegie Endowment for International Peace, February 22, 2012, accessed February 12, 2018, https://bit.ly/2Svftwd.

44. Stacher, *Adaptable Autocrats*, 83.

45. Skocpol, *States and Social Revolutions*.

46. Adam Hanieh, *Lineages of Revolt: Issues of Contemporary Capitalism in the Middle East* (Chicago: Haymarket Books, 2013).

47. Goodwin, *No Other Way Out*.

48. Tilly, *From Mobilization to Revolution*.

49. Charles Tilly, *Regimes and Repertoires* (Chicago: University of Chicago Press, 2006). See also James Jasper who advocated for replacing the concept of agency with that of strategy: "A Strategic Approach to Collective Action: Looking for Agency in Social-Movement Choices," *Mobilization: An International Quarterly* 9, no. 1 (February 2004): 1–16.

50. Laura Nader, "Ethnography as Theory," *Hau: Journal of Ethnographic Theory* 1, no. 1 (2011): 211–219.

51. Goodwin, *No Other Way Out*, 37–40.

52. US Embassy, "Egypt in Transition: Sadat and Mubarak," Wiki Leaks, December 12, 2017, accessed February 14, 2019, https://bit.ly/2E8MdT0.

53. Dina Shehata, "Youth Mobilization in Egypt: New Trends and Opportunities," working paper, Issam Fares Institute for Public Policy and International Affairs, American University in Beirut (2011).

54. Laura Nader's essay admonished anthropologists to "study up" and contribute to understanding how "power and responsibility are exercised in the United States." See: Laura Nader, "Up the Anthropologist: Perspectives Gained from Studying Up," in *Reinventing Anthropology*, ed. Dell H. Hymes (New York: Pantheon Books, 1974), 284–311.

55. If recent "big history" studies challenge conventional periodizations by opening up the timeline to encompass much larger swaths of human history, the focus on "micro-periods" challenges conventional periodizations by zooming in on events within a specific historical period, thereby also destabilizing existing categories. Choosing a historical approach depends naturally in part on the subject under investigation. For example, explaining the decline of feudalism and rise of capitalism requires a longer historical analysis. World-systems scholars argued that not only should the time frame be longer but also that geographical boundaries should be wider in order to account for world-systemic changes (prominent examples being Braudel's *The Mediterranean*, Wallerstein's *The Modern World-System*, and Arrighi's *The Long Twentieth Century*). Long before the distinction between "big history" and "micro-periods," Fernand Braudel distinguished between the *longue durée* and *histoire événementielle*, the study of revolutions falling into the latter category. See P. J. Corfield, *Time and the Shape of History* (New Haven: Yale University Press, 2007); Sergei Bogatyrev, "Bronze Tsars: Ivan the Terrible and Fedor Ivanovich in the Décor of Early Modern Guns," *Slavonic and East European Review* 88 (January 2010): 48–72; Fernand Braudel, *The Mediterranean and the Mediterranean World in the Age of Phillip II* (London: Collins, 1972); Immanuel Maurice Wallerstein, *The Modern World System* (New York: Academic Press, 1976); Giovanni Arrighi, *The Long Twentieth Century: Money, Power and the Origins of Our Times* (London: Verso, 2010).

56. William H. Sewell, "Historical Events as Transformations of Structures: Inventing Revolution at the Bastille," *Theory and Society* 25, no. 6 (1996): 841–881.

57. Aristide R Zolberg, *Moments of Madness* (n.p.: n.p., 1972).

58. Skocpol, *States and Social Revolutions*.

59. See William R. Thompson, *The Grievances of Military Coup-Makers* (Beverly Hills: Sage, 1973); R. W. Jackman, "The Predictability of Coups d'etat: A Model with African Data," *American Political Science Review* 72 (1978): 1262–1275; Jonathan M. Powell and Clayton L. Thyne, "Global Instances of Coups from 1950 to 2010: A New Dataset," *Journal of Peace Research* 48, no. 2 (2011): 249–259; Patrick J. Mcgowan, "African Military Coups détat, 1956–2001: Frequency, Trends and Distribution," *Journal of Modern African Studies* 41, no. 3 (2003): 339–370.

60. Peter Feaver, *Armed Servants: Agency, Oversight, and Civil-Military Relations* (Cambridge, MA: Harvard University Press, 2005).

61. See: Clayton L. Thyne, "Supporter of Stability or Agent of Agitation? The Effect of US Foreign Policy on Coups in Latin America, 1960–99," *Journal of Peace Research* 47, no. 4 (2010): 449–461; Ozan O. Varol, "The Democratic Coup d'État," *Harvard International Law Journal* 53, no. 2 (2012): 291–356.

62. John Foran and Jeff Goodwin, "Revolutionary Outcomes in Iran and Nicaragua: Coalition Fragmentation, War, and the Limits of Social Transformation," *Theory and Society* 22, no. 2 (1993): 209–247.

63. Richard Lachmann, *States and Power* (Cambridge: Polity Press, 2010).

64. Fred Halliday, *Revolution and World Politics: The Rise and Fall of the Sixth Great Power* (Durham: Duke University Press, 1999).

65. Trimberger, *Revolution from Above.*

66. Edward Luttwak, *Coup détat: A Practical Handbook* (Cambridge, MA: Harvard University Press, 2016); Samuel Finer, *Man on Horseback: The Role of the Military in Politics* (New York: Routledge, 2017); Tormod K. Lunde, "Modernization and Political Instability: Coups D'Etat in Africa, 1955–85," *Acta Sociologica* 34, no. 1 (1991): 13–32; Aaron Belkin and Evan Schofer, "Coup Risk, Counterbalancing, and International Conflict," *Security Studies* 14, no. 1 (2005): 140–177.

67. Powell and Thyne, "Global Instances."

68. Nikolay Marinov and Hein Goemans, "Coups and Democracy," *British Journal of Political Science* 44, no. 4 (October 2014), accessed February 14, 2019, https://bit.ly/2DBKFQ5.

69. Holger Albrecht, "The Myth of Coup-Proofing Risk and Instances of Military Coups détat in the Middle East and North Africa 1950–2013" *Armed Forces & Society* 41, no. 4 (2014): 659–687.

70. Charles Tilly, *The Vendée* (Cambridge, MA: Harvard University Press, 1980).

71. Leon Trotsky and Max Eastman, *The History of the Russian Revolution* (New York: Simon & Schuster, 1936).

72. Dan Slater and Nicholas Rush Smith, "The Power of Counterrevolution: Elitist Origins of Political Order in Postcolonial Asia and Africa," *American Journal of Sociology* 121, no. 5 (2016): 1513.

73. Jack A. Goldstone, "Toward a Fourth Generation of Revolutionary Theory," *Annual Review of Political Science* (2001): 173–174.

74. George Lawson, "Within and Beyond the 'Fourth Generation' of Revolutionary Theory," *Sociological Theory* 34, no. 2 (2016): 106–127.

75. At times, however, the decision to disobey orders is not tantamount to a subversion of civil-military relations. Pion-Berlin and Trinkunas (2010) refer to this phenomenon as "shirking": the military is ordered to suppress protesters but instead refuses to deploy and remains quartered in its barracks. As they underline, "the result is a constitutional crisis, not a military takeover." See: David Pion-Berlin and Harold Trinkunas, "Civilian Praetorianism and Military Shirking During Constitutional Crises in Latin America," *Comparative Politics* 42, no. 4 (2010) 395–411.

76. Erica Chenoweth And Maria J. Stephan, *Why Civil Resistance Works: the Strategic Logic of Nonviolent Conflict,* Columbia Studies in Terrorism and Irregular Warfare (New York: Columbia University Press, 2011); Sharon Erickson Nepstad, Nonviolent Revolutions: Civil Resistance in the Late 20th Century (Oxford: Oxford University Press, 2011); Aurel Croissant, Democratization, Democracy and Authoritarian Continuity (London: Routledge, 2014); Zoltan Barany, "Comparing the Arab Revolts: The Role of the Military," *Journal of Democracy* 22, no. 4 (October 2011), accessed February 12, 2016, https://bit.ly/2RXV3a1.

77. Zoltan Barany, *How Armies Respond to Revolution and Why* (Princeton, NJ: Princeton University Press 2016), 138–143.

78. Amy Austin Holmes, "Why Egypt's Military Orchestrated a Massacre," *Washington Post,* August 22, 2014; Amy Austin Holmes and Kevin Kohler, "Myths of Military Defection in Egypt and Tunisia," *Mediterranean Politics,* July 30, 2018, 1–26.

79. For example, in Tunisia the army disobeyed orders to violently suppress the protests, but then stepped aside after Ben Ali was ousted. In Egypt the army disobeyed orders to violently suppress protesters, but then took power after Mubarak was ousted.

80. Cole, "Egypt's Modern Revolutions and the Fall of Mubarak," 72.

81. Guillermo O'Donnell, *Transitions from Authoritarian Rule: Comparative Perspectives* (Baltimore, MD: Johns Hopkins University Press, 1991).

82. Ibid.

83. Paul Collier and Jan Willem Gunning, "Why Has Africa Grown Slowly?" *Journal of Economic Perspectives* 13, no. 3 (1999): 3–22.

84. On the role of the labor movement in the uprising, see Beinin, *Workers and Thieves*; Anne Alexander, "Brothers-in-Arms? The Egyptian Military, the Ikhwan and the Revolutions of 1952 and 2011," *Journal of North African Studies* 16, no. 4 (2011): 533–554.

85. Adam Przeworski, *Democracy and the Market: Political and Economic Reforms in Eastern Europe and Latin America* (Cambridge: Cambridge University Press, 2003).

86. My understanding of Serra's model is that it is not normative; there is no assumption that countries automatically will or should move from one level to another. It is simply meant as a way of distinguishing between different levels of military power. See Narcis Serra, *The Military Transition: Democratic Reform of the Armed Forces* (Cambridge: Cambridge University Press, 2010).

87. Serra, *The Military Transition.*

88. Stepan's distinction between the military-as-government and the military-as-institution will also be used to understand the period of SCAF rule.

89. Alfred Stepan, *The Military in Politics: Changing Patterns in Brazil* (Princeton, NJ: Princeton University Press, 1974).

90. See for example Varol's article (2012) in the *Harvard International Law Journal* comparing Turkey in 1960, Portugal in 1974, and Egypt in 2011, in which he argues that they all represent "democratic coups d'etat": see also Varol, *The Democratic Coup D'Etat*.

91. The European Union and the countries of the Persian Gulf, in particular Saudi Arabia and Qatar, have also attempted to influence the recent course of events in Egypt, including through the provision of financial aid. However, I do not believe that their support, or lack thereof, has an impact on regime survival that is comparable to that of the United States, which has provided military and financial aid to Egypt for three decades, trains its military officers, has close relationships with the highest-ranking members of SCAF, and is still the hegemonic power in the international system.

92. My analysis of regime strategies and protest strategies will draw from, but also expand upon, Charles Tilly's work on contentious politics. See Tilly, *Regimes and Repertoires*.

93. Marc Lynch, *The Arab Uprisings Explained: New Contentious Politics in the Middle East* (New York: Columbia University Press, 2012); Paolo Gerbaudo, *Tweets and the Streets: Social Media and Contemporary Activism* (London: Pluto Press, 2012); Mona Abaza, "Mourning, Narratives and Interactions with the Martyrs through Cairo's Graffiti," E-International Relations, October 7, 2013, accessed March 15, 2016, https://bit.ly/2tm1xFC; Bellin, "Reconsidering the Robustness of Authoritarianism in the Middle East: Lessons from the Arab Spring,"; Barany, *How Armies Respond to Revolution and Why*; Clement M. Henry and Robert Springborg, "A Tunisian Solution for Egypt's Military," *Foreign Affairs*, June 15, 2011, accessed January 5, 2017, https://fam.ag/2Ebc3Ge; Holger Albrecht and Dina Bishara, "Back on Horseback: The Military and Political Transformation in Egypt," *Middle East Law and Governance* 3, no. 1-2 (2011), accessed March 3, 2015; Tewfick Aclimandos, "Reforming the Egyptian Security Services," Arab Reform Initiative, June 1, 2011, accessed August 5, 2015, http://www.arab-reform.net/en/node/567; Philippe Droz-Vincent, "Authoritarianism, Revolutions, Armies and Arab Regime Transitions," *International Spectator* 46, no. 2 (2011): 5–21; Yezid Siyagh, "Above the State: The Officers' Republic in Egypt," Carnegie Endowment for International Peace, August 1, 2012, accessed January 5, 2015, https://bit.ly/2TOq3Ln; Hazem Kandil, *Soldiers, Spies and Statesmen: Egypt's Road to Revolt* (London: Verso Books, 2012); Grawert and Abul-Magd, *Businessmen in Arms*; Steven A. Cook, *The Struggle for Egypt from Nasser to Tahrir Square* (New York: Oxford University Press, 2012); Brownlee, *Democracy Prevention*; Lloyd C. Gardner, *The Road to Tahrir Square: Egypt and the United States from the Rise of Nasser to the Fall of Mubarak* (New York: New Press, 2011); Jean-Pierre Filiu, *From Deep State to Islamic State: The Arab Counter-Revolution and Its Jihadi Legacy* (London: Hurst & Company, 2015); Jeffrey C. Alexander, *Performative Revolution in Egypt: An Essay in Cultural Power* (London: Bloomsbury Academic, 2011); Beinin, *Workers and Thieves*; Rabab El-Mahdi, "Labour Protests in

Egypt: Causes and Meanings," *Review of African Political Economy* 38, no. 129 (2011): 387–402; Wickham, *Muslim Brotherhood: Evolution of an Islamist Movement*; Ashraf El-Sherif, "The Muslim Brotherhood and the Future of Political Islam in Egypt," Carnegie Endowment for International Peace, October 21, 2014, accessed January 5, 2017, https://bit.ly/2E9sL8J; Ashraf El-Sherif, "Egypt's Salafists at a Crossroads," Carnegie Endowment, April 29, 2015, accessed January 5, 2017, https://bit.ly/2DAtlLg; Hazem Kandil, "Why Islamists Count?," *Cambridge Review of International Affairs* 28, no. 2 (2015); Hesham Al-Awadi, *The Muslim Brothers in Pursuit of Legitimacy: Power and Political Islam in Egypt under Mubarak* (London: I. B. Tauris, 2014). Albrecht Holger and Dorothy Ohl, "Exit, Resistance, Loyalty: Military Behavior during Unrest in Authoritarian Regimes," *Perspectives on Politics* 14, no. 1 (March 2016): 38–52; Abul-Magd, *Militarizing the Nation*; Eric Trager, *Arab Fall: How the Muslim Brotherhood Won and Lost Egypt in 891 Days* (Washington, DC: Georgetown University Press, 2017).

94. Brown, "Egypt's Judges in a Revolutionary Age,"; Jeffrey Goldberg, "The Modern King in the Arab Spring," *The Atlantic*, February 19, 2014, accessed August 6, 2016, https://bit.ly/2tktfmh; Dalia Fahmy and Daanish Faruqi, eds., *Egypt and the Contradictions of Liberalism: Illiberal Intelligentsia and the Future of Egyptian Democracy* (London: Oneworld, 2017); Sahar F. Aziz, "(De)liberalizing Judicial Independence in Egypt," in *Egypt and the Contradictions of Liberalism: Illiberal Intelligentsia and the Future of Egyptian Democracy*, ed. Dalia F. Fahmy and Daanish Faruqi (London: Oneworld, 2017).

95. Scholars that offer analyses of more than one Arab Spring country include: Gilbert Achcar and G. M. Goshgarian, *The People Want: A Radical Exploration of the Arab Uprising* (London: Saqi, 2013); Samir Amin, *The People's Spring: The Future of the Arab Revolution* (Nairobi: Pambazuka Press, 2012); Lisa Anderson, "Demystifying the Arab Spring," *Foreign Affairs*, December 20, 2011, accessed June 6, 2015, https://fam.ag/1M9FjGn; James L. Gelvin, *The Arab Uprisings: What Everyone Needs to Know* (New York: Oxford University Press, 2012); Eberhard Kienle and Nadine Mourad Sika, *The Arab Uprisings: Transforming and Challenging State Power* (London: I. B. Tauris, 2015); Lynch, *The Arab Uprisings Explained*; Owen, *The Rise and Fall of Arab Presidents for Life*; Vijay Prashad, *Arab Spring, Libyan Winter* (Oakland, CA: AK Press, 2012). A series of edited volumes have also offered a comparative perspective on the region, including: Joel Beinin and Frédéric Vairel, *Social Movements, Mobilization, and Contestation in the Middle East and North Africa* (Stanford, CA: Stanford University Press, 2013); Rex Brynen, *Beyond the Arab Spring: Authoritarianism and Democratization in the Arab World* (Boulder, CO: Rienner, 2012); Gerges, *The New Middle East*; Bassam Haddad, Rosie Bsheer, and Ziad Abu-Rish, *The Dawn of the Arab Uprisings: End of an Old Order?* (London: Pluto Press, 2012); Mark L. Haas and David W. Lesch, *The Arab Spring: Change and Resistance in the Middle East* (Boulder, CO: Westview Press, 2013); Lina Khatib and Ellen Lust, *Taking to the Streets: The Transformation of Arab Activism* (Baltimore, MD: Johns Hopkins University Press, 2014); Bichara Khader, "Le « printemps arabe »: un premier bilan," ed. Bichara Khader, *CETRI*,

Éditions Syllepse, Alternatives Sud XIX (March 2012), accessed February 8, 2018, https://www.cetri.be/Le-printemps-arabe-un-premier-2644?lang=fr; David A. McMurray and Amanda Ufheil-Somers, *The Arab Revolts: Dispatches on Militant Democracy in the Middle East* (Bloomington: Indiana University Press, 2013); Daniel Ritter, *The Iron Cage of Liberalism: International Politics and Unarmed Revolutions in the Middle East and North Africa* (Oxford: Oxford University Press, 2014).

96. Holger Albrecht, *Raging Against the Machine: Political Opposition under Authoritarianism in Egypt* (Syracuse, NY: Syracuse University Press, 2013); Cook, *The Struggle for Egypt*; Mohamed El-Bendary, *The Egyptian Revolution and Its Aftermath: From Mubarak's Fall to Morsi's Rise* (New York: Algora Publishing, 2013); Adel Iskandar, *Egypt in Flux: Essays on an Unfinished Revolution* (Cairo: American University in Cairo Press, 2013); Kandil, *Soldiers, Spies and Statesmen*; Tarek Osman, *Egypt on the Brink: From Nasser to the Muslim Brotherhood* (New Haven: Yale University Press, 2013); H. A. Hellyer, *A Revolution Undone: Egypt's Road beyond Revolt* (New York: Oxford University Press, 2016); Ketchley, *Egypt in a Time of Revolution*; Brecht De Smet, *Gramsci on Tahrir: Revolution and Counter-Revolution in Egypt* (London: Pluto Press, 2016); M. Cherif Bassiouni, *Chronicles of the Egyptian Revolution and Its Aftermath: 2011–2016* (Cambridge: Cambridge University Press, 2017); Philip Marfleet, *Egypt: Contested Revolution* (London: Pluto Press, 2016).

97. Bahgat Korany and Rabab El-Mahdi, *Arab Spring in Egypt Revolution and Beyond* (Cairo: American University in Cairo Press, 2014); Dan Tschirgi, Walid Kazziha, and Sean F. McMahon, *Egypt's Tahrir Revolution* (Boulder: Lynne Rienner, 2013); Jeroen Gunning and Ilan Zvi Baron, *Why Occupy a Square? People, Protests and Movements in the Egyptian Revolution* (New York: Oxford University Press, 2014).

98. Kandil, *Soldiers, Spies and Statesmen*, 233–234.

99. De Smet, *Gramsci on Tahrir*.

100. Ketchley, *Egypt in a Time of Revolution*.

101. Trager, *Arab Fall: How the Muslim Brotherhood Won and Lost Egypt in 891 Days*.

102. Hellyer, *A Revolution Undone*, 166.

103. Bayat, *Revolution without Revolutionaries*; Chalcraft, *Popular Politics in the Making of the Modern Middle East*; Beinin, *Workers and Thieves*; Fahmy and Faruqi *Egypt and the Contradictions of Liberalism*; Amy Austin Holmes, "They Have a Gun in One Hand and the Media in the Other: The Rise of Anti-Militarist Activism under the Supreme Council of Armed Forces," Project on Middle East Political Science, May 3, 2016, accessed February 17, 2019, https://bit.ly/2SYiioX.

104. Holmes, "They Have a Gun in One Hand and the Media in the Other."

105. Bruce Rutherford, "Egypt's New Authoritarianism under Sisi," *Middle East Institute* 72, no 2 (Spring 2018): 185–208.

106. The issue of why women are often written out of the histories of the Egyptian revolution is a larger phenomenon that cannot be adequately addressed here. To give just one example of how this happens, see Hellyer, *A Revolution Undone*, where a glossary is included of the prominent players in the revolution. Out of 27 people listed in the glossary, only one is a woman.

107. "All According to Plan: The Rab'a Massacre and Mass Killings of Protesters in Egypt," Human Rights Watch, August 12, 2014, accessed February 14, 2019, https://bit.ly/1NaCcCS.

Chapter 3

1. Abigail Hauslohner, "Is Egypt about to have a Facebook Revolution?," *Time*, January 24, 2011, accessed February 1, 2017, https://bit.ly/2SBLW3K; Mike Giglio, "Inside Egypt's Facebook Revolt," *Newsweek*, January 27, 2011, accessed March 1, 2016, http://www.newsweek.com/inside-egypts-facebook-revolt-66791; William Wan, "Egypt's Facebook Revolution Faces Identity Crisis," *Washington Post*, March 23, 2011, accessed August 6, 2016, https://wapo.st/2SSWwCV.

2. Alexander, "Brothers-in-Arms? The Egyptian Military, the Ikhwan and the Revolutions of 1952 and 2011," ; Nahed Eltantawy and Julie B. Wiest, "Social Media in the Egyptian Revolution: Reconsidering Resource Mobilization Theory," *International Journal of Communication* 5 (2011): 1207–1224.

3. Racha Mourtada and Fadi Salem, "Social Media in the Arab World: Influencing Societal and Cultural Change?," report, Dubai School of Government, 1st ed., vol. 2, 5.

4. James DeFronzo, *Revolutions and Revolutionary Movements* (Boulder, CO: Westview Press, 2011).

5. Karl Marx, *The Communist Manifesto* (Ware, Hertfordshire: Wordsworth Editions, 2008).

6. For a critical comparison of Mosca, Pareto, and Michels, see Michael Hartmann, *The Sociology of Elites* (London: Routledge, 2007).

7. Skocpol, *States And Social Revolutions*.

8. Richard Lachmann, "Agents of Revolutions," in *Theorising Revolutions*, ed. John Foran (London and New York: Routledge, 1997), 74.

9. Goodwin, *No Other Way Out*.

10. As will be discussed in chapters 6 and 7, one of the reasons why human rights organizations in Egypt have had to rely extensively on foreign funding is precisely because they receive little to no support from Egyptian elites, who in theory would have the financial means to support them through donations. Their reliance on funds from abroad has also been one of the tools used by the regime to silence them. In December 2011, NGOs were raided and many of their employees received prison sentences ranging from 1 to 5 years with the allegation of having received foreign funds. At the time of writing, the prosecutions continue and some of the most prominent human rights defenders including Hossam Bahgat, Azza Soliman, and Gamal Eid are at risk of having even their private assets frozen. See Background on Case No. 173, the "foreign funding case," Imminent Risk of Prosecution and Closure, report, March 21, 2016, accessed August 4, 2016, http://eipr.org/en/pressrelease/2016/03/21/2569.

11. "The Struggle between Egypt's Business and Military Elite," Stratfor Worldview, February 9, 2011, accessed August 6, 2016, https://bit.ly/2N8kYLd.

12. David E. Cooper, "Equality and Envy," *Journal of Philosophy of Education* 16, no. 1 (1982): 35–47.

13. Grawert and Abul-Magd, *Businessmen in Arms*; Abul Magd 2017.

14. W. J. Dorman, "Exclusion and Informality: The Praetorian Politics of Land Management in Cairo, Egypt," *International Journal of Urban and Regional Research* 37, no. 5 (2013): 1584–1610.

15. Issandr El Amrani, "Electoral Manipulation in Egypt: Revisiting 2005," *The Arabist*, November 5, 2010, accessed April 19, 2016. https://arabist.net/blog/2010/11/5/electoral-manipulation-in-egypt-revisiting-2005.html.

16. Political analyst, interview by author, November 12, 2011.

17. "The Struggle between Egypt's Business and Military Elite."

18. El Amrani, "Electoral Manipulation in Egypt."

19. In 2007 he said, "the party is still riddled with senior officials who resist change and contrive to occupy their positions for life." Cited in ibid.

20. Hussein Sabbour, head of the Egyptian Businessmen's Association (EBA), interview by author, June 7, 2012.

21. "Naguib Sawiris," *Enigma*, May 1, 2011, accessed February 11, 2018, https://bit.ly/2UYn2Ir.

22. "Billionaire Rebel: Naguib Sawiris Is Pushing for an Egypt That Fulfills the Promise of the Arab Spring," *Bloomberg Markets*, December 2011.

23. "Long-sighted: Wealthy Egyptian Business Families Venture Abroad," *The Economist (US)*, July 15, 2010.

24. One of the most popular songs during the uprising was composed by 24-year-old Ramy Essam who decided to turn the people's chants into songs. After Mubarak gave his second speech on February 1 in which he said he would stay in power until elections in the fall, Ramy Essam spontaneously composed a song in which he chanted over and over, "erhal, erhal, erhal" ("leave, leave, leave").

25. According to a confidential US embassy cable, there had been rumors already in the summer of 2005 that Mubarak may appoint Suleiman as vice president. The report noted that although many still believed that Gamal was the intended heir, appointing him as vice president was "almost impossible" due to "very palpable public animosity" in this regard. "Mubarak to Name Vice-President," Wiki Leaks, June 15, 2005, accessed February 15, 2019, https://wikileaks.org/plusd/cables/05CAIRO4534_a.html.

26. The case against Mohamed Abou El Enein has been covered widely in the media, and was also discussed briefly in Cherif Bassiouni, "Corruption Cases Against Officials of the Mubarak Regime," report, Egyptian American Rule of Law Association (2012), accessed October 12, 2017, https://bit.ly/2to4V2Y.

27. Marx, *The Communist Manifesto*.

28. For a history of the Egyptian military see Anouar Abdel-Malek, *Egypt: Military Society: The Army Regime, the Left and Social Change under Nasser* (New York: Random House, 1968); Amos Perlmutter, *Egypt, the Praetorian*

State (New Brunswick, NJ: Transaction Books, 1974); Mark Neal Cooper, *The Transformation of Egypt: State and State Capitalism in Crisis, 1967–1977* (Ann Arbor, MI: University Microfilms International, 1981); Steven A. Cook, *Ruling but Not Governing: The Military and Political Development in Egypt, Algeria, and Turkey* (Baltimore, MD: Johns Hopkins University Press, 2007).

29. Imad Harb, "The Egyptian Military in Politics: Disengagement or Accommodation?," *Middle East Journal* 57, no. 2 (2003): 269–290.

30. Gotowicki, "The Role of the Egyptian Military in Domestic Society."

31. Cooper, *The Transformation of Egypt*.

32. Cook, *Ruling but Not Governing*.

33. Robert Springborg, *Development Models Muslim Contexts: Chinese, "Islamic" and Neo-liberal Alternatives* (Edinburgh: Edinburgh University Press, 2009); Kandil, *Soldiers, Spies and Statesmen*.

34. See for example Barany, *How Armies Respond to Revolution and Why*; Nelly Lahoud et al., "The 'Arab Spring': Investing in Durable Peace," OAI, June 29, 2011, accessed August 7, 2017, https://bit.ly/2Gr5QrR.

35. Zeinab Abul-Magd, "The Army and the Economy in Egypt," Jadaliyya, December 23, 2011, accessed September 9, 2017, https://bit.ly/2GrwxfY.

36. Bellin, "Reconsidering the Robustness of Authoritarianism in The Middle East: Lessons from the Arab Spring,".

37. Jean Lachapelle, Lucan A. Way, and Steven Levitsky, "Crisis, Coercion, and Authoritarian Durability: Explaining Diverging Responses to Anti-Regime Protest in Egypt and Iran," proceedings of The American Political Science Association Annual Meeting, New Orleans, August 31, 2012, accessed September 3, 2017, https://papers.ssrn.com/sol3/papers.cfm?abstract_id=2142721.

38. Barany, *How Armies Respond to Revolution and Why*.

39. Sharon Erickson Nepstad, "Nonviolent Resistance in the Arab Spring: The Critical Role of Military-Opposition Alliances," *Swiss Political Science Review* 17, no. 4 (November 2011): 485–491.

40. Rollanza, "فيديو هام يثبت تورط الجيش فى موقعة الجمل" [An important video that proves the involvement of the army in the Battle of Camel],YouTube video, 12:58, June 8, 2011. https:// www.youtube.com/ watch?v=jR0jCFa773w. [Translation provided by author].

41. See SCAF's statement on January 29 to February 2, 2011 and statements for February 10 and 11 on "١ - بيانات القيادة العامة للقوات المسلحة," [Statements of the General Command of the Armed Forces - 1], Al Moqatel, accessed February 14, 2019, https://bit.ly/ 2SJ3sCL.; "٢ - بيانات القيادة العامة للقوات المسلحة" [Statements of the General Command of the Armed Forces - 2], Al Moqatel, accessed February 14, 2019, https://bit.ly/2IqELHl. [Translation provided by author].

42. "F16 Fighter Jets Fly Extremely Low over Tahrir Square in an Attempt at Intimidation 30 Jan.," YouTube video, 0:33, February 2011, https://www.youtube.com/watch?v=b5xiWEjogNA.

43. At least since the early 1990s American defense officials had been trying to convince their Egyptian counterparts to downsize their force and to discard their remaining

Eastern-bloc equipment in favor of weapons systems built in the United States. At the time they were unwilling to downsize their force, however, because they did not want "to add several hundred thousand individuals with military training and experience to the unemployment lines." See Gotowicki, "The Role of the Egyptian Military in Domestic Society."

44. Razoux, "What to Expect of the Egyptian Army?"

45. "The Egyptian Military Empire," *Middle East Monitor*, July 9, 2014, accessed February 14, 2019, https://bit.ly/2LJtWwX.

46. Aclimandos, "Reforming the Egyptian Security Services."

47. Norvell B. De Atkine, "Why Arabs Lose Wars?," *Middle East Quarterly* 6, no. 4 (December 1999), accessed September 9, 2017, http://www.meforum.org/441/why-arabs-lose-wars.

48. Ibid.

49. Former army officer, interview by author, November 21, 2014.

50. "US Embassy Cables: Egyptian Military's Influence in Decline, US Told," *The Guardian*, February 3, 2011, accessed February 13, 2018, https://bit.ly/2SRWTxr.

51. For an analysis of Egypt's security sector pre- and post-Mubarak, see Aclimandos, "Reforming the Egyptian Security Services."

52. Henry and Springborg, "A Tunisian Solution for Egypt's Military."

53. Mahmoud AlMamlouk, "نص شهادة المشير بقضية قتل المتظاهرين" [The text of the Marshal's testimony in the killing of protestors case], AlYoum7, June 2, 2012, accessed February 14, 2019, https://bit.ly/2S2YEDE. [Translation provided by author].

54. Phil Stewart, "U.S. Praises Military Restraint in Egypt Protests," Reuters, January 30, 2011, accessed September 7, 2017, https://reut.rs/2E8FtV7.

55. "What Tantawi Is Alleged to Have Said at Mubarak's Trial," McClatchy Newspapers, September 27, 2011, accessed September 7, 2017, https://bit.ly/2SWuKWo.

56. Egyptian activist, interview by author, November 11, 2011.

57. Wikithawra, "حصر قتلي الـ18 يوم الأولي من الثورة تفصيليا" [Detailed record of the deaths during the first 18 days of the revolution], Wikithawra, October 23, 2013, accessed February 11, 2019. https://bit.ly/2G3CDT1. [Translation provided by author].

58. A retired major in the Egyptian army, interview by author, November 12, 2011.

59. See SCAF's statement on January 29 to February 2, 2011 at "بيانات القيادة العامة ١ - للقوات المسلحة" [Statements of the General Command of the Armed Forces - 1], Al Moqatel, accessed February 14, 2019, https://bit.ly/2SJ3sCL. [Translation provided by author].

60. Kevin Connolly, "Egypt Crisis: Beleaguered Mubarak Reshuffles Cabinet," BBC News, January 31, 2011, accessed September 7, 2017, https://bbc.in/2N91Ooo.

61. Although this cannot be confirmed, I could not help wondering, as this was the only day I was not allowed onto Tahrir, if it was conceivable that they had some advance warning and therefore had instructions to keep outside observers like myself off the square.

62. Goldstone, "Toward a Fourth Generation of Revolutionary Theory," 74.

63. Ibid.

64. Ibid.

65. Abdel-Rahman Hussein, "Unleashed by the Old Regime, Xenophobia Persists," *Egypt Independent*, July 18, 2011, accessed September 7, 2017, https://bit.ly/2SRX23X.

66. "Omar Suleiman, Egypt's Vice President, Blames Violence on 'Foreign Influences,'" PRI, February 3, 2011, accessed September 5, 2017, https://bit.ly/2GMmIZt.

67. Due to the targeting of foreigners during this time, and the fact that Mubarak was still in power, the author wrote an op-ed under a pen name. See Amy Eskendar, "The Real Force of Stability in Egypt Is Its People, Not Its Government," *Baltimore Sun*, February 8, 2011, accessed September 7, 2017, https://bit.ly/2TOUX6k.

68. "Egypt Shuts Down Al Jazeera Bureau," Al Jazeera English, January 30, 2011, accessed September 7, 2017, https://bit.ly/2GHSmHD.

69. Elliott Abrams, "Egypt Protests Show George W. Bush Was Right about Freedom in the Arab World," *Washington Post*, January 29, 2011, accessed September 7, 2017, https://wapo.st/2DFA2vt.

70. Jeremy M. Sharp, "Egypt in Transition," November 18, 2011, accessed September 9, 2017, https://bit.ly/2SyvnG6.

71. "Obama's Second State of the Union (Text)," *New York Times*, January 25, 2011, accessed September 7, 2017, https://nyti.ms/2TRKEhI.

72. "US Urges Restraint in Egypt, Says Government Stable," Reuters, January 25, 2011, accessed September 7, 2017, https://bit.ly/2BE7jHl.

73. "Exclusive: Biden Discusses Unrest in Egypt, Keeping U.S. Competitive," PBS, June 8, 2015, accessed September 7, 2017, https://to.pbs.org/2BDrVPV.

74. "'This Week' Transcript: Crisis in Egypt," ABC News, January 30, 2011, accessed September 7, 2017, https://abcn.ws/2UYt5g7.

75. Helene Cooper, Mark Landler, and David E. Sanger, "In U.S. Signals to Egypt, Obama Straddled a Rift," *New York Times*, February 12, 2011, accessed September 7, 2017, https://nyti.ms/2TQdWxr.

76. Alyson Krueger, "Senator Patrick Leahy: Egypt Will Lose Aid If Mubarak Does Not Step Down (video)," Huffington Post, February 3, 2011, accessed September 7, 2017, https://bit.ly/2SNJreh.

77. Cooper, Landler, and Sanger, "In U.S. Signals to Egypt."

78. Julian Borger, "The Egyptian Crisis: Another Day, Another Two US Policies," *The Guardian*, February 6, 2011, accessed September 7, 2017, https://bit.ly/2NbXN2U.

79. Robert Fisk, "US Envoy's Business Link to Egypt," *The Independent*, February 6, 2011, accessed September 7, 2017, https://ind.pn/2fMDfAO.

80. Fisk, "US Envoy's Business Link to Egypt."

81. Cooper, Landler, and Sanger, "In U.S. Signals to Egypt."

82. Krueger, "Senator Patrick Leahy."

83. Allam Abdel Ghaffar, "تراكم القمامة بشوارع الجيزة بعد إضراب عمال النظافة" [Garbage piles up in the streets of Giza after custodial workers strike], AlYoum7, February 8, 2011, accessed February 15, 2019, https://bit.ly/2S3vlRB. [Translation provided by author]. Reda Hebishi, "إضراب عمال ورش بولاق يوقف حركة قطارات الصعيد" [Stopping Upper Egypt's trains due to workers strike in Bulaq's workshops], AlYoum7, February 9, 2011, accessed February 15, 2019, https://bit.ly/2SYyYwJ. [Translation provided by author].

84. Mohamed Adel, "الاخوان: لن نشارك في مظاهرات 25 يناير" [The Brotherhood: we will not participate in January 25 protests], YouTube video, 1:49, September 17, 2011. https://www.youtube.com/watch?v=xS3xynR6Mx8. [Translation provided by author].

85. "April 6 Activist on His US Visit and Regime Change in Egypt," Wikileaks Cable, December 13, 2008, accessed February 13, 2018, https://bit.ly/2QUAmvc. See "Egypt Protests: Secret US Document Discloses Support for Protesters," *The Telegraph*, January 28, 2011, accessed October 14, 2017, https://bit.ly/2fAJynm.

86. Shehata, "Youth Mobilization in Egypt: New Trends and Opportunities."

87. Iyad El-Baghdadi, "Meet Asmaa Mahfouz and the Vlog That Helped Spark the Revolution," YouTube video, 4:36. February 2011, http://www.youtube.com/watch?v=SgjIgMdsEuk.

88. Mohamed Rabie, " دور الإخوان في الثورة" [The role of the Muslim Brotherhood in the revolution], Ahram Gate, August 3, 2011, accessed October 12, 2017, https://bit.ly/2SOzWvn. [Translation provided by author].

89. Osama Mansour, "الإخوان وثورة 25 يناير . . . نظرة موضوعية " [The brotherhood and January 25 revolution . . . and objective overview], Yanayer Website, April 19, 2011, accessed April, 11 2016, http:// www.25yanayer.net/نظرة-يناير-25- وثورة-الإخوان-موضوعية/. [Translation provided by author].

90. Rabie claims that a number of leaders of the Muslim Brotherhood were arrested on January 27, and that at least 149 Muslim Brotherhood youth were arrested subsequently. See Rabie, " دور الإخوان في الثورة" [The role of the Muslim Brotherhood in the revolution].

91. Mona El-Ghobashy, "The Praxis of the Egyptian Revolution," Middle East Research and Information Project, Spring 2011, accessed September 8, 2017, http://merip.org/mer/mer258/praxis-egyptian-revolution.

92. "مصر: مقتل ثلاثة أشخاص في مظاهرات ضد الحكومة" [Egypt: Three people killed in demonstrations against the government], BBC News, January 25, 2011, accessed February 15, 2019, https://bbc.in/2S5g6Yj. [Translation provided by author].

93. On the Friday of Rage, 664 were killed. See Wikithawra, "حصر قتلى الـ 18 يوم الأولى من الثورة تفصيليا" [Detailed record of the deaths during the first 18 days of the revolution].

94. Rebecca Fox, "Media Darlings: The Egyptian Revolution and American Media Coverage," MA diss., American University in Cairo, Winter 2012, January 27, 2013, accessed February 14, 2018, https://bit.ly/2V1mtNV.

95. "Egypt Leaves the Internet," Oracle—DYN, January 27, 2011, accessed September 8, 2017, https://dyn.com/blog/egypt-leaves-the-internet/.

96. Some of the foreign residents left behind included refugees who were unable to leave. Although the UNHCR offices in Cairo are tasked with providing relief services to refugees, most of their staff evacuated as well.

97. Shayfeencom was created to monitor the 2005 elections (the name translates to "we are watching you").

98. Pierre Sioufi was featured in several news articles as his apartment became the unofficial "headquarters of the revolution." See Roger Cohen, "Guru of the Revolution," *New York Times*, February 17, 2011, accessed September 8, 2017, https://nyti.ms/

2SyPfca.; Philipp Oehmke, "Egypt's Man in the Moon: The Watchdog of Tahrir Square Fears for the Revolution," Spiegel Online, April 29, 2011, accessed September 8, 2017, https://bit.ly/2TQ8ivd.

99. Bothaina Kamel announced in the spring of 2011 that she would run for president, making her the first female presidential candidate in the history of Egypt.

100. I described this in more detail in an op-ed in the *Baltimore Sun* under a pen name. See Eskendar, "The Real Force of Stability in Egypt Is Its People, Not Its Government."

101. I later learned that his name was Adam Yassin Mekiwi. He was a writer who had grown up in Alexandria, where he attended the French school. I never asked him whether his association of the NDP headquarters with the Bastille was due to his French education, or because it was indeed as hated by Cairenes in 2011 as the Bastille was by Parisians in 1789.

102. Ziad Bakir was one of many killed that night, most likely by a sniper. His body, however, was not found until several months later, and only after his family had launched a campaign to discover his whereabouts. Ziad had worked as a graphic designer for the Cairo Opera House; he had gone out on January 28 and never returned home. His sister Mirette Bakir, with whom I later became friends, described to me how she and her family began to receive threats from anonymous people that they should not make a fuss in the media and that Ziad was simply being detained and would soon be released. When they finally found his body in a morgue in the spring of 2011, it became clear that he had been killed by a sniper because the bullet entered his body from above. During the chaos on January 28, Ziad was one of many who voluntarily blocked the entrance to the Egyptian Museum to prevent it from being looted. He was killed while protecting Egypt's ancient heritage.

103. Many years later, in April 2019, Khaled Abol Naga spoke at a hearing on Capitol Hill about those days during the uprising in 2011. He said "I have never been in my life more proud than anything I have done than being just one of the millions who marched in Tahrir Square and every street in Egypt asking for bread, freedom, and social justice." https://twitter.com/AmyAustinHolmes/status/1115746440821772288.

104. The bulk of the police stations that were attacked were located in poorer neighborhoods of Cairo including Imbaba, Helwan, Bab al-Shi'riyya, Bulaq al-Dakrur, al Matariyya, and al-Gammaliyya. As Salwa Ismail describes, this type of contention during the January 25 Revolution was not new but built off a long history of popular protests against police stations and prisons, including a series of "mini-uprisings" against local police stations in the 1990s and the first decade of the twenty-first century. Ismail. "فيديو... استقالة المكتب التنفيذي لـ "تمرد مطروح" [Video . . . The resignation of the executive office of Tamarod's branch in Matrouh]. Neil Ketchley puts the number of prisons that were burnt down closer to 80. See Ketchley, *Egypt in a Time of Revolution*.

105. Wikithawra, "حصر قتلي الـ 18 يوم الأولي من الثورة تفصيليا" [Detailed record of the deaths during the first 18 days of the revolution].

106. A confidential report by state security was written at the end of February 2011 and described the astonishment of the authorities at the sheer number and organization

of protesters. It attributed the collapse of the police on January 28 as being due to several factors including the fact that many police lost contact with the Interior Ministry due to the communications blackout, and that many apparently felt abandoned by their superiors. See Mostafa Mohie, "Classified Report Reveals State Security's Take on Jan 25 Revolution," Mada Masr, January 12, 2015, accessed September 8, 2017, https://bit.ly/2GJfkxX.

107. Ramadan Ahmed, "العادلي في شهادته بـ«اقتحام السجون»: هروب ٢٣ ألف مسجون خلال أحداث يناير" [El-Adly in his testimony: 23,000 prisoners escaped during the events of January], Veto Gate, October 10, 2018, accessed February 15, 2019, https://bit.ly/2TRy2qP. [Translation provided by author].

108. Mohammed Bamyeh, "The Egyptian Revolution: First Impressions from the Field," Jadaliyya, February 11, 2011, accessed September 10, 2017, https://bit.ly/2GuAwIE.

109. In part due to the difficulty of traveling in Egypt during this time, and in part due to the general tendency to focus on Cairo, the events outside the capital have not been covered nearly as well by either the media or scholars. Because I did not travel to other cities in Egypt during the 18-day uprising, my own observations are limited to Cairo. In subsequent years I did conduct fieldwork in the governorates outside Cairo, which are covered in later chapters. Further research is needed in order to provide a more balanced assessment of what was a nationwide rebellion.

110. Yara Elhemaily conducted a survey of workers in the informal sector and found, among other things, that their earnings increased significantly during this period because they did not have competition from the formal sector as so many businesses had been shut down. Unpublished research paper written at AUC.

111. Michael Schwartz, "The Egyptian Uprising: The Mass Strike in the Time of Neoliberal Globalization," New Labor Forum 20, no. 3 (Fall 2011), accessed September 9, 2017, https://bit.ly/2IcYNVq.

112. According to data from Wikithawra, 1,022 civilians were killed, 49 police officers, and 4 army soldiers. Wikithawra, "حصر قتلي الـ 18 يوم الأولي من الثورة تفصيليا" [Detailed record of the deaths during the first 18 days of the revolution].

113. I discuss these "moments of madness" in Cairo during the protests on Tahrir and in Istanbul during the Gezi protests in my essay. See Amy Austin Holmes, "On Military Coups and Mad Utopias," South Atlantic Quarterly 113, no. 2 (May 1, 2014): 380–395.

Chapter 4

1. To my knowledge it was Issandr El Amrani who put together the first diagram of SCAF members in the English language, including basic information about each general. See Issandr El Amrani, "Egypt's Military Council in a Diagram," The Arabist, March 3, 2011, accessed September 8, 2017, https://bit.ly/2touukA.

2. "Egypt: Retry or Free 12,000 after Unfair Military Trials," Human Rights Watch, September 11, 2011, accessed February 14, 2019, https://bit.ly/2BBmykt.

3. Egyptian Initiative for Personal Rights, "رسالة إلي وزير الصحة" [Letter to the Minister of Health], EIPR, March 20, 2011, accessed February 15, 2019, https://bit.ly/2UYqsuI. [Translation provided by author].

4. "In an Investigation by the EIPR: Bullets of the Ministry of Interior Were Aimed to Leave Demonstrators Permanently Disabled," Egyptian Initiative for Personal Rights, November 25, 2011, accessed October 14, 2017, https://bit.ly/2SV820K.

5. Lucie Ryzova, "The Battle of Cairo's Muhammad Mahmoud Street," Al Jazeera, November 29, 2011, accessed October 14, 2017, https://bit.ly/1ESdamP.

6. "Egypt Football Clash Kills Scores," BBC News, February 2, 2012, accessed February 15, 2019, https://bbc.in/2EbqidQ.

7. A young activist who spoke to Mina Daniel before the Maspero massacre said that Daniel conveyed his fear that the protest could be violently dispersed by the military and sanctioned by the Coptic church because the church felt that the Maspero youth were challenging their old authority. Mina Daniel was killed during the assault on October 9, 2011.

8. Wael Eskandar, "SCAF: A Brief History of Injustice," Ahram Online, November 11, 2011, accessed September 8, 2017, https://bit.ly/2GuHYU8. See "Diaries of a Revolution under Military Rule: Excerpts from 2011 Report," Al Nadeem Center for Rehabilitation of Victims of Violence, June 21, 2016, accessed September 8, 2017, https://bit.ly/2tlDxTj.

9. Wikithawra, "حصر قتلى عهد المجلس العسكرى تفصيليا" [A detailed record of deaths under the SCAF], Wikithawra, November 3, 2013, accessed February 12, 2019, https://bit.ly/2Gd6FUY. [Translation provided by author]. Wikithawra, "حصر مصابي عهد المجلس العسكري عدداً" [A detailed record of the injured under the SCAF], Wikithawra, November 3, 2013, accessed February 12, 2019, https://bit.ly/2SCh4Ab. [Translation provided by author].

10. Wikithawra, "حصر قتلى عهد المجلس العسكرى تفصيليا" [A detailed record of deaths under the SCAF]; "حصر مصابي عهد المجلس العسكري عدداً" [A detailed record of the injured under the SCAF].

11. Ibid.

12. Harriet Sherwood, "Cairo Israeli Embassy Attack: 'Staff Feared for Their Lives,'" The Guardian, September 10, 2011, accessed February 15, 2019, https://bit.ly/2tpy25P.

13. Wikithawra, "حصر قتلى عهد المجلس العسكرى تفصيليا" [A detailed record of deaths under the SCAF].

14. Ibid. "حصر مصابي عهد المجلس العسكري عدداً" [A detailed record of the injured under the SCAF].

15. Ibid.

16. "Egypt Football Clash Kills Scores," BBC News.

17. Issandr El Amrani, "Sightings of the Egyptian Deep State," Middle East Research and Information Project, January 1, 2012, accessed September 8, 2017, http://merip.org/mero/mero010112.

18. As quoted in Jack Shenker, "Fury over Advert Claiming Egypt Revolution as Vodafone's," The Guardian, June 3, 2011, accessed September 8, 2017, https://bit.ly/2UYUgHF.

19. Wikithawra. "حصر قتلي الـ 18 يوم الأولى من الثورة تفصيليا" [Detailed record of the deaths during the first 18 days of the revolution], Wikithawra. October 23, 2013, accessed February 11, 2019, https://bit.ly/2G3CDT1. [Translation provided by author]. Phil Stewart, "U.S. Praises Egyptian Military's 'Professionalism,'" Reuters, January 31, 2011, accessed February 12, 2018, https://reut.rs/2E8FtV7.

20. William B. Quandt, "U.S. Policy and the Arab Revolutions of 2011," in *The New Middle East: Protest and Revolution in the Arab World*, ed. Fawaz A. Gerges (Cambridge: Cambridge University Press, 2013).

21. Brownlee, *Democracy Prevention*, 167.

22. "Remarks with Egyptian Foreign Minister Mohamed Kamel Amr after Their Meeting," US Department of State, September 28, 2011, accessed February 15, 2019, https://bit.ly/2BCgJmB.

23. Marc Lynch and Steven A. Cook, "U.S. Policy on Egypt Needs a Big Shift," *New York Times*, November 30, 2011, accessed September 8, 2017, https://nyti.ms/2SZrTvS.

24. Amy Austin Holmes, "Is US Support for the SCAF Unconditional?," The Atlantic Council, November 25, 2011, accessed September 11, 2017, https://bit.ly/2GFrl7w.

25. In total, four American, one German, and several Egyptian NGOs were raided in 2011. In subsequent years, especially under President Sisi, the crackdown on civil society organizations expanded, as will be discussed in detail in chapters 6 and 7.

26. Todd Ruffner, "Under Threat: Egypt's Systematic Campaign against NGOs," Project on Middle East Democracy, March 2015, accessed September 8, 2017, https://bit.ly/2DGIMBP.

27. In the assessment of Shadi Hamid, the State Department pushed more for the release of the American citizens than their Egyptian colleagues who worked at the same organizations. Shadi Hamid, "The Real Reason the U.S. Should Consider Cutting Military Aid to Egypt," Brookings, July 2, 2012, accessed February 14, 2019, https://brook.gs/2BzyUJy.

28. Brownlee, *Democracy Prevention*, 162.

29. I attended the Coptic mass at Saint Mark's Cathedral together with a colleague from AUC. We had to pass about seven security checks to get inside. It was a long ceremony that went on for several hours, and like watching diplomacy in action with high-ranking SCAF generals sitting next to Coptic priests. On the way out, some young men were walking with arms linked toward the cathedral, chanting "down with military rule" and that Tantawi was a coward because he did not attend.

30. Brownlee, *Democracy Prevention*.

31. Over the course of the transition period, a few generals were added to the SCAF while others stepped down, usually without any justification or explanation to the public.

32. "MPs Denunciation of SCAF Head, Salafist Leader Lands Him Parliament Investigation," Ahram Online, February 19, 2012, accessed September 8, 2017, http://english.ahram.org.eg/News/34916.aspx.

33. "Egypt Military Judiciary Wants MP's Immunity Lifted over Tantawi Insult," Ahram Online, June 12, 2012, accessed September 8, 2017, https://bit.ly/2SxkDYu.

34. Sherif Tarek, "Dramatic Row in Egypt's Parliament over Police Use of Birdshot in Deadly Clashes," Ahram Online, February 6, 2012, accessed September 12, 2017, https://bit.ly/2GtEjGi.

35. Heba Hesham, "Revolutionary Youth to Simulate Parliament," Daily News Egypt, March 15, 2012, accessed February 12, 2018, https://bit.ly/2GJi6n4.

36. Each of the five main political currents was to be represented in the Revolutionary Youth Parliament: Islamists, liberals, leftists, nationalists, and independents were represented by 20%. Ibid.

37. A perhaps even more blunt example of the parliament's weakness was when SCAF general Mukhtar Al-Mulla said to a room full of foreign journalists, "So whatever the majority in the People's Assembly, they are very welcome, because they won't have the ability to impose anything that the people don't want," in reference to the fact that it would no longer be the parliament but the military who would pick the 100 members of the constituent assembly to write the constitution. See David D. Kirkpatrick, "Military Flexes Its Muscles as Islamists Gain in Egypt," New York Times, December 7, 2011, accessed September 8, 2017, https://nyti.ms/2EdgKPQ.

38. Member of No Military Trials in Cairo, interview by author, May 24, 2012.

39. Marc Lynch, "That's It for Egypt's So-Called Transition," Foreign Policy, June 14, 2012, accessed September 8, 2017, https://bit.ly/2EamFow; Nathan J. Brown, "Cairo's Judicial Coup," Foreign Policy, June 14, 2012, accessed September 8, 2017, http://foreignpolicy.com/2012/06/14/cairos-judicial-coup/.

40. Member of the Muslim Brotherhood, interview by author, June 22, 2012.

41. Anne Alexander argues that the Ikhwan and the military had a shared desire to demobilize street protests after both the 1952 and 2011 revolutions in order to secure their own positions in the new political order. See Anne Alexander and Miriyam Aouragh, "Egypt's Unfinished Revolution: The Role of the Media Revisited," International Journal of Communication 8 (2014), accessed September 11, 2017, https://bit.ly/2GKUAWC.

42. Ibid.

43. Anne Alexander, "Brothers-in-arms? The Egyptian Military, the Ikhwan and the Revolutions of 1952 and 2011," Journal of North African Studies 16, no. 4 (2011): 533–554.

44. Noor Ayman Noor, "Egyptian Political Activist: 'Corruption Will be Difficult to End,'" The Guardian, May 19, 2011, accessed September 11, 2017, https://bit.ly/2TS6cuC.

45. The person who had the idea to create a #NoSCAF hashtag sent me a 466-page PDF documenting all the tweets and blogs on that day. When I attempted to print out the PDF in the fall of 2015 at a copy center on the AUC campus, however, I was told that it was "mamnou" or forbidden to print out such materials about the military. Ironically, it was possible to print out materials about the Tantawi-led SCAF while the SCAF was still in power, but not in the fall of 2015 with Sisi at the helm.

46. Issandr El Amrani, "Sightings of the Egyptian Deep State," Middle East Research and Information Project, January 1, 2012, accessed September 10, 2017, http://merip.org/mero/mero010112.

47. My previous research dealt with some of these issues. See Amy Austin Holmes, *Social Unrest and American Military Bases in Turkey and Germany since 1945* (Cambridge: Cambridge University Press, 2016).

48. The survey was conducted in February and March 2012 in order to assess what Egyptians believe have been the accomplishments and setbacks of the transition period and which social forces are driving the contradictory dynamics. A short article based on a small subset of the questions was published already. See Amy Austin Holmes, "Egyptians Blame Military for Failures of Transition Period," Ahram Online, June 28, 2012, accessed September 10, 2017, https://bit.ly/2UWN26X.

49. Lillian Boctor, "Organizing for No Military Trials for Civilians: Interview with Egyptian Activist Shahira Abouellail," Jadaliyya, November 6, 2011, accessed September 8, 2017, https://bit.ly/2SxKBLC.

50. "Diaries of a Revolution under Military Rule: Excerpts from 2011 Report," El-Nadeem Center for the treatment and rehabilitation of victims of violence and torture.

51. Laila Mostafa Soueif, "Testimony for the Detainment of Amr Abdallah ElBehairy Early Saturday," تناتيف من حياة ماعت [Pieces of the life of Ma'et] (web log), February 26, 2011, accessed September 12, 2017, http://ma3t.blogspot.com.eg/2011/02/26-2011.html. [Translation provided by author].

52. "Egypt: Retry or Free 12,000 after Unfair Military Trials." Human Rights Watch.

53. Noor Ayman Noor, interview by author, July 8, 2012.

54. Boctor, "Organizing for No Military Trials for Civilians: Interview with Egyptian Activist Shahira Abouellail."

55. Member of No Military Trials , interview by author, May 24, 2012.

56. "About Us," No Military Trials for Civilians, 2011, http://en.nomiltrials.org/p/about-us.html.

57. Member of No Military Trials, interview by author, May 24, 2012.

58. Noor Ayman Noor, interview by author, July 8, 2012.

59. Tahrir Diaries, "مرشحي الرئاسة المصريين ضد المحاكمات العسكرية للمدنيين" [Egyptian Presidential Candidates against Military Trials of Civilians], YouTube, 1:25, September 2011. https://www.youtube.com/watch?v=gs_5FljIDnU. [Translation provided by author].

60. First member of Mosireen Collective , interview by author, February 19, 2012.

61. In late December 2011, the offices of NDI, IRI, and several other organizations were raided by Egyptian security forces. Forty pro-democracy activists including 20 US citizens were put on trial and charged with working illegally in Egypt. It is believed that Fayza Abou el-Naga, who had been a member of the NDP and who had served as Minister of Planning and International Cooperation both under Mubarak and under the SCAF, was behind the decision to criminally charge the NGO workers. For a good summary see: Khaled Fahmy, "The Truth about Fayza," *Egypt Independent*, February 27, 2012, accessed September 12, 2017, https://bit.ly/2DH6jm8/.

62. Samira Ibrahim, testimony about suing the military for the "virginity test" she and six other women were forced to undergo while in prison. See: Tahrir Diaries, "سميرة و الجيش قصة فتاة مصرية" [Samira and the Army: A story of an Egyptian girl], YouTube,

22:44, November 2011, https:// www.youtube.com/ watch?v=c29CAXR141s. [Translation provided by author].

63. Habiba Mohsen, "What Made Her Go There? Samira Ibrahim and Egypt's Virginity Test Trial," Al Jazeera, March 16, 2012, accessed September 12, 2017, https://bit.ly/ 2N9hQyL.

64. Charlize Theron, "Samira Ibrahim—The World's 100 Most Influential People: 2012," Time Magazine, April 18, 2012, accessed February 15, 2019, https://bit.ly/2N8I44u.

65. Author's transcription of excerpts from Tahrir Diaries, "سميرة و الجيش: قصة فتاة مصرية" [Samira and the Army: A story of an Egyptian girl], YouTube, 22:44, November 2011, https:// www.youtube.com/ watch?v=c29CAXR141s. [Translation provided by author].

66. "Diaries of a Revolution under Military Rule: Excerpts from 2011 Report," El-Nadeem Center for the treatment and rehabilitation of victims of violence and torture, 45.

67. Tahrir Diaries, "شهادة سلوى — تم اعتقالها من الجيش يوم ٩ مارس ٢٠١١" [Testimony of Salwa—Was arrested by the Army on 9 March 2011], YouTube, 3:18, March 17, 2011, https://www.youtube.com/watch?v=ajCe1km7UFM. [Translation provided by author].

68. "Admission of Forced 'Virginity Tests' in Egypt Must Lead to Justice," Human Rights Now, June 1, 2011, accessed September 12, 2017, https://bit.ly/2SA66LE.

69. "Egypt: Military Pledges to Stop Forced 'Virginity Tests,'" Amnesty International, June 27, 2011, accessed September 12, 2017, https://bit.ly/2GuJyFy.

70. Ibid.

71. "Egyptian Women's Views: Verdict in Virginity Test Case," BBC News, March 12, 2012, accessed September 12, 2017, https://bbc.in/2X46ikV.

72. Ibid.

73. "Egypt: Military 'Virginity Test' Investigation a Sham," Human Rights Watch, April 17, 2015, accessed September 12, 2017, https://bit.ly/2GJpZZv.

74. Nada El-Kouny, "Egyptian Activists to Continue Struggle against 'Virginity Test' Perpetrators," Ahram Online, March 11, 2012, accessed September 12, 2017, https:// bit.ly/2SZDpr7.

75. Second member of Mosireen collective, interview by author in Cairo, February 19, 2012.

76. Ziad at the Mosireen office in Cairo, interview by author, February 12, 2012.

77. Salma Shukralla, "Tahrir Sit-in Enters Second Day, to Go on until 7 Demands Are Met," Ahram Online, July 9, 2011, accessed September 12, 2017, https://bit.ly/ 2UVcQAk.

78. Sherif Younis, "The Maspero Massacre: The Military, the Media, and the 1952 Cairo Fire as Historical Blueprint," Jadaliyya, October 17, 2011, accessed September 12, 2017, https://bit.ly/2DCikJe.

79. Third member of Mosireen collective, interview by author in Cairo, February 19, 2012.

80. Amir-Hussein Radjy, "How to Save the Memories of the Egyptian Revolution," The Atlantic, January 25, 2018, accessed February 15, 2019, https://bit.ly/2GL2PCf.

81. The Salafi Front movement was the more antistate or "revolutionary" wing of the Salafi movement, in contrast to the al-Da'wah al Salafiyyah.

82. Robert Mackey, "Video Shows Protesters Were Attacked by Armed Assailants," *New York Times*, May 3, 2012, accessed September 12, 2017, https://nyti.ms/2DKllaN.

83. Second member of Mosireen collective interview by author in Cairo, February 19, 2012.

84. First member of Mosireen collective, interview by author in Cairo, February 19, 2012.

85. Third member of Mosireen collective, interview by author in Cairo, February 19, 2012.

86. First member of Mosireen collective, interview by author in Cairo, June 18, 2012.

87. David D. Kirkpatrick, "Thousands of Women Mass in Major March in Cairo," *New York Times*, December 20, 2011, accessed February 15, 2019, https://nyti.ms/18jQZZY.

88. SCAFreaks, "SCAF General 'Adel Omarah'—'kazeboon'—Liars campaign." YouTube video, 6:37, January 2012, http://www.youtube.com/watch?v=tDF8qctR2tg.

89. Sally Toma is one of the activists Thanassis Cambanis describes in his book. See Thanassis Cambanis, *Once upon a Revolution: An Egyptian Story* (New York: Simon & Schuster Paperbacks, 2016).

90. Amr, a member of Kazeboon, interview by author, February 18, 2012.

91. Menna Taher, "Public Film-Screenings of Army Abuses Attacked in Alexandria and Cairo," Ahram Online, December 30, 2012, accessed September 12, 2017, https://bit.ly/2toAFFi.

92. Amr, a member of Kazeboon, interview by author, February 18, 2012.

93. As one reviewer pointed out, the dissolution of the Muslim Brotherhood-dominated parliament should not be compared to the previously mentioned violent assaults.

Chapter 5

1. Hossam, a blogger and independent activist, interview by author, January 23, 2014.

2. Ibrahim Kassem, "فوز مرسى برئاسة مصر بنسبة ٥١.٧٣%" [Morsi wins the presidency of Egypt with 51.73%], AlYoum7, June 24, 2012, accessed February 15, 2019, https://bit.ly/2SRMDpe. [Translation provided by author].

3. Ahmed, a financial analyst in Cairo, interview by author, May 2014.

4. Wael Kandil, "معاهدة «فيرمونت» بين الرئيس والقوى الوطنية" [The agreement of "Fairmont" between the president and national forces], Shorouk News, July 7, 2012, accessed September 12, 2017, https://bit.ly/2TQMH5V. [Translation provided by author].

5. Ibid.

6. Suleyman Yasar, "As Morsi Takes Over in Egypt, Will Military Allow Economic Reform?," Al-Monitor, June 28, 2012, accessed September 12, 2017, https://bit.ly/2X58kkR.

7. Hamouda Chekir and Ishac Diwan, Crony Capitalism in Egypt, working paper no. 250, Center for International Development at Harvard University, Harvard University (2012), 11, accessed September 12, 2017, https://bit.ly/2X8oPwi.

8. Roll, "Egypt's Business Elite after Mubarak."

9. Hussein Salem was nicknamed the "Father of Sharm el-Sheikh" since he owned much of the resort city in the Sinai. He was closely connected to the Mubarak family and a co-owner of the East Mediterranean Gas Company, which exported Egyptian natural gas to Israel at a fraction of its market price. See Bel Trew and Osama Diab, "The Crooks Return to Cairo," Foreign Policy, February 7, 2014, accessed September 16, 2017, https://bit.ly/2IhJwTj.

10. Chekir and Diwan, Crony Capitalism in Egypt.

11. Noha Moustafa, "In Reconciling with Regime Figures, Officials Opt for Quick Cash over Formal Trials," Egypt Independent, February 23, 2013, accessed September 16, 2017, https://bit.ly/2DKMfiH.

12. Roll, Egypt's Business Elite after Mubarak.

13. One of my interviewees described Hassan Malek as becoming for the FJP what Gamal Mubarak was for the NDP: the "go to person" for business deals. An independent analyst, interview by author, on January 14, 2014.

14. David J. Lynch, "Egypt's Islamists Woo Mubarak Tycoons as Mursi Seeks Funds," Bloomberg, February 14, 2013, accessed September 12, 2017, https://bloom.bg/2DFstVH.

15. Moustafa, "In Reconciling with Regime Figures."

16. Ibid.

17. Roll, Egypt's Business Elite after Mubarak, 13.

18. Ibid., 24.

19. "Mubarak Era Tycoons Join Egypt President in China," Ahram Online, August 28, 2012, accessed September 17, 2017, https://bit.ly/2GMXz0L.

20. Dina Ezzat, "Brotherhood Shater, Former Mubarak-Era Minister Secure Qatari Loan to Egypt," Ahram Online, October 21, 2012, accessed September 17, 2017, https://bit.ly/2BA7Rhq.

21. Janine Zacharia, "Mubarak Ally Watches Egypt from Uncertain Exile," Washington Post, March 3, 2011, accessed September 17, 2017, https://wapo.st/2S0OS53.

22. "Egypt Trials: Mubarak Officials' Charges and Verdicts," BBC News, October 12, 2015, accessed September 17, 2017, https://bbc.in/2TNlYH3.

23. Ezzat, "Brotherhood Shater."

24. In 2013 some observers argued that the fuel shortages and the resulting long lines at gas stations were by design and an attempt to undermine Morsi. The alleged sudden improvement after his ouster was seen as proof that the shortages were engineered. However, this would have been the work of bureaucrats rather than businessmen. Furthermore, another fuel shortage in 2015 would suggest that the fuel crisis was not confined to the Morsi presidency. See Ben Hubbard and David D. Kirkpatrick, "Sudden Improvements in Egypt Suggest a Campaign to Undermine Morsi," New York Times, July 10, 2013, accessed September 17, 2017, https://nyti.ms/2BBguIu.

25. On the economic sabotage that preceded the Chilean coup, Peter Winn wrote: "At bottom, the Paro de Octubre (October Strike) was a general strike of the bourgeoisie, intended to demonstrate their power as a class, stop the advance toward socialism, and create the conditions within which Allende could be ousted—by military coup or congressional impeachment. The October Strike represented the culmination of more than a year of planning, organization, and orchestration by Chile's economic elites, during which they had drawn the social and political center into their strategy for bringing Allende's socialist road to the end." See Peter Winn, *Weavers of Revolution: The Yarur Workers and Chile's Road to Socialism* (Oxford: Oxford University Press, 1989).

26. According to Mohsin Khan, former head of the IMF's Middle East Department, "Businessmen abroad and investors, both domestic and foreign, have a real wait-and-see attitude." See Lynch, "Egypt's Islamists Woo Mubarak Tycoons as Mursi Seeks Funds.".

27. For more on the cabinet reshuffle, see: Nancy Messieh, "Profiling Egypt's New Ministers," Atlantic Council, May 7, 2013, accessed September 17, 2017, https://bit.ly/2EaDuQb.

28. Abigail Hauslohner, "Egypt's Military Expands Its Control of the Country's Economy," *Washington Post*, March 16, 2014, accessed September 17, 2017, https://wapo.st/2tnWPqU.

29. The details of who exactly funded Tamarod are still being revealed at the time of writing. See a summary of the Wikileaks documents relating to Egypt, the UAE, and the Muslim Brotherhood by Hossam Bahgat and Mostafa Mohie, "Wikileaks Cables Trace Ebb and Flow of Egypt-UAE Relations," Mada Masr, July 26, 2015, accessed October 10, 2017, https://bit.ly/2tnXLvq.

30. Of course there were some embarrassing episodes. One particularly egregious case includes comments Morsi had made in 2010, prior to the revolution, about Jews being the descendants of apes and pigs. But since he had taken office, his tone had improved. In what may be considered a dubious attempt to compensate for such statements, in December 2012, Essam El-Erian, deputy chief of the Muslim Brotherhood, called on Egyptian Jews to return to their "homeland" in Egypt. He also offered to return their property that had been confiscated when they were expelled by Gamal Abdel Nasser in the 1950s, claiming this would "make room for Palestinians." See Zvi Bar'el, "Muslim Brotherhood Deputy Chief Calls for the Return of Jews to Egypt," Haaretz.com, March 24, 2013, accessed September 17, 2017, https://bit.ly/2V0GcNI.

31. David D. Kirkpatrick, "Keeper of Islamic Flame Rises as Egypt's New Decisive Voice," *New York Times*, March 11, 2012, accessed September 17, 2017, https://nyti.ms/2EbP11L.

32. Ahmed Eleiba, "F-16 Deal Redefines US Relationship with Egypt's Morsi Administration," Ahram Online, January 13, 2013, accessed September 17, 2017, https://bit.ly/2UZ30NZ.

33. "A Member of the Working Group on the Southern Mediterranean," telephone interview by author, March 2014.

34. Gregg Carlstrom et al., "Egypt's New Dictator Was Made in the USA," *Politico Magazine*, February 18, 2014, accessed October 10, 2017, https://politi.co/23kWgXF.

35. "A Member of the Working Group on the Southern Mediterranean," telephone interview by author, March 2014.

36. United States officials have confirmed in private interviews that the weapons that were withheld from Egypt were not necessary for combatting the insurgency in the Sinai. The United States had been trying to convince the Egyptian military to reconsider their weapons purchases for a long time and to tailor their purchases more toward the threat they were facing, namely a counterinsurgency rather than a land war. Former member of the National Security Council, interview by author, October 4, 2017.

37. In February 2016 the House Judiciary Committee voted along party lines to call on the State Department to designate the Muslim Brotherhood as a terrorist organization. Republican support for the resolution may be related to the anti-Muslim rhetoric of some of the Republican presidential candidates, including Donald Trump's call for banning Muslims from entering the United States until the government can "figure out what's going on." See Marc Lynch, "Is the Muslim Brotherhood a Terrorist Organization or a Firewall against Violent Extremism?," *Washington Post*, March 7, 2016, accessed October 12, 2017, https://wapo.st/21VC4Np.

38. Stéphane Lacroix, "Saudi Arabia's Muslim Brotherhood Predicament," *Washington Post*, March 20, 2014, accessed August 11, 2017, https://wapo.st/2E7TOBw.

39. "Egypt Orders Brotherhood Chief Held, Morsi in 'Safe Place,'" Middle East Institute, 2013, accessed October 12, 2017, https://bit.ly/2TRUSP5.

40. In early December 2014, a series of audio recordings were leaked that, if verified, may provide some insight into the events of his initial incarceration. Morsi's lawyers later challenged the basis for his imprisonment on July 3 because he was essentially kidnapped by the military with no criminal charges until months later. See Esam Al-Amin, "Leaked Audio Shows Egypt's Coup Leaders as a Criminal Syndicate," *Counterpunch*, December 12, 2014, accessed October 13, 2017, https://bit.ly/2tpIDh7.

41. "Egypt's New Shocking and Potentially Indicting Leaks," *Middle East Monitor*, December 5, 2014, accessed October 12, 2017, https://bit.ly/2EcNadi.

42. James T. Quinlivan, "Coup-proofing: Its Practice and Consequences in the Middle East," *International Security* 24, no. 2 (1999): 131–165; Aaron Belkin and Evan Schofer, "Toward a Structural Understanding of Coup Risk," *Journal of Conflict Resolution* 47, no. 5 (2003): 594–620; Terence Lee, "Military Cohesion and Regime Maintenance," *Armed Forces & Society* 32, no. 1 (2005): 80–104; Daron Acemoglu and James Robinson, "Economic Backwardness in Political Perspective," *American Political Science Review* 100, no. 111 (February 2006), accessed October 12, 2017, https://economics.mit.edu/files/4471; Holger Albrecht, "Does Coup-Proofing Work? Political-Military Relations in Authoritarian Regimes amid the Arab Uprisings," *Mediterranean Politics* 20, no. 1 (2014): 36–54.

43. Previously, the military budget was submitted to the parliament as a one-line item, but under the new constitution even this nominal approval was deemed unnecessary.

Instead, the National Defense Council was tasked with approving the military budget. See Yezid Sayigh, "Morsi and Egypt's Military," Al-Monitor, January 8, 2013, accessed October 10, 2017, https://bit.ly/2Xe9Uky.

44. Ibid.

45. Sahar Aziz, "Sinai's Role in Morsi's Ouster," Sada, August 20, 2013, accessed October 12, 2017, https://bit.ly/2TQG7fE.

46. "Source of Egypt's Coup: Morsi Gave Free Hand to Islamic Militants, Ordered Military to Stop Crackdowns on Jihadis," Talking Points Memo, July 18, 2013, accessed October 10, 2017, https://bit.ly/2GJ1xYk.

47. Hossam Bahgat, "Who Let the Jihadis Out?" Mada Masr, February 16, 2017, accessed October 10, 2017, https://bit.ly/2tuKam6.

48. The removal of Tantawi and Anan came as a surprise to US Secretary of Defense Leon Panetta, who had said: "It is my view, based on what I have seen, that President Morsi and Field Marshal Tantawi have a very good relationship and are working together towards the same ends." See Ernesto Londoño, "Egypt's Morsi Replaces Military Chiefs in Bid to Consolidate Power," Washington Post, August 12, 2012, accessed October 10, 2017, https://wapo.st/2SZFLGs.

49. Abdel-Rahman Hussein, "Egypt Defence Chief Tantawi Ousted in Surprise Shakeup," The Guardian, August 13, 2012, accessed October 10, 2017, http://bit.ly/2GtaUMw.

50. An independent analyst in Cairo, interview by author, January 14, 2014.

51. AlMasry AlYoum, "اشتباكات بالتحرير في جمعة كشف الحساب" [Clashes in Tahrir in Friday of "Account Statement"], YouTube video, 2:36, October 12, 2012, https://www.youtube.com/watch?v=ylSFs7_i5mg. [Translation provided by author].

52. Essam Amer, "حركة كفاية تدعو لتوقيعات سحب الثقة من الرئيس تحت شعار تمرد" [Kefaya movement calls for collecting no confidence petitions under the slogan of "rebellion"], AlSherouk News, April 28, 2013, accessed February 15, 2019, http://bit.ly/2GMzdUL. [Translation provided by author].

53. Samar Gaber, "الاشتراكيين الثوريين: تعليق اعتصام عمال المحلة انتصار جزئى لتحقيق مطالبهم" [Revolutionary Socialists: Suspending the Mahalla workers' sit-in a partial victory to achieve their demands], ElFagr, July 24, 2012, accessed February 15, 2019, https://www.elfagr.com/151489. [Translation provided by author].

54. Nada ElKhouly, "على قهوة «الكرنك»: «إحنا بتوع الإنتاج». لا فلول ولا إخوان" [On the Karnak coffeeshop: We are the ones concerned with production. . . . No feloul or brothers], AlSherouk News, July 23, 2012, accessed February 15, 2019, http://bit.ly/2SARNXm. [Translation provided by author].

55. See Mahmoud ElTabbakh, "عمال غزل المحلة:علقنا الإضراب لنثبت للإخوان أننا لسنا فلول" [The Workers of Mahla Spinning: We put the strike on hold to prove to the Muslim Brotherhood we were not feloul], Masrawy, July 23, 2012, accessed October 12, 2017, http://bit.ly/2EaGXhF. [Translation provided by author].

56. "Morsi Meter," Morsi Meter, 2012, accessed February 15, 2019, http://morsimeter.com/en.

57. Josh Levs, "Like 'Obameter,' the 'Morsi Meter' Tracks Egyptian President's Promises," CNN, June 26, 2012, accessed October 12, 2017, https://cnn.it/2SBjX4h.

58. Shaimaa Khalil, "Egypt: President Morsi's 100 Days in Power," BBC News, October 9, 2012, accessed September 20, 2017, https://bbc.in/2X4gE4h.

59. Ibid.

60. Holmes, "In Egypt, Industrial Scale Death Decrees.".

61. Zeinab Abul-Magd, "Morsy and His Brothers: Sleeping in Nasser's Bed," *Egypt Independent*, October 10, 2012, accessed October 12, 2017, http://bit.ly/2SE6gSm.

62. Amira Mikhail, "Tahrir Bodyguard: Fighting Sexual Harassment on Egypt's Streets," Atlantic Council, December 10, 2012, accessed February 15, 2019, https://bit.ly/2DCQI6M; "Operation Anti Sexual Harassment—Opantish By Stephanie Gaspais," Gender and Sexuality Resource Center, November 5, 2015, accessed February 15, 2019, https://bit.ly/2STwQG9.

63. "المبادرة المصرية للحقوق الشخصية تصدر نتائج تحقيقها في أحداث دهشور" [The Egyptian Initiative for Personal Rights publishes its investigation findings in Dhashour's events], Egyptian Initiative for Personal Rights, August 7, 2012, accessed February 15, 2019, https://bit.ly/2TSaXEr. [Translation provided by author].

64. For a list of attacks on Muslim Brotherhood and FJP offices between June 18 and July 3, 2013, see Ketchley, *Egypt in a Time of Revolution*, 114.

65. Peter Beaumont, "Mohamed Morsi Signs Egypt's New Constitution into Law," *The Guardian*, December 26, 2012, accessed February 15, 2019, https://bit.ly/2BBHl7w.

66. Financial analyst in Cairo, interview by author, May 2014.

67. Wikithawra, "حصر قتلى عهد محمد مرسي تفصيلياً" [A detailed report on the number of deaths under Morsi], Wikithawra, June 26, 2013, accessed February 11, 2019, https://bit.ly/1MhzB7X. [Translation provided by author].

68. James Legge, "In Pictures: Jubilation in Cairo, Riots in Port Said," *The Independent*, January 26, 2013, accessed February 15, 2019, https://ind.pn/2SzTgNv.

69. Mossad El-Gohary, "Death Toll at 42 in Two Days of Egypt Violence," *The Times of Israel*, January 27, 2013, accessed February 15, 2019, https://bit.ly/2GM3vay.

70. "Egypt: Officials turn Blind Eye to Port Said Police Abuses," Human Rights Watch, March 2, 2013, accessed September 20, 2017, https://bit.ly/2GJEVXM.

71. Karim Medhat Ennarah, "The Politics of Mobilization and Demobilization," Mada Masr, February 10, 2014, accessed September 12, 2017, https://bit.ly/2V3443z.

72. At one point Morsi allegedly spoke about being concerned that no harm be done to both the captives and kidnappers. See "Source of Egypt's Coup: Morsi Gave Free Hand to Islamic Militants, Ordered Military to Stop Crackdowns on Jihadis," Talking Points Memo, July 18, 2013, accessed October 12, 2017, https://bit.ly/2GJ1xYk.

On June 16, 2013 in a speech at the Cairo International Stadium, Morsi announced that his government would be severing diplomatic ties with Syria, including closing the Syrian embassy in Cairo and withdrawing Egyptian diplomats from Damascus. See Nouran El-Behairy, "Morsi's Syria Speech Angers Opposition," *Daily News Egypt*, June 16, 2013, accessed October 12, 2017, https://bit.ly/2N6Q5H2.

73. As argued in the chapter on the first uprising against Mubarak, January 25 was chosen as the day to begin the protests because it was a national holiday to commemorate the police. Activists decided to turn it into a day of rage instead.

74. Adel Islander, "Tamarod: Egypt's Revolution Hones Its Skills," Jadaliyya, June 30, 2013, accessed October 12, 2017, https://bit.ly/2DLdp99.

75. Hassan Shaheen had taken part in protests against the SCAF. He happened to be captured in a video that went viral showing a woman being stripped by the military and dragged across Tahrir Square. See his testimony here: Mahmoud ElAgami, "شهادة رجل حاول إنقاذ فتاة مجلس الوزراء" [The testimony of a man who tried to save the girl of the minister's council events], YouTube video, 3:37. December 19, 2011, https://bit.ly/2T0sw8t. [Translation provided by author].

76. Samir AlSayed, "عاجل. البرادعي وموسى وصباحي يعلنون إنشاء جبهة إنقاذ وطني لإدارة المرحلة الحالية سياسيًا وشعبيًا" [El- Baradei, Moussa and Sabahi announce the establishment of a national salvation front to manage the current stage], Ahram Gate, November 24, 2012, accessed February 15, 2019, https:// bit.ly/ 2GPTxoe. [Translation provided by author].

77. Amr Moussa told me that he had the idea to convene the National Salvation Front on the same day as Morsi's Constitutional Declaration. While driving from Zagazig back to Cairo, the former head of the Arab League called up a few people, and a few hours later, they held their first meeting, with around 30–35 people in attendance. Amr Moussa, interview by author, August 24, 2017.

78. Basil El-Dabh, "June 30: Tamarod and Its Opponents," Middle East Institute, June 26, 2013, accessed October 12, 2017, http://www.mei.edu/content/june-30-tamarod-and-its-opponents.

79. Activist and blogger, interview by author, January 9, 2014.

80. Shadi Malek, Tamarod cofounder, interview by author, January 12, 2014. Others claim that the turning point was reached already after collecting 2 million signatures.

81. John Pollock, "Rebelbook: A Mix of Technologies Let Dedicated Citizens change Egypt," MIT Technology Review, September 19, 2014, accessed October 12, 2017, https://bit.ly/2IfQoAK.

82. A member of April 6 in Cairo, interview by author, July 2, 2013.

83. One person claimed that he toured around with a businessman who supported Tamarod, and that they were escorted by a high-level security detail wherever they went. Needless to say, activists during the first and second waves never enjoyed protection by the security services.

84. Activist/blogger in Cairo, interview by author, January 9, 2014.

85. Islander, "Tamarod: Egypt's Revolution Hones Its Skills."

86. Ahmed Aboulenein, "Tamarod Rejects Shafiq Endorsement," Daily News Egypt, May 17, 2013, accessed October 12, 2017, https://bit.ly/2ItTbqb.

87. "50 Faces That Made the News in 2011," Ahram Online, January 7, 2012, accessed October 12, 2017, https://bit.ly/2DMeQ71.

88. A member of Tamarod in Cairo, interview by author, January 12, 2014.

89. Mara Revkin, "The Egyptian State Unravels: Meet the Gangs and Vigilantes Who Thrive under Morsi," Foreign Affairs, June 27, 2013, accessed October 12, 2017, https://fam.ag/2S5PdmZ.

90. Two Egyptian police officers, interview by author, January 2014.

91. Khaled Ali, interview by author, May 26, 2014.

92. Salma Abdelaziz and Steve Almasy, "Egypt's Interim Cabinet Labels Muslim Brotherhood a Terrorist Group," CNN, December 25, 2013, accessed October 12, 2017, https://cnn.it/2GsZAjy.

93. "Mubarak Verdict 'Turned Our Dreams into Nightmares,'" *The New Arab*, December 1, 2014, accessed October 12, 2017, https://bit.ly/2tqbySm.

94. Gamal Essam El-Din, "The Quest for Control," Ahram Online, June 21, 2013, accessed October 12, 2017, https://bit.ly/2Ihhh7r.

95. David D. Kirkpatrick, "Egypt, Its Streets a Tinderbox, Braces for a Spark," *New York Times*, June 29, 2013, accessed October 13, 2017, https://nyti.ms/2SzXm8v.

96. Patrick Kingsley, "Egyptian Activists Hope for 'Second Revolution' a Year after Morsi's Election," *The Guardian*, June 27, 2013, accessed October 12, 2017, https:// bit.ly/2GjE28I.

97. Maggie Michael, "Egyptian Activists Angry over US Envoy's Comments," *The Big Story*, June 25, 2013, accessed October 12, 2017, https://bit.ly/2TQYOQm.

98. Erin Delmore, "Morsi Supporters Decry 'Military Coup' Underway in Egypt," MSNBC, July 3, 2013, accessed February 15, 2019, https://on.msnbc.com/2SX1HBO.

99. CBC Egypt, "بيان القوات المسلحة المصرية يوم ١ يوليو ٢٠١٣" [The Statement of the Egyptian Armed Forces on July 1, 2013], YouTube video, 7:09. July 1, 2013, https:// bit.ly/2N7vPoK. [Translation provided by author].

Chapter 6

1. "نص بيان الحكومة لاعتبار «الإخوان» جماعة إرهاب" [The Text of the Government's Statement regarding considering the Muslim Brotherhood a terrorist group], ElMasry ElYoum, December 25, 2013, accessed February 11, 2019, https:// www. almasryalyoum.com/news/details/363925.

2. "مصر—قاض يصدر أحكام إعدام جماعية" [Egypt—A judge issues mass death sentences], Human Rights Watch, December 3, 2014, accessed February 11, 2019, https://www. hrw.org/ar/news/2014/12/03/265064.

3. Hazem Adel and Ahmed Arafa, "الإدارية العليا تقضى بقبول تأسيس حزب سامي عنان ورفض تمرد" [Supreme Administrative Court rules by accepting the establishment of Sami Anan's party and rejecting Tamarod's], AlYoum7, January 28, 2015, accessed February 11, 2019, https://bit.ly/2E5hCG0.

4. Karim Sobhy, "نيابة قصر النيل تبدأ التحقيق مع أحمد ماهر فى أحداث الشورى" [Qasr Al-Nil Prosecution begins investigation with Ahmed Maher in Shura events], AlYoum7, November 30, 2013, accessed February 11, 2019, https://bit.ly/2E2kUtu.

5. Ibrahim Qara'a, "حكم بوقف وحظر أنشطة حركة «6 إبريل» بجميع المحافظات" [Banning the activities of 6 April in all governorates], AlMasryAlYoum, April 28, 2014, accessed February 11, 2019, https://bit.ly/2SNgsXI. [Translation provided by author].

6. Wikithawra, "تقرير فئة "الطلاب" حصر وقائع قتل أو قبض وملاحقة قضائية خلال عهد السيسي عدلي منصور حتي 15 أبريل 2014" [Report on the "Students," Record of murder or arrest and prosecution incidents, during Sisi/ Adly Mansour period, until 15 April 2014],

Wikithawra, May 4, 2014, accessed February 11, 2019, https:// bit.ly/ 2SpBz2V. [Translation provided by author].

7. Wikithawra, "فض تظاهرة مجلس الشوري 26 نوفمبر 2013, صور وشهادات وتقارير," [Dispersing the Shura Council Demonstration 26 November 2013, photos, testimonies and reports], Wikithawra, January 29, 2014, accessed February 11, 2019, https:// bit.ly/2E3q9sV. [Translation provided by author].

8. AlWafd, "نشر نص قانون التظاهر بالجريدة الرسمية" [The text of the Protest Law in the Official Gazette], AlWafd, November 24, 2013, accessed February 11, 2019, https:// bit.ly/2sL8kZN. [Translation provided by author].

9. "وزارة الداخلية المصرية ترفض استئناف دوري كرة القدم" [Egyptian Interior Ministry refuses to resume football league], BBC News, July 15, 2012, accessed February 11, 2019, https://bbc.in/2N4e7Ti. [Translation provided by author].

10. Ashraf Abdel Hamid, "داخلية مصر ترفض عودة الجماهير لمباريات الكرة" [Egypt's interior refuses to return the masses to the matches of the ball], Alarabiya.net, March 18, 2016, accessed February 11, 2019, https:// bit.ly/ 2Dokg84. [Translation provided by author].

11. Trager, *Arab Fall: How the Muslim Brotherhood Won and Lost Egypt in 891 days*, 247. In a televised interview in 2011, Mohamed Badie, former supreme guide of the Muslim Brotherhood, said they are more than 750,000, but did not specify the exact number; see EgyDoctor, "كم يبلغ عدد المنتمين لجماعة الإخوان المسلمين في مصر؟" [How many Muslim Brotherhood members are there in Egypt?], YouTube Video, 2:16, August 31, 2013, https:// www.youtube.com/ watch?v=ofAERYOsZ88 [Translation provided by author].

12. Mohamed Khayal, "حصر سري لأعضاء الإخوان" [A Secret Count of the members of the Brotherhood], *ElSherouk News*, 2011. [Translation provided by author].

13. Ahmed Maher, interview by author, May 2017.

14. Information taken from the Supreme Council of Universities in Egypt. See "Supreme Council of Universities," Supreme Council of Universities, accessed August 11, 2017, http://portal.scu.eun.eg/.

15. A leading member of the Ultras was cited in November 2012 and estimated the number of Ultras at around 20,000. See Ned Parker, "Violent Soccer Youths Cast Chill over Egypt," *Los Angeles Times*, November 3, 2012, accessed August 6, 2017, https://lat.ms/2SBrP64.

16. "ذكرى فض اعتصام رابعة العدوية: تسلسل الأحداث" [The anniversary of the Rabaa sit-in: The sequence of events], BBC News, August 14, 2016, accessed February 11, 2019, https://bbc.in/2GHrkzU. [Translation provided by author].

17. Wikithawra, "حصر قتلى عهد السيسي/عدلي منصور تفصيلياً (مُحَدَّث) حتى 31 يناير 2014" [A detailed report on the number of deaths under Sisi Adly Mansour until January 31, 2014], Wikithawra, March 26, 2014, accessed February 11, 2019, https://bit.ly/ 2N1xXyf. [Translation provided by author].

18. Ibid.

19. The figures are 932 in Rabaa and 90 in Nahda; ibid.

20. AlWafd, "نشر نص قانون التظاهر بالجريدة الرسمية" [The text of the Protest Law in the Official Gazette].

21. Wikithawra, "حصر قتلى عهد السيسي/عدلي منصور تفصيلياً (مُحَدَّث) حتى 31 يناير 2014" [A detailed report on the number of deaths under Sisi Adly Mansour until January 31, 2014].

22. "نص بيان الحكومة لاعتبار «الإخوان» جماعة إرهاب" [The Text of the Government's Statement regarding considering the Muslim Brotherhood a terrorist group].

23. Wikithawra, "حصر قتلى عهد السيسي/عدلي منصور تفصيلياً (مُحَدَّث) حتى 31 يناير 2014" [A detailed report on the number of deaths under Sisi Adly Mansour until January 31, 2014].

24. Dream TV, "خطاب ترشح السيسي للرئاسة كاملا" [Sisi's presidential candidacy full speech], YouTube video, 15:01, March 26, 2014, https:// www.youtube.com/watch?v=2Yqn6U55q9o. [Translation provided by author].

25. Ibrahim Qara'a, "حكم بوقف وحظر أنشطة حركة «6 إبريل» بجميع المحافظات" [Banning the activities of 6 April in all governorates].

26. Samir Omar and Ashraf Saad, "مصر—تمديد انتخابات الرئاسة ليوم ثالث" [Egypt—Extending presidential elections for a third day], Sky News Arabia, May 27, 2014, accessed February 12, 2019, https://bit.ly/2N34nbU. [Translation provided by author].

27. "النتيجة النهائية—السيسي رئيساً لمصر بـ96.91 % مقابل 3.09 % لصباحي" [Final results—Sisi is Egypt's presidents with 96.91% against 3.09% for Sabahi], CNN, June 3, 2014, accessed February 12, 2019, https://cnn.it/2Ss7fVn. [Translation provided by author].

28. Members of the Coptic minority reported that they believed that the status of the Coptic Church had, for the first time, been elevated to the same level of importance as Al-Azhar, at least symbolically. Maspero Youth Union in Cairo, Founding Member, interview by author, August 2017.

29. Holmes and Koehler, "Myths of Military Defection in Egypt and Tunisia."

30. "محمد البرادعي يؤدي اليمين الدستورية لتولي منصب نائب الرئيس للعلاقات الدولية" [Mohamed ElBaradie is sworn in as vice president for international relations], France 24, July 14, 2013, accessed February 12, 2019, https:// bit.ly/ 2BxAcVD. [Translation provided by author].

31. "السيرة الذاتية للدكتور زياد بهاء الدين نائب رئيس مجلس الوزراء وزير التعاون الدولى" [Curriculum Vitae of Dr. Ziad Bahaa Eldin, Deputy Prime Minister and Minister of International Cooperation], Ahram Gate, July 16, 2013, accessed February 12, 2019, https://bit.ly/2StMVTy. [Translation provided by author].

32. "السيرة الذاتية لكمال ابو عيطة وزير القوى العاملة الجديد" [Curriculum Vitae of Kamal Abu Eita, Minister of Manpower], AlBorsa News, July 16, 2013, accessed February 12, 2019, https://bit.ly/2RZ4WEm. [Translation provided by author].

33. Karim Hassan, "بوابة الأهرام تنشر التشكيل الكامل للمجلس القومى لحقوق الإنسان" [Ahram Gate publishes the new formation of the National Council for Human Rights], Ahram Gate, August 22, 2013, accessed February 12, 2019, https://bit.ly/2DBi8u6. [Translation provided by author].

34. Hossam Bahgat, the founder of the Egyptian Initiative for Personal Rights, was reportedly also offered a position in the National Council of Human Rights after the ouster of Morsi, but refused.

35. Amira Wahba, "نص استقالة البرادعي للرئيس منصور: تكبدنا ثمنًا غاليًا كان يمكن تجنب" [The text of ElBaradie's resignation to President Mansour: "We have paid heavily for something that could have been avoided," Ahram Gate, August 14, 2013, accessed February

12, 2019, http://gate.ahram.org.eg/News/382972.aspx. [Translation provided by author]. "قبول استقالة نائب رئيس الوزراء المصر" [Accepting the resignation of the Egyptian Deputy Prime Minister], BBC News, January 30, 2014, accessed February 12, 2019, https://bbc.in/2TLDgEu. [Translation provided by author]. Azza Atiya, "كمال أبوعيطة: استقالة حكومة الببلاوي كانت مفاجأة سارة" [Kamal Abu Eita: The resignation of Beblawi's cabinet was a good surprise], ElWatan News, March 10, 2014, accessed February 12, 2019, https://bit.ly/2SrXMgV. [Translation provided by author].

36. Salwa AlZoghby, "أحمد البرعي وزير التضامن.الاجتماعي. رجل المراحل الانتقالية" [Ahmed El Boraie Minister of Social Solidarity, the man of transitional periods], ElWatan News, July 14, 2013, accessed February 12, 2019, https://bit.ly/2StGobJ. [Translation provided by author].

37. Marwa AlSayed, "حسام بهجت يرفض عضوية قومي حقوق الإنسان" [Hossam Bahgat refuses the national Council for Human Rights' membership], Veto Gate, August 29, 2013, accessed February 12, 2019, https://bit.ly/2BBENpI. [Translation provided by author].

38. Karim Hassan, "بوابة الأهرام تنشر التشكيل الكامل للمجلس القومى لحقوق الإنسان" [Ahram Gate publishes the new formation of the National Council for Human Rights], Ahram Gate.

39. See Ayat Oraby, "انتخبوا_العرص آخر إحصائية لعدد مستخدمي و زائري هاشتاج انتخبوا العرص" [Elect the Pimp: Latest Statistics for the Users of the Hashtag Elect the Pimp], Twitter, April 2, 2014, accessed August 11, 2017, https://bit.ly/2S5hZ79. [Translation provided by author].. Also see Charlotte Alfred, "'Vote for the Pimp' Hashtag Prompts Twitter Battle in Egypt," Huffington Post, March 31, 2014, accessed August 11, 2017, https://bit.ly/1QtDwUo.

40. Wikithawra, "٣١ إحصائيات عامة حول قتلى أول سبع شهور من عهد السيسي/عدلي منصور حتى يناير ٢٠١٤" [General Statistics on the number of deaths during the first seven months under Sisi/Adly Mansour until January 31, 2014], Wikithawra, January 2014, accessed February 12, 2019, https://bit.ly/2DwqzGQ. [Translation provided by author].

41. Yousry ElBadry, "ضبط ٣٥ من مالكي القنوات الدينية وملاحقة ٣٤ من قيادات «الإخوان»" [Arresting 35 Owners of Religious Channels and tracking 34 Muslim Brotherhood Leaders], Al-Masry Al-Youm, July 3, 2013, accessed August 11, 2017, http://www.almasryalyoum.com/news/details/230627. [Translation provided by author].

42. "اغلاق القنوات الدينية: انتهاك لحرية الرأي أم ضرورة أمنية" [The Closure of Religious Channels: Violation of Freedom of Speech or a Security Necessity], BBC Arabic, July 9, 2013, accessed August 11, 2017, https://bbc.in/2BC4Ugr. [Translation provided by author].

43. "صحفيو "الحرية والعدالة" يدينون وقف إصدار الجريدة ويعلنون الاعتصام بمقر نقابة الصحفيين" [Journalists from Freedom and Justice Party Newspaper denounce stopping its publication and announce their sit-in at the Journalists' Syndicate"], Aswat Masriya, December 26, 2013, accessed August 11, 2017, https://bit.ly/2SGjGxj. [Translation provided by author].

44. Sami Anan was prevented from forming a political party. Ahmed Wasfy had gained some popularity for his role in restoring security in the Canal Zone after riots in the spring of 2013, while Morsi was still in power. He had then suggested in an interview in 2014 that if Sisi were promoted or assumed political office, this would be a sign that the removal of Morsi was not a "second revolution" but a

coup. See David D. Kirkpatrick, "General Who Led Takeover of Egypt to Run for President," *New York Times*, March 26, 2014, accessed August 11, 2017, https://nyti.ms/2tp37H6.

45. Sameh Seif Elyazal, "Huge Dueling Demonstrations across Cairo; Mohammed Morsi's Presidency Appears to be Over," interview by Christiane Amanpour, CNN, July 3, 2013, accessed August 11, 2017, https://cnn.it/2UYkutP.

46. Mohamed El-Baradei, "'This Was Not a Coup,'" interview, *Der Spiegel*, July 8, 2013, accessed August 11, 2017, https://bit.ly/2IfVXiC.

47. Mohamed El-Baradei, interview by author, October 2016.

48. William Burns, interview by author, January 2018.

49. "الجيش المصري يقصي الإخوان" [The Egyptian army deposes the Muslim Brotherhood], Sky News Arabia, July 3, 2013, accessed February 15, 2019, https://bit.ly/2Gs1elm. [Translation provided by author].

50. Yousri ElBadry, "القبض على سعد الكتاتني ورشاد بيومي"[Arresting Saad El- Katatni and Rashad Bayoumi], AlMasry AlYoum, July 4, 2013, accessed February 16, 2019, https://bit.ly/2DI1PM2. [Translation provided by author].

51. Ahmed Harby, "القبض على مهدى عاكف المرشد السابق لجماعة الإخوان المسلمين" [Arresting Mahdy Aakef, the former Supreme Guide of the Muslim Brotherhood], AlYoum7, July 4, 2013, accessed February 16, 2019, https://bit.ly/2GS4WUX.[Translation provided by author].

52. "السلطات المصرية تعتقل القيادي في جماعة الاخوان المسلمين حلمي الجزار" [Egyptian authorities arrest Helmy ElGazzar, a leading figure of the Muslim Brotherhood], Kuwait News Agency, July 5, 2013, accessed February 16, 2019, https:// bit.ly/2SSSoD0. [Translation provided by author].

53. Hassan Ahmed, "القبض على خيرت الشاطر في مدينة نصر" [Arresting Khairat Al-Shater in Nasr City], AlMasry AlYoum, July 6, 2013, accessed February 15, 2019, https://bit.ly/2BFlSKS. [Translation provided by author].

54. Gamal Heshmat, "ضبط ابن شقيق جمال حشمت و4 من قيادات «الإخوان» بالبحيرة,="
[Arresting the nephew of Gamal Heshmat and four brotherhood leaders in Behaira], AlMasry AlYoum, August 17, 2013, accessed February 15, 2019, https:// bit.ly/2SXhSz2. [Translation provided by author].

55. Hassan Ahmed, "تفاصيل القبض على قيادات بـ«الإخوان» في عدد من المحافظات" [The details of arresting leading figures of the Brotherhood in a number of governorates], AlMasry AlYoum, August 18, 2013, accessed February 16, 2019, https://bit.ly/2IgrJMj. [Translation provided by author].

56. Ibid.

57. Hassan Ahmed, "القبض على محمد بديع مرشد الإخوان المسلمين في شقة سكنية بـرابعة العدوية" [Arresting Mohamed Badie, the Supreme Guide of the Muslim Brotherhood, in an apartment in Rabaa], AlMasry AlYoum, August 20, 2013, accessed February 16, 2019, https://bit.ly/2TRNpQi. [Translation provided by author].

58. "القبض على محمد البلتاجى القيادي بجماعة الإخوان المسلمين بالجيزة," [Arresting Mohamed ElBeltagy, a leading figure of the Muslim Brotherhood in Giza], Ahram Online, August 29, 2013, accessed February 15, 2019, https:// bit.ly/2T0In6Z. [Translation provided by author].

59. Yousri ElBadry, "القبض على أمين «الحرية والعدالة» بمطروح بتهمة التحريض على أعمال عنف" [Arresting the General Secretary of the Freedom and Justice Party in Matrouh on charges of inciting violence], AlMasry AlYoum, August 29, 2013, accessed February 15, 2019, https://bit.ly/2DNmRtU. [Translation provided by author].

60. Hassan Ahmed, "القبض على أمين «الحرية والعدالة» بالقاهرة خالد حنفي" [Arresting Khaled Hanafy, the General Secretary of the Freedom and Justice Party in Cairo], AlMasry AlYoum, September 9, 2013, accessed February 16, 2019, https://bit.ly/2DM0CmF. [Translation provided by author].

61. "إلقاء القبض على القيادي الإخواني عصام العريان بالقاهرة" [Arresting Essam El- Erian, a leading brotherhood figure in Cairo], AlArabiya, October 30, 2013, accessed February 15, 2019, https://bit.ly/2DNmRtU. [Translation provided by author].

62. Ehab Omar, "القبض على القيادي الإخواني جلال عبد الصادق من منزله في أسيوط" [Arresting Galal Abdel Sadek, a leading figure of the Brotherhood, at his house in Assuit], ElBalad News, November 23, 2013, accessed February 16, 2019, https:// bit.ly/2SD92Hf. [Translation provided by author].

63. Nermin Ibrahim, "القبض على أمين الحرية والعدالة بأسيوط بقرية سياحية بالإسكندرية" [Arresting the General Secretary of the Freedom and Justice Party in Assuit in a touristic compound in Alexandria], Veto Gate, November 30, 2013, accessed February 16, 2019, https://bit.ly/2S67rVm. [Translation provided by author].

64. The number of people killed is taken from Wikithawra. Documentation is available at: "مذبحة دار الحرس الجمهورى 8 يوليو 2013" [Massacre of the Republican Guards July 8, 2013], Wikithawra, July 20, 2013, accessed August 11, 2017, https:// goo.gl/ 86T1WL. [Translation provided by author]. Also see Patrick Kingsley and Leah Green, "Killing in Cairo: The Full Story of the Republican Guards Club Shootings," *The Guardian*, July 18, 2013, accessed August 11, 2017, https://bit.ly/2GMAHP0.

65. Ibid.

66. Max Fisher, "What's the Matter with Egypt's Liberals?" *Washington Post*, August 12, 2013, accessed August 11, 2017, https://wapo.st/2SFGtce.

67. Sharif Abdel Kouddous, "What Happened to Egypt's Liberals after the Coup?" *The Nation*, June 29, 2015, accessed August 11, 2017, https://www.thenation.com/article/what-happened-egypts-liberals-after-coup/.

68. "The Sad State of Egypt's Liberals," *The Economist*, October 10, 2015, accessed August 11, 2017, https://econ.st/2Gsf4UJ.

69. Ebrahem Gamal, "حمزاوي هذا انقلاب وليس ثورة" [Hamzawy: This is a coup and not a revolution], June 17, 2014, accessed August 11, 2017, https:// www.youtube.com/watch?v=bIReOA6-MuM. [Translation provided by author].

70. Amr Hamzawy, "أزمة الليبرالية المصرية وإعادة تأسيسها" [The Crisis of Egyptian Liberalism and its re- structure], Shorouk News, July 31, 2013, accessed August 11, 2017, https://bit.ly/2N9U7yv. [Translation provided by author].

71. "منع عمرو حمزاوي و18 آخرين من السفر لـ"إهانة القضاء" [Banning Amr Hamzawi and 18 others from traveling for "insulting the judiciary"], Alarabiya.net, January 16, 2014, accessed August 11, 2017, https://goo.gl/kEDkpt. [Translation provided by author].

72. "الجنايات» تلغي قرار منع «حمزاوي وقنديل» من السفر بقضية «إهانة القضاء»" [Court of felonies» cancels travel ban for "Hamzawi and Qandil" for their involvement in

"insulting the judiciary" case], *Shorouk News*, October 22, 2014, accessed August 11, 2017, https://goo.gl/vxYkX4 [Translation provided by author].

73. See April 6th Movement Facebook Page, accessed August 11, 2017, https://www.facebook.com/shabab6april

74. April 6 issued the statement on July 31, 2013, two weeks before the sit-ins were besieged by security forces. The statement rejected the decision of the Council of Ministers to give the Ministry of Interior the mandate to disperse the Rabaa and Nahda sit-ins and assigned them the responsibility of the blood that will be shed if the sit-ins were dispersed. See statement: April 6th Movement Facebook Page, accessed August 11, 2017, https://goo.gl/mDHQkn. Another post was showing condolences to a member who was killed at the sit-in and others who were unknown. See statement: April 6th Movement Facebook Page, accessed August 11, 2017, https://goo.gl/Edve3i.

75. Jess Martin, "Freedom Is in the Hands of the People | SocialistWorker.org," Socialistworker.org, July 10, 2013, accessed August 11, 2017, http://socialistworker.org/2013/07/10/freedom-in-the-peoples-hands.

76. See No Military Trials website, accessed August 11, 2017, http://www.nomiltrials.org.

77. Wael Eskandar, "Egypt's Kazeboon: Countering State Narrative," Middle East Institute, July 12, 2013, accessed August 11, 2017, http://www.mei.edu/content/egypts-kazeboon-countering-state-narrative.

78. Egyptian General Calls for Mass Protests", New York Times, July 24, 2013: https://www.nytimes.com/2013/07/25/world/middleeast/egypt.html.

79. Heba AbdelSattar, "٦ إبريل': لن نشارك فى تظاهرات اليوم . . . وأحمد ماهر: الدولة لا تحتاج لتفويض من الشعب للقيام بواجبها" [April 6th: We won't participate in today's protests—Ahmed Maher: the state does not need a permission from the people to do its job], AlAhram Gate, July 26, 2013, accessed August 11, 2017. http:// gate.ahram.org.eg/News/376362.aspx. [Translation provided by author].

80. "مؤسس حركة ٦ أبريل: لم أصرح بأن ما حدث انقلاب" [April 6th Founder: I did not say that what happened is a coup], Alarabiya.net, July 12, 2013, accessed August 11, 2017, https://goo.gl/gkruVi. [Translation provided by author].

81. "إسقاط الإخوان لتعميق الثورة لا لتدعيم النظام . . . لن نفوّض" [Overthrowing the Brotherhood to deepen the revolution not to support the regime . . . we will not authorize], The Socialist Gate, July 25, 2013, accessed August 11, 2017, http://revsoc.me/ statements/ sqt- lkhwn- ltmyq- lthwr- l- ltdym- lnzm- ln- nfwwd/. [Translation provided by author].

82. "'تمرّد' تنشر خريطة مسيرات التفويض تحت شعار 'لا للإرهاب'" [Tamarod publishes a map for the authorization protests under the slogan "No to Terrorism"], Alarabiya.net, July 25, 2013, accessed August 11, 2017, https:// goo.gl/ TmkBeP. [Translation provided by author].

83. "التحالف الشعبي يدعو لتفويض السيسي ويحذر من أي إجراءات استثنائية" [The Popular Coalition calls for authorizing Sisi to fight terrorism and warns against emergency measures], Elgornal.net, July 26, 2013, accessed August 11, 2017, http://elgornal.net/news/news.aspx?id=2948798. [Translation provided by author].

84. "اتحاد العمال فى التحرير...تفويضا للجيش لمحاربة الإرهاب" [Labor Union is in Tahrir Square to authorise the military to fight terrorism], Egyptian Trade Union Federation, July 26, 2013, accessed August 11, 2017, http://etufegypt.com/archives/14971 [Translation provided by author].

85. Fatma Ramadan, "إلي عمال مصر التفويض سم قاتل" [To Egyptian Workers: Authorization is a venom], Elhewar ElMotamaden, July 26, 2013, accessed August 11, 2017, http://www.m.ahewar.org/s.asp?aid=370369&r=0. [Translation provided by author].

86. The Egyptian Current Party Facebook Page, accessed August 11, 2017, https://goo.gl/t2mMsb.

87. The Egyptian Current Party Facebook Page, accessed August 11, 2017, https://goo.gl/4zBWC5.

88. Mostafa Ramadan, "دعوة 'السيسي' للتظاهر قد تؤدى إلى اقتتال أهلي :'القوية مصر'" [Strong Egypt Party: Sisi's call for protest could lead to a civil strife], ONA—ONews Agency, July 24, 2013, accessed August 11, 2017, http://onaeg.com/?p=1082704. [Translation provided by author].

89. Mostafa Nada, "«مصر القوية»: موقف أبو الفتوح من «30 يونيو» ثورة أعقبها انقلاب على شرعية مرسي" [Strong Egypt Party: Aboul Fetouh's position from June 30th events is that it is a revolution followed by a coup], Shorouk News, February 15, 2015, accessed August 11, 2017, https://bit.ly/2N9tj1o. [Translation provided by author].

90. "Mahmoud Abou Zeid (Shawkan)," Committee to Protect Journalists, accessed February 12, 2019, https://bit.ly/2StYGtd.

91. "Egypt releases award-winning photojournalist Shawkan after five years in prison," CNN, March 5, 2019.

92. While my article offers an ethnography of the sit-in itself, two other early pieces described the violent crackdowns and the more general context at the time, including one by my former AUC colleague Emad Shahin. See Amy Austin Holmes, "Before the Bloodletting: A Tour of the Rabaa Sit-In," *Cairo Review of Global Affairs*, August 16, 2013; Emad El-Din Shahin, "Sentenced to Death in Egypt," *The Atlantic*, May 19, 2015, accessed August 11, 2017, https://bit.ly/2Guxrbz. Professor Shahin was sentenced to death in absentia with vague charges of espionage and undermining Egypt's national security. See also Adam Schatz, "Egypt's Counter-Revolution," *London Review of Books*, August 16, 2013, accessed August 11, 2017, https://bit.ly/2GNK5lh.

93. Wikithawra, "تقرير شامل: حصر ضحايا فض اعتصام رابعة تفصيلياً، وآلية الحصر" [Report: A detailed record of deaths from the Rabaa dispersal and the methodology of reporting], Wikithawra, March 17, 2014, accessed February 12, 2019, https://bit.ly/1M8j2hV. [Translation provided by author].

94. According to Wikithawra, there were 83 churches attacked, not 56. See, "توثيق الاعتداءات على دور عبادة وممتلكات الاقباط ما بعد فض الاعتصامين" [Documenting attacks on Coptic houses of worship and properties after the dispersal of the sit- ins], Wikithawra, August 29, 2013, accessed February 12, 2019, https://bit.ly/1XGoADS. [Translation provided by author].

95. Wikithawra, "حصر قتلى عهد المجلس العسكرى تفصيليا" [A detailed record of deaths under the SCAF], Wikithawra, November 3, 2013, accessed February 12, 2019, https://bit.ly/2Gd6FUY. [Translation provided by author].

96. Peter Hessler, "Egypt's Failed Revolutions," *New Yorker*, January 2, 2017, accessed August 11, 2017 https://bit.ly/2ijIeGu.

97. See Amy Austin Holmes, "Why Egypt's Military Orchestrated a Massacre,".

98. Unpublished statement of principles for Tamarod drafted by Mona Seleem.

99. See Mostafa Hashem, "مصر: تمرد داخل حركة "تمرد" يهدد مستقبلها السياسي" [Egypt: Rebellion inside Tamarod Movement threatens its political future], DW.COM, December 25, 2013, accessed August 11, 2017, https://goo.gl/jgsW2f. [Translation provided by author]. Also see El-Shami, Khaled, "تمرد تصحيح المسار» «الجماهير» تعلن انتهاء الحملة. . . وتطلق مشروع «الجماهير»" [The correction of path Tamarod front ends its campaign and starts the "public" project], AlMasryAlYoum, June 9, 2014, accessed February 10, 2018, http://www.almasryalyoum.com/news/details/461087. [Translation provided by author].

100. Tamarod activist in Alexandria, interview by author, December 2016.

101. Activist in Aswan, interview by author, January 2017.

102. See Tamarod Port Said's Facebook Page, accessed August 11, 2017, https://www.facebook.com/TmrodPTS.

103. See Tamarod Minya's Facebook Page, accessed August 11, 2017, https://bit.ly/2GsfCKh.

104. Activist in Tanta, interview by author, May 2017.

105. See Mai Shams El-Din, "Rebellion on the Rocks," Mada Masr, June 30, 2014, accessed February 10, 2018, https://bit.ly/2DMapcp.

106. Abdallah Khalifa, "تمرد' الإسماعيلية تعلن حل الحملة والعودة لصفوف الشعب لاستكمال أهداف الثورة" [Tamarod Ismailia Branch announces dissolving the branch and returning to the people's side to continue achieving the goals of the revolution], ElBadil, November 29, 2013, accessed February 10, 2018, https://elbadil.com/2013/11/تمرد-الإسماعيلية-تعلن-حل-الحملة-والعو/. [Translation provided by author].

107. Moamen Ismail, "فيديو . . . استقالة المكتب التنفيذي لـ "تمرد مطروح"" [Video . . . The resignation of the executive office of Tamarod's branch in Matrouh], Masr AlArabia, November 29, 2013, accessed February 10, 2018, https://bit.ly/2GHvDLT. [Translation provided by author].

108. Mohamed Nassar, "«تمرد كفر الشيخ» تحل مكاتبها التنفيذية بالمحافظة" [Tamarod Kafr El Sheikh's branch dissolves its executive offices], Shorouk News, November 11, 2013, accessed February 10, 2018, https://bit.ly/2X6GXa5. [Translation provided by author].

109. Ketchley, *Egypt in a Time of Revolution*, 111–113.

110. Please refer to the table at the beginning of the chapter that outlines the type of state action or mode of repression against specific target groups within society.

111. Amr Hamzawy, "Legislating Authoritarianism: Egypt's New Era of Repression," Carnegie Endowment for International Peace, March 16, 2017, accessed August 11, 2017, https://goo.gl/JxN4HB.

112. As I witnessed myself as a long-term resident of Cairo, the Protest Law was so draconian that even nonprotest gatherings of more than 10 people became risky. For example, walking tours of downtown Cairo that involved more than a handful of people could become a problem. This curtailed outings with students, tourist

groups, as well as Friday morning walks organized by a group of expats to visit architectural sites in Old Cairo.

113. A member of April 6 political bureau, interview by author, December 2016.

114. BBC News Arabic, "مصر: أزمة بين المجلس العسكري وحركة 6 ابريل" [Egypt: A crisis between the SCAF and April 6 movement], BBC News, July 23, 2011, accessed February 12, 2019, https://bbc.in/2N2w4S2. [Translation provided by author].

115. Ahmed Maher, interview by author, May 2017.

116. A member of April 6 political bureau, interview by author, December 2016.

117. "نص قرار المجلس الأعلى للقوات المسلحة بتعديل قانون الطوارئ" [Text of the SCAF's decision to amend emergency law], AlMogaz, September 16, 2011, accessed February 12, 2019, https:// bit.ly/ 2WYc6wj. [Translation provided by author]. "مركز الأبحاث والدراسات القانونية" [Centre for Research and Legal Studies], Facebook, July 15, 2012, accessed February 12, 2019, https://bit.ly/2Ss648I. [Translation provided by author].

118. Ahmed Mansour was killed on December 16, 2011 during the clashes of Mohamed Mahmoud. See "فى ذكرى ميلاد الشهيد أحمد منصور القصاص من القتلة مازال مفقودا" [On the anniversary of the martyr Ahmed Mansour al-Qassas, the killers are still missing], April 6 Youth, May 27, 2017, accessed August 11, 2017, https:// goo.gl/ ravXHA. [Translation provided by author].

119. Gaber Salah was injured during the second clashes of Mohamed Mahmoud. He died as a result of his injury on November 26, 2012. See "وفاة "جيكا" عضو 6 أبريل إثر إصابته بخرطوش" [The death of "Gika" of April 6 after being hit by bird shots], Alarabiya.net, November 26, 2012, accessed August 11, 2017, https://bit.ly/2DJTdoc. [Translation provided by author].

120. Ibrahim Abul Hassan was killed during Al Abassiya events on May 1, 2011. See Mahmoud Motawea, "6 ابريل تدعو لوقفة أمام محكمة 'مصر الجديدة' في ذكرى استشهاد' أبو الحسن" [April 6th calls for a stand in front of the court of "Heliopolis" on the anniversary of the martyrdom of Abu Hassan], Sada ElBalad, February 20, 2013, accessed August 11, 2017, http://www.elbalad.news/403758. [Translation provided by author].

121. Ahmed Al Masry was injured in clashes that took place after the dispersal of Rabaa. He died on September 1, 2013.

122. Mohamed, a member of April 6 political bureau, interview by author, December 2016.

123. "القبض على علاء عبد الفتاح لاتهامه بأحداث مجلس الشورى" [Arresting Alaa Abdel Fattah for the Shura Council events], AlArabiya, November 29, 2013, accessed February 16, 2019, https://bit.ly/2SBDHEU. [Translation provided by author].

124. "الناشط أحمد ماهر يسلم نفسه للسلطات المصرية" [Activist Ahmed Maher surrenders himself to the Egyptian authorities], Reuters, November 30, 2013, accessed February 16, 2019, https://bit.ly/2S6TWoi. [Translation provided by author].

125. Marwa Morsi and Ahmed Maged, "عضو بـ "الاشتراكيين الثوريين" في الإسكندرية يتهم وكيل نيابة المنشية برفض سماع شهادته في قضية" [A member of the Revolutionary Socialists in Alexandria accuses the Mansheya prosecutor of refusing to hear his testimony in a case], ElWatan News, December 5, 2013, accessed February 16, 2019, https://bit.ly/2SWdd0h. [Translation provided by author].

126. "القبض على الناشط المصري أحمد دومة" [Arresting Egyptian activist Ahmed Douma], BBC News, December 3, 2013, accessed February 16, 2019, https://bbc.in/2IfynTa. [Translation provided by author].

127. Ahmed Ghoneim, "القبض على الناشط خالد السيد أثناء اشتباكات شارع شريف" [Arresting activist Khaled El-Sayed during classes in Sherif Street], ElWatan News, January 25, 2014, accessed February 16, 2019, https://bit.ly/2IhqA7e. [Translation provided by author].

128. Hossam Abdel Rady, "القبض على الناشطة ماهينور المصري بالإسكندرية بتهمة خرق قانون التظاهر" [Arresting activist Mahinour El- Massry in Alexandria for violating the Protest Law], ElWatan News, April 12, 2014, accessed February 16, 2019, https://bit.ly/2GHxi45. [Translation provided by author].

129. "المبادرة المصرية تعرب عن صدمتها ازاء استمرار احتجاز يارا سلام و ٢٢ أخرين" [The Egyptian Initiative for Personal Rights is shocked that Yara Sallam along with 22 other are still detained], The Egyptian Initiative for Personal Rights, June 30, 2014, accessed February 16, 2019, https://bit.ly/2DP9ecy. [Translation provided by author].

130. Amr Hamed, "الأمن يلقي القبض على شقيقة علاء عبد الفتاح في مسيرة الاتحادية" [Security arrests Alaa Abdel Fattah's sister in the Itahdiyya March], ElWatan News, June 21, 2014, accessed February 16, 2019, https://bit.ly/2BOEU1x. [Translation provided by author].

131. Sami Magdy, "هاني الجمل... ذكريات الثورة ومستقبلها" [Hany ElGamal . . . the memory and future of the revolution], Masrawy, December 22, 2015, accessed February 16, 2019, https://bit.ly/2STrqv6. [Translation provided by author].

132. See Mark R. Beissinger, Amaney Jamal, and Kevin Mazur, "Who Participated in the Arab Spring," Princeton.edu, 2012, accessed August 11, 2017, https://bit.ly/2SD7zAR.

133. Sarah Gamil, "التعليم: بدء الدراسة ٢١ سبتمبر" [Ministry of Education: Academic term starts on September 21], AlMasry AlYoum, August 17, 2013, accessed February 16, 2019, https://bit.ly/2tmEAlO. [Translation provided by author]. "جامعة القاهرة - بدء الدراسة بكليات جامعة القاهرة 21 سبتمبر" [Term starts at Cairo University faculties on 21st September], Cairo University Website, September 16, 2013, accessed August 11, 2017, https://cu.edu.eg/ar/Cairo-University-News-3876.html. [Translation provided by author].

134. "جامعة الأزهر: مظاهرات الطلاب خرجت عن سلميتها" [Al-Azhar University: Student demonstrations gone non-peaceful], Masr AlArabia, October 30, 2013, accessed August 11, 2017.,https://goo.gl/E7rMfC. [Translation provided by author].

135. "تأجيل تاريخ موعد بداية الدراسة في جامعة الازهر الترم الثانى" [Postponement of the starting date of the second academic term at Al-Azhar University], Masreat Website, February 15, 2014, accessed August 11, 2017, https:// goo.gl/ bdfwFJ. [Translation provided by author].

136. See Koloud Saber, Ahmed Ezzat, and Emad Mubarak, "الحقوق والحريات الطلابية في ضوء التعديلات القانونية الأخيرة" [Student Rights and Freedoms in Light of the Recent Legal Amendments], The Association for Freedom of Thought and Expression, 2008, accessed August 11, 2017, https://bit.ly/2V0lbmz. [Translation provided by author]. Also see: Essam ElDin Rady and Heba Hassan, "بعد قرار منع النشاط الحزبي بها الجامعات في الحظر" [After the Decision to Ban Party Activities on Campus: Universities

under Curfew], Al-Ahram, March 17, 2013, accessed August 11, 2017, https://bit.ly/2Ec8aR6. [Translation provided by author].

137. Mohamed Saad, former vice president of student union at Cairo University, interview by author, December 2016.

138. For an excellent analysis of the protests led by Students Against the Coup, see chapter 6 in Ketchley, *Egypt in a Time of Revolution*.

139. Two members of Students Against the Coup, interview by author, January 2017.

140. Essam Hashem et al., "جامعة القاهرة تدين أحداث مقتل طالب الهندسة وتحمل أجهزة الأمن المسئولية" [Cairo University condemns the murdering of its engineering student and holds security responsible], Ahram Online, December 1, 2013, accessed February 16, 2019, https://bit.ly/2TSPCL6. [Translation provided by author].

141. Ibid.

142. Wikithawra, "حصر قتلي شهر يناير ٢٠١٤ تفصيلياً" [Detailed report of the deaths during January 2014], Wikithawra. February 8, 2014, accessed February 12, 2019, https://bit.ly/2SEs1S5. [Translation provided by author].

143. A student in the medical faculty at the University of Tanta, interview by author, May 2017.

144. Egypt specialist at the State Department and a member of the Policy Planning Staff under President Obama, interview by author, October 2017.

145. Michael R. Gordon and Kareem Fahim, "Kerry Says Egypt's Military Was 'Restoring Democracy' in Ousting Morsi," *New York Times*, August 1, 2013, accessed August 11, 2017, https://nyti.ms/1mBEcZk.

146. William J. Burns, *The Back Channel: A Memoir of American Diplomacy and the Case for its Renewal* (New York: Random House, 2019), 308.

147. Ibid., 308–309.

148. Martin Chulov, "Egypt's Ousting of Mohamed Morsi Was a Coup, Says John McCain," *The Guardian*, December 1, 2017, accessed February 12, 2019, https://bit.ly/2SJjnRf.

149. Peter Baker, "A Coup? Or Something Else? $1.5 Billion in U.S. Aid Is on the Line," *New York Times*, July 4, 2013, accessed February 12, 2019, https://nyti.ms/2SOm8AQ.

150. Joel Gehrke, "Sen. Patrick Leahy: U.S. Law Requires Pulling Foreign Aid to Egypt Because of Military Coup," *Washington Examiner*, July 3, 2013, accessed February 12, 2019, https://washex.am/2GnPb8O.

151. William Burns, interview by author, January 24, 2018.

152. Andrew Miller and Amy Hawthorne, "Egypt's Sham Election," *Foreign Affairs*, March 23, 2018, accessed February 12, 2019, https://fam.ag/2DvUAGS.

153. Ibid.

154. See Varol, *The Democratic Coup d'État*; and Tansey, *The International Politics of Authoritarian Rule*.

155. In February 2016 the House Judiciary Committee voted along party lines to call on the State Department to designate the Muslim Brotherhood as a terrorist organization. Republican support for the resolution may be related to the anti-Muslim rhetoric of some of the Republican presidential candidates, including Donald Trump's

call for banning Muslims from entering the United States until the government can "figure out what's going on." It has been argued that the bill is "unlikely to become law." See Lynch, "Is the Muslim Brotherhood a Terrorist Organization or a Firewall against Violent Extremism?".

156. See "The U.S. Department of State's International Narcotics and Law Enforcement Affairs (INL): Egypt," U.S. Department of State, 2015, accessed August 11, 2017, https://bit.ly/2N01t7u.

157. Holmes, "In Egypt, Industrial Scale Death decrees."

158. A number of prominent media personalities exhorted the Egyptian people to vote after a low turnout for the presidential elections in May 2014. See Masr Madaneya, "الإعلام المصري بعد اول يوم من التصويت في الإنتخابات الرئاسية" [The Egyptian Media after the first day of voting in the presidential elections], YouTube video, 2:49, May 2014, https://bit.ly/1mlzMBh. [Translation provided by author].

159. Patrick Kingsley, "Egyptian Presidential Election Extended to Third Day," *The Guardian*, May 27, 2014, accessed August 11, 2017, https://bit.ly/2tiPicY

160. Michael Crowley, "John Kerry and Obama Denounce Egypt Verdict on Al Jazeera Journalists," *Time*, June 23, 2014, accessed February 11, 2018, https://bit.ly/2BzbEeP.

161. "Egypt Court Sentences Al Jazeera Journalists," Al Jazeera English, accessed August 11, 2017, https://bit.ly/2TKfpoL; Patrick Kingsley, "Al-Jazeera Journalists Jailed for Seven Years in Egypt," *The Guardian*, June 23, 2014, accessed August 11, 2017, https://bit.ly/2GjE28I

162. "محمود بدر يدعم السيسي في سوهاج" [Mahmoud Badr Supports Sisi in Sohag], ElMasry ElYoum, May 19, 2014, accessed August 11, 2017, http://lens.almasryaly-oum.com/album/5650/212819. [Translation provided by author].

163. Mostafa Hashem, "مصر: تمرد داخل حركة "تمرد" يهدد مستقبلها السياسي" [Egypt: Rebellion inside Tamarod Movement threatens its political future], DW.COM, December 25, 2013, accessed August 11, 2017, https://goo.gl/jgsW2f. [Translation provided by author].

164. Head of a prominent human rights organization in Egypt, interview by author, May 2017.

165. See: Elias Groll, "The Strange Elite Politics Behind Thailand's Military Coup," *Foreign Policy*, May 22, 2014, accessed August 30, 2018, https://bit.ly/2GsezKD; "Thai Junta Charges 50 Anti-Government Activists," VOA, February 16, 2018, accessed August 30, 2018, https://bit.ly/2RYqJft; Duncan McCargo, "Divided and Self-Destructive, Thailand Is a Long Way from Compromise," *The Guardian*, January 24, 2014, accessed August 20, 2018, https://bit.ly/2SpTDdk ; Paul Chambers and Napisa Waitoolkiat, "The Resilience of Monarchised Military in Thailand," *Journal of Contemporary Asia* 46, no. 3 (March 23, 2016), accessed May 17, 2019, https://www.tandfonline.com/doi/abs/10.1080/00472336.2016.1161060?journalCode=rjoc20.

166. See Corinne Dufka, "*By Day We Fear the Army, by Night the Jihadists*": Abuses by Armed Islamists and Security Forces in Burkina Faso, report, May 2018, accessed February 16, 2019, https://bit.ly/2tocBC7. See Bettina Engels, "Political Transition in Burkina Faso: The Fall of Blaise Compaoré," *Governance in Africa* 2, no. 1, July 9, 2018, accessed August 30, 2018, .

167. Koray Caliskan: "Explaining the End of Military Tutelary Regime and the July 15 Coup Attempt in Turkey," *Journal of Cultural Economy* 10, no. 1 (2017): 97–111.

Chapter 7

1. Larry Jay Diamond, "Thinking about Hybrid Regimes," *Journal of Democracy* 13, no. 2 (2002), accessed February 11, 2018, https://bit.ly/2tr1yrT.

2. Maha Abdelrahman (2004) has argued that civil society in Egypt should not be seen as inherently democratic but is riddled with authoritarian tendencies, a point to which I return later in the chapter.

3. See Hazem Kandil, "Sisi's Egypt," *New Left Review* 102 (November/December 2016), accessed February 10, 2018, https://bit.ly/2iPUG5f. Also see Brechenmacher, "Civil Society Under Assault: Repression and Responses in Russia, Egypt, and Ethiopia."

4. Mostafa El Hassan, interview by author, January 2017.

5. Sally Engle Merry, *The Seductions of Quantification: Measuring Human Rights, Gender Violence, and Sex Trafficking* (Chicago: University of Chicago Press, 2016).

6. The PTS scale ranges from 1 (least repressive) to 5 (most repressive). Egypt was ranked at level 4 in both 2012 and 2013, although the Rabaa massacre occurred in 2013 and was the biggest massacre in postcolonial Egyptian history.

7. Stephanie Kirchgaessner, "Why Was He killed? Brutal Death of Italian Student in Egypt Confounds Experts," *The Guardian*, February 24, 2016, accessed February 17, 2019, https://bit.ly/2MbfLBz.

8. Kareem Fahim, "Mohamed Soltan, U.S. Citizen Imprisoned in Egypt, Is Released," *New York Times*, May 30, 2015, accessed February 17, 2019, https://nyti.ms/2GNsYQP; "Newly Released Egyptian-American Charity Worker Visits Trump," Ahram Online, April 21, 2017, accessed February 17, 2019, https://bit.ly/2V83K3D.

9. "Egypt Police Raid Journalists' Syndicate, Arrest Two Journalists," Committee to Protect Journalists, May 2, 2016, accessed February 17, 2019, https://bit.ly/2cjSAFl.

10. Emna Sayadi, "Egypt: More Than 500 Sites Blocked Ahead of the Presidential Election," Access Now, March 14, 2018, accessed February 17, 2019, https://bit.ly/2svR1LY.

11. Tamer Aboarab, "معتز الفجيري: السلطات المصرية تهدد المعارضين في الخارج بالقتل" [Moutaz Al- Fougiri: Egyptian authorities threaten to kill the opposition abroad], YouTube Video, 1:46, October 31, 2018, https://bit.ly/2SDOvCs. [Translation provided by author].

12. Background on Case No. 173—the "Foreign Funding Case," Imminent Risk of Prosecution and Closure, report, March 21, 2016, accessed August 4, 2016, http://eipr.org/en/pressrelease/2016/03/21/2569.

13. Mahmoud Molla, "القبض على ٢٤ فى مسيرة الدفوف النوبية" [Arresting 24 in the Nubian tambourine march], AlMasry AlYoum, September 4, 2017, accessed February 17, 2019, https://bit.ly/2SF7FYM. [Translation provided by author].

14. "EIPR: Authorities Have Systematically Entrapped LGBTQ Individuals Online since 2015," Mada Masr, November 22, 2017, accessed February 17, 2019, https://bit.ly/2BGLeb9.

15. Mohamed Azmy, president of the General Nubian Union, interview by author, January 2017.

16. Molla, "القبض على ٢٤ فى مسيرة الدفوف النوبية" [Arresting 24 in the Nubian tambourine march].

17. On the number of arrests for Protest Law violations see: https://daftarahwal.com/arrests-accusations-protest-law-abstract-ar/.

18. Adel Abdel Ghafar, "Youth Unemployment in Egypt: A Ticking Time Bomb," Brookings, August 1, 2016, accessed February 9, 2018, https://brook.gs/2BGcbeW.

19. Amal Raslan, "التضامن: لدينا ٤٨ ألف جمعية مسجلة ونستعلم عن مصادر التمويل قبل الموافقة" [Ministry of Social Solidarity: we have 48,000 registered NGOs and we are investigating their funding sources before granting approval]. AlYoum7, August 21, 2016, accessed February 16, 2019, https://bit.ly/2DKaOMM. [Translation provided by author].

20. One example of a charity worker who suffered from the crackdown on NGOs is Aya Hegazy, a dual Egyptian American citizen. She had formed a charity to help street children and spent three years in prison, along with her husband and several of their coworkers. See Louisa Loveluck, "Who Is Aya Hijazi, the American Freed from Jail in Egypt?" Washington Post, April 21, 2017, accessed February 9, 2018, https://wapo.st/2DIo0BG.

21. Neither Libya nor Egypt ever claimed responsibility for the forced disappearance of Mansour El-Kikhia, but a CIA report claims that Egyptian agents were involved in his disappearance. See Jim Hoagland, "Egypt, Libya Linked to Abduction," Washington Post, September 28, 1997, accessed February 9, 2018, https://wapo.st/1yrGVpM.

22. Moatez El-Figary discusses the death threats to CIHRS board members in this video: Be tawkit Masr, "بتوقيت مصر معتز الفجيري: منظمات حقوق الإنسان في مصر تواجه أزمة وجودية" [Be tawkit Masr| Moataz El-Figary: In Egypt, Human Rights NGOs face Existential Crisis], YouTube video, 11:24, August 13, 2016, https:// www.youtube.com/watch?v=yWDiKkfieVY. [Translation provided by author].

23. Mohamed Zaree, interview by author, May 2017.

24. Fahmy Howeidy, "نُذر الغارة على المجتمع المدنى فى مصر" [Warnings of a raid on civil society in Egypt], AlWasat Party, November 25, 2014, accessed February 17, 2019, https://bit.ly/2SGRoSY. [Translation provided by author].

25. I had invited Osama Diab from EIPR to speak to my class at AUC, but because of the ultimatum and fear that the security forces may pull another stunt like in December 2011, when they raided NDI, IRI, and other organizations, I asked him to come out to Tagammu instead so as not to take the risk that EIPR would be raided while my students were visiting. The Development course I was teaching had a community-based learning component, and so we were encouraged to bring our students into the community; however, this became an ever more perilous endeavor.

26. "After 20 Years: CIHRS Moves Its Regional and International Programs outside Egypt," Cairo Institute for Human Rights Studies, December 9, 2014, accessed February 17, 2019, https://bit.ly/2Edl5lO.

27. "2017 Martin Ennals Award for Human Rights Defenders goes to Mohamed Zaree," Martin Ennals Award for Human Rights Defenders, October 10, 2017, accessed February 9, 2018, https://bit.ly/2yaZ1DY.

28. Amy Austin Holmes, "The Attack on Civil Society Outside Cairo," The Carnegie Endowment for International Peace, January 26, 2017, accessed February 9, 2018, http://carnegieendowment.org/sada/?fa=67810.

29. "Arrest of Azza Soliman," Front Line Defenders, accessed February 9, 2018, https://bit.ly/2hk7wTg.

30. Background on Case No. 173—the "Foreign Funding Case," Imminent Risk of Prosecution and Closure, Report, March 21, 2016, accessed August 4, 2016, http://eipr.org/en/pressrelease/2016/03/21/2569.

31. S. Mohamed, "Under the State's Gaze: Repression of Women's Organizations in Egypt," Tahrir Institute for Middle East Policy, May 28, 2018, accessed July 29, 2018, https://bit.ly/2D0P8xH.

32. Mohamed Zaree, interview by author, May 2017.

33. "Social Solidarity Ministry Closes 75 NGOs, 121 Childcare Centers in Beheira," Mada Masr, May 26, 2016, accessed February 9, 2018, https://bit.ly/2Ig8Fhk.

34. Lina Attalah, "Laila Soueif," Bidoun, May 14, 2017, accessed February 9, 2018, http://bidoun.org/articles/Laila-Soueif.

35. Mostafa Zaky, "حصر أموال الإخوان تتحفظ على ١٥٨٩ عنصرا داعما للجماعة ١١٨ شركة ١١٣٣ جمعية أهلية" [Confiscating the money of 1589 Brotherhood supporters, 118 companies and 1133 civil society organizations], Ahram Gate, September 11, 2018, accessed February 16, 2019, https://bit.ly/2GuFHZ7 [Translation provided by author], 434; "Muslim Brotherhood NGOs Shutdown," Daily News Egypt, July 8, 2015, accessed February 9, 2018, https://bit.ly/2V2qCBc.

36. "مايو ٢٠١٤ – مايو ٢٠١٦ عامين من الحبس الاحتياطي عقوبة مبادرة لإعادة تأهيل أولاد الشوارع" [From May 2014 to May 2016, two years of temporary detention to punish an initiative that rehabilitates street children], Association for Freedom of Thought and Expression, May 5, 2016, accessed February 16, 2019, https://bit.ly/2WZQ7oG. [Translation provided by author].

37. Mohammad Saif and Ahmed Abdullatif, "بالفيديو | ضبط «أمريكية» وزوجها يديران «جمعية «وهمية» لتدريب أطفال الشوارع على القتال ومهاجمة الشرطة" [In Video: Arrest of American and Her Husband Who Run "Fake" Society to Train Street Children to Fight and Attack Police], Elwatannews, May 4, 2014, accessed February 10, 2018, https://www.elwatannews.com/news/details/475208. [Translation provided by author].

38. Aya Hegazy, interview by author, December 2017.

39. Aya Hegazy, interview by author, December 2017.

40. "Beyer Statement on Acquittal of Aya Hijazi and Her Co-Defendants in Egypt," Congressman Don Beyer, April 16, 2017, accessed February 9, 2018. https://bit.ly/2GsrXy5.

41. Philip Rucker and Karen DeYoung, "Freed Egyptian American Prisoner Returns Home following Trump Intervention," Washington Post, April 20, 2017, accessed February 9, 2018, https://wapo.st/2BEGtPn.

42. Rhana Natour, "Exclusive: Aya Hijazi on Her Surprising Meeting with President Trump after Release from Egypt Prison," PBS, May 26, 2017, accessed February 9, 2018, https://to.pbs.org/2qo47Il.

43. "وقف إصدار جريدة الحرية والعدالة" [Suspending the publication of Freedom and Justice newspaper], AlAhram, December 27, 2013, accessed February 17, 2019, https://bit.ly/2X7P9XG. [Translation provided by author].

44. "نص قانون مكافحة الإرهاب" [The text of antiterrorism law], AlAhram, August 17, 2015, accessed February 17, 2019, https://bit.ly/2Bzurqu. [Translation provided by author].

45. Nour Ali, "النص الكامل لمشروع قانون التنظيم المؤسسى للصحافة والإعلام" [The full text of draft law regulating institutions media and journalism], AlYoum7, December 13, 2016, accessed February 17, 2019, https://bit.ly/2BDQzjB. [Translation provided by author].

46. "Egypt: One of the World's Biggest Prisons for Journalists | Reporters without Borders," RSF, accessed February 9, 2018, https://rsf.org/en/egypt.

47. "The Institute of Politics at Harvard University," Bassem Youssef | The Institute of Politics at Harvard University, accessed February 9, 2018, http://iop.harvard.edu/fellows/bassem-youssef.

48. Jared Malsin, "Bassem Youssef Abruptly Cancels Egyptian Satire Show," *Time*, June 3, 2014, accessed February 9, 2018, https://bit.ly/1yGEbJe.

49. Tweet by Bassem Youssef on July 3, 2013: "Instead of writing numerous tweets here's one to sum it all up MB are the new form of Nazis Got it? I said it on the show and saying it now." Bassem Youssef, "Instead of writing numerous tweets here's one to sum it all up MB are the new form of Nazis got it? I said it on the show and saying it now," Twitter, July 3, 2013, accessed February 9, 2018, https://bit.ly/2DO8OTu.

50. "يسري فودة يعلن توقف برنامج آخر كلام هذا الأسبوع" [Yosri Fouda announces canceling his program Akher Kalam], Masrawy, September 22, 2014, accessed February 17, 2019, https://bit.ly/2GMO5mk. [Translation provided by author].

51. Dreamtvchannel, "النيابة العسكرية تستدعي المذيعة ريم ماجد والمدون حسام الحملاوي للتحقيق" [The Military Prosecution summons the presenter Reem Maged and the blogger Hossam Al- Hamlawy for interrogation], YouTube, 3:55, May 31, 2011, https://bit.ly/2TZpRJr. [Translation provided by author].

52. "Egyptian Presenter Reem Maged's New TV Show Suspended," Ahram Online, May 15, 2015, accessed February 9, 2018, https://bit.ly/2BDxBJH.

53. Conversation with AUC Dean, spring 2017, at AUC New Cairo campus.

54. "ورقة موقف . . . من يملك أوامر "الفرم" بحق الصحف المصرية!؟." مؤسسة حرية الفكر والتعبير" [Position Paper, Who makes the shredding orders regarding Egyptian newspapers], The Association for Freedom of Thought and Expression, August 23, 2015, accessed February 11, 2018. https://bit.ly/2IjCI7H. [Translation provided by author].

55. "Egypt's Al-Ahram Strongly Criticises Interior Ministry after Police Storm Journalists Syndicate," AlAhram English, May 3, 2016, accessed February 11, 2018, https://bit.ly/2SUgQnp.

56. Muhammed Magdy, "Journalists' Syndicate head: Egyptian Press Facing Crisis with the State," Al-Monitor, January 11, 2017, accessed February 11, 2018, https://bit.ly/2X8RW2D.

57. For the list of blocked websites, see https://bit.ly/2tuzoMR.

58. "The news website that's keeping press freedom alive in Egypt," *The Guardian*, January 27, 2015, https://www.theguardian.com/news/2015/jan/27/-sp-online-newspaper-keeping-press-freedom-alive-egypt.

59. "2017 World Press Freedom Index | Reporters Without Borders," RSF, accessed February 11, 2018, https://rsf.org/en/ranking.

60. "Record Number of Journalists Jailed as Turkey, China, Egypt Pay Scant Price for Repression," Committee to Protect Journalists, December 13, 2015, accessed February 11, 2018, https://bit.ly/2V4s9ae.

61. David D. Kirkpatrick, "Renowned Scholar in Egypt Charged with Espionage," *New York Times*, January 22, 2014, accessed February 11, 2018, https://nyti.ms/2S4k6rP.

62. "Statement by Prof. Emad Shahin on His Death Sentence," Official Website—Emad Shahin, June 4, 2015, accessed February 11, 2018, http://emadshahin.com/?p=1839.

63. Both Emad Shahin and Amr Hamzawy were professors in the School of Global Affairs and Public Policy (GAPP) at AUC. Nabil Fahmy was the founding dean of GAPP, and also served as foreign Minister of Egypt after the coup from July 2013 until June 2014.

64. Wikithawra, "حصر المقبوض عليهم والملاحقين قضائياً خلال عهد السيسي/عدلي منصور, مُحَدَّث حتي ١٤ مايو ٢٠١٤" [A detailed record of detainees under Sisi/Adly Mansour, updated May 14, 2014], Wikithawra, January 2014, accessed February 12, 2019, https://bit.ly/2aSqHQJ. [Translation provided by author].

65. Elisabetta Povoledo, "Italian Student in Cairo Was Murdered over His Research, Prosecutor Says," *New York Times*, January 26, 2018, accessed February 11, 2018, https://nyti.ms/2GMHvMu.

66. "Sisi Son May Have Had Role in Regeni," ANSA, July 7, 2016, accessed February 11, 2018, https://bit.ly/2X3i3bk.

67. Alexander Stille, "Who Murdered Giulio Regeni?" *The Guardian*, October 4, 2016, accessed February 11, 2018, https://bit.ly/2TUNKSc.

68. Mai Shams El-Din, "AUC Remembers Giulio Regeni, Protests University's Position on His Death," Mada Masr, February 25, 2016, accessed February 11, 2018, https://bit.ly/2V2pVIh.

69. "Giulio Regeni: Egypt Airs Video of Murdered Italian Student," BBC, January 24, 2017, accessed May 16, 2018, https://bbc.in/2V1wI4R.

70. AlHurra, "قناة "نوبة تيوب" . . . الحلقة الأحدث في سلسلة مبادرات تهدف للحفاظ على التراث النوبي في مصر" ["NubaTube" channel, a channel that aims at preserving the Nubian heritage in Egypt], YouTube, 2:30, July 5, 2016, https://bit.ly/2UY7ODa. [Translation provided by author].

71. Nour Ali and Abdel Latif Sobh, "النص الكامل لقانون الجمعيات الأهلية الجديد بعد موافقة البرلمان عليه" [The full text of NGO law after approval by the Parliament], *AlYoum7*, November 29, 2016, accessed February 17, 2019, https://bit.ly/2GvMzpn. [Translation provided by author].

72. "Statement by Senators John Mccain and Lindsey Graham on Egyptian Legislation Regulating NGOs," Senate.gov, December 1, 2016, accessed February 11, 2018, https://bit.ly/2N8ukqm.

73. Hagar Hosny, "نقيب المحامين: احتجاز خالد علي يومًا يفتقد مبررات الحبس الاحتياطي"
[Bar Association: Khaled Ali's detention lacks justification for pretrial detention],
Masrawy, May 24, 2017, accessed February 17, 2019, https:// bit.ly/ 2DMDKU9.
[Translation provided by author].

74. Ruth Michaelson, "Egypt Blocks Access to News Websites including Al-Jazeera and
Mada Masr," *The Guardian*, May 25, 2017, accessed February 11, 2018, https://bit.ly/
2X9sLNJ.

75. "2017 Martin Ennals Award for Human Rights Defenders Goes to Mohamed Zaree."

76. Noah Gray, "Trump Compliments Egyptian President's Shoes," CNN, May 21, 2017,
accessed February 11, 2018, https://cnn.it/2Ed8UFD.

77. Nada Badawi, "Central Bank Head in Abu Dhabi in Search of Financial Aid," Daily
News Egypt, July 8, 2013, accessed February 11, 2018, https://bit.ly/2GuIrpA.

78. "The UAE Secretly Picked Up the Tab for the Egyptian Dictatorship's D.C. Lobbying,"
The Intercept, October 4, 2017, accessed February 12, 2018, https://bit.ly/2xSV35c.

79. Youssef Abdo, "الكاتب الروائي حجاج أدول للأهرام : النوبة في مواد الدستور الجديد لأول
مرة" [Novelist Haggag Oddoul: Nubia is in the new constitution for the first time],
AlAhram, November 16, 2013, accessed February 17, 2019, https://bit.ly/2TO4BWK.
[Translation provided by author].

80. State Information Service, *Constitution of the Arab Republic of Egypt*, January 18,
2014, Article 236, pp. 63–64, accessed February 11, 2018, http://www.sis.gov.eg/
Newvr/Dustor-en001.pdf.

81. Abdallah Salah, "٣٠ يوم في الأمان" [Suspending protests for 30 days], *AlYoum7*,
December 1, 2016, accessed February 17, 2019, https://bit.ly/2DPRBcB. [Translation
provided by author].

82. Amy Austin Holmes, "Egypt's Nubia: Drowning by Government Decree,"
RealClearWorld, September 27, 2017, accessed February 11, 2018, https://bit.ly/
2GMJOz2.

83. "Human Rights Defenders Mohamed Azmy and Maysara Abdoun Arrested at
Peaceful Protest for Nubian Rights," Front Line Defenders, March 21, 2018, accessed
February 17, 2019, https://bit.ly/2ImmjiS.

84. "Egypt: Torture Epidemic May be Crime against Humanity," Human Rights Watch,
October 30, 2017, accessed February 11, 2018, https://bit.ly/2w57Axs.

85. United Nations Committee Against Torture, report, May 12, 2017, accessed February
11, 2018, https://bit.ly/2GNcKan.

86. Mohamed Amer and Mohamed ElBadry, "حبس ماهينور المصري ومعتصم مدحت على
ذمة قضية تظاهر" [Detaining Mahienour El-Massry and Moatassem Medhat over a
protest], *Masrawy*, November 18, 2017, accessed February 17, 2019, https:// bit.ly/
2S6K3Hl. [Translation provided by author].

87. Asmaa Khalifa, "القصة الكاملة لمعتقلي مسيرة الدفوف بأسوان" [The full story of the
Tambourine March's detainees in Aswan], *Edaatat*, October 15, 2017, accessed
February 17, 2019, https://bit.ly/2GxPsG6. [Translation provided by author].

88. Nasser ElSharkawi, "حبس ماهينور المصري بتهمة التظاهر ضد اتفاقية ترسيم الحدود مع
السعودية" [Sentencing Mahienour El-Massry to two years in prison for protesting

against the border demarcation agreement with Saudi Arabia], *AlMasry AlYoum*, December 30, 2017, accessed February 17, 2019, https://bit.ly/2GLvl6E. [Translation provided by author].

89. "Egypt in the Wake of Presidential Elections," Wilson Center, April 4, 2018. Discussion with Mohamed Anwar Sadat, Nathan Brown, and Amy Austin Holmes. The conversation is available as a podcast here: https://www.wilsoncenter.org/event/egypt-the-wake-presidential-elections.

Chapter 8

1. Some dates are more approximate than others and may have been slightly revised in the process of writing the manuscript.
2. See Cole, "Egypt's Modern Revolutions and the Fall of Mubarak"; Paul Sedra, "The Long Shadow of the 1952 Revolution," *Jadaliyya*, February 13, 2011, accessed October 12, 2017, https://bit.ly/2S8qrmp.
3. See "Former Egyptian MP Mustafa Bakri Threatens to Massacre Americans in Egypt if Sisi Is assassinated," The Middle East Media Research Institute, January 23, 2014, accessed October 12, 2017, https://bit.ly/2V3tSN4.
4. Soliman, *The Autumn of Dictatorship*, 164.
5. The name of the program in Arabic is "Hodou" which translates to "Quietly or Slowly."
6. Patrick Kingsley, "Egyptian PM Dismisses Alleged Sisi Recordings," *The Guardian*, February 9, 2015, accessed October 12, 2017, https://bit.ly/2DLviEV.
7. AlMasry AlYoum, "مصر من الهليكوبتر. الملايين ضد مرسي" [Egypt from the helicopter, millions against Morsi], YouTube video, 12:48, July 2, 2013. https://bit.ly/2DJN8rE; Ashraf Gawdat, "رد فعل المتظاهرين عند الاتحادية عند مرور طائرة الجيش 30 يونيو" [The reactions of Ittihadiya protesters when seeing army helicopters on June 30], YouTube video. 0:54, June 30, 2013. https://bit.ly/2TVRjru.
8. Richard Leiby, "The Rise and Fall of Egypt's Most Despised Billionaire, Ahmed Ezz," *Washington Post*, April 9, 2011, accessed October 12, 2017, https://wapo.st/2SVqTbZ.
9. Patrick Kingsley, "Will #SisiLeaks be Egypt's Watergate for Abdel Fattah El-Sisi?" *The Guardian*, March 5, 2015, accessed October 12, 2017, https://bit.ly/2SPZYOM.
10. As discussed in more detail in chapter 6, Moheb Doss was one of the Tamarod leaders who claims that the UAE offered him money, which he refused. When he became aware that other members of Tamarod may have accepted the bribe, he demanded that they be investigated for corruption.
11. Their meeting place was referred to by members of April 6 not as their headquarters or office, but rather as "Hamza's villa."
12. Author interview with an exiled member of the Brotherhood in London, March 2015.
13. Acemoglu and Robinson, "Economic Backwardness in Political Perspective."

14. In "The Eighteenth Brumaire of Louis Napoleon," Marx describes in an evocative passage the hypocrisy of calling upon the military to save French society: "Similarly, after the coup d'état the French bourgeoisie cried out: Only the Chief of the Society of December 10 can still save bourgeois society! Only theft can still save property; only perjury, religion; bastardy, the family; disorder, order!" See Karl Marx, *The Eighteenth Brumaire of Louis Bonaparte* (New York: International Publishers, 1994).

15. See "Global Wealth Databook 2014," Paris School of Economics, October 2014, accessed October 12, 2017, https://bit.ly/2FlYvFb.

16. Soliman, *The Autumn of Dictatorship*, 164.

17. David D. Kirkpatrick, *Into the Hands of the Soldiers: Freedom and Chaos in Egypt and the Middle East* (London: Bloomsbury, 2018), 227.

18. Ibid., 228.

19. Philip Gordon, White House Coordinator for the Middle East, North Africa, and Persian Gulf Region 2013–2015, interview by author, February 6, 2019.

20. Member of the National Security Council under Obama, interview by author, October 4, 2017.

21. David D. Kirkpatrick, "The White House and the Strongman," *New York Times*, July 27, 2018, accessed February 15, 2019, https://nyti.ms/2K2Iwy9.

22. Member of the National Security Council under Obama, interview by author, October 4, 2017.

23. Charles Kurzman, "Structural Opportunity and Perceived Opportunity in Social-Movement Theory: The Iranian Revolution of 1979," *American Sociological Review* 61, no. 1 (1996): 153–170.

24. Ibid.

25. Philip Gordon, White House Coordinator for the Middle East, North Africa, and Persian Gulf Region 2013–2015, interview by author, February 6, 2019.

26. See Bellin, "Reconsidering the Robustness of Authoritarianism in The Middle East: Lessons from the Arab Spring,"; Lachapelle, Way, and Levitsky, "Crisis, Coercion, and Authoritarian Durability: Explaining Diverging Responses to Anti-Regime Protest in Egypt and Iran."

27. For discussion of the state's position on freedom of independent organization and workers' rights during the transitional period, see Fatima Ramadan and Amr Adly, "Low-Cost Authoritarianism: The Egyptian Regime and Labor Movement since 2013," Carnegie Middle East Center, September 17, 2015, accessed October 12, 2017, https://bit.ly/2TOVogQ.

For a detailed analysis of the NGO Law debate and the legislative proposal that went into parliamentary deliberations in the Shura Council before the ouster of president Morsi, see "Egypt—Civic Freedom Monitor," The International Centre for Non-for-Profit Law, June 27, 2017, accessed October 22, 2017, http://www.icnl.org/research/monitor/egypt.html.

28. As discussed in chapter 7, in the fall of 2017 the LGBTQ community was subjected to a harsh crackdown that ensued after a group of young people waved a rainbow flag at a Mashrou Leila concert in Cairo. Men who were suspected of being homosexual were arrested, and five of them were forced to undergo rectal examinations. "Egypt

Jails 16 as LGBT Crackdown Goes On," BBC News, November 28, 2017, accessed February 15, 2019, https://bbc.in/2BtoNVd.

29. Zolberg, *Moments of Madness.*

30. I described both the utopian dreamscapes of the protests in Egypt and Turkey as well as the nightmarish violence of the coups in a recent article. See Holmes, "On Military Coups and Mad Utopias."

Glossary

Kamal Abbas: is a lifelong labor activist who served as general coordinator of the Center for Trade Union and Workers Services, an organization advocating for independent unions in Egypt. In 2013, he was chosen for membership in the National Council for Human Rights.

Mohamed Abdel Aziz: was a founding member of the Tamarod ("rebellion") campaign that opposed Morsi and called for early presidential elections. He was later suspended from the campaign for supporting Hamdeen Sabahi in the 2014 presidential elections.

Gamal Abdel Nasser: was a founding member of Egypt's Free Officers Movement, which deposed King Farouk in 1952, abolishing the monarchy and establishing a republic. Nasser became the second president of Egypt, advocating for Arab nationalism, implementing land reform, and expropriating the Suez Canal.

Kamal Abu Eita: is an Egyptian labor activist who led several labor strikes in 2007 and 2008. He served as the Minister of Manpower and Immigration in the post-Morsi interim government headed by former Prime Minister Hazem el-Beblawi.

Mahmoud Abu Zeid (Shawkan): is an Egyptian freelance photojournalist who was arrested during his coverage of the Rabaa massacre on August 14, 2013 and charged with six offenses. He was sentenced to a five-year term in September 2018.

Habib El-Adly: was the former Minister of Interior in Egypt from 1997 to 2011. After the 2011 Egyptian revolution, he faced a trial for conspiring to kill demonstrators during the 18 days of the revolution as well as corruption charges.

Mohamed El-Baradei: is an Egyptian diplomat who served as general director of the International Atomic Energy Agency. Following the 2011 revolution, he established the Constitution Party and became an interim vice president in 2013 upon Morsi's ouster.

Mohamed Al-Beltagy: is a Muslim Brotherhood politician, a parliamentarian from 2005 to 2010, and the secretary general of the Muslim Brotherhood's Freedom and Justice Party after the 2011 revolution.

Ahmed El-Borei: was the former minister of manpower and immigration in Essam Sharaf's cabinet, formed following the 2011 Egyptian revolution. He also served as minister of social solidarity in Hazem el-Beblawi's interim cabinet after Morsi's ouster.

Moataz Al-Fogairy: is a member of the international human rights organization Front Line Defenders and the former executive director of the Cairo Institute for Human Rights Studies, one of Egypt's oldest human rights organizations.

Hossam Al-Hamalawy: is an Egyptian activist, a journalist, a blogger, and a member of the Revolutionary Socialists. His blog *3arabawy,* concerned with covering social movements and workers' activism, was among the most famous blogs in Egypt.

Khaled Ali: is a prominent lawyer and human rights activists and the former head of the Egyptian Centre for Economic and Social Rights, an Egyptian NGO concerned with socioeconomic issues. He ran for the 2012 and the 2018 presidential elections.

Shaimaa Al-Sabbagh: was a poet, political activist, and leading member of the Socialist Popular Alliance Party. She was killed by security forces during a march to commemorate the revolution on its fourth anniversary on January 24, 2015.

Mohamed Anwar El-Sadat (Anwar El-Sadat): was Egypt's third president from 1970 until his assassination in 1981. He launched Egypt's economic opening up, the *Infitah* policies, and signed the Camp David Accords with Israel in 1978.

Mohamed Anwar Esmat El-Sadat: is the nephew of former President Anwar al-Sadat and former parliamentarian under Mubarak and after the 2011 revolution. In 2017, he was expelled from the parliament for allegedly leaking information to foreign diplomats.

Khaled El-Sayed: is an activist and a member of the Youth for Freedom and Justice movement and the Coalition of the Youth of the Revolution. As a result of his activism, he was arrested several times, tortured, imprisoned, and banned from traveling in 2015.

Khairat al-Shater: is a businessman and the Deputy Supreme Guide of the Muslim Brotherhood (now imprisoned since 2013). He was the Brotherhood's presidential candidate for the 2012 presidential elections before he was disqualified from the race.

Kamal El-Shazly: a politician and parliamentarian since 1964 (from Nasser to Mubarak). He also served as the secretary general of the National Democratic Party and the Minister of State for the Affairs of the Shura Council and Parliament.

Abdel Fattah El-Sisi: is the sixth president of Egypt, elected in 2014 after deposing Mohamed Morsi. He served as the director of military intelligence after 2011 and as the commander-in-chief and minister of defence under Morsi. Under his leadership there were virginity tests of female protesters in 2011 and the 2013 Rabaa massacre.

Sami Anan: is an Egyptian military officer who was the Chief of Staff of the Armed Forces since 2005 until former President Mohamed Morsi's dismissal from his position in 2012. He ran for the 2018 presidential elections before he was arrested for breaching military rules regarding his candidacy.

Lina Attallah: was the founder and editor-in-chief of *Mada Masr*, a news website that *The Guardian* in 2015 described as keeping press freedom alive in Egypt. *Mada Masr* was one of the first websites to be blocked in 2017 and is still censored at the time of writing.

Mohamed Azmy: is a Nubian activist and the founder of NubaTube, a YouTube channel that aims at preserving Nubian heritage. He was the president of the General Nubian Union, an Aswan-based movement concerned with the rights of the Nubian community.

Mohammed Badei: is the eighth Supreme Guide of the Muslim Brotherhood. He was arrested after the Rabaa massacre along with other Brotherhood leaders and received a life sentence and death penalty for several charges, including murder and inciting violence.

Mahmoud Badr: was a founding member of the Tamarod ("rebellion") campaign that opposed Morsi and called for early presidential elections. He became a member of General Abdel Fattah El-Sisi's presidential campaign in 2014.

Ziad Bahaa El-Din: is an economist, lawyer, politician, and a member of the Egyptian Social Democratic Party. He was appointed deputy prime minister under Hazem el-Beblawi's cabinet in July 2013 until his resignation in January 2014.

Hossam Bahgat: is a human rights activist and journalist for the independent online news website *Mada Masr*. He founded the Egyptian Initiative for Personal Rights in 2002, an independent human rights organization based in Cairo.

William J. (Bill) Burns: is the president of the Carnegie Endowment for International Peace and a former foreign service officer. He served as deputy secretary of state from

2011 to 2014 and was sent to Egypt in July 2013 as part of an envoy to hold talks with Egypt's interim government after the deposition of Mohamed Morsi.

Amr Darrag: is an academic, politician, and the Secretary General of the Freedom and Justice Party, Giza office. He served as the minister of planning and international co-operation under Mohamed Morsi in 2013.

Moheb Doss: was a founding member of the Tamarod ("rebellion") campaign that opposed Morsi and called for early presidential elections.

Ahmed Douma: is a prominent activist (currently imprisoned) and a member of the Egyptian Popular Current. He was arrested under consecutive regimes from Mubarak to Morsi, and he received several sentences for his activism, including a 15-year sentence.

Hazem El-Beblawi: is an economist and a politician who served as an interim prime minister under Adly Mansour from July 2013 to March 2014. He, along with his cabinet, declared the Muslim Brotherhood a terrorist organization on December 21, 2013.

Aida Seif El-Dawla: is a psychiatrist, feminist, and founding member of al-Nadeem Center for Rehabilitation of Victims of Violence, a Cairo-based NGO concerned with supporting and treating victims of violence and torture.

Ziad El-Elaimy: is a lawyer, activist, member of the Egyptian Social Democratic Party, and former member of the parliament of 2012. He was also a member of the executive office of the Coalition of the Youth of the Revolution and served as its official spokesperson.

Essam El-Erian: is a Muslim Brotherhood parliamentarian who served as the vice chairman of the Freedom and Justice Party. He was arrested after the Rabaa massacre in October 2013 and received a life sentence and a death penalty.

Anas El-Fiqqi: was the former minister of information under Mubarak from 2004 to February 12, 2011. He faced corruption charges, including squandering public funds, from which he was acquitted in 2016.

Hany El-Gamal: is a founding member of *al-Dostor* (Constitution Party). He was imprisoned for over two years for his participation in the *Shura* demonstration against the Protest Law in 2013. In 2015, he received a presidential pardon.

Waleed El-Masry: was a founding member of the Tamarod ("rebellion") campaign that opposed Morsi and called for early presidential elections. He left the campaign after the June 30 protests and criticized some of its founders.

Mahienour El-Massry: is a prominent human rights lawyer who has been defending the rights of protesters and workers. She was imprisoned several times for her activism and was awarded the Ludovic Trarieux International Human Rights Prize in 2014.

Safwat El-Sherif: is an Egyptian politician who served as minister of information from 1982 to 2004, as head of the State Information Service, and as secretary general of the National Democratic Party.

Fatma Emam: is a Nubian human rights activist who worked on the constitution-drafting committee in 2014 and succeeded in having Nubia mentioned for the first time in the Egyptian constitution.

Ahmed Ezz: is a businessman who owned Ezz Steel, the biggest steel company in Egypt, and also a National Democratic Party politician. After the 2011 revolution, he was sentenced to 37 years in prison on corruption charges.

Alaa Abdel Fattah (Alaa Seif): is a prominent Egyptian blogger and a human rights activist who has been imprisoned under consecutive regimes for his activism and protest organization and participation. He is currently serving a five-year sentence from 2015.

Zoheir Garranah: is a National Democratic Party politician who served as a minister of tourism from 2006 to 2011. He received a five-year sentence for squandering public funds and was acquitted in 2013.

Boutros Boutros Ghali: was an Egyptian academic, politician, and diplomat who served as minister of foreign affairs in 1977 and as the sixth secretary-general of the United Nations from 1992 to 1996.

Dalia Abdel Hamid: is a researcher at the Egyptian Initiative for Personal Rights and an advocate of the rights of women and the LGBTQ community. She denounced the crackdown on the LGBTQ community in 2017, including the execution of forced anal exams.

Bahey El-Din Hassan: is an Egyptian human rights activist, director, and cofounder of the Cairo Institute for Human Rights Studies. Shortly after Sisi assumed the presidency, he received a death threat for his meetings with international officials on the human rights situation, and as a result he left Egypt and moved to France.

Mozn Hassan: is an Egyptian activist and a women's rights advocate. She's the founder of Nazra for Feminist Studies, a Cairo-based NGO concerned with gender-related issues. Her assets were frozen and she has been banned from traveling since 2016.

Mohamed Hassanein: is a cofounder of Belady Foundation, an NGO concerned with street children, and also the husband of Egyptian American activist Aya Hegazy. He was arrested and detained, along Hegazy (2014–2017), over allegations of child abuse.

Aya Hegazy: is an Egyptian American activist who was arrested and detained, along with her husband, from May 2014 until April 2017 over allegations that her NGO, Belady, provided shelter for street children, was operating illegally, and was involved in child abuse.

Samira Ibrahim: is an Egyptian activist who reported having been subjected to beatings of detained female protestors and the execution of virginity tests by the military during the dispersal of sit-in in March 2011.

Loay Kahwagy: is an Egyptian activist and a member of the Revolutionary Socialists in Egypt, Alexandria branch. He was arrested along with activist Mahienour El Massry and poet Omar Hazeq for allegedly violating the Protest Law and served over a year in prison.

Bothaina Kamel: is an activist, Egyptian TV anchor, and politician. She is also a founding member of *Shayfeencom* ("we are watching you"), a movement established in 2005 that worked on monitoring elections and introducing accountability in Egypt.

Mohamed Lotfy: is an Egyptian human rights activist and the executive director and cofounder of the Egyptian Commission for Rights and Freedoms. He was banned from traveling in 2015.

Ahmed Maher: is an Egyptian activist and a cofounder and coordinator of the April 6 Youth Movement, which led nationwide protests against the Mubarak regime in 2008. He received a three-year prison sentence for demonstrating against the Protest Law in 2013.

Asmaa Mahfouz: is an Egyptian activist and one of the founding members of the April 6 Youth Movement. She became one of the faces of the 2011 Egyptian revolution and a member of the Coalition of the Youth of the Revolution.

Adly Mansour: is an Egyptian judge and was the president of the Supreme Constitutional Court of Egypt from 2013 to 2016. He served as the interim president of Egypt from 2013 to 2014, until the election of Abdel Fattah El-Sisi.

Heba Morayef: was the Human Rights Watch country director for Egypt and among the activists who led the campaign to end the practice of virginity tests.

Mohamed Morsi: is a Muslim Brotherhood politician who served as the chairman of the Freedom and Justice Party from 2011 to 2012 and as the fifth president of Egypt from 2012 until he was ousted in July 2013.

Amr Moussa: was the Egyptian Minister of Foreign Affairs (1991–2001). He served as the secretary general of the Arab League. He ran in the 2012 presidential elections and was among the key leaders of the Egyptian National Salvation Front.

Gamal Mubarak: is one of former Egyptian president Hosni Mubarak's sons, a businessman and politician who was being prepared to succeed his father. He was the deputy secretary general of the ruling National Democratic Party.

Mohamed Hosni Mubarak (Hosni Mubarak): is the former commander of the Air Force and a politician who served as the fourth president of Egypt from 1981 to 2011. He stepped down after the eruption of nationwide protests for 18 days in January 2011.

Ahmed Nazif: is an Egyptian politician who served as a prime minister from 2004 to 2011 and as the first minister of communications and information technology from 1999 to 2004. In 2011, he was accused of squandering public funds, but he was acquitted in 2016.

Noor Ayman Nour: is an Egyptian activist and son of opposition figures Ayman Nour, former head of the al-Ghad Party, and Gamila Ismail. He was also an active member of the No to Military Trials for Civilians advocacy group.

Haggag Oddoul: is a Nubian novelist and vocal activist of the Nubia cause. He is one of the driving forces behind including "Nubia" for the first time in the 2014 constitution.

Ragia Omran: is a lawyer and a human rights activist who endorsed workers protests and supported the April 6 Movement. She cofounded the Front to Defend Egyptian Protesters in 2010 and became a member of the National Council for Human Rights in 2013.

Seham Osman: is a Nubian activist. In 2017, she was the first woman to announce her intention to run for president of the General Nubian Union, a Nubian movement based in Aswan, before she had to withdraw after coming under severe pressures.

Anne Patterson: is an American diplomat and the former US ambassador to Egypt from 2011 to 2013. During the 2013 protests, Patterson was censured by protesters for her close relationship with the Morsi government, which implicated support for the Muslim Brotherhood.

Rachid Mohamed Rachid: is a businessman and a former National Democratic Party politician who served as the minister of trade and industry from 2004 to 2011. After the 2011 revolution, he was tried in absentia and charged with squandering public funds.

Mohamed Reda: was a first-year engineering student at Cairo University who was killed by the Egyptian security forces on campus during clashes between students and security forces on November 28, 2013.

Giulio Regeni: was an Italian Cambridge University PhD student who was kidnapped in January 2016 and tortured to death. Independent investigations implicated the Egyptian security forces in his death. His case sparked international outrage and raised questions about academic safety and freedoms in Egypt.

Hamdeen Sabahi: is a Nasserist Egyptian politician, a former parliamentarian, and the leader of the Egyptian Popular Current. He was arrested and imprisoned several times under al-Sadat and Mubarak. He ran as a presidential candidate in 2014 against Sisi.

Salma Said: is an Egyptian blogger, activist, and one of the founders of *Mosireen* ("we are determined"), a nonprofit media activism collective that documents events since Egypt's 2011 revolution.

Yara Sallam: is an Egyptian feminist, human rights activist, and researcher who works for the Egyptian Initiative for Personal Rights. In 2014, she was tried and imprisoned for almost two years for protesting against Morsi near the Ittihadiya presidential palace.

Naguib Sawiris: is an Egyptian businessman and billionaire who owns Orascom Telecom Media and Technology Holding. After Egypt's 2011 revolution, he founded the Free Egyptians Party.

Margaret Scobey: is a US diplomat and the former US ambassador to Egypt from 2008 to 2011. During her term, she met with representatives from Egyptian human rights organizations and opposition figures.

Essam Sharaf: is an academic and National Democratic Party (NDP) politician who formerly served as a minister of transportation from 2004 to 2005. After 2005, he left the NDP, returned to academia, and became the prime minister of Egypt after 2011.

Mona Seif: is an Egyptian human rights activist and sister of blogger and activist Alaa Abdel Fattah. She is a founding member of No to Military Trials for Civilians, an advocacy group to end the practice of subjecting civilians to military tribunals.

Sanaa Seif: is an Egyptian activist and sister of blogger and activist Alaa Abdel Fattah. In 2014, she was tried and imprisoned for almost two years for her participation in a march against Morsi near the Ittihadiya presidential palace.

Mona Seleem: is a journalist and founding member of the Tamarod ("rebellion") campaign that opposed Morsi and called for early presidential elections. She was arrested briefly while covering protests of Muslim Brotherhood supporters in 2014.

Ahmed Shafik: is an Egyptian politician and a former commander in the Air Force. He served as a prime minister for two months after Egypt's 2011 revolution and ran as a presidential candidate in 2012, but he lost to Morsi.

Hassan Shaheen: was a founding member of the Tamarod ("rebellion") campaign that opposed Morsi and called for early presidential elections. He was suspended from the campaign for supporting Hamdeen Sabahi in the 2014 presidential elections.

Emad Shahin: is an Egyptian political scientist whose work focuses on comparative politics, political Islam, and political economy. He was allegedly involved in an espionage case in 2014 and as a result he received a death sentence in 2015.

Sedki Sobhy: is an Egyptian former general who served as the minister of defence from 2014 to 2018. In 2017, there was an attempt to assassinate him, along with the Minister of Interior, at Arish Airport by an attack that the Islamic State of Iraq and the Levant-Sinai Province claimed responsibility for.

Azza Soliman: is an Egyptian lawyer and women's rights advocate who founded the Centre for Egyptian Women's Legal Assistance, a Cairo-based women's rights NGO. In 2016, her bank accounts were frozen and she was banned from leaving Egypt.

Mohamed Soltan: is a former Egyptian American political prisoner who was sentenced to life in prison for his participation and support of the Rabaa sit-in. In reaction to his imprisonment, he went on an open-ended hunger strike that lasted over 450 days.

Ahmed Fathi Sorour: is an Egyptian lawyer and politician who served as the speaker of the people's assembly from 1990 to 2011. He was arrested and imprisoned over charges of planning for the Battle of the Camel.

Mohamed Hussein Tantawi: is an Egyptian field marshal and the former defense minister and commander-in-chief of the Egyptian Armed forces under Mubarak. He was the chairman of the Supreme Council of the Armed Forces from February 11, 2011 until June 30, 2012.

Sally Toma: cofounded *Kazeboon* ("Liars"), a grassroots media campaign that exposed human rights violations committed by the military during the Supreme Council of the Armed Forces' rule through projecting video clips of such crimes against walls and buildings.

Yousef Waly: is an Egyptian politician who served as deputy chairman of the National Democratic Party and a minister of agriculture and land reclamation from 1982 to 2004. He faced several corruption charges after 2011 and was sentenced to 10 years in jail.

Ahmed Wasfy: is an Egyptian lieutenant-general and the former commander of the second field army. In 2014, he commented in a TV interview that if the army in Egypt sought a political position in Egypt then July 3 can be considered a military coup.

Frank G. Wisner: is a former American diplomat who was sent by Obama to Egypt on January 31, 2011 to advise Hosni Mubarak on his resignation in order to defuse anti-government protests. He later supported Mubarak's stay in power, which the US State Department said did not "reflect the official policy" of the Obama administration.

Mohamed Zaree: is an Egyptian human rights activist and director of the Cairo Institute for Human Rights Studies, one of Egypt's oldest human rights organizations. In 2017, he received the Martin Ennals Award for Human Rights Defenders.

Activist Groups, NGOs, and Civil Society Associations

April 6 Youth Movement (April 6): An activist group founded in 2008 by a group of political activists, including Asmaa Mahfouz, to support the workers in Mahalla who called and held a nationwide strike. After 2011 April 6 expanded and then split into two fronts: the April 6 movement led by Ahmed Maher and the Democratic Front led by Abdel Rahman Ezz.

Cairo Institute for Human Rights Studies (CIHRS): One of Egypt's oldest independent human rights organizations. After 2014, CIHRS relocated its headquarters to Tunis due to the crackdown on NGOs in Egypt.

Egyptian Commission for Rights and Freedoms (ECRF): An independent human rights organization founded in 2013 by activists Ahmed Abdallah, Mohamed Lotfy, and Mohamed Sameh.

Egyptian Initiative for Personal Rights (EIPR): An independent human rights organization in Cairo founded by Hossam Bahgat in 2002.

Hisham Mubarak Law Center: A law firm based in Cairo and Aswan founded by Ahmed Seif El-Islam in 1999.

Kazeboon (Liars): A grassroots media campaign that exposed human rights violations committed by the military during the transitional period under the Supreme Council of the Armed Forces through projecting video clips of such crimes against walls and buildings. It was founded by a group of independent activists, such as Sally Toma, in December 2011.

Mosireen (We Are Determined): A nonprofit media activism collective that documents events since Egypt's 2011 revolution. It was founded by a group of activists including Salma Said.

No to Military Trials for Civilians: An advocacy group that demanded an end to the practice of subjecting civilians to military tribunals after the 2011 revolution. It was founded by several activists including Mona Seif and Shahira Abou Leil.

Operation Anti-Sexual Harassment (Op-Antish): A group formed to prevent sexual harassment and assault during protests due to the inaction of the police to help victims of assault.

Tahrir Bodyguards: An antisexual harassment initiative founded in 2011 by a coalition of different rights-based groups and anti–sexual harassment campaigns. It used the technique of roaming Tahrir Square to protect women and prevent mob attacks on women.

Tamarod (Rebellion): A campaign that opposed former president Mohamed Morsi and aimed at collecting 15 million signatures to hold early presidential elections. It was founded in 2013 by a group of activists including Mahmoud Badr, Hassan Shaheen, Mohamed Abdel Aziz, and Moheb Doss.

Ultras Ahlawy: An Ultras group founded in 2007 to support one of Egypt's biggest football clubs, Al Ahly. The members of the group played a key role in Egypt's 2011 protests and they have had several confrontations with the Egyptian police.

Ultras White Knights (UWK): An Ultras group founded in 2007 to support one of Egypt's biggest football clubs, Al Zamalek SC. The members of the group played a key role in Egypt's 2011 protests and had several confrontations with the Egyptian police, including the Friday of Rage on January 28 and the Battle of Mohamed Mahmoud in November 2011.

Political Parties or Coalitions

Al Wafd Party: One of Egypt's oldest political parties that adopted a nationalist liberal ideology. It was founded in 1919 by a group of political leaders including Saad Zaghloul, and it was dissolved in 1952. It was succeeded by the New Wafd Party founded in 1978.

Bread and Freedom Party: A socialist political party founded in 2014 by the former members of the Socialist Popular Alliance Party, including Khaled Ali.

Gabhet el enkaz (Egyptian National Salvation Front): A coalition of political parties that opposed the constitutional declaration Mohamed Morsi issued in 2013. It included several opposition figures and leaders, including Hamdeen Sabahi, Mohamed el-Baradie, and Amr Moussa.

Freedom and Justice Party (FJP): An Islamist political party founded by the Muslim Brotherhood movement in 2011 and headed by Dr. Mohamed Morsi who became the Brotherhood's presidential candidate in 2012. The party was dissolved in 2014.

Muslim Brotherhood (Brotherhood): A Sunni Islamist movement/organization founded originally in Egypt by Hassan el-Banna in 1928 and expanded in later years to other Arab and Muslim countries. In Egypt, the Brotherhood provides social institutions and charity activities, and after Egypt's 2011 revolution it established itself as a separate political party.

National Democratic Party (NDP): A centrist political party founded by Egypt's late president Mohamed Anwar Al-Sadat in 1978. It became the ruling party that supported the regime of Mohamed Hosni Mubarak.

Revolutionary Socialists: A Marxist-Trotskyist organization in Egypt founded in 1995 by members of the Egyptian left. The organization supports the labor movement in Egypt and has contributed greatly in organizing strikes and marches during the 2011 revolution.

Bibliography

"2017 Martin Ennals Award for Human Rights Defenders Goes to Mohamed Zaree." Martin Ennals Award. October 9, 2017. Accessed February 11, 2018. https://bit.ly/2yaZ1DY.

"2017 World Press Freedom Index | Reporters Without Borders." RSF. Accessed February 11, 2018. https://rsf.org/en/ranking.

"434 Muslim Brotherhood NGOs Shutdown." Daily News Egypt. July 8, 2015. Accessed February 9, 2018. https://bit.ly/2V2qCBc.

"50 Faces That Made the News in 2011." Ahram Online. January 7, 2012. Accessed October 12, 2017. https://bit.ly/2DMeQ71.

Abaza, Mona. "Mourning, Narratives and Interactions with the Martyrs through Cairo's Graffiti." E-International Relations, October 7, 2013. Accessed March 15, 2016. https://bit.ly/2tm1xFC.

Abdelaziz, Salma, and Steve Almasy. "Egypt's Interim Cabinet Labels Muslim Brotherhood a Terrorist Group." CNN. December 25, 2013. Accessed October 12, 2017. https://cnn.it/2GsZAjy.

Abdel Ghafar, Adel. "Youth Unemployment in Egypt: A Ticking Time Bomb." Brookings. August 1, 2016. Accessed February 9, 2018. https://brook.gs/2BGcbeW.

Abdel Ghaffar, Allam. "تراكم القمامة بشوارع الجيزة بعد إضراب عمال النظافة." [Garbage piles up in the streets of Giza after custodial workers strike.] AlYoum7. February 8, 2011. Accessed February 15, 2019. https://bit.ly/2S3vlRB. [Translation provided by author].

Abdel Hamid, Ashraf. "داخلية مصر ترفض عودة الجماهير لمباريات الكرة." [Egypt's interior refuses to return the masses to the matches of the ball.] Alarabiya.net. March 18, 2016. Accessed February 11, 2019. https://bit.ly/2Dokg84. [Translation provided by author].

Abdel-Malek, Anouar. *Egypt: Military Society: The Army Regime, the Left and Social Change under Nasser.* New York: Random House, 1968.

Abdel Rady, Hossam. "القبض على الناشطة ماهينور المصري بالإسكندرية بتهمة خرق قانون التظاهر." [Arresting activist Mahinour ElMassry in Alexandria for violating the Protest Law.] ElWatan News. April 12, 2014. Accessed February 16, 2019. https://bit.ly/2GHxi45.

Abdelrahman, Maha M. *Civil Society Exposed: The Politics of NGOs in Egypt.* London: Tauris Academic, 2004.

Abdel Sabour, Maher. "إحالة أوراق ٥٢٩ متهما للمفتي وبراءة ١٦ آخرين في أحداث عنف المنيا عقب فض رابعة والنهضة." [Transferring the papers of 529 defendants to the Mufti and acquitting 16 others in the Minya Case.] AlSherouk News. March 24, 2014. Accessed February 14, 2019. https://bit.ly/2DGvMMg. [Translation provided by author].

AbdelSattar, Heba. "لتفويض تحتاج لا الدولة :ماهر وأحمد .اليوم تظاهرات فى نشارك لن ":إبريل ٦"
بواجبها للقيام الشعب من." [April 6th: We won't participate in today's protests—Ahmed
Maher: the state does not need a permission from the people to do its job]. AlAhram
Gate. July 26, 2013. Accessed August 11, 2017. http://gate.ahram.org.eg/News/376362.
aspx. [Translation provided by author].

Abdo, Youssef. "لأول الجديد الدستور مواد في النوبة :للأهرام أدول حجاج الروائي الكاتب
مرة." [Novelist Haggag Oddoul: Nubia is in the new constitution for the first time.]
AlAhram. November 16, 2013. Accessed February 17, 2019. https://bit.ly/2TO4BWK.
[Translation provided by author].

Aboulenein, Ahmed. "Tamarod Rejects Shafiq Endorsement." *Daily News Egypt*. May 17,
2013. Accessed October 12, 2017. https://bit.ly/2ItTbqb.

"About Us." No Military Trials for Civilians. 2011. http://en.nomiltrials.org/p/
about-us.html.

Abrams, Elliott. "Egypt Protests Show George W. Bush Was Right about Freedom in the
Arab World." *Washington Post*. January 29, 2011. Accessed September 7, 2017. https://
wapo.st/2DFA2vt.

Abul-Magd, Zeinab. "The Army and the Economy in Egypt." Jadaliyya. December 23,
2011. Accessed September 9, 2017. https://bit.ly/2GrwxfY.

Abul-Magd, Zeinab. "The Egyptian Republic of Retired Generals." *Foreign Policy*. May 8,
2012. Accessed September 16, 2017. https://bit.ly/2N7013h.

Abul-Magd, Zeinab. *Militarizing the Nation: The Army, Business, and Revolution in
Egypt*. New York: Columbia University Press, 2017.

Abul-Magd, Zeinab. "Morsy and His brothers: Sleeping in Nasser's Bed." *Egypt
Independent*. October 10, 2012. Accessed October 12, 2017. http://bit.ly/
2SE6gSm.

Acemoglu, Daron, and James Robinson. "Economic Backwardness in Political
Perspective." *American Political Science Review* 100, no. 111 (February 2006): 115–
131. Accessed October 12, 2017. https://economics.mit.edu/files/4471.

Achcar, Gilbert, and G. M. Goshgarian. *The People Want: A Radical Exploration of the
Arab Uprising*. London: Saqi, 2013.

Aclimandos, Tewfick. "Reforming the Egyptian Security Services." Arab Reform
Initiative. June 1, 2011. Accessed August 5, 2015. http://www.arab-reform.net/en/
node/567.

Activist/blogger. Interview by author. January 9, 2014.

Activist in Aswan. Interview by author. January 2017.

Activist in Tanta. Interview by author. May 2017.

Adel, Hazem, and Ahmed Arafa. "عنان سامى حزب تأسيس بقبول تقضى العليا الإدارية
تمرد ورفض" [Supreme Administrative Court rules by accepting the establishment of
Sami Anan's party and rejecting Tamarod's]. AlYoum7. January 28, 2015. Accessed
February 11, 2019. https://bit.ly/2E5hCG0. [Translation provided by author].

"Admission of Forced 'Virginity Tests' in Egypt Must Lead to Justice." Human Rights Now. June 1, 2011. Accessed September 12, 2017. https://bit.ly/2SA66LE.

"After 20 Years: CIHRS Moves Its Regional and International Programs outside Egypt." Cairo Institute for Human Rights Studies. December 9, 2014. Accessed February 17, 2019. https://bit.ly/2Edl5lO.

Ahmed, a financial analyst. Interview by author. May 2014.

Ahmed, Hassan. "القبض على أمين «الحرية والعدالة» بالقاهرة خالد حنفي." [Arresting Khaled Hanafi, the General Secretary of the Freedom and Justice Party in Cairo]. AlMasry AlYoum. September 9, 2013. Accessed February 16, 2019. https://bit.ly/2DM0CmF. [Translation provided by author].

Ahmed, Hassan. "القبض على محمد بديع مرشد الإخوان المسلمين في شقة سكنية برابعة العدوية." [Arresting Mohamed Badie, the Supreme Guide of the Muslim Brotherhood in an apartment in Rabaa]. AlMasry AlYoum. August 20, 2013. Accessed February 16, 2019. https://bit.ly/2TRNpQi. [Translation provided by author].

Ahmed, Hassan. "تفاصيل القبض على قيادات بـ«الإخوان» في عدد من المحافظات." [The details of arresting leading figures of the Brotherhood in a number of governorates]. AlMasry AlYoum. August 18, 2013. Accessed February 16, 2019. https://bit.ly/2IgrJMj. [Translation provided by author].

Ahmed, Hassan. "القبض على خيرت الشاطر في مدينة نصر." [Arresting Khairat El-Shater in Nasr City]. AlMasry AlYoum. July 6, 2013. Accessed February 15, 2019. https://bit.ly/2BFlSKS. [Translation provided by author].

Ahmed, Maher. Interview by author. May 2017.

Ahmed, Ramadan. "العادلي في شهادته بـ«اقتحام السجون»: هروب ٢٣ ألف مسجون خلال أحداث يناير." [El-Adly in his testimony: 23 thousand prisoners escaped during the events of January]. Veto Gate. October 10, 2018. Accessed February 15, 2019. https://bit.ly/2TRy2qP. [Translation provided by author].

Al-Amin, Esam. "Leaked Audio Shows Egypt's Coup Leaders as a Criminal Syndicate." Counterpunch. December 12, 2014. Accessed October 13, 2017. https://bit.ly/2tpIDh7.

Al-Anani, Khalil. "Upended Path: The Rise and Fall of Egypt's Muslim Brotherhood." Middle East Journal 69, no. 4 (2015): 527–543.

Al-Awadi, Hesham. The Muslim Brothers in Pursuit of Legitimacy: Power and Political Islam in Egypt under Mubarak. London: I. B. Tauris, 2014.

Albrecht, Holger. Contentious Politics in the Middle East. Gainesville: University Press of Florida, 2010.

Albrecht, Holger. "Does Coup-Proofing Work? Political-Military Relations in Authoritarian Regimes amid the Arab Uprisings." Mediterranean Politics 20, no. 1 (2014): 36–54.

Albrecht, Holger. "The Myth of Coup-proofing Risk and Instances of Military Coups d'état in the Middle East and North Africa 1950–2013." Armed Forces & Society 41, no. 4 (2014): 659–687.

Albrecht, Holger. *Raging against the Machine: Political Opposition under Authoritarianism in Egypt*. Syracuse, NY: Syracuse University Press, 2013.

Albrecht, Holger, and Dina Bishara. "Back on Horseback: The Military and Political Transformation in Egypt." *Middle East Law and Governance* 3, no. 1-2 (2011): 13–23.

Albrecht, Holger, and Dorothy Ohl. "Exit, Resistance, Loyalty: Military Behavior during Unrest in Authoritarian Regimes." *Perspectives on Politics* 14, no. 1. (March 2016): 38–52.

Alexander, Anne. "Brothers-in-arms? The Egyptian Military, the Ikhwan and the Revolutions of 1952 and 2011." *Journal of North African Studies* 16, no. 4 (2011): 533–554.

Alexander, Anne, and Miriyam Aouragh. "Egypt's Unfinished Revolution: The Role of the Media Revisited." *International Journal of Communication* 8 (2014): 890–915. Accessed September 11, 2017. https://bit.ly/2GKUAWC.

Alexander, Jeffrey C. *Performative Revolution in Egypt: An Essay in Cultural Power*. London: Bloomsbury Academic, 2011.

Alfred, Charlotte. "'Vote For The Pimp' Hashtag Prompts Twitter Battle In Egypt." Huffington Post. March 31, 2014. Accessed August 11, 2017. https://bit.ly/1QtDwUo.

AlHurra. "الحفاظ على التراث في سلسلة مبادرات تهدف للحفاظ على التراث" . . . الحلقة الأحدث في سلسلة مبادرات تهدف للحفاظ على التراث" قناة " نوبة تيوب" النوبي في مصر" ["NubaTube" channel, a channel that aims at preserving the Nubian heritage in Egypt]. YouTube. 2:30. July 5, 2016. https://bit.ly/2UY7ODa. [Translation provided by author].

Ali, Nour. "النص الكامل لمشروع قانون التنظيم المؤسسى للصحافة والإعلام". [The full text of draft law regulating institutions of media and journalism]. AlYoum7. December 13, 2016. Accessed February 17, 2019. https://bit.ly/2BDQzjB. [Translation provided by author].

Ali, Nour, and Abdel Latif Sobh. "النص الكامل لقانون الجمعيات الأهلية الجديد بعد موافقة البرلمان عليه." [The full text of NGO law after approval by the Parliament]. AlYoum7. November 29, 2016. Accessed February 17, 2019. https://bit.ly/2GvMzpn. [Translation provided by author].

"All According to Plan: The Rab'a Massacre and Mass Killings of Protesters in Egypt." Human Rights Watch. August 12, 2014. Accessed February 14, 2019. https://bit.ly/1NaCcCS.

AlMamlouk, Mahmoud. "نص شهادة المشير بقضية قتل المتظاهرين". [The text of the Marshal's testimony in the killing of protesters' case]. AlYoum7. June 2, 2012. Accessed February 14, 2019. https://bit.ly/2S2YEDE. [Translation provided by author].

AlMasry AlYoum. "مصر من الهليكوبتر. الملايين ضد مرسي" [Egypt from the helicopter, millions against Morsi]. YouTube video. 12:48. July 2, 2013. https://bit.ly/2DJN8rE. [Translation provided by author].

AlMasry AlYoum. "اشتباكات بالتحرير في جمعة كشف الحساب" [Clashes in Tahrir in Friday of "Account Statement"]. YouTube video, 2:36. October 12, 2012. https://www.youtube.com/watch?v=ylSFs7_i5mg. [Translation provided by author].

AlSayed, Hala. "ثقوب تعوق العمل الخيري." [Holes impeding charity work]. AlAhram. October 29, 2016. Accessed February 13, 2019. http://www.ahram.org.eg/NewsPrint/558304.aspx. [Translation provided by author].

AlSayed, Marwa. "حسام بهجت يرفض عضوية قومي حقوق الإنسان." [Hossam Bahgat refuses the national Council for Human Rights membership]. Veto Gate. August 29, 2013. Accessed February 12, 2019. https://bit.ly/2BBENpI. [Translation provided by author].

AlSayed, Samir. "عاجل. البرادعي وموسى وصباحي يعلنون إنشاء جبهة إنقاذ وطني لإدارة المرحلة الحالية سياسيًا وشعبيًا." [ElBaradei, Moussa, and Sabahi announce the establishment of a national salvation front to manage the current stage]. Ahram Gate. November 24, 2012. Accessed February 15, 2019. https://bit.ly/2GPTxoe. [Translation provided by author].

AlWafd. "ننشر نص قانون التظاهر بالجريدة الرسمية." [The text of the Protest Law in the Official Gazette]. AlWafd. November 24, 2013. Accessed February 11, 2019. https://bit.ly/2sL8kZN. [Translation provided by author].

AlZoghby, Salwa. "أحمد البرعي وزير التضامن الاجتماعي. رجل المراحل الانتقالية." [Ahmed El Boraie Minister of Social Solidarity, the man of transitional periods]. ElWatan News. July 14, 2013. Accessed February 12, 2019. https://bit.ly/2StGobJ. [Translation provided by author].

Amar, Paul, and Vijay Prashad. *Dispatches from the Arab Spring: Understanding the New Middle East*. Minneapolis: University of Minnesota Press, 2013.

Amer, Essam. "حركة كفاية تدعو لتوقيعات سحب الثقة من الرئيس تحت شعار تمرد." [Kefaya movement calls for collecting no confidence petitions under the slogan of "rebellion"]. AlSherouk News. April 28, 2013. Accessed February 15, 2019. http://bit.ly/2GMzdUL.[Translation provided by author].

Amer, Mohamed, and Mohamed ElBadry. "حبس ماهينور المصري ومعتصم مدحت على ذمة قضية تظاهر." [Detaining Mahienour El Massry and Moatassem Medhat over a protest]. Masrawy. November 18, 2017. Accessed February 17, 2019. https://bit.ly/2S6K3Hl.[Translation provided by author].

Amin, Samir. *The People's Spring: The Future of the Arab Revolution*. Nairobi: Pambazuka Press, 2012.

Amr, Member of Kazeboon. Interview by author. February 18, 2012.

Anderson, Betty S. *A History of the Modern Middle East: Rulers, Rebels, and Rogues*. Stanford, CA: Stanford University Press, 2016.

Anderson, Lisa. "Demystifying the Arab Spring." *Foreign Affairs*. December 20, 2011. Accessed June 6, 2015. https://fam.ag/1M9FjGn.

Andreski, Stanislav. "On the Peaceful Disposition of Military Dictatorships." *Journal of Strategic Studies* 3, no. 3 (1980): 3–10.

An exiled member of the Brotherhood in London. Interview by author. March 2015.

An independent analyst in Cairo. Interview by author. January 14, 2014.

"April 6 Activist on His US Visit and Regime Change in Egypt." Wiki Leaks. December 13, 2008. Accessed February 13, 2018. https://bit.ly/2QUAmvc.

April 6th Movement Facebook Page, accessed August 11, 2017. https://goo.gl/Edve3i.

April 6th Movement Facebook Page, accessed August 11, 2017. https://goo.gl/mDHQkn.

April 6th political bureau member. Interview by author. December 2016.

A retired major in the Egyptian army. Interview by author. November 12, 2011.

"Arrest of Azza Soliman." Front Line Defenders. Accessed February 9, 2018. https://bit.ly/2hk7wTg.

Arrighi, Giovanni. *The Long Twentieth Century: Money, Power and the Origins of Our Times*. London: Verso, 2010.

Ashraf Gawdat. "رد فعل المتظاهرين عند الاتحادية عند مرور طائرة الجيش 30 يونيو" [The reactions of Itahadiyya protestors when seeing army helicopters on June 30]. YouTube video. 0:54. June 30, 2013. https://bit.ly/2TVRjru. [Translation provided by author].

Atiya, Azza. "كمال أبوعيطة: "استقالة حكومة البلاوي كانت مفاجأة سارة" [Kamal Abou Eita: The resignation of Beblawi's cabinet was a good surprise]. ElWatan News. March 10, 2014. Accessed February 12, 2019. https://bit.ly/2SrXMgV. [Translation provided by author].

Attalah, Lina. "Laila Soueif." Bidoun. May 14, 2017. Accessed February 9, 2018. http://bidoun.org/articles/Laila-Soueif.

Ayubi, Nazih N. M. *Over-Stating the Arab State*. London: I. B. Tauris, 1995.

Aziz, Sahar. "Sinai's Role in Morsi's Ouster." Sada. August 20, 2013. Accessed October 12, 2017. https://bit.ly/2TQG7fE.

Aziz, Sahar F. "(De)liberalizing Judicial Independence in Egypt." In *Egypt and the Contradictions of Liberalism: Illiberal Intelligentsia and the Future of Egyptian Democracy*. Edited by Dalia F. Fahmy and Daanish Faruqi. London: Oneworld, 2017.

Background on Case No. 173—the "Foreign Funding Case." Imminent Risk of Prosecution and Closure. Report. March 21, 2016. Accessed August 4, 2016. http://eipr.org/en/pressrelease/2016/03/21/2569.

Badawi, Nada. "Central Bank Head in Abu Dhabi in Search of Financial Aid." *Daily News Egypt*. July 8, 2013. Accessed February 11, 2018. https://bit.ly/2GuIrpA.

Bahgat, Hossam. "Who Let the Jihadis Out?" Mada Masr. February 16, 2017. Accessed October 10, 2017. https://bit.ly/2tuKam6.

Bahgat, Hossam, and Mostafa Mohie. "Wikileaks Cables Trace Ebb and Flow of Egypt-UAE Relations." Mada Masr. July 26, 2015. Accessed October 10, 2017. https://bit.ly/2tnXLvq.

Baker, Peter. "A Coup? Or Something Else? $1.5 Billion in U.S. Aid Is on the Line." *New York Times*. July 4, 2013. Accessed February 12, 2019. https://nyti.ms/2SOm8AQ.

Bamyeh, Mohammed. "The Egyptian Revolution: First Impressions from the Field." Jadaliyya. February 11, 2011. Accessed September 10, 2017. https://bit.ly/2GuAwIE.

Barany, Zoltan. "Comparing the Arab Revolts: The Role of the Military." *Journal of Democracy* 22, no. 4 (October 2011): 24–35. Accessed February 12, 2016. https://bit.ly/2RXV3a1.

Bar'el, Zvi. "Muslim Brotherhood Deputy Chief Calls for the Return of Jews to Egypt." Haaretz.com. March 24, 2013. Accessed September 17, 2017. https://bit.ly/2V0GcNI.

Bassal, Mohamed. "The President Exercises the Power of Legislation: Sisi Issues 263 Laws in 420 days." AlShorouk News, August 4, 2015. Accessed March 5, 2017. http://www.shorouknews.com/news/view.aspx?cdate=04082015&id=e1aee73e-be2f-49ee-926c-8e2bad0c4a95.

Bassiouni, Cherif. "Corruption Cases against Officials of the Mubarak Regime." Report. Egyptian American Rule of Law Association. 2012. Accessed October 12, 2017. https://bit.ly/2to4V2Y.

Bassiouni, M. Cherif. *Chronicles of the Egyptian Revolution and Its Aftermath: 2011–2016.* Cambridge: Cambridge University Press, 2017.

Bayat, Asef. *Revolution without Revolutionaries: Making Sense of the Arab Spring.* Stanford, CA: Stanford University Press, 2017.

BBC News Arabic. "مصر: أزمة بين المجلس العسكري وحركة 6 ابريل" [Egypt: A crisis between the SCAF and April 6 movement]. BBC News. July 23, 2011. Accessed February 12, 2019. https://bbc.in/2N2w4S2. [Translation provided by author].

Beaumont, Peter. "Mohamed Morsi Signs Egypt's New Constitution into Law." *The Guardian.* December 26, 2012. Accessed February 15, 2019. https://bit.ly/2BBHl7w.

Beck, Colin J. Reflections on the Revolutionary Wave in 2011. *Theory and Society* 43, no. 2 (2014): 197–223.

Beinin, Joel. *Workers and Thieves: Labor Movements and Popular Uprisings in Tunisia and Egypt.* Stanford, CA: Stanford Briefs, 2016.

Beinin, Joel, and Zachary Lockman. *Workers on the Nile: Nationalism, Communism, Islam and the Egyptian Working Class, 1882–1954.* Princeton, NJ: Princeton University, 1987.

Beinin, Joel, and Frédéric Vairel. *Social Movements, Mobilization, and Contestation in the Middle East and North Africa.* Stanford, CA: Stanford University Press, 2013.

Beissinger, Mark R. "Structure and Example in Modular Political Phenomena: The Diffusion of Bulldozer/Rose/Orange/Tulip Revolutions." *Perspectives on Politics* 5, no. 2 (2007): 259–276.

Beissinger, Mark R., Amaney Jamal, and Kevin Mazur. "Who Participated in the Arab Spring?" Princeton.edu. 2012. Accessed August 11, 2017. https://bit.ly/2SD7zAR.

Belkin, Aaron, and Evan Schofer. "Coup Risk, Counterbalancing, and International Conflict." *Security Studies* 14, no. 1 (2005): 140–177.

Belkin, Aaron, and Evan Schofer. "Toward a Structural Understanding of Coup Risk." *Journal of Conflict Resolution* 47, no. 5 (2003): 594–620.

Bellin, Eva. "Reconsidering the Robustness of Authoritarianism in The Middle East: Lessons from the Arab Spring." *Comparative Politics* 44, no. 2 (2012): 127–149.

Be tawkit Masr. "بتوقيت مصر | معتز الفجيري: منظمات حقوق الإنسان في مصر تواجه أزمة وجودية." [Be tawkit Masr | Moataz El-Figary: In Egypt, Human Rights NGOs Face

Existential Crisis]. YouTube video, 11:24. August 13, 2016. https://www.youtube.com/watch?v=yWDiKkfieVY. [Translation provided by author].

"Beyer Statement on Acquittal of Aya Hijazi and Her Co-Defendants in Egypt." Congressman Don Beyer. April 16, 2017. Accessed February 9, 2018. https://bit.ly/2GsrXy5.

"Billionaire Rebel: Naguib Sawiris Is Pushing for an Egypt That Fulfills the Promise of the Arab Spring." *Bloomberg Markets*, December 2011.

Blaydes, Lisa. *Elections and Distributive Politics in Mubarak's Egypt.* Cambridge: Cambridge University Press, 2011.

Blumenthal, Paul. "Lobbying Contacts by Egypt's Washington Lobbyists." Sunlight Foundation. January 30, 2011. Accessed October 12, 2017. https://sunlightfoundation.com/2011/01/31/lobbying-contacts-by-egypts-washington-lobbyists/.

Boctor, Lillian. "Organizing for No Military Trials for Civilians: Interview with Egyptian Activist Shahira Abouellail." Jadaliyya. November 6, 2011. Accessed September 8, 2017. https://bit.ly/2SxKBLC.

Bogatyrev, Sergei. "Bronze Tsars: Ivan the Terrible and Fedor Ivanovich in the Décor of Early Modern Guns." *Slavonic and East European Review* 88 (January 2010): 48–72.

Borger, Julian. "The Egyptian Crisis: Another Day, Another Two US Policies." *The Guardian.* February 6, 2011. Accessed September 7, 2017. https://bit.ly/2NbXN2U.

Bove, Vincenzo, and Mauricio Rivera. "Elite Co-optation, Repression, and Coups in Autocracies." *International Interactions* 41, no. 3 (2015): 453–479.

Braudel, Fernand. *The Mediterranean and the Mediterranean World in the Age of Phillip II.* London: Collins, 1972.

Brechenmacher, Saskia. "Civil Society under Assault: Repression and Responses in Russia, Egypt, and Ethiopia." Report. Carnegie Endowment for International Peace. Washington, DC, 2017. Accessed February 10, 2018. https://bit.ly/2qAFOK1

Brown, Nathan. "Egypt's Judges in a Revolutionary Age." Carnegie Endowment for International Peace. February 22, 2012. Accessed August 5, 2015. https://bit.ly/2Svftwd

Brown, Nathan J. "Cairo's Judicial Coup." *Foreign Policy.* June 14, 2012. Accessed September 8, 2017. http://foreignpolicy.com/2012/06/14/cairos-judicial-coup/.

Brownlee, Billie Jeanne, and Maziyar Ghiabi. "Passive, Silent and Revolutionary: The 'Arab Spring' Revisited." *Middle East Critique* 25, no. 3 (2016): 299–316.

Brownlee, Jason. *Democracy Prevention: The Politics of the U.S.-Egyptian Alliance.* New York: Cambridge University Press, 2012.

Brownlee, Jason, Tarek E. Masoud, and Andrew Reynolds. *The Arab Spring: Pathways of Repression and Reform.* Oxford: Oxford University Press, 2015.

Brynen, Rex. *Beyond the Arab Spring: Authoritarianism and Democratization in the Arab World.* Boulder, CO: Rienner, 2012.

Burns, William J. *The Back Channel: A Memoir of American Diplomacy and the Case for its Renewal*. New York: Random House, 2019.

Cambanis, Thanassis. *Once Upon a Revolution: An Egyptian Story*. New York: Simon & Schuster Paperbacks, 2016.

Carlstrom, Gregg, Edward Lazear, Christopher Ingalls Haugh, David Dayen, Jack Shafer, Bill Scher, and Zach Hambrick. "Egypt's New Dictator Was Made in the USA." *Politico Magazine*. February 18, 2014. Accessed October 10, 2017. https://politi.co/23kWgXF.

CBC Egypt. "بيان القوات المسلحة المصرية يوم ١ يوليو ٢٠١٣" [The Statement of the Egyptian Armed Forces on July 1, 2013]. YouTube video, 7:09. July 1, 2013. https:// bit.ly/ 2N7vPoK. [Translation provided by author].

Chalcraft, John. *Popular Politics in the Making of the Modern Middle East*. Cambridge: Cambridge University Press, 2016.

Chambers, Paul, and Napisa Waitoolkiat. "The Resilience of Monarchised Military in Thailand." *Journal of Contemporary Asia* 46, no. 3 (2016): 425–444. Accessed August 30, 2018. doi:10.1080/00472336.2016.1161060.

Chang, Leslie T. "The News Website That's Keeping Press Freedom Alive in Egypt." *The Guardian*. January 27, 2015. Accessed May 13, 2019. https://bit.ly/30dtizr.

Chekir, Hamouda, and Ishac Diwan. "Crony Capitalism in Egypt." Working paper no. 250. Center for International Development at Harvard University, Harvard University. 2012. https://bit.ly/2X8oPwi.

Chenoweth, Erica, and Maria J. Stephan. *Why Civil Resistance Works: The Strategic Logic of Nonviolent Conflict (Columbia Studies in Terrorism and Irregular Warfare)*. New York: Columbia University Press, 2011.

Chulov, Martin. "Egypt's Ousting of Mohamed Morsi Was a Coup, Says John McCain." *The Guardian*. December 1, 2017. Accessed February 12, 2019. https://bit.ly/2SJjnRf.

Cohen, Roger. "Guru of the Revolution." *New York Times*. February 17, 2011. Accessed September 8, 2017. https://nyti.ms/2SyPfca.

Cole, Juan. "Egypt's Modern Revolutions and the Fall of Mubarak." In *The New Middle East: Protest and Revolution in the Arab World*. Edited by Fawaz A. Gerges. 60–79. Cambridge: Cambridge University Press, 2014.

Cole, Juan Ricardo. *Napoleon's Egypt: Invading the Middle East*. New York: Palgrave Macmillan, 2008.

Colgan, Jeff D. "Domestic Revolutionary Leaders and International Conflict." *World Politics* 65, no. 4 (2013): 656–690.

Collier, Paul, and Jan Willem Gunning. "Why Has Africa Grown Slowly?" *Journal of Economic Perspectives* 13, no. 3 (1999): 3–22.

Connolly, Kevin. "Egypt Crisis: Beleaguered Mubarak Reshuffles Cabinet." BBC News. January 31, 2011. Accessed September 7, 2017. https://bbc.in/2N91Ooo.

Cook, Steven A. *False Dawn: Protest, Democracy, and Violence in the New Middle East*. New York: Oxford University Press, 2017.

Cook, Steven A. *Ruling but Not Governing: The Military and Political Development in Egypt, Algeria, and Turkey.* Baltimore: Johns Hopkins University Press, 2007.

Cook, Steven A. *The Struggle for Egypt from Nasser to Tahrir Square.* New York: Oxford University Press, 2012.

Cooper, David E. "Equality and Envy." *Journal of Philosophy of Education* 16, no. 1 (1982): 35–47.

Cooper, Helene, Mark Landler, and David E. Sanger. "In U.S. Signals to Egypt, Obama Straddled a Rift." *New York Times.* February 12, 2011. Accessed September 7, 2017. https://nyti.ms/2TQdWxr.

Cooper, Mark Neal. *The Transformation of Egypt: State and State Capitalism in Crisis, 1967–1977.* Ann Arbor, MI: University Microfilms International, 1981.

Corfield, P. J. *Time and the Shape of History.* New Haven: Yale University Press, 2007.

Croissant, Aurel. *Democratization, Democracy and Authoritarian Continuity.* London: Routledge, 2014.

Cronin, Stephanie. *Armies and State-Building in the Modern Middle East: Politics, Nationalism and Military Reform.* London: I. B. Tauris, 2014.

Crowley, Michael. "John Kerry and Obama Denounce Egypt Verdict on Al Jazeera Journalists." *Time.* June 23, 2014. Accessed February 11, 2018. https://bit.ly/2BzbEeP.

Dabashi, Hamid. *Corpus Anarchicum: Political Protest, Suicidal Violence, and the Making of the Posthuman Body.* New York: Palgrave Macmillan, 2012.

Daigle, Craig. *The Limits of Détente: The United States, the Soviet Union, and the Arab-Israeli Conflict, 1969–1973.* New Haven: Yale University Press, 2012.

"Diaries of a Revolution under Military Rule: Excerpts from 2011 Report." Al Nadeem Center for Rehabilitation of Victims of Violence. June 21, 2016. Accessed September 8, 2017. https://bit.ly/2tlDxTj.

De Atkine, Norvell B. "Why Arabs Lose Wars?" *Middle East Quarterly* 6, no. 4 (December 1999). Accessed September 9, 2017. http://www.meforum.org/441/why-arabs-lose-wars.

DeFronzo, James. *Revolutions and Revolutionary Movements.* Boulder, CO: Westview Press, 2011.

Della Porta, Donatella, and Sidney Tarrow. "Interactive Diffusion: The Coevolution of Police and Protest Behavior with an Application to Transnational Contention." *Comparative Political Studies* 45, no. 1 (2012): 119–152.

Delmore, Erin. "Morsi Supporters Decry 'Military Coup' Underway in Egypt." MSNBC. July 3, 2013. Accessed February 15, 2019. https://on.msnbc.com/2SX1HBO.

Diamond, Larry Jay. "Thinking about Hybrid Regimes." *Journal of Democracy* 13, no. 2 (2002): 21–35. Accessed February 9, 2018. https://bit.ly/2tr1yrT.

Dorman, W. J. "Exclusion and Informality: The Praetorian Politics of Land Management in Cairo, Egypt." *International Journal of Urban and Regional Research* 37, no. 5 (2013): 1584–1610.

Dream TV. "خطاب ترشح السيسي للرئاسة كاملا" [Sisi's presidential candidacy full speech]. YouTube video, 15:01, March 26, 2014. https:// www.youtube.com/watch?v=2Yqn6U55q9o. [Translation provided by author].

Dreamtvchannel. "النيابة العسكرية تستدعي المذيعة ريم ماجد والمدون حسام الحملاوي للتحقيق" [The Military Prosecution summons the presenter Reem Maged and the blogger Hossam Al-Hamlawy for interrogation]. YouTube. 3:55. May 31, 2011. https://bit.ly/2TZpRJr.

Droz-Vincent, Philippe. "Authoritarianism, Revolutions, Armies and Arab Regime Transitions." *International Spectator* 46, no. 2 (2011): 5–21.

Dufka, Corinne. "'By Day We Fear the Army, by Night the Jihadists': Abuses by Armed Islamists and Security Forces in Burkina Faso." Report. May 2018. Accessed February 16, 2019. https://bit.ly/2tocBC7.

Dunne, Michele, and Thomas Carothers. "Egypt's Evolving Governance Is No 'Democratic Transition.'" Carnegie Endowment. January 23, 2014. Accessed January 20, 2017. http://carnegieendowment.org/2014/01/23/egypt-s-evolving-governance-is-no-democratic-transition/gz99.

EgyDoctor. "كم يبلغ عدد المنتمين لجماعة الإخوان المسلمين في مصر؟" [How many Muslim Brotherhood members are there in Egypt?]. YouTube Video. 2:16. August 3, 2013. https://www.youtube.com/watch?v=ofAERYOsZ88 [Translation provided by author].

"Egypt—Civic Freedom Monitor." The International Centre for Non-for-profit Law. June 27, 2017. Accessed October 22, 2017. http://www.icnl.org/research/monitor/egypt.html.

"Egypt Court Sentences Al Jazeera Journalists." Al Jazeera English. Accessed August 11, 2017. https://bit.ly/2TKfpoL

"Egypt: Five Years since 'Rabaa Massacre.'" Al Jazeera. August 14, 2018. Accessed February 15, 2019. https://bit.ly/2IeYObn.

"Egypt Football Clash Kills Scores." BBC News. February 2, 2012. Accessed February 15, 2019. https://bbc.in/2EbqidQ.

Egyptian activist. Interview by author. November 11, 2011.

The Egyptian Current Party Facebook Page. Accessed August 11, 2017. https://goo.gl/t2mMsb.

Egyptian Initiative for Personal Rights. "رسالة إلي وزير الصحة." [Letter to the Minister of Health]. EIPR. March 20, 2011. Accessed February 15, 2019. https://bit.ly/2UYqsuI. [Translation provided by author].

"The Egyptian Military Empire." *Middle East Monitor*. July 9, 2014. Accessed February 14, 2019. https://bit.ly/2LJtWwX.

"Egyptian Presenter Reem Maged's New TV Show Suspended." Ahram Online. May 15, 2015. Accessed February 9, 2018. https://bit.ly/2BDxBJH.

"Egyptian Women's Views: Verdict in Virginity Test Case." BBC News. March 12, 2012. Accessed September 12, 2017. https://bbc.in/2X46ikV.

"Egypt Jails 16 as LGBT Crackdown Goes on." BBC News. November 28, 2017. Accessed February 15, 2019. https://bbc.in/2BtoNVd.

"Egypt Leaves the Internet." Oracle—DYN. January 27, 2011. Accessed September 8, 2017. https://dyn.com/blog/egypt-leaves-the-internet/.

"Egypt Military Judiciary Wants MP's Immunity Lifted over Tantawi Insult." Ahram Online. June 12, 2012. Accessed October 8, 2017. https://bit.ly/2SxkDYu.

"Egypt: Military Pledges to Stop Forced 'Virginity Tests.'" Amnesty International. June 27, 2011. Accessed September 12, 2017. https://bit.ly/2GuJyFy.

"Egypt: Military 'Virginity Test' Investigation a Sham." Human Rights Watch. April 17, 2015. Accessed September 12, 2017. https://bit.ly/2GJpZZv.

"Egypt's New Shocking and Potentially Indicting Leaks." *Middle East Monitor*. December 5, 2014. Accessed October 12, 2017. https://bit.ly/2EcNadi.

"Egypt: Officials Turn Blind Eye to Port Said Police Abuses." Human Rights Watch. March 2, 2013. Accessed September 20, 2017. https://bit.ly/2GJEVXM.

"Egypt: One of the World's Biggest Prisons for Journalists | Reporters without Borders." RSF. Accessed February 9, 2018. https://rsf.org/en/egypt.

"Egypt Orders Brotherhood Chief Held, Morsi in 'Safe Place.'" Middle East Institute. 2013. Accessed October 12, 2017. https://bit.ly/2TRUSP5.

"Egypt Police Raid Journalists' Syndicate, Arrest Two Journalists." Committee to Protect Journalists. May 2, 2016. Accessed February 17, 2019. https://bit.ly/2cjSAFl.

"Egypt Protests: Secret US Document Discloses Support for Protesters." The Telegraph. January 28, 2011. Accessed October 14, 2017. https://bit.ly/2fAJynm.

"Egypt: Retry or Free 12,000 after Unfair Military Trials." Human Rights Watch. September 11, 2011. Accessed February 14, 2019. https://bit.ly/2BBmykt.

"Egypt's Al-Ahram Strongly Criticizes Interior Ministry after Police Storm Journalists Syndicate." AlAhram English, May 3, 2016. Accessed February 11, 2018. https://bit.ly/2SUgQnp.

"Egypt Shuts Down Al Jazeera Bureau." Al Jazeera English. January 30, 2011. Accessed September 7, 2017. https://bit.ly/2GHSmHD.

Egypt Specialist at the State Department and a Member of the Policy Planning Staff under President Obama. Interview by author. October 2017.

"Egypt: Torture Epidemic May be Crime against Humanity." Human Rights Watch. October 30, 2017. Accessed February 11, 2018. https://bit.ly/2w57Axs.

"Egypt Trials: Mubarak Officials' Charges and Verdicts." BBC News. October 12, 2015. Accessed September 17, 2017. https://bbc.in/2TNlYH3.

"EIPR: Authorities Have Systematically Entrapped LGBTQ Individuals Online since 2015." Mada Masr. November 22, 2017. Accessed February 17, 2019. https://bit.ly/2BGLeb9.

El Amrani, Issandr. "Egypt's Military Council in a Diagram." *The Arabist*. March 3, 2011. Accessed September 8, 2017. https://bit.ly/2touukA.

El Amrani, Issandr. "Electoral Manipulation in Egypt: Revisiting 2005." *The Arabist* (web log), November 5, 2010. Accessed April 19, 2016. https://arabist.net/blog/2010/11/5/electoral-manipulation-in-egypt-revisiting-2005.html.

El Amrani, Issandr. "Sightings of the Egyptian Deep State." Middle East Research and Information Project. January 1, 2012. Accessed September 8, 2017. http://merip.org/mero/mero010112.

ElBadry, Yousri. "القبض على أمين «الحرية والعدالة» بمطروح بتهمة التحريض على أعمال عنف." [Arresting the General Secretary of the Freedom and Justice Party in Matrouh on charges of inciting violence]. AlMasry AlYoum. August 29, 2013. Accessed February 15, 2019. https://bit.ly/2DNmRtU. [Translation provided by author].

ElBadry, Yousri. "القبض على سعد الكتاتني ورشاد بيومي." [Arresting Saad ElKatatny and Rashad Bayoumi]. AlMasry AlYoum. July 4, 2013. Accessed February 16, 2019. https://bit.ly/2DI1PM2. [Translation provided by author].

ElBadry, Yousry. "ضبط ٣٥ من مالكي القنوات الدينية وملاحقة ٣٤ من قيادات «الإخوان»" [Arresting 35 Owners of Religious Channels and Tracking 34 Muslim Brotherhood Leaders]. Al-Masry Al-Youm, 3 July 2013. Accessed August 11, 2017. http://www.almasryalyoum.com/news/details/230627. [Translation provided by author].

El-Baghdadi, Iyad. "Meet Asmaa Mahfouz and the Vlog That Helped Spark the Revolution." YouTube video, 4:36. February 2011. http://www.youtube.com/watch?v=SgjIgMdsEuk.

El-Baradei, Mohamed. Interview by author. October 2016.

El-Baradei, Mohamed. "'This Was Not a Coup.'" Interview. *Der Spiegel*. July 8, 2013. Accessed August 11, 2017. https://bit.ly/2IfVXiC.

El-behairy, Nouran. "Morsi's Syria Speech Angers Opposition." *Daily News Egypt*. June 16, 2013. Accessed October 12, 2017. https://bit.ly/2N6Q5H2.

El-Bendary, Mohamed. *The Egyptian Revolution and Its Aftermath: From Mubarak's Fall to Morsi's Rise*. New York: Algora, 2013.

El-Dabh, Basil. "June 30: Tamarod and Its Opponents." Middle East Institute. June 26, 2013. Accessed October 12, 2017. http://www.mei.edu/content/june-30-tamarod-and-its-opponents.

Eleiba, Ahmed. "F-16 Deal Redefines US Relationship with Egypt's Morsi Administration." Ahram Online. January 13, 2013. Accessed September 17, 2017. https://bit.ly/2UZ30NZ.

El-Ghobashy, Mona. "Constitutionalist Contention in Contemporary Egypt." *American Behavioral Scientist* 51, no. 11 (2008): 1590–1610.

El-Ghobashy, Mona. "The Praxis of the Egyptian Revolution." Middle East Research and Information Project. Spring 2011. Accessed September 8, 2017. http://merip.org/mer/mer258/praxis-egyptian-revolution.

El-Gohary, Mossad. "Death Toll at 42 in Two Days of Egypt Violence." *The Times of Israel*. January 27, 2013. Accessed February 15, 2019. https://bit.ly/2GM3vay.

ElKhouly, Nada. "على قهوة «الكرنك»: «إحنا بتوع الإنتاج» . . . لا فلول ولا إخوان" [On the Karnak coffeeshop: We are the ones concerned with production . . . No feloul or brothers]. AlSherouk News. July 23, 2012. Accessed February 15, 2019. http://bit.ly/2SARNXm. [Translation provided by author].

El-Kouny, Nada. "Egyptian Activists to Continue Struggle against 'Virginity Test' Perpetrators." Ahram Online. March 11, 2012. Accessed September 12, 2017. https://bit.ly/2SZDpr7.

El-Mahdi, Rabab. "Labour Protests in Egypt: Causes and Meanings." *Review of African Political Economy* 38, no. 129 (2011): 387–402. Accessed January 4, 2015.

El-Shami, Khaled. "«تمرد تصحيح المسار» تعلن انتهاء الحملة. وتطلق مشروع «الجماهير»" [The correction of path Tamarod front ends its campaign and starts the "public" project]. AlMasryAlYoum. June 9, 2014. Accessed February 10, 2018. http://www.almasryalyoum.com/news/details/461087. [Translation provided by author].

ElSharkawi, Nasser. "حبس ماهينور المصري بتهمة التظاهر ضد اتفاقية ترسيم الحدود مع السعودية" [Sentencing Mahienour El Massry to two years in prison for protesting against the border demarcation agreement with Saudi Arabia]. AlMasry AlYoum. December 30, 2017. Accessed February 17, 2019. https://bit.ly/2GLvl6E. [Translation provided by author].

El-Sherif, Ashraf. "Egypt's Salafists at a Crossroads." Carnegie Endowment. April 29, 2015. Accessed January 5, 2017. https://bit.ly/2DAtlLg.

El-Sherif, Ashraf. "The Muslim Brotherhood and the Future of Political Islam in Egypt." Carnegie Endowment. October 21, 2014. Accessed January 5, 2017. https://bit.ly/2E9sL8J.

ElTabbakh, Mahmoud. "عمال غزل المحلة:علقنا الإضراب لنثبت للإخوان أننا لسنا فلول" [The Workers of Mahla Spinning: We put the strike on hold to prove to the Muslim Brotherhood we were not feloul]. Masrawy. July 23, 2012. Accessed October 12, 2017. http://bit.ly/2EaGXhF. [Translation provided by author].

Eltantawy, Nahed, and Julie B. Wiest. "Social Media in the Egyptian Revolution: Reconsidering Resource Mobilization Theory." *International Journal of Communication* 5 (2011): 1207–1224.

Elyachar, Julia. "Upending Infrastructure: Tamarod, Resistance, and Agency after the January 25th Revolution in Egypt." *History and Anthropology* 25, no. 4 (2014): 452–471.

Elyazal, Sameh Seif. "Huge Dueling Demonstrations across Cairo; Mohammed Morsi's Presidency Appears to be Over." Interview by Christiane Amanpour. CNN. July 3, 2013. Accessed August 11, 2017. https://cnn.it/2UYkutP.

Engels, Bettina. "Political Transition in Burkina Faso: The Fall of Blaise Compaoré." *Governance in Africa* 2, no. 1 (2015): 3.

Ennarah, Karim Medhat. "The Politics of Mobilization and Demobilization." Mada Masr. February 10, 2014. Accessed September 12, 2017. https://bit.ly/2V3443z.

Eren, Baris. "The Trajectory of Democracy: The Social Roots of Regime Change in Turkey." PhD diss., Johns Hopkins University, 2014.

Eskendar, Amy. "The Real Force of Stability in Egypt Is Its people, Not Its government." *Baltimore Sun.* February 8, 2011. Accessed September 7, 2017. https://bit.ly/2TOUX6k.

Eskandar, Wael. "SCAF: A Brief History of Injustice." Ahram Online. November 11, 2011. Accessed September 8, 2017. https://bit.ly/2GuHYU8.

Eskandar, Wael. "Egypt's Kazeboon: Countering State Narrative." Middle East Institute. July 12, 2013. Accessed August 11, 2017. http://www.mei.edu/content/egypts-kazeboon-countering-state-narrative.

Essam El-Din, Gamal. "The Quest for Control." Ahram Online. June 21, 2013. Accessed October 12, 2017. https://bit.ly/2Ihhh7r.

Evans, Peter B., and Dietrich Rüschemeyer. *Bringing the State Back In.* Cambridge: Cambridge University Press, 2010.

"Exclusive: Biden Discusses Unrest in Egypt, Keeping U.S. Competitive." PBS. June 8, 2015. Accessed September 7, 2017. https://to.pbs.org/2BDrVPV.

Ezzat, Dina. "Brotherhood Shater, Former Mubarak-era Minister Secure Qatari Loan to Egypt." Ahram Online. October 21, 2012. Accessed September 17, 2017. https://bit.ly/2BA7Rhq.

"F16 Fighter Jets Fly Extremely Low over Tahrir Square in an Attempt at Intimidation 30 Jan." YouTube video, 0:33. February 2011. https://www.youtube.com/watch?v=b5xiWEjogNA.

Fahim, Kareem. "Mohamed Soltan, U.S. Citizen Imprisoned in Egypt, Is Released." *New York Times.* May 30, 2015. Accessed February 17, 2019. https://nyti.ms/2GNsYQP.

Fahmy, Dalia, and Daanish Faruqi. Eds. *Egypt and the Contradictions of Liberalism: Illiberal Intelligentsia and the Future of Egyptian Democracy.* London: Oneworld, 2017.

Fahmy, Khaled. *All the Pasha's Men: Mehmed Ali, His Army and the Making of Modern Egypt.* Cairo: American University in Cairo Press, 1997.

Fahmy, Khaled. "The Truth about Fayza." *Egypt Independent.* February 27, 2012. Accessed September 12, 2017. https://bit.ly/2DH6jm8.

Fatima Ramadan, and Amr Adly. "Low-Cost Authoritarianism: The Egyptian Regime and Labor Movement since 2013." Carnegie Middle East Center. September 17, 2015. Accessed October 12, 2017. https://bit.ly/2TOVogQ.

Feaver, Peter. *Armed Servants: Agency, Oversight, and Civil-Military Relations.* Cambridge, MA: Harvard University Press, 2005.

Filiu, Jean-Pierre. *From Deep State to Islamic State: The Arab Counter-revolution and Its Jihadi Legacy.* London: Hurst & Company, 2015.

Finer, Samuel. *Man on Horseback: The Role of the Military in Politics.* New York: Routledge, 2017.

Fisher, Max. "What's the Matter with Egypt's Liberals?" *Washington Post*. August 12, 2013. Accessed August 11, 2017. https://wapo.st/2SFGtce.

Fishman, Robert M. "Rethinking State and Regime: Southern Europe's Transition to Democracy." *World Politics* 42, no. 3 (April 1990): 422–440. Accessed August 12, 2017. https://ntrda.me/2RZcWoM.

Fisk, Robert. "US Envoy's Business Link to Egypt." *The Independent*. February 6, 2011. Accessed September 7, 2017. https://ind.pn/2fMDfAO.

Foran, John. *Theorizing Revolutions*. London and New York: Routledge, 1997.

Foran, John, and Jeff Goodwin. "Revolutionary Outcomes in Iran and Nicaragua: Coalition Fragmentation, War, and the Limits of Social Transformation." *Theory and Society* 22, no. 2 (1993): 209–247.

Former army officer. Interview by author. November 21, 2014.

"Former Egyptian MP Mustafa Bakri threatens to Massacre Americans in Egypt if Sisi is assassinated." The Middle East Media Research Institute. January 23, 2014. Accessed October 12, 2017. https://bit.ly/2V3tSN4.

Fox, Rebecca. "Media Darlings: The Egyptian Revolution and American Media Coverage." MA diss., American University in Cairo. Winter 2012. January 27, 2013. Accessed February 14, 2018. https://bit.ly/2V1mtNV.

Francisco, Ronald. "After the Massacre: Mobilization in the Wake of Harsh Repression." *Mobilization* 9, no. 2 (2004): 107–126.

Frisch, Hillel. "Guns and Butter in the Egyptian Army." *Middle East Review of International Affair* 5, no. 2 (June 2001): 1–12.

Gaber, Samar. "الاشتراكيين الثوريين: تعليق اعتصام عمال المحلة انتصار جزئي لتحقيق مطالبهم" [Revolutionary Socialists: Suspending the Mahalla workers' sit-in a partial victory to achieve their demands]. ElFagr. July 24, 2012. Accessed February 15, 2019. https://www.elfagr.com/151489. [Translation provided by author].

Gamal, Ebrahem. "حمزاوي هذا انقلاب و ليس ثورة" [Hamzawy: This is a coup and not a revolution]. YouTube video, 4:07. June 2014. https:// www.youtube.com/watch?v=bIReOA6-MuM. [Translation by .author]

Gamal, Wael. "العسكري: مشروعاتنا (عرق) وزارة الدفاع. ولن نسمح للدولة بالتدخل فيها" [The SCAF: Our projects are the fruits of the Ministry of Defence's work and we will not let the state intervene in them] AlSherouk News. March 27, 2012. Accessed February 14, 2019. https://bit.ly/2tnmYq4. [Translation provided by author].

Gamil, Sarah. "التعليم: بدء الدراسة ٢١ سبتمبر" [Ministry of Education: Academic term starts on September 21]. AlMasry AlYoum. August 17, 2013. Accessed February 16, 2019. https://bit.ly/2tmEAlO. [Translation provided by author].

Gardner, Lloyd C. *The Road to Tahrir Square: Egypt and the United States from the Rise of Nasser to the Fall of Mubarak*. New York: New Press, 2011.

Gehrke, Joel. "Sen. Patrick Leahy: U.S. Law Requires Pulling Foreign Aid to Egypt Because of Military Coup." *Washington Examiner*. July 3, 2013. Accessed February 12, 2019. https://washex.am/2GnPb8O.

Gelvin, James L. *The Arab Uprisings: What Everyone Needs to Know.* New York: Oxford University Press, *2012.*

Gerbaudo, Paolo. *Tweets and the Streets: Social Media and Contemporary Activism.* London: Pluto *Press*, 2012.

Gerges, Fawaz A. "ISIS and the Third Wave of Jihadism." *Current History,* December 2014. Accessed February 12, 2016. http://currenthistory.com/Gerges_Current_History.pdf.

Ghoneim, Ahmed. "القبض على الناشط خالد السيد أثناء اشتباكات شارع شريف." [Arresting activist Khaled AlSayed during classes in Sherif Street]. ElWatan News. January 25, 2014. Accessed February 16, 2019. https://bit.ly/2IhqA7e. [Translation provided by author].

Giglio, Mike. "Inside Egypt's Facebook Revolt." *Newsweek.* January 27, 2011. Accessed March 1, 2016. http://www.newsweek.com/inside-egypts-facebook-revolt-66791.

"Giulio Regeni: Egypt Airs Video of Murdered Italian Student." BBC. January 24, 2017. Accessed May 16, 2018. https://bbc.in/2V1wI4R.

"Global Wealth Databook 2014." Paris School of Economics. October 2014. Accessed October 12, 2017. https://bit.ly/2FlYvFb.

Goldberg, Ellis. "Mubarakism Without Mubarak." Foreign Affairs. February 11, 2011. Accessed May 12, 2019. https://fam.ag/30eZRNv.

Goldberg, Jeffrey. "The Modern King in the Arab Spring." *The Atlantic.* February 19, 2014. Accessed August 6, 2016. https://bit.ly/2tktfmh.

Goldstone, Jack A. *States, Parties, and Social Movements.* New York: Cambridge University Press, 2003.

Goldstone, Jack A. "Toward a Fourth Generation of Revolutionary Theory." *Annual Review of Political Science* (2001): 173–174.

Goodwin, Jeff. *No Other Way Out.* Cambridge [u.a.]: Cambridge University Press, 2001.

Goodwin, Jeff, James M. Jasper, and Francesca Polletta. *Passionate Politics: Emotions and Social Movements.* Chicago: University of Chicago Press, 2001.

Gordon, Joel. *Nasser's Blessed Movement: Egypt's Free Officers and the July Revolution.* Oxford: Oxford University Press, 1992.

Gordon, Michael R., and Kareem Fahim. "Kerry Says Egypt's Military Was 'Restoring Democracy' in Ousting Morsi." *New York Times.* August 1, 2013. Accessed August 11, 2017. https://nyti.ms/1mBEcZk.

Gordon, Philip. White House Coordinator for the Middle East, North Africa, and Persian Gulf Region 2013–2015. Interview by author. February 6, 2019.

Gotowicki, Stephen H. *The Role of the Egyptian Military in Domestic Society.* Foreign Military Studies Office Publications. 1997. Accessed October 12, 2017. https://bit.ly/2Eayew4.

Grawert, Elke, and Zeinab Abul-Magd. *Businessmen in Arms: How the Military and Other Armed Groups Profit in the MENA Region.* Lanham: Rowman & Littlefield, 2016.

Gray, Noah. "Trump Compliments Egyptian President's Shoes." CNN. May 21, 2017. Accessed February 11, 2018. https://cnn.it/2Ed8UFD.

Groll, Elias. "The Strange Elite Politics Behind Thailand's Military Coup." *Foreign Policy.* May 22, 2014. Accessed August 30, 2018. https://bit.ly/2GsezKD.

Gunning, Jeroen, and Ilan Zvi Baron. *Why Occupy a Square? People, Protests and Movements in the Egyptian Revolution.* New York: Oxford University Press, 2014.

Haas, Mark L., and David W. Lesch. *The Arab Spring: Change and Resistance in the Middle East.* Boulder, CO: Westview Press, 2013.

Haddad, Bassam. "Syria's Stalemate: The Limits of Regime Resilience." *Middle East Policy* 19, no. 1 (2012): 85–95.

Haddad, Bassam, Rosie Bsheer, and Ziad Abu-Rish. *The Dawn of the Arab Uprisings: End of an Old Order?* London: Pluto Press, 2012.

Halliday, Fred. *Revolution and World Politics: The Rise and Fall of the Sixth Great Power.* Durham: Duke University Press, 1999.

Hamed, Amr. "الأمن يلقي القبض على شقيقة علاء عبد الفتاح في مسيرة الاتحادية" [Security arrests Alaa Abdel Fattah's sister in the Itahdiyya March]. ElWatan News. June 21, 2014. Accessed February 16, 2019. https://bit.ly/2BOEU1x. [Translation provided by author].

Hamid, Shadi. "The Real Reason the U.S. Should Consider Cutting Military Aid to Egypt." Brookings. July 2, 2012. Accessed February 14, 2019. https://brook.gs/2BzyUJy.

Hamzawy, Amr. "Legislating Authoritarianism: Egypt's New Era of Repression." Carnegie Endowment for International Peace. March 16, 2017. Accessed August 11, 2017. https://goo.gl/JxN4HB.

Hamzawy, Amr. "أزمة الليبرالية المصرية وإعادة تأسيسها" [The Crisis of Egyptian Liberalism and its re-structure]. Shorouk News. 31 July 2013. Accessed August 11, 2017. https://bit.ly/2N9U7yv. [Translation provided by author].

Hanieh, Adam. *Lineages of Revolt: Issues of Contemporary Capitalism in the Middle East.* Chicago: Haymarket Books, 2013.

Hanieh, Adam. "Middle East, Labor Migration." In *The Encyclopedia of Global Human Migration,* edited by Immanuel Ness. Hoboken, NJ: Wiley Publishers, 2013.

Harb, Imad. "The Egyptian Military in Politics: Disengagement or Accommodation?" *Middle East Journal* 57, no. 2 (Spring, 2003): 269–290.

Harby, Ahmed. "مصدر: القبض على مهدى عاكف المرشد السابق لجماعة الإخوان المسلمين" [Arresting Mahdy Aakef, the former Supreme Guide of the Muslim Brotherhood]. AlYoum7. July 4, 2013. Accessed February 16, 2019. https:// bit.ly/ 2GS4WUX. [Translation provided by author].

Hartmann, Michael. *The Sociology of Elites.* London: Routledge, 2007.

Hashem, Essam, Marwa Haitham, Heba Hafez, and Rami Yassin. "جامعة القاهرة تدين أحداث مقتل طالب الهندسة وتحمل أجهزة الأمن المسئولية" [Cairo University condemns the murdering of its engineering student and holds security responsible]. Ahram Online.

December 1, 2013. Accessed February 16, 2019. https://bit.ly/2TSPCL6. [Translation provided by author].

Hashem, Mostafa. "مصر: تمرد داخل حركة "تمرد" يهدد مستقبلها السياسي" [Egypt: Rebellion inside Tamarod Movement threatens its political future]. DW.COM. December 25, 2013. Accessed August 11, 2017. https://goo.gl/jgsW2f. [Translation provided by author].

Hassan, Karim. "بوابة الأهرام تنشر التشكيل الكامل للمجلس القومى لحقوق الإنسان" [Ahram Gate publishes the new formation of the National Council for Human Rights]. Ahram Gate. August 22, 2013. Accessed February 12, 2019. https://bit.ly/2DBi8u6.

Hauslohner, Abigail. "Egypt's Military Expands Its Control of the Country's Economy." *Washington Post*. March 16, 2014. Accessed September 17, 2017. https://wapo.st/2tnWPqU.

Hauslohner, Abigail. "Is Egypt about to Have a Facebook Revolution?" *Time*. January 24, 2011. Accessed February 1, 2017. https://bit.ly/2SBLW3K.

Head of a prominent human rights organization in Egypt. Interview by author. May 2017.

Hebishi, Reda. "إضراب عمال ورش بولاق يوقف حركة قطارات الصعيد" [Stopping Upper Egypt's trains due to workers strike in Bulaq's workshops]. AlYoum7. February 9, 2011. Accessed February 15, 2019. https://bit.ly/2SYyYwJ. [Translation provided by author].

Hellyer, H. A. *A Revolution Undone: Egypt's Road Beyond Revolt*. Oxford: Oxford University Press, 2017.

Henry, Clement M., and Robert Springborg. "A Tunisian Solution for Egypt's Military." *Foreign Affairs*. June 15, 2011. Accessed January 5, 2017. https://fam.ag/2Ebc3Ge.

Herb, Michael. *All in the Family*. Albany: State University of New York Press, 1999.

Hesham, Heba. "Revolutionary Youth to Simulate Parliament." *Daily News Egypt*. March 15, 2012. Accessed February 12, 2018. https://bit.ly/2GJi6n4.

Heshmat, Gamal. "ضبط ابن شقيق جمال حشمت و4 من قيادات «الإخوان» بالبحيرة" [Arresting the nephew you Gamal Heshmat and four brotherhood leaders in Behaira]. AlMasry AlYoum. August 17, 2013. Accessed February 15, 2019. https:// bit.ly/ 2SXhSz2. [Translation provided by author].

Hessler, Peter. "Egypt's Failed Revolutions." *New Yorker*. January 2, 2017. Accessed August 11, 2017. https://bit.ly/2ijIeGu.

Hilal, Jamil, and Katja Hermann. Eds. *Mapping of the Arab Left: Contemporary Leftist Politics in the Arab East*. Publication. March 2014. Accessed February 10, 2016. https://www.rosalux.de/publikation/id/7637/.

Hintze, Otto. "Military Organization and the Organization of the State." In *The Historical Essays of Otto Hintze*, 175–215. New York: Oxford University Press, 1975.

Hoagland, Jim. "Egypt, Libya Linked to Abduction." *Washington Post*. September 28, 1997. Accessed February 9, 2018. https://wapo.st/1yrGVpM.

Hobsbawm, Eric John. *The Age Of Revolution 1789–1800*. London: Weidenfeld & Nicolson, 1962.

Holmes, Amy Austin. "The Attack on Civil Society Outside Cairo." The Carnegie Endowment for International Peace. January 26, 2017. Accessed February 9, 2018. http://carnegieendowment.org/sada/?fa=67810.

Holmes, Amy Austin. "Before the Bloodletting: A Tour of the Rabaa Sit-in." *Cairo Review of Global Affairs*. August 16, 2013. Accessed August 11, 2017. https://www.thecairor-eview.com/tahrir-forum/before-the-bloodletting-a-tour-of-the-rabaa-sit-in/.

Holmes, Amy Austin. "Egyptians Blame Military for Failures of Transition Period." Ahram Online. June 28, 2012. Accessed September 10, 2017. https://bit.ly/2UWN26X.

Holmes, Amy Austin. "Egypt's Nubia: Drowning by Government Decree." RealClearWorld. September 27, 2017. Accessed February 11, 2018. https://bit.ly/2GMJOz2.

Holmes, Amy Austin. "In Egypt, Industrial Scale Death Decrees." Providencejournal. com. May 5, 2014. Accessed August 11, 2017. https://bit.ly/2E6tY0H.

Holmes, Amy Austin. "Is US Support for the SCAF Unconditional?" The Atlantic Council. November 25, 2011. Accessed September 11, 2017. https://bit.ly/2GFrl7w.

Holmes, Amy Austin. "On Military Coups and Mad Utopias." *South Atlantic Quarterly* 113, no. 2 (May 1, 2014): 380–395.

Holmes, Amy Austin. *Social Unrest and American Military Bases in Turkey and Germany since 1945*. Cambridge: Cambridge University Press, 2016.

Holmes, Amy Austin. "They Have a Gun in One Hand and the Media in the Other: The Rise of Anti-Militarist Activism under the Supreme Council of Armed Forces." Project on Middle East Political Science. May 3, 2016. Accessed February 17, 2019. https://bit.ly/2SYiioX.

Holmes, Amy Austin. "Why Egypt's Military Orchestrated a Massacre." *Washington Post*. August 22, 2014. Accessed November 28, 2017. https://wapo.st/2V2f697.

Holmes, Amy Austin, and Hussein Baoumi. "Egypt's Protests by the Numbers." Sada. January 29, 2016. Accessed August 11, 2017. http://carnegieendowment.org/sada/62627.

Holmes, Amy Austin, and Kevin Koehler. "Myths of Military Defection in Egypt and Tunisia." *Mediterranean Politics* (2018): 1–26.

Hosny, Hagar. "نقيب المحامين: احتجاز خالد علي يومًا يفتقد مبررات الحبس الاحتياطي" [Bar Association: Khaled Ali's detention lacks justification for pre- trial detention]. Masrawy. May 24, 2017. Accessed February 17, 2019. https://bit.ly/2DMDKU9.

Hossam, a blogger and independent activist. Interview by author. January 23, 2014.

Howeidy, Fahmy. "نُذُر الغارة على المجتمع المدنى فى مصر" [Warnings of a raid on civil society in Egypt]. AlWasat Party. November 25, 2014. Accessed February 17, 2019. https://bit.ly/2SGRoSY. [Translation provided by author].

Hubbard, Ben, and David D. Kirkpatrick. "Sudden Improvements in Egypt Suggest a Campaign to Undermine Morsi." *New York Times*. July 10, 2013. Accessed September 17, 2017. https://nyti.ms/2BBguIu.

"Human Rights Defenders Mohamed Azmy and Maysara Abdoun Arrested at Peaceful Protest for Nubian Rights." Front Line Defenders. March 21, 2018. Accessed February 17, 2019. https://bit.ly/2ImmjiS.

Hussein, Abdel-Rahman. "Egypt Defence Chief Tantawi Ousted in Surprise Shakeup." *The Guardian.* August 13, 2012. Accessed October 10, 2017. http://bit.ly/2GtaUMw.

Hussein, Abdel-Rahman. "Unleashed by the Old Regime, Xenophobia Persists." *Egypt Independent.* July 18, 2011. Accessed September 7, 2017. https://bit.ly/2SRX23X.

Hussein, Sabbour. Head of the Egyptian Businessmen's Association (EBA). Interview by author. June 7, 2012.

Ibrahim, Nermin. "القبض على أمين الحرية والعدالة بأسيوط بقرية سياحية بالإسكندرية." [Arresting the General Secretary of the Freedom and Justice Party in Assuit in a touristic compound in Alexandria]. Veto Gate. November 30, 2013. Accessed February 16, 2019. https://bit.ly/2S67rVm. [Translation provided by author].

"In an Investigation by the EIPR: Bullets of the Ministry of Interior Were Aimed to Leave Demonstrators Permanently Disabled." Egyptian Initiative for Personal Rights. November 25, 2011. Accessed October 14, 2017. https://bit.ly/2SV820K.

"Infographics." The Tahrir Institute for Middle East Policy. Accessed October 14, 2017. https://timep.org/esw/infographics/.

"The Institute of Politics at Harvard University." Bassem Youssef | The Institute of Politics at Harvard University. Accessed February 9, 2018. http://iop.harvard.edu/fellows/bassem-youssef.

Iskandar, Adel. *Egypt in Flux: Essays on an Unfinished Revolution.* Cairo: American University in Cairo Press, 2013.

Iskander, Adel. "Tamarod: Egypt's Revolution Hones its Skills." Jadaliyya. June 30, 2013. Accessed October 12, 2017. https://bit.ly/2DLdp99.

Ismail, Moamen. "فيديو استقالة المكتب التنفيذي لـ "تمرد مطروح." [Video . . . The resignation of the executive office of Tamarod's branch in Matrouh]. Masr AlArabia. November 29, 2013. Accessed February 10, 2018. https://bit.ly/2GHvDLT. [Translation provided by author].

Jackman, R. W. "The Predictability of Coups d'etat: A Model with African data." *American Political Science Review* 72 (1978): 1262–1275.

Jadallah, Dina. *US Economic Aid in Egypt.* London and New York: I. B. Tauris, 2016.

Jasper, James. "A Strategic Approach to Collective Action: Looking for Agency in Social-Movement Choices." *Mobilization: An International Quarterly* 9, no. 1 (February 2004): 1–16.

Jentleson, Bruce W., Andrew M. Exum, Melissa G. Dalton, and J. Stuster. "Strategic Adaptation: Toward a New U.S. Strategy in the Middle East." Report. June 2012. Accessed January 15, 2016. http://www.cnas.org/strategicadaptation.

Jessop, Bob. *State Theory: Putting the Capitalist State in Its Place.* Oxford: Wiley, 2013.

Kagan, Robert, and Michele Dunne. "Obama Embraces the Nixon Doctrine in Egypt." *Washington Post*. April 3, 2015. Accessed October 14, 2017. https://wapo.st/2TNrBVI.

Kandeh, Jimmy D. *Coups from Below: Armed Subalterns and State Power in West Africa*. New York: Palgrave Macmillan, 2004.

Kandil, Hazem. *Inside the Brotherhood*. Cambridge: Polity Press, 2016.

Kandil, Hazem. "Sisi's Egypt." *New Left Review* 102 (November–December 2016). Accessed February 10, 2018. https://bit.ly/2iPUG5f.

Kandil, Hazem. *Soldiers, Spies and Statesmen: Egypt's Road to Revolt*. London: Verso Books, 2012.

Kandil, Hazem. "Why Islamists Count?" *Cambridge Review of International Affairs* 28, no. 2 (2015).

Kandil, Wael. "معاهدة «فيرمونت» بين الرئيس والقوى الوطنية." [The agreement of "Fairmont" between the president and national forces]. Shorouk News. July 7, 2012. Accessed September 12, 2017. https://bit.ly/2TQMH5V. [Translation provided by author].

Kaplan, Temma. *Democracy: A World History*. Oxford: Oxford University Press, 2015.

Karatasli, Sahan Savas, Sefika Kumral, Ben Scully, and Smriti Upadhyay. "Class, Crisis, and the 2011 Protest Wave: Cyclical and Secular Trends in Global Labor Unrest." In *Overcoming Global Inequalities*, edited by Immanuel Maurice Wallerstein and Christopher K. Chase-Dunn, 184–200. London: Paradigm Publishers, 2015. https://bit.ly/2tp0kgI.

Kassab, Bessan. "Tahya Masr: How Sisi bypassed Auditing a Multi-billion Pound Fund." Mada Masr. April 6, 2016. Accessed February 8, 2018. https://bit.ly/2SJ0sWZ.

Kassem, Ibrahim. "فوز مرسى برئاسة مصر بنسبة ٥١ ٪٧٣." [Morsi wins the presidency of Egypt with 51.73%]. AlYoum7. June 24, 2012. Accessed February 15, 2019. https://bit.ly/2SRMDpe. [Translation provided by author].

Katz, Mark N. *Revolutions and Revolutionary Waves*. New York: St. Martin's Press, 1999.

Ketchley, Neil. *Egypt in a Time of Revolution: Contentious Politics and the Arab Spring*. Cambridge: Cambridge University Press, 2017.

Khader, Bichara. "Le « printemps arabe »: un premier bilan." Edited by Bichara Khader. *CETRI, Éditions Syllepse, Alternatives Sud* XIX (March 2012). Accessed February 8, 2018. https://www.cetri.be/Le-printemps-arabe-un-premier-2644?lang=fr.

Khaled, Ali. Interview by author. May 26, 2014.

Khalifa, Abdallah. "تمرد' الإسماعيلية تعلن حل الحملة والعودة لصفوف الشعب لاستكمال أهداف الثورة." [Tamarod Ismailia Branch announces dissolving the branch and returning to the people's side to continue achieving the goals of the revolution]. ElBadil. November 29, 2013. Accessed February 10, 2018. https://elbadil.com/2013/11/-تمرد-الإسماعيلية-تعلن-حل-الحملة-والعو/. [Translation provided by author].

Khalifa, Asmaa. "القصة الكاملة لمعتقلي مسيرة الدفوف بأسوان." [The full story of the tambourine march's detainees in Aswan]. Edaatat. October 15, 2017. Accessed February 17, 2019. https://bit.ly/2GxPsG6. [Translation provided by author].

Khalil, Shaimaa. "Egypt: President Morsi's 100 days in Power." BBC News. October 9, 2012. Accessed September 20, 2017. https://bbc.in/2X4gE4h.

Khatib, Lina, and Ellen Lust. *Taking to the Streets: The Transformation of Arab Activism*. Baltimore: Johns Hopkins University Press, 2014.

Kienle, Eberhard. *A Grand Delusion: Democracy and Economic Reform in Egypt*. London: I. B. Tauris, 2001.

Kienle, Eberhard, and Nadine Mourad Sika. *The Arab Uprisings: Transforming and Challenging State Power*. London: I. B. Tauris, 2015.

Kingsley, Patrick. "Al-Jazeera Journalists Jailed for Seven Years in Egypt." *The Guardian*. June 23, 2014. Accessed August 11, 2017. https://bit.ly/2E5WBug.

Kingsley, Patrick. "Egyptian Activists Hope for 'Second Revolution' a Year after Morsi's Election." *The Guardian*. June 27, 2013. Accessed October 12, 2017. https://bit.ly/2GjE28I.

Kingsley, Patrick. "Egyptian PM Dismisses Alleged Sisi Recordings." *The Guardian*. February 9, 2015. Accessed October 12, 2017. https://bit.ly/2DLviEV.

Kingsley, Patrick. "Egyptian Presidential Election Extended to Third Day." *The Guardian*. May 27, 2014. Accessed August 11, 2017. https://bit.ly/2tiPicY

Kingsley, Patrick. "Will #SisiLeaks be Egypt's Watergate for Abdel Fatah El-Sisi?" *The Guardian*. March 5, 2015. Accessed October 12, 2017. https://bit.ly/2SPZYOM.

Kingsley, Patrick, and Leah Green. "Killing in Cairo: The Full Story of the Republican Guards Club Shootings." *The Guardian*. July 18, 2013. Accessed August 11, 2017. https://bit.ly/2GMAHP0.

Kirchgaessner, Stephanie. "Why Was He killed? Brutal Death of Italian Student in Egypt Confounds Experts." *The Guardian*. February 24, 2016. Accessed February 17, 2019. https://bit.ly/2MbfLBz.

Kirkpatrick, David D. "Egypt, Its Streets a Tinderbox, Braces for a Spark." *New York Times*. June 29, 2013. Accessed October 13, 2017. https://nyti.ms/2SzXm8v.

Kirkpatrick, David D. "General Who Led Takeover of Egypt to Run for President." *New York Times*. March 26, 2014. Accessed August 11, 2017. https://nyti.ms/2tp37H6.

Kirkpatrick, David D. *Into the Hands of the Soldiers: Freedom and Chaos in Egypt and the Middle East*. London: Bloomsbury, 2018.

Kirkpatrick, David D. "Keeper of Islamic Flame Rises as Egypt's New Decisive Voice." *New York Times*. March 11, 2012. Accessed September 17, 2017. https://nyti.ms/2EbP11L.

Kirkpatrick, David D. "Military Flexes Its Muscles as Islamists Gain in Egypt." *New York Times*. December 7, 2011. Accessed September 8, 2017. https://nyti.ms/2EdgKPQ.

Kirkpatrick, David D. "Renowned Scholar in Egypt Charged with Espionage." *New York Times*. January 22, 2014. Accessed February 11, 2018. https://nyti.ms/2S4k6rP.

Kirkpatrick, David D. "Thousands of Women Mass in Major March in Cairo." *New York Times*. December 20, 2011. Accessed February 15, 2019. https://nyti.ms/18jQZZY.

Kirkpatrick, David D. "The White House and the Strongman." *New York Times.* July 27, 2018. Accessed February 15, 2019. https://nyti.ms/2K2Iwy9.

Korany, Bahgat, and Rabab El-Mahdi. *Arab Spring in Egypt: Revolution and Beyond.* Cairo: The American University in Cairo Press, 2014.

Korotayev, Andrey, Leonid Issaev, and Alisa Shishkina. "Egyptian Coup of 2013: An 'Econometric' Analysis." *Journal of North African Studies* 21, no. 3 (2016): 341–356.

Kostiner, Joseph. *Middle East Monarchies.* Boulder, CO: Lynne Rienner, 2000.

Kouddous, Sharif Abdel. "What Happened to Egypt's Liberals after the Coup?" *The Nation.* June 29, 2015. Accessed August 11, 2017. https://bit.ly/2GxqkPU.

Krueger, Alyson. "Senator Patrick Leahy: Egypt Will Lose Aid If Mubarak Does Not Step Down (video)." *Huffington Post.* February 3, 2011. Accessed September 7, 2017. https://bit.ly/2SNJreh.

Kurzman, Charles. "Structural Opportunity and Perceived Opportunity in Social-Movement Theory: The Iranian Revolution of 1979." *American Sociological Review* 61, no. 1 (1996): 153–170.

Kurzman, Charles. *The Unthinkable Revolution in Iran.* Cambridge, MA: Harvard University Press, 2004.

Lachapelle, Jean, Lucan A. Way, and Steven Levitsky. "Crisis, Coercion, and Authoritarian Durability: Explaining Diverging Responses to Anti-Regime Protest in Egypt and Iran." Proceedings of The American Political Science Association Annual Meeting, New Orleans. August 31, 2012. Accessed September 3, 2017. https://bit.ly/2SEjwX6.

Lachmann, Richard. "Agents of Revolutions." In *Theorising Revolutions.* Edited by John Foran, 73–101. London and New York: Routledge, 1997.

Lacroix, Stéphane. "Saudi Arabia's Muslim Brotherhood Predicament." *Washington Post.* March 20, 2014. Accessed August 11, 2017. https://wapo.st/2E7TOBw.

Lahoud, Nelly, David DiMeo, Cindy Jebb, Arie Perliger, Ruth Beitler, and John Ringquist. "The 'Arab Spring': Investing in Durable Peace." OAI. June 29, 2011. Accessed August 7, 2017. https://bit.ly/2Gr5QrR.

Lawson, George. "Within and Beyond the 'Fourth Generation' of Revolutionary Theory." *Sociological Theory* 34, no. 2 (2016): 106–127.

Lee, Terence. *Defect or Defend: Military Responses to Popular Protests in Authoritarian Asia.* Baltimore: Johns Hopkins University Press, 2015.

Lee, Terence. "Military Cohesion and Regime Maintenance." *Armed Forces & Society* 32, no. 1 (2005): 80–104.

Legge, James. "In Pictures: Jubilation in Cairo, Riots in Port Said." *The Independent.* January 26, 2013. Accessed February 15, 2019. https://ind.pn/2SzTgNv.

Lehoucq, Fabrice, and Aníbal Pérez-Liñán. "Breaking Out of the Coup Trap." *Comparative Political Studies* 47, no. 8 (2013): 1105–1129.

Leiby, Richard. "The Rise and Fall of Egypt's Most Despised Billionaire, Ahmed Ezz." *Washington Post*. April 9, 2011. Accessed October 12, 2017. https://wapo.st/2SVqTbZ.

Levitsky, Steven, and Lucan A. Way. *Competitive Authoritarianism: Hybrid Regimes after the Cold War*. New York: Cambridge University Press, 2010.

Levs, Josh. "Like 'Obameter,' the 'Morsi Meter' tracks Egyptian president's promises." CNN. June 26, 2012. Accessed October 12, 2017. https://cnn.it/2SBjX4h.

Linz, Juan J., and Alfred Stepan. *Problems of Democratic Transition and Consolidation: Southern Europe, South America, and Post-Communist Europe*. Baltimore: Johns Hopkins University Press, 1998.

Lobna Darwish. Interview by author. February 19, 2012.

Londoño, Ernesto. "Egypt's Morsi Replaces Military Chiefs in Bid to Consolidate Power." *Washington Post*. August 12, 2012. Accessed October 10, 2017. https://wapo.st/2SZFLGs.

"Long-sighted: Wealthy Egyptian Business Families Venture Abroad." *The Economist (US)*, July 15, 2010. Accessed May 14, 2019. https://econ.st/2HjmiZg.

Loveluck, Louisa. "Who Is Aya Hijazi, the American Freed from Jail in Egypt?" *Washington Post*. April 21, 2017. Accessed February 9, 2018. https://wapo.st/2DIo0BG.

Lunde, Tormod K. "Modernization and Political Instability: Coups d'Etat in Africa 1955–85." *Acta Sociologica* 34, no. 1 (1991): 13–32.

Lust-Okar, Ellen. "Divided They Rule: The Management and Manipulation of Political Opposition." *Comparative Politics* 36, no. 2 (2004): 159.

Luttwak, Edward. *Coup détat: A Practical Handbook*. Cambridge, MA: Harvard University Press, 2016.

Lynch, David J. "Egypt's Islamists Woo Mubarak Tycoons as Mursi Seeks Funds." Bloomberg. February 14, 2013. Accessed September 12, 2017. https://bloom.bg/2DFstVH.

Lynch, Marc. *The Arab Uprisings Explained: New Contentious Politics in the Middle East*. New York: Columbia University Press, 2012.

Lynch, Marc. "Is the Muslim Brotherhood a Terrorist Organization or a Firewall against Violent Extremism?" *Washington Post*. March 7, 2016. Accessed August 11, 2017. https://wapo.st/21VC4Np.

Lynch, Marc. "That's It for Egypt's So-Called Transition." *Foreign Policy*. June 14, 2012. Accessed September 8, 2017. https://bit.ly/2EamFow.

Lynch, Marc, and Steven A. Cook. "U.S. Policy on Egypt Needs a Big Shift." *New York Times*. November 30, 2011. Accessed September 8, 2017. https://nyti.ms/2SZrTvS.

Mackey, Robert. "Video Shows Protesters Were Attacked by Armed Assailants." *New York Times*. May 3, 2012. Accessed September 12, 2017. https://nyti.ms/2DKllaN.

Magdy, Muhammed. "Journalists' Syndicate Head: Egyptian Press Facing Crisis with the State." Al-Monitor. January 11, 2017. Accessed February 11, 2018. https://bit.ly/2X8RW2D.

Magdy, Sami. "هاني الجمل... ذكريات الثورة ومستقبلها." [Hany ElGamal . . . the memory and future of the revolution]. Masrawy. December 22, 2015. Accessed February 16, 2019. https://bit.ly/2STrqv6. [Translation provided by author].

"Mahmoud Abou Zeid (Shawkan)." Committee to Protect Journalists. Accessed February 12, 2019. https://bit.ly/2StYGtd.

Mahmoud, ElAgami. "شهادة رجل حاول إنقاذ فتاة مجلس الوزراء" [The testimony of a man who tried to save the girl of the minister's council events]. YouTube video, 3:37. December 19, 2011. https://bit.ly/2T0sw8t [Translation provided by author].

Malaparte, Curzio. *The Technique of Revolution*. Aurora: Morris Productions, 2014.

Malsin, Jared. "Bassem Youssef Abruptly Cancels Egyptian Satire Show." *Time*. June 3, 2014. Accessed February 9, 2018. https://bit.ly/1yGEbJe.

Mann, Michael. "The Roots and Contradictions of Modern Militarism." *New Left Review* 1, no. 162 (March–April 1987): 35–51.

Mann, Michael. "Ruling Class Strategies and Citizenship." *Sociology* 21, no. 3 (1987): 339–354.

Mansour, Osama. "الإخوان وثورة 25 يناير نظرة موضوعية" [The brotherhood and January 25 revolution . . . and objective overview]. Yanayer Website. April 19, 2011. Accessed April, 11 2016. http:// www.25yanayer.net/الإخوان-وثورة-25-يناير-نظرة-موضوعية/. [Translation provided by author].

Marfleet, Philip. *Egypt: Contested Revolution*. London: Pluto Press, 2016.

Marinov, Nikolay, and Hein Goemans. "Coups and Democracy." *British Journal of Political Science* 44, no. 4 (October 2014): 799–825. Accessed February 14, 2019. https://bit.ly/2DBKFQ5.

Marshall, Shana, and Joshua Stacher. "Egypt's Generals and Transnational Capital." Middle East Research and Information Project. Spring 2012. Accessed September 16, 2017. https://bit.ly/2Sz0zoJ.

Martin, Jess. "Freedom is in the hands of the people | SocialistWorker.org." Socialistworker.org. July 10, 2013. Accessed August 11, 2017. http://socialistworker.org/2013/07/10/freedom-in-the-peoples-hands.

Marx, Karl. *The Communist Manifesto*. Ware, Hertfordshire: Wordsworth Editions, 2008.

Marx, Karl. *The Eighteenth Brumaire of Louis Bonaparte*. New York: International Publishers, 1994.

Maspero Youth Union in Cairo, Founding Member. Interview by author. August 2017.

Masr Madaneya. "الإعلام المصري بعد اول يوم من التصويت في الإنتخابات الرئاسية" [The Egyptian Media after the first day of voting in the presidential elections]. YouTube video, 2:49. May 2014. https://bit.ly/1mlzMBh. [Translation provided by author].

McCargo, Duncan. "Divided and Self-destructive, Thailand Is a Long Way from Compromise | Duncan McCargo." *The Guardian*. January 24, 2014. Accessed August 30, 2018. https://bit.ly/2SpTDdk.

McGowan, Patrick J. "African Military Coups Détat, 1956–2001: Frequency, Trends and Distribution." *Journal of Modern African Studies* 41, no. 3 (2003): 339–370.

McMurray, David A., and Amanda Ufheil-Somers. *The Arab Revolts: Dispatches on Militant Democracy in the Middle East*. Bloomington: Indiana University Press, 2013.

Member of April 6. Interview with author. July 2, 2013.

Member of the Boycott Army Products Campaign. Interview by author. July 8, 2012.

Member of the Muslim Brotherhood. Interview by author. June 22, 2012.

Member of the Working Group on the Southern Mediterranean. Telephone interview by author. March 2014.

Merry, Sally Engle. *The Seductions of Quantification: Measuring Human Rights, Gender Violence, and Sex Trafficking*. Chicago: University of Chicago Press, 2016.

Messieh, Nancy. "Profiling Egypt's New Ministers." Atlantic Council. May 7, 2013. Accessed September 17, 2017. https://bit.ly/2EaDuQb.

Meyer, David S. "Political and Political Opportunities." Annual Review Sociology 30 (2004): 125–145.

Michael, Maggie. "Egyptian Activists Angry over US Envoy's Comments." The Big Story. June 25, 2013. Accessed October 12, 2017. https://bit.ly/2TQYOQm.

Michaelson, Ruth. "Egypt Blocks Access to News Websites including Al-Jazeera and Mada Masr." *The Guardian*. May 25, 2017. Accessed February 11, 2018. https://bit.ly/2X9sLNJ.

Mikhail, Amira. "Tahrir Bodyguard: Fighting Sexual Harassment on Egypt's Streets." The Atlantic Council. December 10, 2012. Accessed February 15, 2019. https://bit.ly/2DCQI6M.

Miller, Andrew, and Amy Hawthorne. "Egypt's Sham Election." *Foreign Affairs*. March 23, 2018. Accessed February 12, 2019. https://fam.ag/2DvUAGS.

Mohamed, Adel. "الاخوان: لن نشارك في مظاهرات 25 يناير" [The Brotherhood: we will not participate in January 25 protests]. YouTube video, 1:49, September 17, 2011. https://www.youtube.com/watch?v=xS3xynR6Mx8. [Translation provided by author].

Mohamed, Azmy. President of the General Nubian Union. Interview by author. January 2017.

Mohamed, Khayal. "حصر سري لأعضاء الاخوان" [A Secret Count of the members of the Brotherhood]. *ElSherouk News*, 2011. [Translation provided by author].

Mohamed, Nassar. "تمرد كفر الشيخ» تحل مكاتبها التنفيذية بالمحافظة" [Tamarod Kafr El Sheikh's branch dissolves its executive offices]. Shorouk News. November 11, 2013. Accessed February 10, 2018, https://bit.ly/2X6GXa5. [Translation provided by author].

Mohamed, S. "Under the State's Gaze: Repression of Women's Organizations in Egypt." Tahrir Institute for Middle East Policy. May 28, 2018. Accessed July 29, 2018. https://bit.ly/2D0P8xH.

Mohamed, Zaree. Interview by author. May 2017.

Mohie, Mostafa. "Classified report reveals State Security's take on Jan 25 Revolution." Mada Masr. January 12, 2015. Accessed September 8, 2017. https://bit.ly/2GJfkxX.

Mohsen, Habiba. "What made her go there? Samira Ibrahim and Egypt's Virginity Test Trial." Al Jazeera. March 16, 2012. Accessed September 12, 2017. https://bit.ly/2N9hQyL.

Molla, Mahmoud. "القبض على 24 فى مسيرة الدفوف النوبية." [Arresting 24 in the Nubian tambourine march]. AlMasry AlYoum. September 4, 2017. Accessed February 17, 2019. https://bit.ly/2SF7FYM. [Translation provided by author].

"Morsi Meter." Morsi Meter. 2012. Accessed February 15, 2019. http://morsimeter.com/en.

Morsi, Marwa, and Ahmed Maged. "عضو بـ "الاشتراكيين الثوريين" في الإسكندرية يتهم وكيل نيابة المنشية برفض سماع شهادته في قضية." [A member of the Revolutionary Socialists in Alexandria accuses the Mansheya prosecutor of refusing to hear his testimony in a case]. ElWatan News. December 5, 2013. Accessed February 16, 2019. https://bit.ly/2SWdd0h. [Translation provided by author].

"Morsi's Private Conversations and Coordination with Magariaf." Wikileaks Cable. September 13, 2012. Accessed February 13, 2018. https://wikileaks.org/clinton-emails/emailid/12389.

Mostafa El Hassan. Interview by author. January 2017.

Motawea, Mahmoud. "6 ابريل تدعو لوقفة أمام محكمة 'مصر الجديدة'في ذكرى استشهاد'أبو الحسن'" [April 6th calls for a stand in front of the court of "Heliopolis" on the anniversary of the martyrdom of Abu Hassan]. Sada ElBalad. February 20, 2013. Accessed August 11, 2017. http://www.elbalad.news/403758. [Translation provided by author].

Mourad, Mary. "AUC discusses Marxist Movement in Egypt." AlAhram English. December 12, 2010. Accessed February 11, 2018. https://bit.ly/2DKtCLG.

Mourtada, Racha, and Fadi Salem. "Social Media in the Arab World: Influencing Societal and Cultural Change?" Report. Dubai School of Government. 1st ed. Vol. 2.

Moustafa, Noha. "In Reconciling with Regime Figures, Officials Opt for Quick Cash over Formal Trials." *Egypt Independent*. February 23, 2013. Accessed September 16, 2017. https://bit.ly/2DKMfiH.

"MPs denunciation of SCAF head, Salafist leader lands him Parliament investigation." Ahram Online. February 19, 2012. Accessed September 8, 2017. http://english.ahram.org.eg/News/34916.aspx.

"Mubarak Era Tycoons Join Egypt President in China." Ahram Online. August 28, 2012. Accessed September 17, 2017. https://bit.ly/2GMXz0L.

"Mubarak to Name Vice-President." Wiki Leaks. June 15, 2005. Accessed February 15, 2019. https://wikileaks.org/plusd/cables/05CAIRO4534_a.html.

"Mubarak Verdict 'Turned Our Dreams into Nightmares,'" *The New Arab*. December 1, 2014. Accessed October 12, 2017. https://bit.ly/2tqbySm.

Nada, Mostafa. "على شرعية» ثورة أعقبها انقلاب «30 يونيو» موقف أبو الفتوح من «مصر القوية»: مرسي." [Strong Egypt Party: Aboul Fetouh's position from June 30th events is that it is a revolution followed by a coup]. Shorouk News. February 15, 2015. Accessed August 11, 2017. https://bit.ly/2N9tj1o. [Translation provided by author].

Nader, Laura. "Ethnography as Theory." *Hau: Journal of Ethnographic Theory* 1, no. 1 (2011): 211–219.

Nader, Laura. "Up the Anthropologist: Perspectives Gained from Studying Up." In *Reinventing Anthropology*, edited by Dell H. Hymes, 284–311. New York: Pantheon Books, 1974.

Nafei, Said, and Tereza Kamel. "للمفتي «بديع» بينهم جديدا «إخوانيا» ٦٨٤ قاضي إعدام المنيا يحيل." [The Minya judge refers 683 new defendants including Badei to the Mufti]. AlSherouk News. April 28, 2014. Accessed February 14, 2019. https://bit.ly/2N5D0xQ. [Translation provided by author].

"Naguib Sawiris." *Enigma*. October 5, 2017. Accessed February 11, 2018. https://www.enigma-mag.com/naguib-sawiris/.

Nassar, Mohamed. "تمرد كفر الشيخ تحل مكاتبها التنفيذية بالمحافظة." [Tamarod Kafr el-Sheikh's branch dissolves its executive offices]. Shorouk News. November 11, 2013. Accessed February 10, 2018. https://bit.ly/2X6GXa5. [Translation provided by author].

Natour, Rhana. "Exclusive: Aya Hijazi on her surprising meeting with President Trump after release from Egypt prison." PBS. May 26, 2017. Accessed February 9, 2018. https://to.pbs.org/2qo47Il.

Nepstad, Sharon Erickson. "Nonviolent Civil Resistance and Social Movements." *Sociology Compass* 7, no. 7 (July 2013): 590–598.

Nepstad, Sharon Erickson. "Nonviolent Resistance in the Arab Spring: The Critical Role of Military-Opposition Alliances." *Swiss Political Science Review* 17, no. 4 (December 2011): 485–491.

Nepstad, Sharon Erickson. *Nonviolent Revolutions: Civil Resistance in the Late 20th Century*. Oxford: Oxford University Press, 2011.

"Newly Released Egyptian-American Charity Worker Visits Trump." Ahram Online. April 21, 2017. Accessed February 17, 2019. https://bit.ly/2V83K3D.

No Military Trials Website. Accessed August 11, 2017. http://www.nomiltrials.org.

Noor Ayman Noor. Interview by author. July 8, 2012.

Nour, Noor Ayman. "Egyptian Political Activist: 'Corruption Will be Difficult to End.'" *The Guardian*. May 19, 2011. Accessed September 11, 2017. https://bit.ly/2TS6cuC.

"Obama's Second State of the Union (Text)." *New York Times*. January 25, 2011. Accessed September 7, 2017. https://nyti.ms/2TRKEhI.

O'Donnell, Guillermo. *Transitions from Authoritarian Rule: Comparative Perspectives.* Baltimore: Johns Hopkins University Press, 1991.

Oehmke, Philipp. "Egypt's Man in the Moon: The Watchdog of Tahrir Square Fears for the Revolution." Spiegel Online. April 29, 2011. Accessed September 8, 2017. https:// bit.ly/2TQ8ivd.

Omar, Ehab. "القبض على القيادي الإخواني جلال عبد الصادق من منزله في أسيوط." [Arresting Galal Abdel Sadek, a leading figure of the Brotherhood from his house in Assuit]. ElBalad News. November 23, 2013. Accessed February 16, 2019. https:// bit.ly/ 2SD92Hf. https://bit.ly/2TQ8ivd. [Translation provided by author].

Omar, Samir, and Ashraf Saad. "مصر- تمديد انتخابات الرئاسة ليوم ثالث." [Egypt—Extending presidential elections for a third day]. Sky News Arabia. May 27, 2014. Accessed February 12, 2019. https://bit.ly/2N34nbU. [Translation provided by author].

"Omar Suleiman, Egypt's Vice President, blames violence on 'foreign influences.'" PRI. February 3, 2011. Accessed September 5, 2017. https://bit.ly/2GMmIZt.

"Operation Anti Sexual Harassment—Opantish by Stephanie Gaspais." Gender and Sexuality Resource Center. November 5, 2015. Accessed February 15, 2019. https:// bit.ly/2STwQG9.

Oraby, Ayat. "انتخبوا_العرص آخر إحصائية لعدد مستخدمي و زائري هاشتاج انتخبوا العرص." [Elect the Pimp: Latest Statistics for the Users of the Hashtag Elect the pimp]. Twitter. April 2, 2014. Accessed August 11, 2017. https://bit.ly/2BG31iQ. [Translation provided by author].

Osman, Tarek. *Egypt on the Brink: From Nasser to the Muslim Brotherhood.* New Haven: Yale University Press, 2013.

Owen, Roger. *The Rise and Fall of Arab Presidents for Life: With a New Afterword.* Cambridge, MA: Harvard University Press, 2012.

Parker, Ned. "Violent Soccer Youths Cast Chill over Egypt." *Los Angeles Times.* November 3, 2012. Accessed August 6, 2017. https://lat.ms/2SBrP64.

Parsa, Misagh. *States, Ideologies, and Social Revolutions: A Comparative Analysis of Iran, Nicaragua, and the Philippines.* Cambridge: Cambridge University Press, 2000.

Perlmutter, Amos. *Egypt, the Praetorian State.* New Brunswick, NJ: Transaction Books, 1974.

Pion-Berlin, David, and Harold Trinkunas. "Civilian Praetorianism and Military Shirking during Constitutional Crises in Latin America." *Comparative Politics* 42, no. 4 (2010): 395–411.

Political analyst. Interview by author. November 12, 2011.

Pollock, John. "Rebelbook: A Mix of Technologies Let Dedicated Citizens Change Egypt." *MIT Technology Review.* September 19, 2014. Accessed October 12, 2017. https://bit.ly/2IfQoAK.

Povoledo, Elisabetta. "Italian Student in Cairo Was Murdered over His Research, Prosecutor Says." *New York Times.* January 26, 2018. Accessed February 11, 2018. https://nyti.ms/2GMHvMu.

Powell, Jonathan M., and Clayton L. Thyne. "Global Instances of Coups from 1950 to 2010: A New Dataset." *Journal of Peace Research* 48, no. 2 (2011): 249–259.

Prashad, Vijay. *Arab Spring, Libyan Winter*. Oakland, CA: AK Press, 2012.

Przeworski, Adam. *Democracy and the Market: Political and Economic Reforms in Eastern Europe and Latin America*. Cambridge: Cambridge University Press, 2003.

Qara'a, Ibrahim. "حكم بوقف وحظر أنشطة حركة «6 إبريل» بجميع المحافظات" [Banning the activities of 6 April in all governorates]. AlMasryAlYoum. April 28, 2014. Accessed February 11, 2019. https://bit.ly/2SNgsXI. [Translation provided by author].

Quandt, William B. "U.S. Policy and the Arab Revolutions of 2011." In *The New Middle East: protest and revolution in the Arab World*, edited by Fawaz A. Gerges, 418–428. Cambridge: Cambridge University Press, 2014.

Quinlivan, James T. "Coup-proofing: Its Practice and Consequences in the Middle East." *International Security* 24, no. 2 (1999): 131–165.

Rabie, Mohamed. " دور الإخوان في الثورة." [The role of the Muslim Brotherhood in the revolution]. Ahram Gate. August 3, 2011. Accessed October 12, 2017. https://bit.ly/2SOzWvn. [Translation provided by author].

Radjy, Amir-Hussein. "How to Save the Memories of the Egyptian Revolution." *The Atlantic*. January 25, 2018. Accessed February 15, 2019. https://bit.ly/2GL2PCf.

Rady, Essam ElDin, and Heba Hassan. "بعد قرار منع النشاط الحزبي بها الجامعات في الحظر" [After the Decision to ban Party Activities on Campus: Universities under Curfew]. Al- Ahram, March 17, 2013. Accessed August 11, 2017. https:// bit.ly/ 2Ec8aR6. [Translation provided by author].

Ramadan, Fatma. "إلي عمال مصر التفويض سم قاتل" [To Egyptian Workers: Authorization is a venom]. Elhewar ElMotamaden. July 26, 2013. Accessed August 11, 2017. http://www.m.ahewar.org/s.asp?aid=370369&r=0. [Translation provided by author].

Ramadan, Mostafa. " 'مصر القوية' : دعوة 'السيسي' للتظاهر قد تؤدي إلى اقتتال أهلي" [Strong Egypt Party: Sisi's call for protest could lead to a civil strife]. ONA—ONews Agency. July 24, 2013. Accessed August 11, 2017. http://onaeg.com/?p=1082704. [Translation provided by author].

Raouf, Rami. "Egypt: Timeline of Communication Shutdown during the Revolution. مدونة رامي رؤوف " (Rami Raouf's blog). June 9, 2011. Accessed February 13, 2019. https://bit.ly/2TLlq4x. [Translation provided by author].

Raslan, Amal. "التضامن: لدينا 48 ألف جمعية مسجلة ونستعلم عن مصادر التمويل قبل الموافقة" [Ministry of Social Solidarity: we have 48,000 registered NGOs and we are investigating their funding sources before granting approval]. AlYoum7. August 21, 2016. Accessed February 16, 2019. https://bit.ly/2DKaOMM. [Translation provided by author].

Razoux, Pierre. "What to Expect of the Egyptian Army?" Technical paper. February 14, 2011. Accessed February 20, 2017. http://www.ndc.nato.int/news/news.php?icode=244.

"Record Number of Journalists Jailed as Turkey, China, Egypt Pay Scant Price for Repression." Committee to Protect Journalists. December 13, 2015. Accessed February 11, 2018. https://bit.ly/2V4s9ae.

"Remarks at the American University in Cairo." US Department of State. June 20, 2005. Accessed February 14, 2019. https://bit.ly/2AEDlCo.

"Remarks with Egyptian Foreign Minister Mohamed Kamel Amr after Their Meeting." US Department of State. September 28, 2011. Accessed February 15, 2019. https://bit.ly/2BCgJmB.

Revkin, Mara. "The Egyptian State Unravels: Meet the Gangs and Vigilantes Who Thrive under Morsi." *Foreign Affairs*. June 27, 2013. Accessed October 12, 2017. https://fam.ag/2S5PdmZ.

Ritter, Daniel. *The Iron Cage of Liberalism: International Politics and Unarmed Revolutions in the Middle East and North Africa*. Oxford: Oxford University Press, 2014.

Roberts, Adam, Michael J. Willis, Rory McCarthy, and Timothy Garton Ash. *Civil Resistance in the Arab Spring: Triumphs and Disasters*. Oxford: Oxford University Press, 2016.

Roll, Stephan. "Egypt's Business Elite after Mubarak: A Powerful Player between Generals and Brotherhood." Report. German Institute for International and Security Affairs. September 2013. Accessed February 11, 2018. https://bit.ly/2BARtgK.

Rollanza. "فيديو هام يثبت تورط الجيش فى موقعه الجمل" [An important video that proves the involvement of the army in the Battle of Camel]. YouTube video, 12:58, June 8, 2011. https://www.youtube.com/watch?v=jR0jCFa773w. [Translation provided by author].

Roston, Aram, and David Rohde. "Egyptian Army's Business Side Blurs Lines of U.S. Military Aid." *New York Times*. March 5, 2011. Accessed September 16, 2017. https://nyti.ms/2GMMVHl.

Rubinstein, Alvin Z. *Red Star on the Nile: The Soviet-Egyptian Influence Relationship since the June War*. Princeton, NJs: Princeton University Press, 1977.

Rucker, Philip, and Karen DeYoung. "Freed Egyptian American Prisoner Returns Home Following Trump Intervention." *Washington Post*. April 20, 2017. Accessed February 9, 2018. https://wapo.st/2BEGtPn.

Ruffner, Todd. "Under Threat Egypt's Systematic Campaign against NGOs." Project on Middle East Democracy. March 2015. Accessed September 8, 2017. https://bit.ly/2DGIMBP.

Rugh, William A. "Egyptian Politics and American Diplomacy." *Middle East Policy* 19, no. 2 (2012): 36–48.

Rutherford, Bruce. "Egypt's New Authoritarianism under Sisi." *Middle East Institute* 72, no. 2 (Spring 2018): 185–208.

Ryzova, Lucie. "The Battle of Cairo's Muhammad Mahmoud Street." Al Jazeera. November 29, 2011. Accessed October 14, 2017. https://bit.ly/1ESdamP.

Saad, Mohamed. Former Vice President of Student Union at Cairo University. Interview by author. December 2016.

Saber, Koloud, Ahmed Ezzat, and Emad Mubarak. "الحقوق والحريات الطلابية في ضوء التعديلات القانونية الأخيرة" [Student Rights and Freedoms in Light of the Recent Legal Amendments]. The Association for Freedom of Thought and Expression, 2008. Accessed August 11, 2017. https://bit.ly/2V0lbmz. [Translation provided by author].

"The Sad State of Egypt's Liberals." The Economist. October 10, 2015. Accessed August 11, 2017. https://econ.st/2Gsf4UJ.

Saif, Mohammad, and Ahmed Abdullatif. "بالفيديو | ضبط «أمريكية» وزوجها يديران جمعية «وهمية» لتدريب أطفال الشوارع على القتال ومهاجمة الشرطة" [In Video: Arrest of American and her Husband Who Run 'Fake' Society to Train Street Children to Fight and Attack Police]. Elwatannews, May 4, 2014. Accessed February 10, 2018. https://www.elwatannews.com/news/details/475208. [Translation provided by author].

Salah, Abdallah. "٣٠.يوم في الأمان" [Suspending protests for 30 days]. AlYoum7. December 1, 2016. Accessed February 17, 2019. https://bit.ly/2DPRBcB.

Sallam, Hesham. "The Egyptian Revolution and the Politics of Histories." PS: Political Science & Politics 46, no. 2 (2013): 248–258.

Sassoon, Joseph. Anatomy of Authoritarianism in the Arab Republics. Cambridge: Cambridge University Press, 2016.

Sayadi, Emna. "Egypt: More Than 500 Sites Blocked Ahead of the Presidential Election." Access Now. March 14, 2018. Accessed February 17, 2019. https://bit.ly/2svR1LY.

Sayigh, Yezid. "Morsi and Egypt's Military." Al-Monitor. January 8, 2013. Accessed October 10, 2017. https://bit.ly/2Xe9Uky.

SCAFreaks. "SCAF General 'Adel Omarah'—'kazeboon'—Liars campaign." YouTube video, 6:37. January 2012. http://www.youtube.com/watch?v=tDF8qctR2tg.

Schatz, Adam. "Egypt's Counter-Revolution." London Review of Books. August 16, 2013. Accessed August 11, 2017. https://bit.ly/2GNK5lh.

Schlumberger, Oliver. Debating Arab Authoritarianism. Johanneshov: TPB, 2007.

Schwartz, Michael. "The Egyptian Uprising: The Mass Strike in the Time of Neoliberal Globalization." New Labor Forum 20, no. 3 (Fall 2011): 33–43. Accessed September 9, 2017. https://bit.ly/2IcYNVq.

Schwedler, Jillian. The Political Geography of Protest in Neoliberal Jordan. Middle East Critique 21, no. 3 (2012): 259.

Sedra, Paul. "The Long Shadow of the 1952." Jadaliyya. February 13, 2011. Accessed October 12, 2017. https://bit.ly/2S8qrmp.

Selbin, Eric. Revolution, Rebellion, Resistance. London: Zed, 2010.

Selim, Gamal M. "Egypt under SCAF and the Muslim Brotherhood: The Triangle of Counter-Revolution." Arab Studies Quarterly 37, no. 2 (2015): 177–199.

Serra, Narcis. The Military Transition: Democratic Reform of the Armed Forces. Cambridge: Cambridge University Press, 2010.

Sewell, William H. "Historical Events as Transformations of Structures: Inventing Revolution at the Bastille." Theory and Society 25, no. 6 (1996): 841–881.

Sfakianakis, John. "The Whales of the Nile: Networks, Businessmen, and Bureaucrats During the Era of Privatization in Egypt." In Networks of Privilege in the Middle East: The Politics of Economic Reform Revisited. Edited by Steven Heydemann, 77–100. New York: Palgrave Macmillan, 2004.

Shahin, Emad El-Din. "Sentenced to Death in Egypt." The Atlantic. May 19, 2015. Accessed August 11, 2017. https://bit.ly/2Guxrbz.

Shahira (activist). Interview by author. May 24, 2012.

Shams El-Din, Mai. "AUC Remembers Giulio Regeni, Protests University's Position on His Death." Mada Masr. February 25, 2016. Accessed February 11, 2018. https://www.madamasr.com/en/2016/02/25/feature/politics/auc-remembers-giulio-regeni-protests-universitys-position-on-his-murder/.

Shams El-Din, Mai. "Rebellion on the Rocks." Mada Masr. June 30, 2014. Accessed February 10, 2018. https://bit.ly/2DMapcp.

Sharp, Jeremy M. "Egypt in Transition." November 18, 2011. Accessed September 9, 2017. https://bit.ly/2SyvnG6.

Shehata, Dina. "Youth Mobilization in Egypt: New Trends and Opportunities." Working paper. Issam Fares Institute for Public Policy and International Affairs, American University in Beirut. 2011.

Shenker, Jack. The Egyptians: A Radical Story. London: Penguin Books, 2017.

Shenker, Jack. "Fury over Advert Claiming Egypt Revolution as Vodafone's." The Guardian. June 3, 2011. Accessed September 8, 2017. https://bit.ly/2UYUgHF.

Sherief, Gaber. Interview by author. February 19, 2012.

Sherwood, Harriet. "Cairo Israeli Embassy Attack: 'Staff Feared for Their Lives.'" The Guardian. September 10, 2011. Accessed February 15, 2019. https://bit.ly/2tpy25P.

Shukralla, Salma. "Tahrir sit-in enters second day, to go on until 7 demands are met." Ahram Online. July 9, 2011. Accessed September 12, 2017. https://bit.ly/2UVcQAk.

Singh, Naunihal. Seizing Power: The Strategic Logic of Military Coups. Baltimore: Johns Hopkins University Press, 2014.

"Sisi Is a Killer." Digital image. ElBehira. 2014. Accessed August 11, 2017. https://bit.ly/2X7swTk.

"Sisi Son May Have Had Role in Regeni." ANSA. July 7, 2016. Accessed February 11, 2018. https://bit.ly/2X3i3bk.

Siyagh, Yezid. "Above the State: The Officers' Republic in Egypt." Carnegie Endowment for International Peace. August 1, 2012. Accessed January 5, 2015. http://carnegie-mec.org/2012/08/01/above-state-officers-republic-in-egypt-pub-48972.

Skocpol, Theda. "Rentier State and Shi'a Islam in the Iranian Revolution." Theory and Society 11, no. 3 (1982): 265–283.

Skocpol, Theda. *Social Revolutions in the Modern World*. Cambridge: Cambridge University Press, 1994.

Skocpol, Theda. *States and Social Revolutions: A Comparative Analysis of France, Russia, and China*. Cambridge: Cambridge University Press, 1979.

Slater, Dan. *Ordering Power: Contentious Politics and Authoritarian Leviathans in Southeast Asia*. Cambridge: Cambridge University Press, 2011.

Slater, Dan, and Sofia Fenner. "State Power and Staying Power: Infrastructural Mechanisms and Authoritarian Durability." *Journal of International Affairs* 65, no. 1 (2011): 15–29. http://www.jstor.org/stable/24388179.

Slater, Dan, and Nicholas Rush Smith. "The Power of Counterrevolution: Elitist Origins of Political Order in Postcolonial Asia and Africa." *American Journal of Sociology* 121, no. 5 (2016): 1472–1516.

Smet, Brecht De. *Gramsci on Tahrir: Revolution and Counter-Revolution in Egypt*. London: Pluto Press, 2016.

Sobhy, Karim. "نيابة قصر النيل تبدأ التحقيق مع أحمد ماهر فى أحداث الشورى" [Qasr Al-Nil Prosecution begins investigation with Ahmed Maher in Shura events]. AlYoum7. November 30, 2013. Accessed February 11, 2019. https://bit.ly/2E2kUtu. [Translation provided by author].

"Social Solidarity Ministry closes 75 NGOs, 121 childcare centers in Beheira." Mada Masr. May 26, 2016. Accessed February 9, 2018. https://bit.ly/2Ig8Fhk.

Soest, Christian Von, and Michael Wahman. "Not All Dictators Are Equal." *Journal of Peace Research* 52, no. 1 (2014): 17–31.

Soliman, Samer. *The Autumn of Dictatorship: Fiscal Crisis and Political Change in Egypt under Mubarak*. Stanford, CA: Stanford University Press, 2011.

Soueif, Laila Mostafa. "Testimony for the Detainment of Amr Abdallah ElBehairy Early Saturday." تناتيف من حياة ماعت [Pieces of the Life of Ma'et] (web log). February 26, 2011. Accessed September 12, 2017. https://bit.ly/2BDpsF1. [Translation provided by author].

"Source of Egypt's Coup: Morsi Gave Free Hand to Islamic Militants, Ordered Military to Stop Crackdowns on Jihadis." Talking Points Memo. July 18, 2013. Accessed October 10, 2017. https://bit.ly/2GJ1xYk.

Springborg, Robert. "Arab Militaries." In *The Arab Uprisings Explained: New Contentious Politics in the Middle East*. Edited by Marc Lynch, 142–159. New York: Columbia University Press, 2014.

Springborg, Robert. *Development Models in Muslim Contexts: Chinese, "Islamic" and Neo-liberal Alternatives*. Edinburgh: Edinburgh University Press, 2009.

Springborg, Robert. *Egypt*. Cambridge: Polity Press, 2018.

Springborg, Robert. *Mubarak's Egypt: Fragmentation of the Political Order*. Boulder, CO: Westview Press, 1989.

Stacher, Joshua. *Adaptable Autocrats Regime Power in Egypt and Syria*. Cairo: American University in Cairo Press, 2012.

State Information Service. *Constitution of the Arab Republic of Egypt*. January 18, 2014. Accessed February 11, 2018. http://www.sis.gov.eg/Newvr/Dustor-en001.pdf.

"Statement by Prof. Emad Shahin on His Death Sentence." Official Website—Emad Shahin. June 4, 2015. Accessed February 11, 2018. http://emadshahin.com/?p=1839.

"Statement by Senators John Mccain and Lindsey Graham on Egyptian Legislation Regulating NGOs." Senate.gov. December 1, 2016. Accessed February 11, 2018. https://bit.ly/2N8ukqm.

Stepan, Alfred. *The Military in Politics: Changing Patterns in Brazil*. Princeton: Princeton University Press, 1974.

Stewart, Phil. "U.S. praises military restraint in Egypt protests." Reuters. January 30, 2011. Accessed September 7, 2017. https://reut.rs/2E8FtV7.

Stille, Alexander. "Who Murdered Giulio Regeni?" *The Guardian*. October 4, 2016. Accessed February 11, 2018. https://bit.ly/2TUNKSc.

"The Struggle Between Egypt's Business and Military Elite." Stratfor Worldview. February 9, 2011. Accessed August 6, 2016. https://bit.ly/2N8kYLd.

A student in the Medical Faculty at the University of Tanta. Interview by author. May 2017.

"Supreme Council of Universities." Supreme Council of Universities. Accessed August 11, 2017. http://portal.scu.eun.eg/.

Svolik, Milan W. *The Politics of Authoritarian Rule*. New York: Cambridge University Press, 2013.

Taher, Menna. "Public film-screenings of army abuses attacked in Alexandria and Cairo." *Ahram Online*, December 30, 2012. Accessed September 12, 2017. https://bit.ly/2toAFFi.

Tahrir Diaries. "مرشحي الرئاسة المصريين ضد المحاكمات العسكرية للمدنيين" [Egyptian Presidential Candidates against Military Trials of Civilians]. YouTube. 1:25. September 2011. https://www.youtube.com/watch?v=gs_5FljIDnU. [Translation provided by author].

Tahrir Diaries. "سميرة و الجيش: قصة فتاة مصرية " [Samira and the Army: A story of an Egyptian girl]. YouTube. 22:44. November 2011. https://bit.ly/2Xasgml. [Translation provided by author].

Tahrir Diaries. " شهادة سلوى – تم اعتقالها من الجيش يوم ٩ مارس ٢٠١١ " [Testimony of Salwa— Was arrested by the Army on 9 March 2011]. YouTube. 3:18. March 17, 2011. https://www.youtube.com/watch?v=ajCe1km7UFM. [Translation provided by author].

Tamarod activist in Alexandria. Interview by author. December 2016.

Tamarod cofounder Shadi Malek. Interview by author. January 12, 2014.

Tamarod Minya's Facebook Page. Accessed August 11, 2017. https://bit.ly/2GsfCKh.

Tamarod Port Said's Facebook Page. Accessed August 11, 2017. https://www.facebook.com/TmrodPTS.

Tamer Aboarab. " السلطات المصرية تهدد المعارضين في الخارج بالقتل :معتز الفجيري" [Moutaz Al-Fougiri: Egyptian authorities threaten to kill the opposition abroad]. YouTube Video. 1:46. October 31, 2018. https://bit.ly/2SDOvCs.

Tansey, Oisin. *The International Politics of Authoritarian Rule*. New York: Oxford University Press, 2016.

Tarek, Sherif. "Dramatic row in Egypt's parliament over police use of birdshot in deadly clashes." Ahram Online. February 6, 2012. Accessed September 12, 2017. https://bit.ly/2GtEjGi.

Taub, Amanda. "The unsexy truth about why the Arab Spring failed." Vox. January 27, 2016. Accessed August 11, 2017. https://www.vox.com/2016/1/27/10845114/arab-spring-failure.

"Thai Junta Charges 50 Anti-Government Activists." VOA. February 16, 2018. Accessed August 30, 2018. https://bit.ly/2RYqJft.

Theron, Charlize. "Samira Ibrahim—The World's 100 Most Influential People: 2012." *Time*. April 18, 2012. Accessed February 15, 2019. https://bit.ly/2N8I44u.

"'This Week' Transcript: Crisis in Egypt." ABC News. January 30, 2011. Accessed September 7, 2017. https://abcn.ws/2UYt5g7.

Thomassen, Bjørn. "Notes towards an Anthropology of Political Revolutions." *Comparative Studies in Society and History* 54, no. 3 (2012): 679–706.

Thompson, William R. *The Grievances of Military Coup-Makers*. Seymour Martin Lipset Collection. Beverly Hills: Sage Publications, 1973.

Thyne, Clayton L. "Supporter of Stability or Agent of Agitation? The Effect of US Foreign Policy on Coups in Latin America, 1960–99." *Journal of Peace Research* 47, no. 4 (2010): 449–461.

Tilly, Charles. *European Revolutions: 1492–1992*. Oxford: Basil Blackwell, 1995.

Tilly, Charles. *From Mobilization to Revolution*. Reading, MA: Addison-Wesley, 1978.

Tilly, Charles. *Regimes and Repertoires*. Chicago: University of Chicago Press, 2006.

Tilly, Charles. *The Vendée*. Cambridge, MA: Harvard University Press, 1980.

Trager, Eric. *Arab Fall: How the Muslim Brotherhood Won and Lost Egypt in 891 Days*. Washington, DC: Georgetown University Press, 2017.

Trew, Bel, and Osama Diab. "The Crooks Return to Cairo." *Foreign Policy*. February 7, 2014. Accessed September 16, 2017. https://bit.ly/2IhJwTj.

Trimberger, Ellen Kay. *Revolution from Above: Military Bureaucrats and Development in Japan, Turkey, Egypt, and Peru*. New Brunswick, NJ: Transaction Books, 1978.

Trotsky, Leon, and Max Eastman. *The History of the Russian Revolution*. New York: Simon & Schuster, 1936.

Tschirgi, Dan, Walid Kazziha, and Sean F. McMahon. *Egypt's Tahrir Revolution*. Boulder, CO: Lynne Rienner, 2013.

Two Egyptian police officers. Interview by author. January 2014.

Two members of Students Against the Coup. Interview by author. January 2017.

"The UAE Secretly Picked Up the Tab for the Egyptian Dictatorship's D.C. Lobbying." *The Intercept*. October 4, 2017. Accessed February 12, 2018. https://bit.ly/2xSV35c.

United Nations Committee Against Torture. Report. May 12, 2017. Accessed February 11, 2018. https://bit.ly/2GNcKan.

"The U.S. Department of State's International Narcotics and Law Enforcement Affairs (INL): Egypt." U.S. Department of State. 2015. Accessed August 11, 2017. https://bit.ly/2N01t7u.

US Embassy. "Egypt in Transition: Sadat and Mubarak." Wiki Leaks. December 12, 2017. Accessed February 14, 2019. https://bit.ly/2E8MdT0.

"US Embassy Cables: Egyptian Military's Influence in Decline, US Told." *The Guardian*. February 3, 2011. Accessed February 13, 2018. https://bit.ly/2SRWTxr.

"US urges restraint in Egypt, says government stable." Reuters. January 25, 2011. Accessed September 7, 2017. https://bit.ly/2BE7jHl.

Varol, Ozan. *The Democratic Coup d'État*. Oxford: Oxford University Press, 2017.

Varol, Ozan O. "The Democratic Coup d'État." *Harvard International Law Journal* 53, no. 2 (2012): 291–356.

Vogelsang, Susan S. "U.S.-Egypt Security Cooperation after Egypt's January 2011 Revolution." Report. United States Army Command and General Staff College Fort Leavenworth, School of Advanced Military Studies. 2011.

Wahba, Amira. "نص استقالة البرادعي للرئيس منصور: تكبدنا ثمنًا غاليًا كان يمكن تجنبه" [The text of ElBaradie's resignation to President Mansour: We have paid heavily for something that could have been avoided]. Ahram Gate. August 14, 2013. Accessed February 12, 2019. http://gate.ahram.org.eg/News/382972.aspx. [Translation provided by author].

Wallerstein, Immanuel Maurice. *The Modern World System*. New York: Academic Press, 1976.

Wan, William. "Egypt's Facebook Revolution Faces Identity Crisis." *Washington Post*. March 23, 2011. Accessed August 6, 2016. https://wapo.st/2SSWwCV.

Waterbury, John, and Gamal Abdel Nasser. *The Egypt of Nasser and Sadat*. Princeton, NJ: Princeton University Press, 1983.

Weber, Max. *Economy and Society*. Berkeley: University of California Press, 1978.

Weyland, Kurt. "Crafting Counterrevolution: How Reactionaries Learned to Combat Change in 1848." *American Political Science Review* 110, no. 2 (May 2016): 215–231.

"What Tantawi Is Alleged to Have Said at Mubarak's Trial." *McClatchy Newspapers*. September 27, 2011. Accessed September 7, 2017. https://bit.ly/2SWuKWo.

Wickham, Carrie Rosefsky. *Muslim Brotherhood: Evolution of an Islamist Movement*. Princeton, NJ: Princeton University Press, 2013.

Wikithawra. "حصر قتلى عهد المجلس العسكري تفصيليا." [A detailed record of deaths under the SCAF]. Wikithawra. November 3, 2013. Accessed February 12, 2019. https://bit.ly/2Gd6FUY. [Translation provided by author].

Wikithawra. "حصر قتلى الـ 18 يوم الأولي من الثورة تفصيليا" [Detailed record of the deaths during the first 18 days of the revolution]. Wikithawra. October 23, 2013. Accessed February 11, 2019. https://bit.ly/2G3CDT1. [Translation provided by author].

Wikithawra. "حصر المقبوض عليهم والملاحقين قضائياً خلال عهد السيسي/عدلي منصور, مُحَدَّث حتى ١٤ مايو ٢٠١٤" [A detailed record of detainees under Al-Sisi/Adly Mansour, updated 14 May 2014]. Wikithawra. January 2014. Accessed February 12, 2019. https://bit.ly/2aSqHQJ. [Translation provided by author].

Wikithawra. "حصر مصابي عهد المجلس العسكري عددياً." [A detailed record of the injured under the SCAF]. Wikithawra. November 3, 2013. Accessed February 12, 2019. https://bit.ly/2SCh4Ab. [Translation provided by author].

Wikithawra. "حصر قتلى عهد محمد مرسي تفصيلياً." [A detailed report on the number of deaths under Morsi]. Wikithawra. June 26, 2013. Accessed February 11, 2019. https://bit.ly/1MhzB7X. [Translation provided by author].

Wikithawra. "حصر قتلي شهر يناير ٢٠١٤ تفصيلياً." [Detailed report of the deaths during January 2014]. Wikithawra. February 8, 2014. Accessed February 12, 2019. https://bit.ly/2SEs1S5. [Translation provided by author].

Wikithawra. "حصر قتلى عهد السيسي/عدلي منصور تفصيلياً (مُحَدَّث) حتي 31 يناير 2014" [A detailed report on the number of deaths under Sisi Adly Mansour until January 31, 2014]. Wikithawra. March 26, 2014. Accessed February 11, 2019. https://bit.ly/2N1xXyf.

Wikithawra. "فض تظاهرة مجلس الشوري 26 نوفمبر 2013 , صور وشهادات وتقارير" [Dispersing the Shura Council Demonstration 26 November 2013, photos, testimonies and reports]. Wikithawra. January 29, 2014. Accessed February 11, 2019. https://bit.ly/2E3q9sV. [Translation provided by author].

Wikithawra. "توثيق الاعتداءات على دور عبادة وممتلكات الاقباط ما بعد فض الاعتصامين" [Documenting attacks on Coptic worship houses and properties after the dispersal of the sit-ins]. Wikithawra. August 29, 2013. Accessed February 12, 2019. https://bit.ly/1XGoADS.

Wikithawra. "إحصائيات عامة حول قتلى أول سبع شهور من عهد السيسي/عدلى منصور حتى ٣١ يناير ٢٠١٤" [General Statistics on the number of deaths during the first seven months under Sisi/ Adly Mansour until January 31, 2014]. Wikithawra. January 2014. Accessed February 12, 2019. https://bit.ly/2DwqzGQ. [Translation provided by author].

Wikithawra. "تقرير شامل: حصر ضحايا فض اعتصام رابعة تفصيليا وآلية الحصر" [Report: A detailed record of deaths from the Rabaa dispersal and the methodology of reporting]. Wikithawra. March 17, 2014. Accessed February 12, 2019. https://bit.ly/1M8j2hV. [Translation provided by author].

Wikithawra. "تقرير فئة "الطلاب" حصر وقائع قتل أو قبض وملاحقة قضائية خلال عهد السيسي/عدلي منصو حتي 15 أبريل 2014" [Report on the "Students." Record of murder or arrest and prosecution incidents, during Sisi/ Adly Mansour period, until 15 April 2014]. Wikithawra. May 4, 2014. Accessed February 11, 2019. https://bit.ly/2SpBz2V. [Translation provided by author].

Winn, Peter. *Weavers of Revolution: The Yarur Workers and Chile's Road to Socialism.* Oxford: Oxford University Press, 1989.

Yasar, Suleyman. "As Morsi Takes Over in Egypt, Will Military Allow Economic Reform?." Al-Monitor. June 28, 2012. Accessed September 12, 2017. https://bit.ly/2X58kkR.

Young, Lindsay. "Egypt's transitional government lobbies on seeking funds, debt reduction." Sunlight Foundation Reporting Group. August 18, 2011. Accessed October 12, 2017. https://bit.ly/2NfDgds.

Younis, Sherif. "The Maspero Massacre: The Military, the Media, and the 1952 Cairo Fire as Historical Blueprint." Jadaliyya. October 17, 2011. Accessed September 12, 2017. https://bit.ly/2DCikJe.

Younis, Sherif. "A Military Coup?" *Egypt Independent.* February 11, 2011. Accessed September 9, 2017. http://www.egyptindependent.com/opinion/military-coup.

Youssef, Bassem. "Instead of writing numerous tweets here's one to sum it all up MB are the new form of Nazis got it? I said it on the show and saying it now." Twitter. July 3, 2013. Accessed February 9, 2018. https://bit.ly/2DO8OTu.

Zacharia, Janine. "Mubarak Ally Watches Egypt from Uncertain Exile." *Washington Post.* March 3, 2011. Accessed September 17, 2017. https://wapo.st/2S0OS53.

Zaki, Moheb. *Civil Society & Democratization in Egypt, 1981–1994.* Cairo: Ibn Khaldoun Center, 1995.

Zaky, Mostafa. "حصر أموال الإخوان تتحفظ على ١٥٨٩ عنصرا داعما للجماعة ١١٨ شركة ١١٣٣ جمعية أهلية." [Confiscating the money of 1589 Brotherhood supporters, 118 companies and 1133 civil society organizations]. Ahram Gate. September 11, 2018. Accessed February 16, 2019. https://bit.ly/2GuFHZ7. [Translation provided by author].

Ziyad. Interview by author. February 19, 2012.

Zolberg, Aristide R. *Moments of Madness.* N.p.: N.p., 1972.

"قبول استقالة نائب رئيس الوزراء المصري." [Accepting the resignation of the Egyptian Deputy Prime Minister]. BBC News. January 30, 2014. Accessed February 12, 2019. https://bbc.in/2TLDgEu. [Translation provided by author].

"الناشط أحمد ماهر يسلم نفسه للسلطات المصرية." [Activist Ahmed Maher surrenders himself to the Egyptian authorities]. Reuters. November 30, 2013. Accessed February 16, 2019. https://bit.ly/2S6TWoi. [Translation provided by author].

"جامعة الأزهر: مظاهرات الطلاب خرجت عن سلميتها." [Al-Azhar University: Student demonstrations gone non-peaceful]. Masr AlArabia. October 30, 2013. Accessed August 11, 2017. https://goo.gl/E7rMfC. [Translation provided by author].

"مؤسس حركة ٦ أبريل: لم أصرح بأن ما حدث انقلاب" [April 6th Founder: I did not say that what happened is a coup]. Alarabiya.net. July 12, 2013. Accessed August 11, 2017. https://goo.gl/gkruVi. [Translation provided by author].

"القبض على علاء عبد الفتاح لاتهامه بأحداث مجلس الشورى" [Arresting Alaa Abdel Fattah for the Shura Council events]. AlArabiya. November 29, 2013. Accessed February 16, 2019. https://bit.ly/2SBDHEU. [Translation provided by author].

"القبض على الناشط المصري أحمد دومة." [Arresting Egyptian activist Ahmed Douma]. BBC News. December 3, 2013. Accessed February 16, 2019. https://bbc.in/2IfynTa. [Translation provided by author].

"إلقاء القبض على القيادي الإخواني عصام العريان بالقاهرة." [Arresting Essam El-Erian, a leading brotherhood figure in Cairo]. AlArabiya. October 30, 2013. Accessed February 15, 2019. https://bit.ly/2DNmRtU[SE1] .

"القبض على محمد البلتاجى القيادى بجماعة الاخوان المسلمين بالجيزة." [Arresting Mohamed ElBeltagy, a leading figure of the Muslim Brotherhood in Giza]. Ahram Online. August 29, 2013. Accessed February 15, 2019. https://bit.ly/2T0In6Z. [Translation provided by author].

"منع عمرو حمزاوي و١٨ آخرين من السفر لإهانة القضاء" [Banning Amr Hamzawi and 18 others from traveling for "insulting the judiciary"]. Alarabiya.net. January 16, 2014. Accessed August 11, 2017. https://goo.gl/kEDkpt. [Translation provided by author].

"مركز الأبحاث والدراسات القانونية." [Centre for Research and Legal Studies]. Facebook. July 15, 2012. Accessed February 12, 2019. https://bit.ly/2Ss648I. [Translation provided by author].

"الجنايات تلغي قرار منع "حمزاوي وقنديل" من السفر بقضية إهانة القضاء." [Court of felonies cancels travel ban for "Hamzawy and Qandil" for their involvement in "insulting the judiciary" case]. Shorouk News. October 22, 2014. Accessed August 11, 2017. https://goo.gl/vxYkX4. [Translation provided by author].

"السيرة الذاتية للدكتور زياد بهاء الدين نائب رئيس مجلس الوزراء وزير التعاون الدولى." [Curriculum Vitae of Dr. Ziad Bahaa Eldin, Deputy Prime Minister and Minister of International Cooperation]. Ahram Gate. July 16, 2013. Accessed February 12, 2019. https://bit.ly/2StMVTy. [Translation provided by author.

"السيرة الذاتية لكمال ابو عيطة وزير القوى العاملة الجديد" [Curriculum Vitae of Kamal Abou Eita, Minister of Manpower]. AlBorsa News. July 16, 2013. Accessed February 12, 2019. https://bit.ly/2RZ4WEm. [Translation provided by author].

"مصر- قاض يصدر أحكام إعدام جماعية." [Egypt—A judge issues mass death sentences]. Human Rights Watch. December 3, 2014. Accessed February 11, 2019. https://www.hrw.org/ar/news/2014/12/03/265064. [Translation provided by author].

"مصر: مقتل ثلاثة أشخاص في مظاهرات ضد الحكومة." [Egypt: Three people killed in demonstrations against the government]. BBC News. January 25, 2011. Accessed February 15, 2019. https://bbc.in/2S5g6Yj. [Translation provided by author].

"السلطات المصرية تعتقل القيادي في جماعة الاخوان المسلمين حلمي الجزار." [Egyptian authorities arrest Helmy ElGazzar, a leading figure of the Muslim Brotherhood]. Kuwait News Agency. July 5, 2013. Accessed February 16, 2019. https://bit.ly/2SSSoD0. [Translation provided by author].

"وزارة الداخلية المصرية ترفض استئناف دوري كرة القدم." [Egyptian Interior Ministry refuses to resume football league] BBC News. July 15, 2012. Accessed February 11, 2019. https://bbc.in/2N4e7Ti. [Translation provided by author].

"النتيجة النهائية - السيسي رئيساً لمصر 96.91% مقابل 3.09% لصباحي" [Final results— Sisi is Egypt's presidents with 96.91% against 3.09% for Sabahi]. CNN. June 3, 2014. Accessed February 12, 2019. https://cnn.it/2Ss7fVn. [Translation provided by author].

"مايو ٢٠١٤ – مايو ٢٠١٦ عامين من الحبس الاحتياطي عقوبة مبادرة لإعادة تأهيل أولاد الشوار" [From May 2014 to May 2016, two years of temporary detention to punish an initiative that rehabilitates street children]. Association for Freedom of Thought and Expression. May 5, 2016. Accessed February 16, 2019. https://bit.ly/2WZQ7oG.

"صحفيو "الحرية والعدالة" يدينون وقف إصدار الجريدة ويعلنون الاعتصام بمقر نقابة الصحفيين" [Journalists from Freedom and Justice Party Newspaper denounce stopping its Publication and announce Their Sit-in at the Journalists' Syndicate."]. Aswat Masriya. December 26, 2013. Accessed August 11, 2017. https://bit.ly/2SGjGxj. [Translation provided by author].

"اتحاد العمال فى التحرير . . .تفويض الجيش لمحاربة الإرهاب" [Labor Union is in Tahrir Square to authorize the military to fight terrorism]. Egyptian Trade Union Federation. July 26, 2013. Accessed August 11, 2017. http://etufegypt.com/archives/14971. [Translation provided by author].

"محمود بدر يدعم السيسي في سوهاج" [Mahmoud Badr Supports Sisi in Sohag]. ElMasry ElYoum. May 19, 2014. Accessed August 11, 2017. https://bit.ly/2V4Njor. [Translation provided by author].

"خريطة انتشار الحكم العسكرى" [Map of Military Rule Diffusion]. Kazeboon. March 3, 2012. Accessed February 14, 2019. https://bit.ly/2GJnuqk. [Translation provided by author].

"مذبحة دار الحرس الجمهورى ٨ يوليو ٢٠١٣" [Massacre of the Republican Guards July 8, 2013]. Wikithawra. July 20, 2013. Accessed August 11, 2017. https://goo.gl/86T1WL. [Translation provided by author].

"محمد البرادعي يؤدي اليمين الدستورية لتولي منصب نائب الرئيس للعلاقات الدولية" [Mohamed ElBaradie is sworn in as vice president for international relations]. France 24. July 14, 2013. Accessed February 12, 2019. https://bit.ly/2BxAcVD. [Translation provided by author].

"فى ذكرى ميلاد الشهيد أحمد منصور القصاص من القتلة مازال مفقودا" [On the anniversary of the martyr Ahmed Mansour al-Qassas, retribution from his killers is still unfulfilled]. April 6 Youth. May 27, 2017. Accessed August 11, 2017. https://goo.gl/ravXHA. [Translation provided by author].

"إسقاط الإخوان لتعميق الثورة لا لتدعيم النظام. لن نفوض" [Overthrowing the Brotherhood was to deepen the revolution and not to support the regime . . . we will not authorize]. The Socialist Gate. July 25, 2013. Accessed August 11, 2017. https://bit.ly/2NcGPkQ. [Translation provided by author].

"من يملك أوامر الفرم بحق الصحف المصرية؟" [Who gives the shredding orders of Egyptian newspapers]. The Association for Freedom of Thought and Expression. August 23, 2015. Accessed February 11, 2018. https://bit.ly/2IjCI7H. [Translation provided by author].

"تأجيل تاريخ موعد بداية الدراسة في جامعة الأزهر الترم الثاني" [Postponing the starting date of the second academic term at Al-Azhar University]. Masreat Website. February 15, 2014. Accessed August 11, 2017. https://goo.gl/bdfwFJ. [Translation provided by author].

"١-بيانات القيادة العامة للقوات المسلحة" [Statements of the General Command of the Armed Forces—1]. Al Moqatel. Accessed February 14, 2019. https://bit.ly/2SJ3sCL. [Translation provided by author].

"٢-بيانات القيادة العامة للقوات المسلحة" [Statements of the General Command of the Armed Forces—2]. Al Moqatel. Accessed February 14, 2019. https://bit.ly/2IqELHl. [Translation provided by author].

"وقف إصدار جريدة الحرية والعدالة" [Suspending the publication of Freedom and Justice newspaper]. AlAhram. December 27, 2013. Accessed February 17, 2019. https://bit.ly/2X7P9XG. [Translation provided by author].

"«لا للإرهاب»تمرد تنشر خريطة مسيرات التفويض تحت شعار" [Tamarod publishes a map for the authorization protests under the slogan "'No to Terrorism'"]. Alarabiya.net. July 25, 2013. Accessed August 11, 2017. https://goo.gl/TmkBeP. [Translation provided by author].

"جامعة القاهرة - بدء الدراسة بكليات جامعة القاهرة ٢١ سبتمبر" [Term starts at Cairo University faculties on 21st September]. Cairo University Website. September 16, 2013. Accessed August 11, 2017. https://cu.edu.eg/ar/Cairo-University-News-3876.html [Translation provided by author].

"نص قرار المجلس الاعلى للقوات المسلحة بتعديل قانون الطوارى" [Text of the SCAF's decision to amend emergency law]. AlMogaz. September 16, 2011. Accessed February 12, 2019. https://bit.ly/2WYc6wj. [Translation provided by author].

"ذكرى فض اعتصام رابعة العدوية: تسلسل الأحداث" [The anniversary of the Rabaa sit-in: The sequence of events]. BBC News. August 14, 2016. Accessed February 11, 2019. https://bbc.in/2GHrkzU. [Translation provided by author].

"اغلاق القنوات الدينية:انتهاك لحرية الرأي آم ضرورة أمنية؟" [The Closure of Religious Channels: Violation of Freedom of Speech or a Security Necessity?]. BBC Arabic. July 9, 2013. Accessed August 11, 2017. https://bbc.in/2BC4Ugr. [Translation provided by author].

"وفاة "جيكا" عضو ٦ أبريل إثر إصابته بخرطوش" [The death of "Gika" of April 6 after being hit by bird shots]. Alarabiya.net. November 26, 2012. Accessed August 11, 2017. https://bit.ly/2DJTdoc. [Translation provided by author].

[The Egyptian army deposes the Muslim Brotherhood]. Sky News Arabia. July 03 3, 2013. Accessed February 15, 2019. https://bit.ly/2Gs1elm.

"المبادرة المصرية تعرب عن صدمتها ازاء استمرار احتجاز يارا سلام و ٢٢ أخرين" [The Egyptian Initiative for Personal Rights is shocked that Yara Sallam along with 22 others are still detained]. The Egyptian Initiative for Personal Rights. June 30, 2014. Accessed February 16, 2019. https://bit.ly/2DP9ecy. [Translation provided by author].

"المبادرة المصرية للحقوق الشخصية تصدر نتائج تحقيقها في أحداث دهشور" [The Egyptian Initiative for Personal Rights publishes its investigation findings in Dhashour's events]. Egyptian Initiative for Personal Rights. August 7, 2012. Accessed February 15, 2019. https://bit.ly/2TSaXEr. [Translation provided by author].

"التحالف الشعبي يدعو لتفويض السيسي ويحذر من أي إجراءات استثنائية" [The Popular Coalition calls for authorizing Sisi to fight terrorism and warns against emergency measures]. Elgornal.net. July 26, 2013. Accessed August 11, 2017. http://elgornal.net/news/news.aspx?id=2948798. [Translation provided by author].

"نص قانون مكافحة الإرهاب" [The text of anti-terrorism law]. AlAhram. August 17, 2015. Accessed February 17, 2019. https://bit.ly/2Bzurqu. [Translation provided by author].

"نص بيان الحكومة لاعتبار «الإخوان» جماعة إرهابية" [The Text of the Government's Statement regarding the Muslim Brotherhood as a terrorist group]. ElMasry ElYoum. December 25, 2013. Accessed February 11, 2019. https:// www.almasryalyoum.com/ news/ details/363925. [Translation provided by author].

"يسري فودة يعلن توقف برنامج آخر كلام هذا الأسبوع" [Yosri Fouda announces cancelling his program Akher Kalam]. Masrawy. September 22, 2014. Accessed February 17, 2019. https://bit.ly/2GMO5mk. [Translation provided by author].

Index

Note: Tables and figures are indicated by *t* and *f* following the page number